ELECTORAL REFORM IN
ENGLAND AND WALES

ELECTORAL REFORM IN ENGLAND AND WALES [1915]

THE DEVELOPMENT AND OPERATION OF THE PARLIAMENTARY FRANCHISE 1832-1885

by
CHARLES SEYMOUR

A Reprint with an Introduction by
Michael Hurst
MA, FRSA, FRHistS, Fellow and Tutor in Modern History and Politics, St John's College, Oxford

DAVID & CHARLES REPRINTS

ISBN 0 7153 4982 1

*This work was first published in 1915
by Yale University Press, New Haven
and Humphrey Milford, London
Oxford University Press*

*Reprinted by the present publishers, with a new introduction,
1970*

© 1970 INTRODUCTION BY MICHAEL HURST

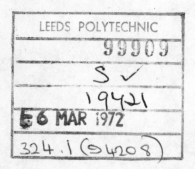
Printed in Great Britain by
Latimer Trend & Company Limited Whitstable
for David & Charles (Publishers) Limited
South Devon House   Newton Abbot
Devon

INTRODUCTION
1970

The value of Seymour's work has not diminished with the years. Indeed, in some respects it has actually risen. Whereas little else existed on the subject in 1915, much has been produced since, not all of it beyond serious criticism. So what was essentially a book of exposition must now also be treated as a vital corrective of weaker material. On the time span alone it remains in a class of its own. Nothing else properly comparable covers the whole period from the First to the Third Reform Acts and it is all too easy to lose the thread of development in jumping from one narrowly specialist work to another. Seymour fills the role of indispensable companion, not only to the student of electoral technicalities, but to the whole range of the historical profession right through to the political philosopher attempting to plumb the mysteries of why and how England and Wales found an almost wholly peaceful road from electoral oligarchy and imperfect liberalism to something approaching a full parliamentary democracy. At a time when clear appreciation of grand trends has become ever more a paramount need and the tendency for researchers to narrow their fields of work is becoming depressingly stronger, the argument for reproducing a volume like this, albeit unchanged, is particularly cogent.

By keeping the triple factors of franchise width, distribution of seats and registration regulations in constant and concomitant play, and by stressing the irregular elements at work for so long, Seymour presents his themes with a fine sense of proportion. And the very depth of his research saves him from the superficiality so prominent among the faults of some later writers. No one of keen perception could swallow the contention of Professor Gash, in his *Politics in the Age of Peel*, that the Tory fears of 1832 proved justified in the event, after an intelligent reading of these pages. Even the moderately endowed will wonder at Robert Blake's points about compounders and personal payment as laid out in his *Disraeli*. Few will linger to admire those who have suddenly come across the importance of registration as a prime factor in influencing the complexion of the House of Commons. For those who have cared to comb through these pages the whole affair was clear anyway.

Changes in the franchise had, of course, irregular effects according to the varying social structures and economic levels of different districts. Prosperity and rising values could produce a broadly based electorate such as that which backed Wilkes in Middlesex in the eighteenth century. With time the same phenomenon spread into other areas some years before 1832. These unending possibilities of electorate expansion have often been forgotten. Facts in Seymour bring the point forcefully home. Concurrently, the superlative importance of seat redistribution and facilitated registration emerge again and again with crystal clarity. Then too the number of county seats increased with each reform Act, but their nature changed profoundly, and with the single-seat system of the 1885 Act the pattern of politics again underwent a considerable reconstruction. But the whole process was one of slow motion. And what comes slowly can be tolerated and adjusted to so much more easily than dramatic and revolutionary shifts of power, affecting not one or two, but the whole gamut of social classes. Yet though there was no great haste, there was speed in the tortoise as opposed to the hare sense. By the time registration became almost painless in 1918 and women flooded on to the electoral lists, fully liberal constitutionalism had captured virtually Britain's whole society. What had been added at the bottom of society had not, as so often elsewhere, resulted in losses at the top. During the long course of change, legislation at the various stages had more often than not resembled something one might have expected from the next rather than the current state of the franchise. Beginning with reforms of itself, the House of Commons had generally contrived to be ahead of much of community opinion and behind only a relatively small portion of it. In the successful evolution of liberal constitutionalism timing may be almost all. Timing was on its side in England and Wales – and in Scotland. Time was not the balm for Ireland, and Seymour offers no study of it. Nevertheless, he contributes much to the proper understanding of the major portion of the United Kingdom at a highly crucial stage of political, social and economic development. As such the work is invaluable to devotees of history, politics and sociology. Hence this reprinting.

May 1970   Michael Hurst
                                                St John's College
                                                Oxford

YALE
HISTORICAL PUBLICATIONS
STUDIES
III

ISSUED UNDER THE DIRECTION OF THE
DEPARTMENT OF HISTORY

―――

THE FIRST VOLUME PUBLISHED ON THE
FOUNDATION ESTABLISHED BY THE
KINGSLEY TRUST ASSOCIATION

ELECTORAL REFORM IN ENGLAND AND WALES

THE DEVELOPMENT AND OPERATION OF THE
PARLIAMENTARY FRANCHISE, 1832-1885

By

CHARLES SEYMOUR, M.A. (Cantab.), Ph.D.

Assistant Professor of History in Yale College

NEW HAVEN: YALE UNIVERSITY PRESS
LONDON: HUMPHREY MILFORD
OXFORD UNIVERSITY PRESS
MDCCCCXV

TO
THE MEMORY OF
THOMAS DAY SEYMOUR

PREFACE

The study which follows attempts to trace in a single field the extraordinary transformation which took place in English political conditions during the nineteenth century. It was first inspired by the difficulty of obtaining exact information upon the effects of the reforms in the electoral franchise and of the redistribution of seats; and it has been developed in the hope of determining the changes in the practical operation of the electoral system which were effected by these and supplementary reforms. It makes no claim to be a history of the popular movement for parliamentary reform, nor does it attempt to describe the parliamentary tactics incident to the passing of the Reform Bills. I have sought to confine myself to a clear statement of electoral conditions and the democratic development resulting from the reforms in the franchise, distribution of seats, registration, and methods of electioneering.

Two facts stand out as the result of such a study. In the first place, very obviously, there was a constant advance towards democracy in elections, so that the continual transfer, bit by bit, of electoral power from the land-owning classes and the commercial plutocracy to the masses, becomes inevitably the *leit-motif* of the whole movement. It is the thread which runs through the various phases of electoral development, connecting the different aspects of the reforms; aspects which at the time and since, have not always been correlated in the popular mind.

In the second place, and it is a fact less generally recognized, the progress of democracy in the electoral system, if it was constant, was extremely slow. We find the aristocracy in practical control long after the first Reform Act, and the power of the middle classes between 1832 and 1867 was often merely titular. Even the enfranchisement of 1867 left the characteristic of privilege strongly embedded in the electoral system. Democracy did not actually control elections before the extension of the franchise to the counties in 1884, the drastic redistribution of the following year, the elimination of the worst of corrupt practices, and the granting of control of registration to the democratic party associations. If we are to understand the success of democracy in winning final power in the electoral system, we must realize that the changes came gradually and were in every sense a development and not a revolution.

The difficulty of tracing such changes in a single volume has not been small, and I wish to express my deep gratitude to those who have given their assistance. The kindly and inspiring advice and supervision of Professor W. C. Abbott is largely accountable for the gathering of material into a doctoral dissertation, much of which has been included in the present volume. My thanks are also due especially to Professors C. M. Andrews, Allen Johnson, H. S. Canby, and S. B. Hemingway, who have read parts of the manuscript and offered many valuable suggestions and criticisms. I am also indebted for constant and untiring assistance to Mr. E. Byrne Hackett and his assistants of the Yale Press, to the authorities of the Yale University Library, as well as to the authorities of the British Museum and of the Columbia University and New York Public Libraries.

Finally, I wish to acknowledge the invaluable help in the compilation of material rendered by my sister, Mrs. John Angel, and above all that of my wife, whose keen criticism, encouragement, and practical assistance in the completion of the manuscript and reading of proof, has more than anything else made possible the publication of this volume.

New Haven, August 6, 1915.

TABLE OF CONTENTS

ELECTORAL REFORM IN ENGLAND AND WALES

CHAPTER I

INTRODUCTION

"UPON the matter of regulating the suffrage," said Montesquieu, "depends the destruction or salvation of States," and more than a century later the same thought is reëchoed in one of Gladstone's speeches. During that century Europe saw the truth of the dictum constantly and vehemently asserted by every class in every nation. Paris labourers inveighing against the suffrage restrictions of the Constitution of 1791, and, later, demanding universal suffrage on the barricades of 1848; British shopkeepers threatening revolution in 1832; philosophical Germans in their discussions at Frankfort; all upheld the vital importance of the question. Nor did those who resisted the onward march of liberalism regard the matter in less serious light, for to them the advent of democratic or even middle class suffrage meant the loosening of the bond that held society together, the speedy dissolution of the forces of order and discipline. And the importance of the question has not faded in recent years, as will be witnessed by those who have seen Austrian suffrage riots, demonstrations against the Prussian electoral system, and the activities of British feminists.

It may be that both liberals and reactionaries have exaggerated the practical importance of the arrangement of the suffrage. We know that the will of the masses may be carried into effect through the force of public opinion, even though the labourers have not the right to elect the lawmakers. And a nation which chooses its representatives by universal suffrage may yet be under the firm control of autocracy. But even if that is so, none will deny that the determination of the electoral franchise has invariably been regarded as of vital importance; and the growth of a system of elective representation has been the basis of political development in nearly all the states of Europe during the nineteenth century. Especially is this true of England, where the transfer of control in elections from the aristocracy to the masses furnishes a clear norm and test of the notable advance of democracy in the most democratic of European nations.

It is well known that previous to 1832 the power of selecting the members of the House of Commons lay practically with a small group of influential persons. In many of the electoral constituencies the number of voters was trifling and their choice of a representative was dictated by the peer or wealthy commoner whose influence in the community was supreme. The restrictions placed upon the right to vote were such that even in the more populous constituencies the electorate was generally confined to a small knot of voters who obeyed implicitly the orders of their landlord. And the distribution of seats was so arranged that large and important centres of population and industrial activity had no direct representation, while unimportant villages, absolutely controlled by a single person, returned two members to Westminster.

The process by which electoral power was transferred from the landed and commercial aristocracy to the mass of the people, forms the subject of the study that follows. It was a gradual process and can be rightly understood only if we appreciate that it was accomplished in various different aspects of the electoral system. No one piece of legislation accounts for even a major part of the transformation; and the series of acts that popularized voting qualifications cannot be regarded as explaining by themselves the conquest of electoral power by the democracy.

It is true that the reforms which removed the restrictions on the exercise of the suffrage played a vital, although it was not an all-important, part in the democratic advance. The legislation of 1832, 1867, and 1884, by enacting new and more popular voting rights, gradually increased the electorate so that from a small and unevenly distributed number of voters it grew to include all but a comparatively slight portion of the adult male population. This growth in size of itself weakened the aristocratic control.

The reforms also rearranged electoral constituencies in the interests of the democracy by redistributing the parliamentary seats. The populous and industrial districts were given an influence in the House of Commons which was roughly proportionate to their importance, and the equality of voting values in the different constituencies varied far less in 1885 than it ever had before. Such redistribution weakened the sway of the upper classes in elections very directly. For the prevailing power that belonged to the aristocracy before 1832, through their control of the small boroughs, largely disappeared when those boroughs were enlarged or merged in the more populous constituencies.

The growth in the number of electors and the redistribution of electoral power, although the most salient characteristics of parliamentary reform, constituted only a part of a wide transformation of the representative system. Important changes were made at the same time in details of the system, which did much to deprive the aristocracy of its power and to make of England a true electoral democracy. Of these changes the most signifi-

cant took place in methods of electioneering and in the
process of electoral registration.

The most obvious and direct method by which the aristocracy controlled the votes of electors after 1832, was by
corruption of various kinds. So successful were the agents
of the upper classes in thus maintaining the power of the
"governing families" and the new business aristocracy,
that until 1854 the electoral franchise of the people often
remained merely an academic definition. And notwithstanding the Corrupt Practices Act of 1854 and the
introduction of secret voting in 1872, it is clear that many
electors habitually cast their votes according to the instructions of vote-buyers, who acted in behalf of aristocratic influences. As a result of such corruption and because of the enormous expense of contesting a seat, the
electorate of many boroughs was almost as completely
under the control of the upper classes as it had been before
1832.

It was not until 1883, when methods of electioneering
were thoroughly transformed, that the power of the plutocracy was broken. As under all democratic political systems, corruption was not entirely eliminated. But the
opportunities for bribery were largely destroyed, and the
direct purchase of votes became an antiquated mode of
influencing elections. The expense of contesting a seat
was also diminished, a fact which tended to weaken the
aristocratic electoral hegemony. Without question the
upper classes continued to exercise great influence in elections. But it was generally confined to the influence that
naturally belongs to a popular and respected member of
the aristocracy; and it was of a far less compelling nature
than when it had rested mainly upon electoral corruption.

The various reforms in methods of electioneering are
thus worthy of attention in a study of parliamentary reform. Of almost equal importance in the transfer of elec-

toral power to the masses was the development of the
registration system. The Reform Act of 1832 had for
the first time introduced a permanent system of listing
the names of voters, much to the bewilderment and annoyance of the voters. The process of registration was complicated and involved much red tape, so that a very large
proportion of persons who were actually qualified, never
became voters. The electoral agents soon perceived their
opportunity. Utilizing the apathy of prospective
electors, they brought the names of the latter on the lists
on the condition that they would vote as they were told;
on the other hand, they were able, by means of chicanery,
to disfranchise large numbers of the opposing party. The
composition of the electoral lists was accordingly to a
large extent in the hands of agents of aristocratic
interests.

Although the complexities of the system were by no
means removed in the process of reform, they were to a
certain extent simplified. And the control of registration
was taken over from the agents of the aristocracy by the
democratic party associations. The intricacies of electoral registration still constitute a formidable barrier to
complete democracy in elections, but to a far lower degree
than formerly.

In the study that follows emphasis is laid upon the
importance of the reforms in electioneering and registration, partly because the true relation of these reforms to
the increase of democratic power has not always been
fully recognized; partly because of their vital importance.
The student of electoral institutions in England ought
certainly to recognize the basic necessity of the reforms in
the franchise and of redistribution, if the democracy was
to win ultimate control. He ought also to remember that
the three "Reform Acts" did not of themselves make the
English electoral system democratic. And the prime

object of investigation in the following study has been the
actual operation of the franchise, the dynamic forces
determining electoral power, rather than the mere exter-
nals of legislation.

CHAPTER II

THE REFORMED FRANCHISES OF 1832

The Reform Act of 1832—Conditions under which it was passed—
Its general character—Electoral franchises in counties and
boroughs—The 40s. freehold qualification in counties—Retained
in 1832—Question of borough freeholders voting in counties—
Triumph of the Whigs—New franchises in counties—Leaseholders
and copyholders—The tenant-at-will qualification—Protests of
the Radicals—Increased electoral power of the great landholders—
Borough franchises, new and old—The ancient rights—Scot and
lot, burgage, corporation, and freeman qualifications—Suggested
abolition of ancient rights—Opposition of the ministers to freeman franchise—Freeman franchise retained—The new £10 qualification—Opposition of the Tories—Of the Radicals—General
characteristics of the new qualifications.

THE long and gradual process by which electoral
institutions in England have become democratic
was inaugurated by the Reform Act of 1832. This measure was the first ever passed in England that dealt with
the system of elections and parliamentary representation
as a whole. Piecemeal legislation had been attempted and
wholesale revision suggested for many years, but it was
not until the beginning of the second third of the nineteenth century that conditions, political, social, and economic, culminated in thoroughgoing reform. These conditions have often been described.[1] The misery of the
masses, consequent upon the termination of the great war,
gave rise to general discontent with the governing classes.
This discontent crystallized in a demand that the govern-

[1] Grego, *Elections in England;* Porritt, *The Unreformed House
of Commons;* Veitch, *The Genesis of Reform.*

ment be brought into closer touch with the people by a reform of parliamentary and electoral institutions.

The reformers complained that the electoral franchise was complex and irregular in its operation, and in general so restricted that the electorate was small and easily controlled by aristocratic interests. The distribution of seats, they pointed out, was such that direct representation in the House of Commons was denied to populous and thriving towns, although it was granted to many hamlets of the least importance. In the smaller represented boroughs the seats were controlled by peers or wealthy commoners, who either sent their own nominees to parliament or sold the seat to the highest bidder. In either case popular opinion was not consulted and the members of the House of Commons, with few exceptions, represented the aristocracy and their interests. The separation of the government from the middle and lower classes which resulted, was believed by many to be largely accountable for the social and economic misery of the time. It was certainly an important factor in the continually increasing discontent.

In the midst of this discontent the Tories, who were torn by private quarrels, fell from that power which they had held for many years. They were succeeded by a ministry composed of conservative Whigs and Canningites, and led by Earl Grey. Moderate in their opinions and, with few exceptions, belonging to the landowning aristocracy, the members of the new government abhorred radical change; they were nevertheless pledged to a general reform of the representative system, and the willingness of their chief to respond, in part at least, to the popular demand was the strength of their party. Amid difficulties arising on the one side from Tory opposition to any change, and on the other from Radical dissatisfaction at the moderation of the government's proposals, they introduced and carried

a bill of general electoral reform. The excitement and
clamour which accompanied first the refusal of the bill by
the House of Commons, then a succeeding general election,
a second refusal by the Lords, and the final surrender of
the latter, made of the years 1831 and 1832 a notably
critical period in English history.

The Reform Act was revolutionary only in so far as
it began the series of organic changes in the English
representative system. Designed to break down the electoral power vested in a small coterie of plutocrats, it was
not intended to inaugurate a truly democratic régime.
The measure abolished many of the old complex and
restricted franchises and introduced a new general qualification intended to confer the suffrage upon what the
ministers called the "respectable mass of the nation." But
although the new qualification was more liberal in character than some of the earlier franchises, it was not such
as to provide for a very material increase in the number
of voters. More extensive was the rearrangement of seats,
according to which the privilege of sending members to
Westminster was taken from numerous small boroughs and
granted to communities of greater importance. The act
of 1832 also introduced a system of registration, having
for its object the compilation of electoral lists, which was
later to affect the practical exercise of the franchise in a
very high degree.

The present chapter is concerned primarily with the
various types of franchise existent in England in 1832
and with the alterations made in the franchise by the act
of that year. As is generally known, England and Wales
are divided for the purposes of representation into a
number of constituencies, each returning one or more
members to serve in the House of Commons. These constituencies are mainly of two kinds: counties and boroughs.
Formerly the county constituencies corresponded to the

ancient civil divisions, called shires; whereas the borough constituencies had their origin in towns which by royal charter, by prescription, by writ of summons, or by act of parliament, enjoyed the privilege of representation in the national council. County and borough constituencies were also distinguished from each other by their area, by the size of their electorate, and by the nature of the qualifications which conferred the franchise. Since 1885 such distinctions have practically ceased to exist, but in 1832 they still persisted.

As might be inferred from its name, as well as from a knowledge of the English character, the Reform Act did not attempt to build up a new electoral system; nor in reforming the old did it succeed in simplifying the complexities which had always characterized voting qualifications. It left intact the ancient distinction between electoral franchises in counties and boroughs, so that after 1832, as before, the right of vote differed in the two types of constituencies. It also preserved some of the old qualifications, at the same time that it authorized the new. Thus in both counties and boroughs there were after 1832 two classes of franchise: the new rights created by the act of 1832, and the ancient rights which had until then given the suffrage to parliamentary electors. It is obvious that voting qualifications were exceedingly complicated, and the nature of both the old and the new demands explanation.

In the county constituencies the ancient franchise which depended upon a freehold qualification was left untouched; according to this, the vote was granted to every person who held a freehold worth at least 40s. a year, above all charges. This qualification dated back to 1430, when for the first time a restriction had been placed upon the county suffrage. Previous to that year it is probable that all free inhabitant householders voted and that the parlia-

mentary qualification was, like that which compelled
attendance in the county court, merely a "resiance" or
residence qualification.[1] As seats in parliament became
more desirable, and the value and privilege of the suffrage
more generally recognized, there resulted naturally a
restriction of the franchise. The act of 1430,[2] after declaring that elections had been crowded by many persons
of low estate, and that confusion had thereby resulted,
accordingly enacted that the suffrage should be limited to
persons qualified by a freehold of 40s.

This qualification was broader in practice than would
appear at first glance, since the term freehold was applicable to many kinds of property. An explanatory act
of parliament, it is true, confined it to lands of purely
freehold tenure; but notwithstanding this formal declaration, the wider interpretation of the meaning of freeholder
persisted, and we read of many freehold voters who were
enfranchised by such qualifications as annuities and rent
charges issuing out of freehold lands, and even dowers of
wives and pews in churches.[3] After the Restoration the
electoral rights of clergymen were recognized by statute,
and church offices were held to confer a county franchise;
this interpretation widened commensurately with the financial possibilities and value of a vote. A chorister of Ely
cathedral, the butler and brewer of Westminster Abbey,
the bell-ringer, the gardener, the cook, and the organ-
blower, all voted by virtue of their supposedly ecclesiasti-

---

[1] Non-freeholders were assessed for the payment of the knight
of the shire's wages, and they certainly voted in the elections for
sheriffs, Prynne, *Brevia,* iv, 381.

[2] 8 Henry VI, c. 7.

[3] Porritt, *The Unreformed House of Commons,* 22.

Claims to vote in respect of pew rights have been made in the
19th century but refused by the courts, "Hinde v. Charlton" (1866),
Law Reports, 2 Common Pleas, 104; "Brumfitt v. Roberts" (1870),
Ibid., 5 Common Pleas, 224.

cal offices.[1] In 1835 the members of a vestry in Marylebone succeeded in qualifying as electors from a burial
ground attached to the parish.[2]

When the question of voting rights came up in 1832
general sentiment in the House of Commons favoured
retaining the freehold qualification in counties, notwithstanding the well-known desires of the king, who regarded
this franchise as too democratic and would have liked to
see it raised to a £10 value, if it was not to be entirely
abolished.[3] Royal wishes did not, however, coincide with
the interests of either party. The electoral strength of
the Whigs in many county constituencies depended upon
the freeholder vote of the large urban communities, whereas
the Tories, on the other hand, looked to the support of the
small freeholder in the country districts. Neither party
favoured the abolition or the increase in value of the freeholder qualification; but though the Commons voted a
continuance of the 40s. franchise, they agreed to impose
certain limitations upon it: freehold estates lesser than
estates of inheritance were to confer the vote only under
certain conditions; and when the estate was for life (or
lives) only, there must be actual and bona fide occupation
if it were to serve as a qualification.[4] The wider interpre-

---

[1] Porritt, *op. cit.,* 22; *House of Commons Journal,* xi, 93; Peck-
well, *County Election Law,* ii, 102.

[2] *Parliamentary Debates,* T. Hansard, ed. 3d Series, xx, 196.

Taxpaying qualifications in connection with this freehold franchise
were first required in 1712. In that year the exercise of the franchise became contingent upon the assessment of the land or tenements,
in respect of which the vote was conferred, (10 Anne, c. 31). In
1781 the right to vote in counties was made dependent upon a charge,
laid within six months of the election, "toward some aid granted or
to be granted to his Majesty by a land-tax or an assessment, in the
name of the person claiming to vote," (20 George III, c. 17).

[3] Grey, *Correspondence with King William IV,* i, 104.

[4] If however the land was vested in the owner by act of marriage
or marriage settlement, devise, or promotion to a benefice or an

tation of the meaning of freehold, which admitted as qualifications such holdings as pew rights, annuities, and church offices, was not restricted by the act of 1832.[1]

Though the general principle of the freehold franchise was accepted without debate, one aspect of the question gave rise to much discussion at the time and has formed a notable issue in party politics to the present day. The bill provided that the freeholders in boroughs who did not occupy their property should vote in the counties in which the borough was situated.[2] This clause drew forth a torrent of complaint, especially from the Conservatives. Peel pointed out that it would be far simpler for the freeholders in the represented boroughs to vote in the borough where their property was situate instead of being forced to travel to the county polling place; moreover, if the borough freeholders were allowed to vote in the counties, he felt that the boroughs would have an unfair influence in county elections and the rural element would be submerged by the urban.[3] Sir Edward Sugden supported him warmly and complained that the bill would deluge agricultural interests with votes from the town.[4]

When the bill came to committee the youthful and brilliant Praed led the Tory movement for the exclusion of

office, the estate need not be held either by inheritance or by occupation in order to qualify, 2 & 3 Will. IV, c. 45, sec. 18.

[1] Such wide interpretations have, however, been limited by the courts, "Kirton v. Dear," (1869), *Law Reports, 5 Common Pleas,* 217; "Robinson v. Ainge," (1869), *Ibid.,* 4 *Common Pleas,* 429.

[2] According to the early system, the same persons seem to have participated in the election of knights and burgesses; thus in the indentures of return in various cases, the returns both of knights and burgesses were signed by the same electors.

[3] 3 Hansard, vi, 350; ix, 982.

[4] Others pointed out that Birmingham contained 2000 freeholders and by their votes would command the return of at least one of the members for Warwick county, and that Leeds with its 1700 freeholders would control one of the ridings of Yorkshire, 3 Hansard, vi, 167.

borough freeholders from the county constituencies. He
argued with some keenness and much applause. Claiming
that the ministers were treating the agricultural interests
unfairly in the redistribution of seats by disfranchising a
large number of small rural boroughs, he begged that
they would not weaken further the agricultural element
by giving the towns a share in county elections. He insisted that country and town interests were distinct and
should be kept so. Such separation, he claimed, was a
principle that had always formed part of the representative system; the knights of the shire were supposed to
represent the agricultural interest and their return ought
not to be influenced by those who had no direct connection
with that interest: "Let the town freeholders have votes
in the towns with which they are connected and with which
they have a common interest. Do not send them into the
county to vote, from which they have separate and distinct
interests. . . . The only mode in which the county representation can be kept distinct and independent is by
excluding altogether the freeholders in towns from any
share in the county representation."[1]

The Whigs, on the other hand, objected to his principles
and argued that such division of interests between the
inhabitants of towns and counties should not be encouraged. If Praed's theory were correct, said Russell, the
members of the House would represent distinct classes; and
a division and a feeling of jealousy would be created between the agricultural and the manufacturing interests,
the union and combination of which should be the object of
the legislature: "Let us beware of separating the members
of this House into two distinct and hostile parties, the one

[1] 3 Hansard, vi, 356; ix, 1129. Wharncliffe and Eldon argued in
the same manner, the latter claiming with force that plural voting was
undesirable and that "residence on premises out of which the claim
to vote arises, should be indispensable," *Ibid.*, xii, 21, 1113.

in behalf of agriculture, the other of commerce."[1] Russell feared, moreover, that votes could easily be created by the splitting of freeholds; four hundred or five hundred created votes would swamp a town constituency, but would not affect the county. He showed that in Tavistock, where there were originally one hundred and twenty freeholders, they had been reduced to twenty-seven when the Duke of Bedford bought up most of the property included in the borough limits. If the freeholders had the right to vote in the borough, the Duke by reviving these freeholds as electoral qualifications would control the constituency; the large size of the county electorate, however, would prevent any number that he might create from having a material effect on county elections.[2] Althorp, who naturally supported the same side, pointed out that until 1832 freeholders in the unrepresented towns always had voted in the counties, so that the Tories could hardly complain that the ministers were introducing new principles to favour urban interests; he showed also that occupying freeholders with a £10 qualification would vote in the borough under the newly created borough franchise.[3]

The ministers triumphed and the clause which allowed freeholders in towns to vote in the county constituencies became part of the act, with the result that since 1885 there has been no election at which the Liberals have not bitterly complained of exactly those conditions which the Tories then prophesied. As a matter of fact the issues debated in this question were of a strictly party nature. The landowning Tories hoped that their electoral interests in the counties would be advanced by the exclusion of the

1 3 Hansard, ix, 984.
2 3 Hansard, v, 1236; ix, 984.
3 3 Hansard, ix, 1141. The difficulties of the question and the perplexity of the ministers are clearly displayed in the debates, *Ibid.*, iv, 788; v, 1317; vi, 162.

men occupied in industry, trade, and commerce, who were freeholders in boroughs. On the other hand the Whigs, who owed their success in many counties to the votes of just these men, were anxious to see them voting at the county polling places.[1]

The act of 1832, besides preserving the freeholder franchise, introduced in counties three new kinds of qualifications. Two of these, like the qualification of the freeholders, were derived from the ownership of property: they were the copyholders[2] and leaseholders, for a term of sixty years, who might vote in respect of their tenures, provided that the clear yearly value of their land, above all rents and charges, amounted to £10 or more. Where the term of the lease was shorter than sixty, but not less than twenty years, the minimum clear yearly value which was to confer the right to vote, was set at £50.[3] The other qualification introduced was the £50 rental. This was the starting point of an occupation qualification in counties, which marks as distinct a step in the development of the suffrage as the granting of household suffrage in boroughs a generation later. Under this qualification, a person claiming the vote must actually occupy as tenant, and the liability required must be an entire liability for a yearly rent of not less than £50, under a tenancy to the same landlord. Sub-lessees or assignees of such tenants might

---

[1] Porritt, "Barriers against Democracy in the British Electoral System," in *Political Science Quarterly*, xxvi, 1.

[2] Tenants by the general form of customary tenure are called copyholders. "Tenant by copy of court roll is as if a man be seized of a manor, within which manor there is a custom which hath been used time out of mind of man, that certain tenants within the same manor have used to have lands and tenements to hold to them and their heirs in fee simple or fee tail or for term of life, etc., at the will of the lord, according to the custom of the manor," cited in Mackenzie and Lushington, *Registration Manual*, 80.

[3] 2 & 3 Will. IV, c. 45, sec. 19, 20.

vote under this qualification when they were in actual occupation.[1]

The copyhold and leasehold qualifications were generally acceptable to the Tories, and were regarded as compensation offered to the landowning classes for the loss of that influence which they were to suffer through the general disfranchisement of the small boroughs. For this reason they were attacked both by the industrials and by those who posed as the defenders of the small farmers against the great landlords. Lord Milton complained that the leasehold qualification "would produce a class most dependent on the landlords, and was likely to overbalance the independent interest in the counties."[2] The opponents of this franchise also feared that the effect on agriculture would be bad, since the landlords would be tempted to cut up their estates into £50 leaseholds. They believed, moreover, that an excellent opportunity was offered for the creation of fictitious votes.[3] Baring objected to the leasehold and copyhold qualifications because of the complicated nature of the tenure, which would result in much perplexity as to whether or not any particular tenure would confer a qualification. Such franchises, he said, would give employment to all the lawyers throughout the country, when it came to a settlement of disputed rights and claims.[4] The justice of this criticism is appreciated when we discover that there were 400 different kinds of

[1] 2 & 3 Will. IV, sec. 20. "Burton v. Langham" (1848), 5 *Common Bench Reports,* 92; "Gadsby v. Barrow" (1844), 8 *Jurist Reports,* 1031.

[2] 3 Hansard, vi, 200. A writer in the *Westminster Review* (xxv, 502) insisted that the leaseholders were absolutely dependent upon the good will of their landlords; in general they had broken some of the formal covenants so that they could be legally evicted at any time.

[3] 3 Hansard, vi, 200.

[4] 3 Hansard, vi, 277.

title which conferred a copyhold qualification, and 250
which established a leasehold.[1]

The £50 rental qualification aroused still more violent
opposition and was passed only with difficulty and in the
face of ministerial disapproval. This franchise was embodied in an amendment that was made and carried by the
Marquis of Chandos, and the clause setting forth the qualification has invariably borne the name of its author. The
latter represented the electoral interests of the landlords;
according to a contemporary estimate, he was the "im-
personation of the corn-laws, the high priest of the temple
of Ceres . . . the acknowledged leader of the ultra malt-
tax repealing, commerce taxing squirearchy."[2] He was
generally known as the "Farmers' Friend," and it was
directly in the interest of agriculture that he brought forward the qualification: "If the landed interest was of any
value to the country, if any commiseration was due to the
farmers for their patient and loyal sufferings of late
years, they ought not in point of representation to be
worse treated than the householders in towns."[3] All the
Tories developed this argument, and often with skill and
plausibility.

In answer, Althorp showed that the £50 rental franchise
was not in reality designed to benefit the farmers, but
rather the landlords, who could force their tenants to vote
as they wished, under pain of ejection. To those who
said that the agricultural tenant-at-will was quite as
respectable as the £10 householder in boroughs, whom the
Whigs planned to enfranchise, he replied: "The Committee
were not called to decide upon their [the tenants'] respec-

[1] *Parliamentary Papers*, 1846, no. 451, "Minutes of Evidence,"
§ 3306.

[2] "Mask," *Pencillings of Politicians*, 99, 105; Fowler, *Echoes of
Old Country Life*, 23.

[3] 3 Hansard, vi, 273.

tability, but whether they were in that situation which would make them independent county electors. . . . It was in the power of the landlord to do his tenant a greater injury than the landlord of the householder could do to his. . . . If a man thus circumstanced should vote contrary to the wish of his landlord and he was turned out for it, he would lose all the capital he had embarked in the land."[1] Althorp feared also that the control of the landlord would result in the ballot. Milton also opposed the £50 tenant franchise on the same ground that he had opposed the leasehold; as being in reality unfair to the small farmer. Most of the country people, he said, did not want the vote; they often divested themselves of freehold property in order to avoid voting against their conscience at the bidding of the landlord.[2] The other Whig leaders, especially the ministers, also opposed the Chandos clause. Grey announced in the Lords that it was projected and carried by persons not connected with the government, and the government would not be responsible for it, though they accepted it, to save the bill. Like Althorp he especially disliked the tenant qualification as it gave such power to the landlords that it must ultimately result in the ballot. Durham's hostility to it was also open and pronounced.[3]

The great mass of the Whig squires, however, made common cause with the Tories, realizing the electoral strength that would accrue in their individual constituencies. They were assisted by Hume and the Radicals, who favoured the extension of the suffrage in all directions. The latter, moreover, believed that the dependence of the

[1] 3 Hansard, vi, 281.

[2] 3 Hansard, vi, 277. The freeholders in many counties objected to the new franchise fearing that their own votes would now be swamped by the influx of suffrages controlled by the landlords; cf. a petition from the freeholders of Cumberland, *Ibid.*, vi, 699.

[3] 3 Hansard, vii, 940; Reid, *Life of Durham*, i, 406.

tenants on the landlords was exaggerated; and that even without the ballot, landlords were likely in the future to be more anxious to let their land than the tenants to rent it. The tenants would then have sufficient power to send their own representatives to promote the interests of the farmer as distinct from those of the landlord.[1] Hunt voted for the tenant qualification on the same grounds that led Althorp and Grey to oppose it; namely, that it would give such power to the landlords that the ballot must result.[2] His political foresight as well as the forebodings of the Whig leaders were fully justified by the report of the committee that investigated electoral conditions in the counties in 1870.[3]

The combination of the agricultural interests, whether Whig or Tory, with the Radicals was too great for the ministers, who in this instance found the support of the urban element insufficient for the rejection of the £50 tenant qualification. Rather than to alienate an important section of their party, the government finally accepted the Chandos clause, which for the next generation proved a mighty bulwark of agricultural strength in elections.

The introduction of the leasehold, copyhold, and £50 tenancy qualifications greatly increased the complexity of the county franchise. Previous to 1832 there was only one path to the county suffrage afforded by the freeholder

---

[1] Le Marchant, *Memoir of Lord Althorp*, 339; Roebuck, *History of the Whig Ministry*, ii, 198.

[2] 3 Hansard, vi, 278. It has been suggested (Hunt and Poole, *History of England*, xi, 295) that Grey did not seriously lament the intervention of Chandos because of the support offered to aristocratic dominion. But the fear of the ballot, expressed by the Whig leaders, was certainly sincere; even a Tory, like Wharncliffe, although he approved of the increased control of the landlords, disapproved of the Chandos clause because he felt that if such control was exercised it would immediately lead to secret voting.

[3] *Parliamentary Papers*, 1870, no. 115.

qualification, and notwithstanding the variety of forms which that qualification assumed there was generally little question as to whether or not a person were qualified. But with three new franchises, each of which was dependent upon a variety of tenures, there was a danger lest voting rights should be so complicated as to require technical information and the services of election experts.[1] The complications were increased by the provision that a person who held property which would give him either a county or a borough qualification must vote in the borough; it resulted that persons in the same place with similar property but of different value must vote in different constituencies. Thus a 40s. freeholder in a borough was to vote for the representative of the county in which the borough was situated; but if his qualification were a £10 freehold which he occupied, he thereby held a borough qualification as well, and accordingly lost his county vote, which was transferred to the borough.[2] If a man had a house worth £5 in a borough, and land in the county worth £45, so that conjointly they completed his £50 qualification, he could vote for the county. But if the house in the borough was worth £10, he lost his county vote.

The opponents of the bill were not slow to seize upon such complexities as an excuse for its rejection or mutilation. With much foresight they pointed out that the proving of a qualification would involve such litigation that the ordinary man would hardly consider it worth his while to

---

[1] Freehold tenure, serving as an electoral qualification, was in reality by no means simple: there were 570 different kinds establishing such a qualification, and for land alone, without any building upon it, 150. Such qualifications, however, were well known, and do not seem to have caused much litigation, whereas the 50 different kinds of tenancy-at-will, and the 650 kinds conferring a copyhold and lease-hold vote would be strange to the voters and the courts, and cause endless difficulty, *Parliamentary Papers,* 1846, no. 451, "Minutes of Evidence," § 3306; 3 Hansard, xcii, 399.

[2] 3 Hansard, vi, 304.

claim his vote. Baring, who understood electioneering, and was appalled by the prospect of confusion which the county franchise seemed to present, suggested that a single uniform franchise be adopted for the counties. Let occupancy alone be the sole qualification; this, he insisted, would do away with all the complications and would frustrate the hopes of the election attorneys, who expected to control elections absolutely.[1] Baring's suggestion, made in desperation and without expectation of acceptance, passed unnoticed. The succeeding generation, however, was to prove that Baring's fear of electoral complications was justified; and it is curious that the most important class of county franchise, after 1885, should have been suggested by one of the chief anti-reformers of 1832.

On the whole the Tories and the landholders felt that they "had not come out so badly" [*sic*] as a result of the reformed county vote. While they fought every change in boroughs and gave the impression of utter disgust at the result of the new franchises there, they at least gained one substantial advantage in the counties. The permission granted to the non-occupying urban freeholder to vote in counties had possibly given strength to the Liberals. But the carrying of the £50 tenant clause was bound to assure the Tory landowners equal balance, if not something more. This was also the belief of the Liberals, who foresaw that the farmers would be handed over entirely to the aristocracy. The general effect of the county franchise, as seen in their eyes, was noted by Gore Langton: "The small independent freeholders, who are at once the honour and security of the country, will lose their comparative weight; while the influence of the large landed proprietor will be increased."[2]

In boroughs, as in counties, two categories of voters

1 3 Hansard, vi, 310.
2 3 Hansard, ix, 985.

were left by the Reform Act: those exercising the franchise under the new qualification introduced in 1832 and
those known as the ancient right voters, who voted under
qualifications existent before the passing of the act. Only
one class of new rights was created by the act of 1832.
This was the £10 occupation qualification. According to
the act, the franchise was granted to all male persons
who for a year before registration had occupied as owners
or tenants "any house, warehouse, country house, shop,
or other building, either separately or jointly with any
land" of a clear yearly value of not less than £10. The
land must be within the electoral limits of the borough;
and in order to qualify, the occupier must have been rated,
in respect of such premises, to all rates for the relief of the
poor; and he must have paid at the time of registration
all rates and taxes due from him the preceding April.[1]

This occupation franchise was the characteristic of the
borough suffrage after 1832. As ownership furnished the
ordinary qualification for franchise in the counties, so in
the boroughs, occupation, actual or constructive, was the
basis of the suffrage. While, however, in the counties no
provision was made for ascertaining the true value or
bona fide rent which was to qualify for the franchise; in
the boroughs, assessment to the taxes was embodied with
the condition of value, and actual payment was superadded. There was another difference between the character of the county and borough franchise, as determined
by the Reform Act. In the latter no claimant could be
registered as a voter if he had received parochial relief

---

[1] 2 & 3 Will. IV, c. 45, sec. 27. "The poor rate is primarily a
tax towards the necessary relief of the lame, impotent, old, blind, and
other such persons within a township or parish, being poor and not
able to work, and for the putting out of poor children to be appren-
tices, levied upon the inhabitants and occupiers of land, houses,
tithes, sporting rights, and mines within the parish or township,"
43 Eliz. c. 2, (The Poor Relief Act, 1601).

within the past twelve months; in the counties, no disqualification was attached to the receipt of poor-relief. This distinction arose from the fact that in counties the franchise was annexed to the tenement in every case; the law therefore presumed the voter not to be in a state of disqualifying indigence, so long as he continued in possession of the land. In boroughs, however, the franchise was annexed in many cases to the person and not to the tenement.[1]

This personal franchise was the characteristic of most of the ancient rights which had conferred a vote in boroughs before 1832, and which were preserved under certain conditions by the act of that year. These ancient voting rights were far more numerous and confused in boroughs than in counties. Originally the borough franchise, like that of the county, had depended on residence alone, and no general measure, comparable to the 40s. freeholder act of 1430, was passed to limit and restrict the suffrage. In some boroughs, however, the franchise was closely defined and limited by custom; in others, local acts for the remodelling of the franchise and the reduction of the electorate were passed.[2] The Tudors and the first Stuarts were, moreover, quick to make use of the royal prerogative of granting and annulling, by charter, the liberties of parliamentary elections, and in this way the various types of borough franchise became more and more differentiated and generally more restricted.[3]

After the Revolution of 1688 the House of Commons began to assume the power of determining, upon pretext of usage, the rights of electoral franchise in all the boroughs

1 Rogers, *Election Law,* i, 179-180; Anstey, *Notes upon the Representation of the People Act,* 60.

2 VI *Rot. Parl.* 431, b; 433, a.

3 *Commons Journals,* i, *passim* (1623-1626); particularly cf. 108. For the electoral methods of James II, see Reresby, *Memoirs, passim.*

of England. Several acts[1] gave the force of law to these "last determinations," but the resolutions of the Commons were so often rescinded and varied that, instead of giving stability or harmony to the newly restricted franchise, they merely made confusion worse confounded. By the end of the eighteenth century the unevenly developed restrictions on the franchise, which resulted from the increasing demand for seats in the House of Commons and the growing desire of the patrons to control elections, had produced a tangled skein of electoral rights. The complexities of the borough franchise became the bane of parliamentary committees and a mine and a mint of inspiration for Radical orators and writers. To describe in detail the characteristics of voting rights before 1832 would pass the scope of this chapter; the chief qualifications, however, demand rough explanation. The most important of them were preserved by the Reform Act, some are still in use, and all persisted for many years after 1832.[2]

There were, in a broad sense, four general classes of borough qualifications.[3] First of all, the type which still remained closely akin to the original franchise; under this all resident householders, or all persons paying scot and lot, might vote, provided they did not receive alms or parochial relief. In the same class stood the potwaller or potwalloper, whose euphonious title has given him an interest hardly warranted by his numbers or importance.[4]

[1] 7 & 8 Will. III, c. 7; 12 & 13 Will. III, c. 5; 12 Anne, c. 16; 2 Geo. II, c. 24; 28 Geo. III, c. 52; 9 Geo. IV, c. 22.

[2] The best description of the unreformed borough franchises is to be found in Porritt, *The Unreformed House of Commons;* a mass of material is still to be sifted from Oldfield, *The Representative History of Great Britain and Ireland,* and Merewether and Stephens, *The History of Boroughs.*

[3] *Parliamentary Papers,* 1866, nos. 3626, 284.

[4] Inhabitants paying scot and lot are the predecessors of the rated occupiers of the present day. According to Stubbs, scot refers

Under the householder, the scot and lot, and potwaller qualifications, the suffrage depended to the last upon residence and contribution to the charges of municipal government. There were, before 1832, sixty-six boroughs in which this franchise was practically the sole means of obtaining the suffrage. These boroughs ranged in size from villages like Gatton and Aldborough to such metropolitan boroughs as Westminster and Southwark.[1] The smaller boroughs in which this sort of franchise existed, were easily controlled by the borough patron. If he once possessed himself of a larger part of the property within the parliamentary area, he had merely to fill the houses with tenants who would obey his instructions as the elections recurred.[2]

Another type of borough franchise was that conferred by a burgage hold.[3] There were twenty-seven boroughs in which such tenure formed the avenue to the suffrage. They were essentially the rotten boroughs and were largely responsible for the outcry made before the reform against nomination. Many of them were disfranchised by the act

to the rate, or impost, and lot to the apportioned amount of the same. In the 18th century the House of Commons declared that it meant simply poor-rate, (2 Geo. I, c. 18). A potwaller has been defined as one, whether he be a householder or a lodger, who has the sole dominion of a room with a fireplace in it, and who furnishes and cooks his own diet at such fireplace. Heaton (*The Three Reforms of Parliament*, 7) says that the word is derived from the English *pot* and the Saxon *wealan*.

[1] Oldfield, *op. cit., passim.* Porrit (op. cit., 30) says there were only 59 boroughs in this group, but a later parliamentary return endorses Oldfield's estimate, *Parliamentary Papers*, 1866, nos. 3626, 284.

[2] Porrit, *op. cit.*, 38.

[3] A burgage was "a tenure of lands in England, by the performance of certain services, distinguished both from knight service in which the render was uncertain, and from villeinage where the service was of the meanest kind." Hemmeon, in his study, *Burgage Tenure in Mediæval England,* discusses the characteristics of this form of tenure.

of 1832; in some boroughs, however, a burgage hold conferred a qualification even as late as 1884. Closely related to this franchise was the freehold qualification, exercised in towns which assumed the county and not the municipal form of government and were known as counties of cities or towns.[1] There were seventeen of these at the time of the passing of the Reform Act, of which four were then disfranchised.[2]

There were also before the reform some thirty or more boroughs in which the right of choosing a member for parliament was vested in the municipal corporation. Of these, eight were disfranchised and those that remained were of small importance. In larger cities like Bath, where the inhabitants could formerly win the suffrage only through membership in the corporation, the reformed electorate was, as will be seen, composed almost entirely of those voting under new qualifications.[3]

The most important of all classes of ancient voting rights was the freeman qualification. Although the most common, it was by no means popular in its character; for when the term freeman was used in municipal or parliamentary connection it borrowed all the exclusiveness, all the sense of bourgeois monopoly which hung about the trade guilds. This franchise existed in one hundred and seven boroughs at the beginning of the nineteenth century, and only ten of these were disfranchised in 1832. Freedom might be obtained in many ways. The unreformed system allowed the creation of freemen by the corporation,

---

[1] The right annexed to a burgage tenement was probably the more ancient; from this there grew up the right of freeholders generally, within certain cities and boroughs, to vote, whether their tenement was held in burgage or not, Heywood, *Borough Elections,* iv.

[2] *Parliamentary Papers,* 1866, no. 284.

[3] Thus in Bath after 1832 there was but one person voting as a capital burgess in an electorate of more than three thousand, *Parliamentary Papers,* 1866, no. 3626.

and in most cases this right was abused thriftily and
effectively.[1] After the reform, freedom might be acquired
through inheritance or servitude.[2] In the former case the
sons of freemen acquired their freedom upon arriving at
the age of twenty-one; in the latter, apprenticeship for
seven years to a freeman brought the privilege through
"servitude." In unreformed days, marriage with a freeman's daughter gave the parliamentary franchise,[3] but
after 1832, although freedom might be acquired in certain
boroughs by marriage, in none was it allowed to confer
the right to vote.[4]

The act of 1832 accepted all the existent forms of
franchise in use at the time, and kept them alive with distinctions as to perpetuity for some and limited duration
for others. Residence was, however, to be in future a
necessary condition of the borough suffrage. Resident
freemen and London liverymen were to hand down their
electoral rights to their descendants; and in certain
boroughs a freehold or a burgage tenure was to confer
the franchise in perpetuity. All the other classes of the
franchise were to continue for the lives of their respective
possessors only.

It was after long debate and much acrimonious discus-

---

[1] *House of Commons Journals,* xii, 527; Merewether and Stephens,
op. cit., iii, 2000.

[2] *Parliamentary Papers,* 1867, no. 72.

[3] Lambert, "Parliamentary Franchises, Past and Present," in
The Nineteenth Century, December, 1889; Porritt, *op. cit.,* i, 59, 78.

[4] In eight boroughs freedom might be acquired by marriage as
late as 1867, *Parliamentary Papers,* 1867, no. 72. In London the
quality of liveryman, which conferred the franchise, might be
acquired through purchase or redemption, as well as by patrimony
or servitude, *Ibid.,* 1876, no. 454. In 1835 the municipal corporations
lost the right of creating freemen (by 5 & 6 Will. IV, c. 26), a right
which was not restored until 1885 (by 48 & 49 Vict., c. 29), and then
under conditions which protected both the parliamentary and
municipal franchises.

sion that the Whig ministers permitted the continuation of the freeman franchise. In their original scheme the ministers had planned the complete abolition of all the ancient rights of franchise in boroughs, merely reserving the rights of the existing holders for their lives. In presenting the ministerial plan, Russell emphasized the differences of franchise in the various boroughs and the electoral complications which resulted therefrom. The House of Commons' determinations, he pointed out, had always been coloured by political bias and were still founded to a certain extent on the iniquity of party conflict. Moreover, in many cases the electors qualified by these franchises came from the lowest class. It was notorious that in the small boroughs no part of the electorate was more corrupt than the scot and lot voters, and their disfranchisement would be an advantage. "I contend," he concluded, "that it is important to get rid of these complicated rights, of these vexatious questions, and to give to the real property and to the real respectability of the different cities and towns the right of voting."[1]

In committee the Whig leaders pointed out that their plan entailed no personal injustice to voters, since all existing rights were preserved for the lives of their possessors. But as the ancient rights were liable to the greatest abuse, it was dangerous to preserve them in perpetuity. The government admitted that in the large towns the scot and lot franchise was exercised very usefully; but its abolition would occasion no practical disfranchisements, since the new £10 franchise would serve to qualify the majority of the former electors. In the small towns the ancient right voters were disreputable and a much better class would be substituted.[2] Stanley showed that the forfeiture of rights was deferred to a future

[1] 3 Hansard, ii, 1069.
[2] 3 Hansard, vi, 737.

generation and also that it was applied to a class and not to an individual so that none could complain; such forfeiture, moreover, was justifiable on the principle that it was essential to a sound system of representation. The government also believed that the abolition of the ancient complex franchises would help to put the electoral attorneys out of business, thus answering Baring's complaint that England would be transformed by the bill into a hodge-podge of litigation.[1]

The attack upon the ancient rights was, however, strenuously opposed by the Tories. Sir Charles Wetherell pursued his customary line of stigmatizing their abolition as nothing but robbery: "The right of freemen to vote . . . was an hereditary right, and that principle once adopted of attacking and spoliating hereditary rights no man could take it upon him to say where it would end."[2] Other Tories contended that since the county franchise had been permanently preserved, it was only fair to the borough electors that theirs should be also. In answer to Russell's argument that the complications of this franchise caused the House infinite trouble, they asserted that there were on an average barely four disputed cases a year. A sentimental argument also was introduced, claiming that the ancient right voters were honestly attached to their quaint and ancient rights and that they should be permitted this simple enjoyment which their ancestors had possessed before them.[3]

The Tory amendment for the preservation of all the

[1] 3 Hansard, vi, 896, 901.
[2] 3 Hansard, vi, 898.
[3] 3 Hansard, vi, 723. It was true, certainly, that electors with several qualifications preferred the ancient right for voting purposes. There is one case after 1832 where an elector with a freeholder and an occupation qualification always voted as a potwalloper; the latter right was apparently always regarded as a special privilege, Fowler, *Echoes of Old Country Life*, 22.

ancient rights was defeated without difficulty, but a determined and ultimately successful effort was made to save at least the freeman franchise. The Tories in their opposition to the ministerial plan of complete disfranchisement were assisted by the Radicals and many of the Whigs. Edmund Peel led the movement and pointed out that the Whigs' position was wholly untenable on logical grounds: "As it is admitted that there is no danger in allowing the resident freemen to retain their rights for the next forty or fifty years . . . where, I would ask, would be the danger in allowing these ancient rights to be permanent?" He emphasized, moreover, the value of a close connection between the working classes and the House of Commons, and the danger of estranging those classes by the aristocratic colour of the bill. By severing this connection there would be produced "not conciliation, not union, not satisfaction, but indifference, if not dislike, to the future constituted and parliamentary authorities of the country."[1]

This argument was developed by many who usually supported the ministers. Lord Milton thought "it most desirable that those who had no property should yet feel they had an interest in the constitution." Others twitted the ministers with their inconsistency: the government claimed that the great principle of the bill was to open and not to close boroughs, to extend and not to contract the franchise. But the disappearance of the freemen as electors would in some boroughs render the number of electors extremely small; in one at least it would reduce the constituency from 1500 voters to 325.[2] And certainly the registers after 1832 showed boroughs, such as Coventry and Lancaster, where four-fifths of the electorate was composed of freemen, and where the new qualification by itself would have enfranchised only a small proportion of the

[1] 3 Hansard, vi, 892.
[2] 3 Hansard, vi, 887.

inhabitants. Several Tories argued that those who acquired their freedom through servitude had justly earned the franchise and that the Commons had no right to deprive them or their descendants of the privilege. Trevor conceived it "unjust to deprive freemen of a privilege they had obtained by the sweat of their brows, a privilege which created an honourable spirit of emulation. . . . A right so obtained was as much the property of the freeman as was the coronet of the peer."[1] Another argument was that the acquisition of freedom acted as a sort of insurance; when a freeman died, his widow and children participated in certain charities. But it was feared that without the elective franchise there would be no inducement for the ordinary man to take up his freedom; becoming a freeman entailed a fee and, without the suffrage, would result in no immediate recompense.[2]

The government at first refused absolutely to concede that the freeman franchise should be allowed to remain. In the absence of Althorp, whose tact and easy good nature softened many a refusal on the part of the ministers, Russell replied brusquely that to admit the freeman voting right in perpetuity was quite impossible. He believed that the £10 franchise gave a sufficient share in representation and sufficient power to the industrial classes. The freemen were corrupt and their disfranchisement would be distinctly a benefit. And if the privilege of voting were allowed to freemen, it must also be granted to the other classes of ancient right voters.[3] A very large number of ardent reformers expressed themselves as hostile to government on this point, generally because of the disfranchising effects of the abolition clause. In the division, however, many of them renounced their convic-

1 3 Hansard, vi, 734.
2 3 Hansard, vi, 885.
3 3 Hansard, vi, 886, 903.

tions for the sake of party weal, and Peel's amendment was lost.[1]

The exigencies of parliamentary tactics, however, induced the ministers to reconsider the freeman franchise. After the Lords had thrown out the bill in the autumn of 1831, certain provisions were recast in the hope of overcoming the fears and prejudices of the peers. Grey and Althorp, rather against their own judgment, decided that a modification of the freeman abolition clause would go far towards reconciling some of the "waverers."[2] Accordingly, when the third Reform Bill was introduced, provision was made that while all other classes of ancient rights should lapse with the lives of their possessors, the freeman franchise should be continued, with the condition, however, that all freemen created since March, 1831, should be excluded; it was a generally recognized fact that a large number of freemen electors had been created by anti-reform corporations, during the months of excitement, with the express object of defeating reform.

This concession was hailed with joy by those who, in the preceding session, had fought vainly for the freemen. Sir Robert Peel believed that it would operate well in breaking down the dead uniformity which would otherwise be established by the £10 qualification, and he was pleased at the recognition of hereditary privilege. The final consent of the ministers to the change was granted grudgingly, and Althorp admitted that they made it as a politic concession rather than as an actual improvement on their previous determination.[3] From the opportunist point of view they acted wisely, for the retention of the freeman franchise served to reconcile many of the working classes with the

---

[1] 3 Hansard, vi, 908.
[2] Le Marchant, *Althorp,* 373.
[3] 3 Hansard, x, 52.

£10 clause, and that too at a moment when the popularity of the Whigs in the country was waning.[1]

Encouraged by the government's surrender of their plan to abolish the freeman qualification, the Tories attempted to extend that franchise further by abrogating the condition of residence. Wetherell complained that it was unfair to demand residence from a glazier or a plumber and not from a Master of Arts voting for his university.[2] Members representing the services also objected that all freemen in the army and navy would be disfranchised. As was generally acknowledged, however, non-residence of electors had been a main factor in the egregious expense of elections, for it led to the payment of travelling expenses, which also served as a convenient cloak for wholesale bribery. The attempt to permit non-residence was accordingly met with strong arguments and was defeated by a large majority.[3]

The creation of freemen electors was carefully restricted by the Reform Act, as well as by the Municipal Corporations Act of 1835.[4] Such restrictions made it impossible for any corporation to increase suddenly the number of voters in the interest of the predominant party, as had been the custom in unreformed days. Nor was the franchise to be secured by marriage with a freeman's widow or daughter as in times past. Many petitions came in to the House from the London liverymen and from boroughs

---

[1] Wallas, *Life of Place*, 279. On the other hand, the ministers had been fortified in their project of abolition by the receipt of addresses from the classes about to be disfranchised, offering to sacrifice their privileges if such action would assist in passing the bill; such addresses were sent by the Taunton potwallers, the London liverymen, and the corporations of Gloucester, Calne, Chichester, and Salisbury.

[2] 3 Hansard, vi, 726.

[3] 3 Hansard, vi, 911; x, 55.

[4] 5 & 6 Will. IV, c. 26.

where freemen were numerous, begging that the daughters of freemen might be allowed to bring the suffrage as their marriage portion to the altar. And it appeared that the ancient privilege was highly valued. The ladies of Bristol, we read, had been granted the right, as a dowry, by Queen Elizabeth, apparently because they possessed insufficient personal charms to win husbands unless aided by material inducements. But Althorp was obdurate, and ungallantly refused to permit the continuance of the custom; he explained, with absence of humour, that it had given rise to many abuses, and described seriously the cases where ladies had been shut up in a room at election time, ready to marry any person disposed to vote in a certain interest.[1]

The discussion which raged over the retention of the freeman franchise was, however, overshadowed by the debates upon the new £10 householder qualification in boroughs. On the one hand the Tories centred their attack upon this franchise, since it was designed to enfranchise a large number of new electors, and they regarded it as the opening wedge of the coming democracy. On the other hand the Whigs defended the new qualification as the corner-stone of their whole scheme. And the conflict was confused by the Radicals, who regarded the scope of the £10 suffrage as altogether inadequate, but who were unwilling to wreck the bill entirely by refusing to assist the government.

In the eyes of the ministers the chief fault of the old electoral system was the absolute power of individuals and

---

[1] 3 Hansard, vi, 698; x, 62. At one closely contested election it is said that a trick was devised for the same woman to marry several men. When the ceremony was completed and the temporary husband had duly recorded his vote the two shook hands over a grave, saying, "Now death do us part," which was considered a divorce; after which the woman proceeded to qualify another husband at another church, *Chambers Journal,* lviii, 710.

corporations in the small boroughs. A large majority of the borough seats were controlled so completely that the borough patron had only to nominate his favoured client to ensure his election. Seats might be given by the patron or the corporation on condition that their interests were furthered by the member; more often they were sold to the highest bidder. In any case such a system was not what is usually implied by the term representative. The Whigs planned to destroy, or at least attack, the nomination system in two ways: the smallest boroughs they would disfranchise absolutely, in the larger ones they would so increase the number of voters that control of their suffrages would be difficult if not impossible.[1]

To fix upon a qualification that would enfranchise sufficient numbers without creating a thoroughly popular or radically inclined constituency, was the problem of the ministers in their drafting of the bill. The Whigs, by tradition, had even less confidence in the poorer classes than the Tories, and while they were willing to admit a very few of the artisans they were determined to avoid a low property franchise, which, as they frankly insisted, would admit classes which had been shown to be corrupt and untrustworthy. Russell solemnly warned the House of Commons to beware of a body of electors "hostile to property and debased by ignorance."[2] It is therefore not surprising that the first qualification considered was as high as £20. This was favoured by both the king and Grey, and was proposed to the small sub-committee which had been commissioned to draft the first bill. Althorp on the other hand believed this qualification too high, and induced Graham, who represented his opinions on the sub-

[1] 3 Hansard, ii, 1066. The elimination of corruption was another object; the ministers hoped to swamp the venal scot and lot voters by the new ten pounders, *Ibid.*, xiii, 558.

[2] 3 Hansard, ix, 497-498.

committee, to obtain a lower rate if possible. This he did, with the assistance of Brougham, by advocating the ballot, not in the hope of obtaining it, but in order to secure the lower rate of franchise by way of compromise.[1] A £20 qualification, it was soon discovered, would have been pitiably ineffective as a measure of enfranchisement. In the large boroughs the electorate would have been extremely limited, and in some of the small boroughs there would have been but three, seven, or ten electors.[2]

The £10 qualification which the sub-committee ultimately presented had all the disadvantages of a compromise. While the more conservative members of the cabinet felt that it was too democratic, Brougham would have preferred giving the vote to all householders. This qualification, however, had been tried for municipal voting purposes, notably at Norwich, and had proved satisfactory. And so far as could be estimated from the inaccurate and incomplete returns, it would admit to voting privileges about the number and the class that the Whigs had in mind.

The Tories, naturally, were opposed to the new qualification on principle and in practice. To destroy the prescriptive rights of the artisans and grant new rights to the lower middle class was at total variance with all their ideas. And in practice the latter class had shown itself inclined to support the Whigs, whose chief electoral strength in towns was supposed to lie among the smaller shopkeepers. The Tories asserted that not merely the

---

[1] Parker, *Life of Sir James Graham,* 101; Le Marchant, *Althorp,* 292.

[2] 3 Hansard, ii, 1070. It is rather surprising to learn that Thomas Attwood was willing to induce the Birmingham Political Union to accept the £20 franchise; such weakness was prevented by the refusal of the more robust politicians from Newcastle, Holyoake, *Sixty Years of an Agitator's Life,* i, 26.

lower classes but the upper and upper middle classes as well were deprived of the vote; that in nearly all boroughs the majority of voters would be qualified by property qualifications of between £10 and £20; power would thus be in the hands of those whom Sibthorp called the "dregs of the community," Croker, "a vulgar, privileged pedlary," and Wetherell, "the oligarchy of shopkeepers."[1] In proof of the dependence and unfitness of the £10 householders for the suffrage, their opponents pointed out that on the very night on which the measure was introduced, a bill which was to exempt from poor rates all whose property was less than £12 annual value reached its second reading. A person unable to pay his rates was surely not entitled to the vote.[2]

Peel's chief objection was that the new qualification was too uniform, and would leave power in the hands of one class; in his eyes the great advantage of the old system was that it represented all classes. He feared that this very uniformity would cause unfairness; in the large towns and metropolitan boroughs, the result would be almost universal suffrage, whereas in the small towns many of the most respectable inhabitants would be excluded.[3] He agreed, also, with the statement that a £5 householder in a small borough was the equal in fitness of a £15 householder in a larger one, and he advocated a proportional franchise. Of the ratepayers in a borough, he argued, let the first third be electors; this would provide for a respectable constituency both in small and in large towns.[4] To this Russell and Milton objected that the

---

[1] Croker, *Diaries and Correspondence,* ii, 115; 3 Hansard, vi, 575, 612; ix, 1214; xii, 37.

[2] 3 Hansard, iv, 1232.

[3] 3 Hansard, vi, 581; x, 948.

[4] 3 Hansard, vi, 576, 607; ix, 371, 1212, 1260. Exactly the same point was brought out by a Radical journalist in July, 1831. The

nominal uniformity introduced a virtual variety; that the proportional franchise would bring on the register the one class that the Tories professed to fear; whereas the £10 qualification offered a wide suffrage where it was safe, and a more restricted one in the smaller places, where experience had proved that corruption resulted from the exercise of the franchise by the old scot and lot voters.[1]

The objections of the Tories to the £10 electors, on the ground of their dangerous tendencies, were numerous. Such electors, they said, were for the most part dissenters, and would send to Westminster "Presbyterians of the lowest class."[2] The first results of their introduction as voters would be the dissolution of the union with Ireland.[3] The repeal of the corn laws could no longer be postponed.[4] "Members would be nothing but delegates," was the prediction of Sir James Scarlett.[5] And numerous were the foreign examples of disaster adduced to show the danger of a lower middle class electorate; the horrors of the French Revolution were ascribed to just this sort of a constituency, which alienated alike noble and peasant; it was lower middle class suffrage which led to the corruption and inefficiency of government in America.[6] If democratic principles were to be introduced at all, let scot and lot, the only logical democratic franchise, be the means of introduction, and not this attempt to attain the kind of *juste milieu* which was bringing disrespect on the July

proposed franchise, he felt, would restrict the electorate in the small towns, which were the very places where they should be admitted, since they were less under the influence of the wealthy classes than the £10 occupiers, *Westminster Review*, xv, 170-172.

1 3 Hansard, vi, 577, 579.
2 3 Hansard, xii, 37.
3 3 Hansard, xii, 70.
4 3 Hansard, v, 756.
5 3 Hansard, vii, 161.
6 3 Hansard, iv, 714, 1140; xi, 677.

Monarchy.[1] In fact, both the moderate and extreme Tories lost no opportunity of opposing the new qualification. And so strongly did they feel that when in the autumn of 1831 the wavering Lords attempted a compromise with Grey, one of the points on which they were most insistent was that the new qualification should be introduced only into the newly represented boroughs.[2]

The Radicals, and the mass of the working classes, looked on the new qualifications either with indifference or with dislike. For most of them reform meant a thoroughly democratic measure, and one which was certain to bring in its train social and economic redress. Croker (a prejudiced witness, certainly) tells of meeting a crowd of workmen on their way to London to help pass reform, which was "to put down machinery and enable the poor man to make a living."[3] And the majority of the petitions upon reform which came into the House were directed towards such measures as the ballot, triennial parliaments, the abolition of tithes and the corn laws, and other social reforms. To the working classes reform meant something far different from the enfranchisement of one or two hundred thousand shopkeepers. To exchange the domination of the landowning aristocracy for that of the lower middle class was certainly no improvement; it might prove a far less sympathetic and wise domination. "To keep the Whigs in power the lion must give place to the rat, and the tiger to the leech."[4]

The attitude of the more violent members of the political societies was dangerously hostile to the £10 qualifica-

---

[1] 3 Hansard, vii, 975. Ellenborough said that he preferred household suffrage to the £10 qualification, Broughton, *Recollections of a Long Life*, iv, 218.

[2] *Melbourne Papers*, 142.

[3] Croker, *Diaries and Correspondence*, ii, 170.

[4] Holyoake, *Sixty Years of an Agitator's Life*, i, 279.

tion. Manchester and London were the centres of revolutionary feeling among the working classes and of middle class intolerance, and in both of those places the destruction of the bill, as embodying provisions unfair to the poor, was openly demanded. In London the most revolutionary of the societies, the Rotundanists, denounced the qualification as liable to do more harm than good. The working class journals fulminated against it in violent and coarse invective.[1] According to Francis Place, the bill was in greater danger from the revolutionary Radicals than from the Tories.[2]

Some of the more extreme of the working classes doubtless opposed the bill in order to bring about a violent revolution. But even amongst the more moderate Radicals who supported the bill in order to prevent a revolution, dissatisfaction with the £10 clause was acute. The new electors were termed the "Worshipful Company of Ten-pound Householders." The qualification was denounced as "a damnable delusion, giving us as many tyrants as there are shopkeepers."[3] One of the working class leaders, Doherty, told Place that the qualification would do the people no good; and another, Lovett, said that the middle classes were merely going to use the workmen as tools for their own purposes.[4] So little enthusiasm was aroused by the prospect of this qualification that the political associations which supported the bill were almost forced to disband and, in the autumn of

[1] "The bill is the most illiberal, the most tyrannical, the most abominable, the most infamous, the most hellish measure that ever could or can be proposed. . . . I therefore conjure you to prepare your coffins, if you have the means. You will be starved to death by thousands if this bill passes, and thrown on the dunghill, or on the ground, naked like dogs," *Poor Man's Guardian*, March 19, 1832.

[2] Wallas, *Life of Place*, 275.

[3] Kent, *The English Radicals*, 332.

[4] Wallas, *Life of Place*, 266, 282.

1831, the Birmingham Political Union was at the point of death from apathy; according to Place, who told it to Hobhouse, three £50 subscriptions, alone, prevented its dissolution. In London the National Political Union was unable to rouse its members from their indifference.[1]

In the House the Radicals were also dissatisfied, although for the most part they supported the ministerial plan. Both Hobhouse and Burdett feared that their Westminster electors would forbid their support of the bill from dislike of the £10 clause. Russell's presentation of the defects of the system and his remedy of this middle class franchise were regarded by them as generally inadequate.[2] The most violent of the attacks on the new qualification was made by Hunt, who, although disliked by Place and Cobbett, was in a position to know the ideas of many of the working classes. He asserted that the masses considered themselves tricked, and if they were to be excluded themselves, would have preferred that the peers and gentry rather than the £10 householders should choose their representatives.[3] His attempts, however, to amend the borough qualification to one of household suffrage were supported by few, even the Radicals voting for the qualification which was distasteful to the masses.

The £10 qualification, as passed, was by no means liberal; it was intended for a time that it should be made still less so. The ministry at first insisted that in order to qualify, the claimant must show that he paid his rent in half yearly installments. Those who paid rent more

---

[1] Broughton, *Recollections,* iv, 164.

[2] 3 Hansard, ii, 1154; Roebuck, *History of the Whig Ministry,* ii, 70. The majority of the Westminster electors, however, did accept the clause in order to assist in passing the bill, Broughton, *Recollections,* iv, 88.

[3] 3 Hansard, iii, 1246.

frequently, it was supposed, were of a transient and migratory class and unfit for the suffrage. The effect of this provision would have been to exclude at least half, if not more, of the prospective electorate; for the custom of paying rent quarterly was general. The ministers discovered their mistake, or their restrictive manœuvre was exposed, and the condition was removed. The tenement must be held for a year, however, instead of for six months as had been originally proposed.[1]

The general character of the new qualifications evinced very plainly the fear of radical change that hung over the reforming ministry. The new franchises introduced in the counties were calculated to bring greater power than ever to the landowning classes; and though it is true that these were proposed by the enemies of reform, the new qualification in boroughs showed little tendency on the part of the government to grant extensive rights to the masses. In fact the disfranchisement of non-resident voters and the gradual extinction of ancient rights struck directly at the electoral power of the working classes. The ministers themselves believed that the effect of the reform qualifications would not be to weaken the influence of the aristocracy, even as they doubtless hoped that it would strengthen the Whig merchants and landowners. Grey asserted that the government would soon be generally assailed, not for having gone too far but for having passed too aristocratic a measure. Althorp prophesied that the composition of the House would remain unchanged.[2] And even the Tories, notwithstanding their dire forebodings, accepted the situation as not

---

[1] 3 Hansard, v, 1376. Althorp ascribed the action of the ministers to the mistake of an under-secretary, who had been appointed by Peel, and who failed to explain the disfranchising effects of the provision for semi-annual payments, Le Marchant, *Althorp*, 325.

[2] 3 Hansard, ix, 443.

absolutely desperate and began to organize their methods for the damming of the democratic flood.

The Radicals naturally regarded the new qualifications as a timid compromise and, even after the act had been carried, spared no epithets in reference to those who had proposed it. Molesworth called the Whig policy "debasing" and described the Whigs as "miserable wretches"; Duncombe said they had "the voice of lions and the timidity of hares"; the London Working Man's Association condemned "the hypocritical, conniving, and liberty-undermining Whigs."[1] The attitude of the less outspoken Radicals toward the qualifications of 1832 was that their value lay rather in what they promised for the future; as Place said, it was the "commencement of the breaking up of the old, rotten system." It is with this latter estimate that the opinion of posterity will doubtless concur. Notwithstanding the immediate and notable alterations which resulted in the electoral system from the new qualifications, their importance lay not so much in themselves, but in the fact that they were the first of a series of innovations; for, as Mill said, they broke the spell that had kept men bound to the fear of change.

[1] Kent, *The English Radicals*, 347.

CHAPTER III

THE REDISTRIBUTION OF SEATS

Importance of the redistribution of 1832—Distribution of county seats before 1832—Distribution of borough seats—Advantage of the South—Numerical anomalies—Nomination—Disfranchisement proposed by the government—Opposition of the Tories—Their arguments—The disfranchising clauses—Schedule A—Schedule B—Character of the disfranchised boroughs—Difficulties in passing the disfranchising clauses—Charges of gerrymandering—The enfranchising clauses—Schedule C—Opposition to the new metropolitan seats—Schedule D—Division of the counties—Opposition of the Tories and Radicals—University representation—Principle of the redistribution.

THE determination of voting rights was by no means the most important task attempted by the legislators of 1832. It is true that the power of the aristocracy in elections rested largely upon the restricted character of the franchise and that the new qualifications, by increasing the number of voters, did much to break the control of the borough patrons. But of equal or greater importance was the redistribution of seats. This provided for the representation of the populous industrial districts of the Northwest, and deprived the southern boroughs, most of which were controlled by proprietors, of much of their preponderant influence in the House of Commons. The redistribution was certainly tentative and incomplete, leaving the industrial sections of the country inadequately represented; but as the first assault upon the electoral predominance of the small boroughs, and thus upon aristocratic influence, it may be regarded as a significant factor in the democratization of representative institutions.

As we have noted, the electoral divisions or constituencies of England and Wales are of two sorts: the large areas, generally of a rural character in 1832, known as counties; and the boroughs, which at that time might be villages, large industrial towns, or even the bare sites of vanished hamlets. Besides counties and boroughs, the two English universities, Cambridge and Oxford, had also the privilege of representation. At the time of the Reform Act the population or wealth of a constituency had nothing to do with the number of members which represented it in the Commons. Each of the English counties,[1] regardless of its size, returned two members who were known as knights of the shire; the Welsh counties each elected a single representative. The influence of a small county, like Rutland, in the national council thus counterbalanced that of Lancashire, with all its factories and millions of inhabitants.

Originally the county members were regarded as superior in dignity to the borough representatives, and something of this distinction may still be discerned in the early nineteenth century. Representing large rural areas, the knights were also, at least in theory, the spokesmen for the agricultural element. Since their constituencies were large and populous, they were generally supposed to voice the popular feeling to a greater extent than the burgesses. In practice, however, this was not invariably the case, and Russell considered that only a small proportion of the knights could be considered as truly popular representatives, since the large number of compromises and uncontested elections in the counties threw the power into the hands of the great landowners.[2]

But the claims of the knights to representative character could certainly be more easily justified than those

1 Except Yorkshire, which returned four.
2 Russell, *Speeches*, 212.

of the burgesses. The constituencies which returned the latter were often of little or no importance, and in many cases it is difficult to ascertain the original cause for granting representation to the borough. Some boroughs were represented because they had once been of size and importance; others, doubtless, for the very reason that they were small and easily controlled, and so might be used to further the aims of the monarch. Thus East and West Looe in Cornwall, always inconsiderable places, had been enfranchised by Elizabeth as a protection to the crown and to Protestantism.[1] Other parliamentary boroughs were probably created at the request of royal favorites whose influence in the towns or villages was sufficient to ensure control of their seats in the House of Commons.[2] As it lay with the crown to decide what boroughs should be represented, the right of sending members to Westminster depended upon the policy or whim of a monarch who, by 1832, had been dead from two to five hundred years.

The vast majority of the represented boroughs lay in the southern counties. These were the districts where the royal power was generally supreme and which the king preferred to see represented; in particular the royal county of Cornwall would naturally be favoured. The southern counties moreover had in olden times held the first place in commerce and industry. Of the ten counties lying to the south of the Severn and Thames, seven have extensive coast lines and the other three are so near the Bristol and English Channels as to be powerfully affected by the economic conditions of the seaboard. Here, during the fourteenth, fifteenth, and sixteenth centuries, before

[1] 3 Hansard, v, 228.
[2] Thus Corfe Castle and Bishop's Castle were said to have been created parliamentary boroughs by Elizabeth for Sir Christopher Hatton, 3 Hansard, ii, 1103.

coal and machinery had come to their own, trade and
population had been concentrated. All through the forma-
tive period of parliament the industrial life of all England
had been centred in the South. Cornwall appears in the
earliest haze of British tradition with its tin mines; it was
the Durham or Glamorgan of old England and the
deserted shafts and rotting timbers still, in 1830, bore as
strong witness to former industrial glories as do the
stones of the Coliseum to Rome's imperial grandeur.
Before Lancashire gained renown for its cotton manufactures, Wiltshire and Somerset were famous as seats of
the woolen trade.[1] It was natural that the South with its
concentration of wealth and population should enjoy
more complete representation than the rest of England.
Thus under the unreformed system, the balance of electoral
power lay most decidedly in the southernmost portion and
decreased almost regularly toward the North. Of the
two hundred and three enfranchised boroughs in England
and Wales, one hundred and five lay in the southern coast
counties. In the twenty-two counties to the north of a
line drawn from the Thames to the Mersey there were
only sixty-eight parliamentary boroughs, while the eight
great counties of the North could show but thirty-five—
less than the two counties of Wiltshire and Cornwall.

By the nineteenth century the industrial revolution,
amongst other causes, had shifted the centre of population and industry far to the north. Following the inven-
tions of Arkwright and Watts, the Midlands, Lancashire,
and Yorkshire, began to claim for themselves a title to
importance. The distribution of members, however, remained unchanged. As a result, conditions of representa-

[1] These counties "were full of rivers and towns and infinitely
prosperous, insomuch so that some of the market towns are equal to
cities in bigness and superior to many in number of people," Defoe,
Travels, ii, 35.

tion had grown up which seem unfair and anomalous to modern and especially to American eyes. Nor was there any relation between the population or wealth of a locality and its representation in parliament. The new large towns, such as Leeds and Manchester, sprung up in the wake of the industrial revolution, were not directly represented. The small boroughs of the South, however, still held their old parliamentary position; towns, as Burke said, whose "streets can only be traced by the colour of their corn, and whose only manufacture is in the members of Parliament."[1] A part of Cornwall, which since 1885 has formed but one parliamentary division and has been represented by only one member, contained, in 1830, nine boroughs and returned eighteen members.[2] In Yorkshire two small towns in the same parish, Aldborough and Boroughbridge, although they were but half a mile apart, were each represented by two members. Steyning and Bramber, in Sussex, were so much the same town that they had but one common street, and none but the expert could tell where one began and the other ended; yet each sent its two members to Westminster and together enjoyed as much representation as London city.[3] The representatives of the small boroughs thus controlled the House of Commons. There were thirty-six boroughs of which the population was in each case less than twenty-five persons; one hundred and fifteen boroughs had less than two hundred inhabitants each; and a clear majority of the House was returned by towns of less than five thousand inhabitants.[4]

In the eyes of the Radicals this system was naturally

[1] 3 Hansard, iii, 648. Burke's rhetoric is naturally exaggerated, for with the exception of a half dozen, the small boroughs were at least respectable villages.

[2] Porritt, *The Unreformed House of Commons*, i, 18.

[3] Oldfield, *Representative History*, v, 42.

[4] Hansard, iii, 224; Oldfield, *Representative History*, v, 330.

wrong, since it was inconsonant with democratic theory. In their opinion there should be a direct connection between population and representation. But the practical effects of the system affected not merely the Radicals, who voiced a very small proportion of legislatorial opinion in 1831, but also many of the moderate reformers. For the representation of the small boroughs made possible the wholesale practice of nomination to seats in the Commons, either by peers or by commoners of wealth.

Practically a majority of the members secured their seats either as a gift or by purchase from the proprietor of the borough. Of the twenty-eight members returned by Cornwall, eighteen were regularly appointed by the patrons of the small Cornish boroughs, and the other seats were generally bought up by borough-mongers from time to time.[1] In towns where the electorate was too large to be easily controlled by private influence the seat was often sold; in Shoreham the electors formed a club for the disposal of the borough to the highest bidder, and divided the profits.[2] But in the smaller boroughs the patron held undisputed right to appoint the member; the property right in the seat was generally acknowledged openly, and like other property, seats might be transmitted to heirs, or sold in the market.[3] Several peers or wealthy common-

---

[1] 3 Hansard, ii, 457.

[2] Russell, *Recollections*, 36.

[3] Thus we read in the *Magna Britannia* (vi, 139), under the heading "Old Sarum": "It has been lately purchased by Mr. Pitt, commonly known by the name of Governor Pitt, who had the famous large diamond. His posterity now have an hereditary right to sit in the House of Commons as owners of it, as the Earls of Arundel have to sit in the House of Peers as Lords of Arundel Castle." Russell says that a peer on being asked who should be returned for one of his boroughs named a waiter of White's Club; but as he did not know the man's exact name the election was declared void. A new election was then held, when the name having been ascertained, the waiter was declared duly elected, *Recollections*, 35.

ers controlled a large number of seats; the Duke of Norfolk returned eleven members, Lord Lonsdale nine, and
Lord Darlington seven. Russell tells of a noble lord who
used to go out hunting followed by a tail of six or seven
members of parliament of his own making. It was claimed
in 1793 that seventy persons secured the return of one
hundred and fifty members, and Lambton said in 1821 that
one hundred and eighty persons appointed three hundred
and fifty members.[1] The influence of peers and plutocrats
over the House of Commons was thus almost complete, and
Sir Francis Burdett could say with justice that the question in 1832 was at bottom whether the power of nomination to the House should be vested in the peers or the
people.[2]

Thus while manufacturers of the large industrial towns
complained that their interests had not fair representation,
and the philosophical Radicals protested that popular
rights were infringed, the system of nomination was
attacked by many reformers who were unaffected by other
arguments. Dissatisfaction with the representative system, and especially with the distribution of seats, was
accordingly partly of a political and partly of an economic character. Gathering force all through the latter
years of the eighteenth century, and intensified by the
social unrest which agitated England after the close of
the great war, it finally proved irresistible.

Believing that the chief fault of the electoral system
was the power of nomination, the ministers of 1832 concentrated all their efforts upon its elimination. They
planned to meet the evil by two forms of attack. The
larger close boroughs, which were controlled by a patron
or corporation, they would liberate, or in the parlance of

[1] *Chambers Journal,* lviii, 711; Heaton, *The Three Reforms of Parliament,* 5.
[2] 3 Hansard, iv, 819-823.

the day "open," by increasing the electorate. The smaller boroughs they would disfranchise and give the seats thus made available to more populous towns.[1] By such redistribution of seats they would gain the approval of those who opposed the system of nomination, would satisfy the claims of the industrial centres which had hitherto been unrepresented, and would please the Radicals, who believed that representation should be based upon population and wealth.

The real struggle of 1832 was fought around the question of redistribution and especially the schedules that determined which town should lose, and which gain, representation.[2] In comparison with the redistribution, the introduction of the new voting qualifications was for most of the politicians a secondary matter. The saving or winning of seats was the vital issue. For a member or a patron to have his borough swamped by a mass of new voters was bad enough; but to have the borough disfranchised entirely was naturally very much worse. The disfranchisement clauses were the first object of Tory attack, just as to the reformers the abolition of the small close boroughs and the representation of the large towns was the heart of the whole matter.[3]

The discussion of the disfranchisement clauses lasted a fortnight, the Tories fighting bitterly both the principle and the details of the schedules. In their eyes the right of representation, once granted to a borough, could not

1 3 Hansard, ii, 1066.

2 In Schedule A were listed the boroughs about to lose both members; in Schedule B were the boroughs from which one member was to be taken; Schedule C contained the names of the towns which for the first time were to have the right to return two members; and Schedule D included the list of those receiving one member.

3 "Schedule A was the banner under which was fought and won the great battle of Reform," Roebuck, *History of the Whig Ministry,* ii, 81.

be taken away; such rights were property which could not
be violated, and disfranchisement was little else than
unjustified confiscation, or as Wetherell put it, "corporation robbery." The Tories also, with great wealth of
argument, dwelt upon the excellent practical effects of the
system of nomination in boroughs, as well as the inconvenience that would be suffered through the disappearance
of the smaller constituencies. By means of the nomination
boroughs, they asserted, the landed and moneyed interests
received the representation that would otherwise be denied
them; the power of nomination vested in the great landholders was the best means for preserving the legislative
connection between the Lords and Commons; the deficiency
of Scottish representation was not felt, merely because of
the virtual representation of Scotland through the
English close boroughs; nomination constituencies were
essential to the smooth functioning of government, since
through them alone could cabinet ministers find certain
means of entering the Commons, when rejected by the
independent boroughs.[1]

The argument, however, on which the Tories laid most
emphasis was the value of close boroughs as nurseries for
nascent statesmen. This point was elaborated by all who
spoke against disfranchisement; lists of the great parliamentary figures of the past generation were drawn up, and
their path to the House by way of close boroughs pointed
out. The Tories insisted that without nomination young
men of talent would find it impossible to enter parliament,
and that the quality of government must suffer, if indeed
government could be carried on at all. They turned the
very speeches of the Whigs into proof of their contention.

[1] 3 Hansard, iv, 180, 848; v, 1351. The value of close boroughs
to the government was especially emphasized by Peel, who took as
his example the exclusion of Palmerston in 1831, and his subsequent
reëntrance by means of a nomination borough.

The brilliant rhetoric of Hawkins, the Whig member for the close borough of St. Michael's, was declared by his opponents to be the best evidence of the value of his constituency; when Macaulay finished a speech which was admitted on both sides to be the best of the session, the Tories triumphantly pointed out that he came from the rotten borough of Calne; and the brilliance of Stanley, they asserted, would have been lacking to the Whigs, were it not for the government's power of nomination in Windsor.[1]

Another Tory argument emphasized the fact that the colonies were virtually represented by the close boroughs and that the interests of the empire overseas would be endangered by the disfranchisement of the nomination constituencies. India especially, they claimed, would suffer, as her interests were taken care of by the members of the East India Company who owned close boroughs. At least eight boroughs—Sandwich, Rochester, Cricklade, Hythe, Bridgewater, Bristol, Old Sarum, and Malmesbury—furnished ready places for Indian "Nabobs."[2]

Such confidence in the value of nomination boroughs was not confined to the reactionary section of the Tories, and many of the moderates in each party doubted the wisdom and the legality of disfranchisement. A large number of members were anxious to grant representation to the large industrial towns of the Northwest, but felt that no borough should be disfranchised except in cases of indubitable corruption or where the borough proprietor consented to a sale of his rights. To obtain the necessary seats without the destruction of vested rights they advocated the grouping of boroughs as in Wales, where several combined to elect a single representative.[3]

[1] 3 Hansard, ii, 1206; iii, 1631-1632.
[2] 3 Hansard, ii, 735; ix, 178.
[3] 3 Hansard, ii, 1177; iv, 1209, 1244, 1327.

Some of the Whig ministers themselves were privately
doubtful of the wisdom of wide disfranchisement, and
cautious in their expressions of opinion, although as members of the cabinet they supported the policy adopted by
the government. Brougham, then suspected and now
convicted of secret fondness for the close boroughs, told
Althorp that they were by no means the worst part of the
representative system, but were indeed very helpful to
practical statesmanship.[1] Melbourne also, according to
Greville, was extremely doubtful, and said that he did not
see how government was to be carried on without them.[2]
Even Althorp believed in the value of close boroughs,
although he declared that strong men could enter parliament by other means, and that such boroughs were injuri-
ous, in that they allowed the rich to dictate to the
ministers.[3]

Grey and Russell, however, were strongly opposed to
the system of nomination and determined upon the disfranchisement of the small close boroughs. The former
asserted that so far from being of assistance to the ministers, the nomination boroughs might, and did, offer great
hindrance to the carrying on of government; for a new
ministry frequently found the needed seats in the hands
of the opposition. As parliament, he said, was chosen by
their opponents, the seats which would naturally be at the
command of the ministers were filled by those most bitterly

[1] Broughton, *Recollections,* iv, 256; Grey, *Correspondence with
King William IV,* i, 81-82. Brougham advocated leaving one member
to all the close boroughs, Roebuck, *History of the Whig Ministry,*
i, 240.

[2] Greville, *Memoirs,* ii, 277; Melbourne's family had in several
instances entered the House of Commons through close boroughs,
Torrens, *Life of Melbourne,* i, 12, 14, 115, 150.

[3] Hansard, ii, 1140.

hostile to them. Hence, as in 1807, a new ministry might be forced to dissolve and appeal to the country.[1]

The most effective opponent of the small boroughs and the system of nomination was Macaulay, whose rhetoric on this occasion furnished the sensation of the debates. He elaborated upon the electoral anomaly which allowed the same weight in the national council to Liverpool as to a deserted village, and depicted the astonishment of a stranger visiting England, when told that the green mound called Gatton had two representatives and the wealthy commercial centre of Manchester none at all. But more important than the anomalous character of the system, said Macaulay, was the fact that it did not work well in practice. The virtues ascribed to it by the Tories were entirely imaginary, and the failure of government, which he asserted was clear during the years following the war, was due to the fact that those who held the reins of power were separated from the mass of the nation.

With the exception of Macaulay, the Whigs took little time for eloquence in their advocacy of disfranchisement: some of them in doubt as to its advisability, some fearing to play into the hands of their opponents, who attempted delay and obstruction at every opportunity. But when the principle of disfranchisement was brought to a division, they supported the policy of the government with very few exceptions.

The Tories were thus forced to shift their opposition from the principle of disfranchisement to the details of the ministerial proposals. They brought forward a mass of statistics in defence of each borough and employed every possible device for purposes of delay. During the debates on the first bill their most effective move was to oppose the diminution of seats in England, which the government

[1] Grey, *Correspondence with King William IV*, i, 186-187, 198.

proposed in order to provide for new Scotch and Irish representation. They contended that England was being stripped to the advantage of the Irish and Catholics.[1] This opposition took concrete form in an amendment of General Gascoyne, which resulted in a defeat for the ministry and led to the dissolution of 1831. This amendment stipulated that there should be no diminution in the number of representatives for England and Wales.[2] The Whigs stood out firmly against it, realizing that it was made for purposes of obstruction, and that once carried, it would lead to such further alteration as to destroy the whole character of the bill.[3] Though Gascoyne and others denied, in the course of debate, that this amendment was intended as an indirect means for the defeat of the bill, he afterwards confessed to Hobhouse that in reality such was the object of the proposal.[4] As will be seen, the principle underlying his motion was later adopted by the cabinet.

The ministers' plan for disfranchisement was greatly strengthened by their overwhelming victory in the election of 1831. In Tory eyes this plan was so absurd that when the original bill was first brought in, the reading of the list of condemned boroughs was greeted by laughter and ironical cheers; and when, just before the first debate, Althorp told the plan to Stanley, the latter burst into an incredulous laugh.[5] According to the first bill, all boroughs with a population of less than two thousand were to be absolutely disfranchised. Numbering sixty-two in all, their names were placed in a list which was known as Schedule A. Russell having taken as his guide the antiquated cen-

[1] 3 Hansard, iii, 690, 1574.
[2] 3 Hansard, iii, 1540.
[3] Grey, *Correspondence with King William IV,* i, 216.
[4] Broughton, *Recollections,* iv, 101.
[5] Broughton, *Recollections,* iv, 93.

sus returns made in 1821, laid himself open to Tory attack
and gave them opportunity for constant criticism of his
figures. Russell replied that the returns of 1831 not being
published, it would be unwise to await their appearance;
if the schedules were to be based on them there would be
strong temptation to falsification in order to avoid disfranchisement.[1] In moving for returns on population after
he had described his plan, however, Russell made a tactical
mistake; and he made another mistake, as he later admitted, when he confused the limits of the parishes with
those of the parliamentary boroughs, thus vitiating his
statistics.[2]

After the dissolution of 1831 the ministers changed the
standard which determined what boroughs should be disfranchised. Instead of taking a minimum population they
entered upon a complicated calculation in order to determine the relative importance of boroughs. The number of
houses in any one borough was divided by the average
number per borough in one hundred and ten boroughs;
the assessed taxes in that borough were also divided by the
average, and the two results were then added to give the
relative importance of the borough in points.[3] The
returns for 1831 were utilized and though many of them
were doubtless inaccurate, the general result was a fair
and comprehensive list of the boroughs of least importance
from the point of view of wealth and population.[4]

[1] 3 Hansard, ii, 1264. Russell's fears were not without justification; in one constituency in Lanark the population increased by
50,000 in ten years according to the returns, 3 Hansard, v, 39.

[2] Russell, *Recollections, 92.*

[3] 3 Hansard, x, 546. For the plan of the government and the
method of determining the comparative importance of the boroughs,
see *Parliamentary Papers,* 1831-1832, nos. 17, 44. Modern historians
have not always observed that the basis of disfranchisement was not
population solely, cf. Lowell, *Government of England,* i, 198.

[4] 3 Hansard, iii, 1237-1239.

Schedule A, as finally amended and passed, absolutely disfranchised fifty-six boroughs. All but fifteen of these boroughs were in the southern counties, and Cornwall and Wiltshire were the chief sufferers, for it was there that the boroughs of small population and infinitesimal electorate had been close packed. And while all the counties on the southern seaboard found their borough representation reduced, the counties of the Midlands and Northwest lost very few borough seats.[1] In nearly all the boroughs listed in Schedule A the number of inhabitants was small, so that even with an extended suffrage there could be no expectation of a large and representative constituency. According to the rule laid down by the ministers, no borough was worthy of representation where at least three hundred electors could not be qualified. In many of the disfranchised boroughs the total number of inhabitants, male, female, and children, fell far below this standard.[2] In some of them, it is true, a population of two thousand or more was to be found; but these boroughs were selected for disfranchisement in preference to smaller boroughs, because in property they were not so wealthy.[3]

In addition to the boroughs chosen for absolute disfranchisement the ministry planned to deprive a number of boroughs of one of their seats. According to the original bill, all boroughs of not more than four thousand inhabitants were to be placed in this category, which was

[1] Cornwall lost 15, Wiltshire, 7, Sussex, 5, and Hampshire, 4. The other counties of the southern seaboard, Surrey, Kent, and Devon, lost 2 or 3 each. The other boroughs absolutely disfranchised were scattered: Suffolk and Yorkshire lost 3 boroughs apiece, Buckinghamshire and Northamptonshire lost 2 apiece, and one borough was disfranchised in each of five other counties.

[2] Old Sarum had no inhabitants and a constituency of 11; Hindon in Wiltshire had but 120 inhabitants, Gatton in Surrey, 145, Bramber in Sussex had 175, and Dunwich in Suffolk had about 200.

[3] *Parliamentary Papers*, 1831, nos. 201, 204.

known as Schedule B. But in the amendments and the reconstruction of the Reform Bill, the standard of population was discarded, as in the case of the disfranchised boroughs, and the combined criterion of number of houses and assessed taxes was adopted. As finally passed Schedule B contained the names of thirty boroughs; seventeen of those which had been originally listed were saved, owing partly to the expostulations of the Tories, and partly to the fact that the Whigs themselves were none too enthusiastic over this part of the bill. As in the case of the disfranchised boroughs, those losing one seat were for the most part in the southern counties.[1]

Schedule B was popular in no section of the House of Commons or the country. Grey attempted to find an excuse for it on the plea that the boroughs contained in it, being chiefly of the nomination type, really deserved complete disfranchisement; but as a measure of conciliation the ministers would allow them to retain half of their representation.[2] Later, however, he admitted openly that this schedule was the weakest spot in the Whig case.[3] As late as December, 1831, he proposed to lessen still further the number of boroughs losing one seat, and to leave to eleven of the most important their full representation; as a counterpoise he wanted to grant ten additional members to the large towns. But Russell would not agree, being unwilling to tinker with the schedule, while Palmerston and Melbourne disliked the idea of additional popular representation.[4]

Lord Milton expressed the attitude of many Liberals

[1] Twenty-one of the 30 boroughs in Schedule B were in the counties on the southern seaboard. Cornwall, Wiltshire, and Sussex each contributed 4 boroughs to this schedule, Dorset, 3, Hampshire and Devon, 2 apiece, and Kent and Surrey, 1 apiece.

[2] 3 Hansard, vii, 938.

[3] 3 Hansard, viii, 326.

[4] Grey, *Correspondence with King William IV*, ii, 8-9.

when he objected to these boroughs which would have but one member, and insisted strongly on the value of double member constituencies, as furthering the interests of the minority and avoiding contested elections.[1] The Tories followed the same argument under the leadership of Peel, declaring that Schedule B was an anomaly and that the boroughs included in it, if of the nomination variety, should be put in Schedule A; if this were not done, why should they not have two members? To most of the Tories Schedule B was the realization of that most hateful of Radical principles: that representation depended upon population.[2] Sir Francis Burdett, it is true, approved of the single member constituency as giving merely a just influence to the majority. But the greater part of the Radicals regarded Schedule B as the "worst blot" on the bill, and were grieved that so many nomination boroughs should be only scotched and not annihilated.[3]

The boroughs completely disfranchised were almost without exception of the "pocket" variety and were either regularly controlled by a patron or sold to the highest bidder. Curiously enough some of them were the very constituencies through which the reformers themselves had first entered parliament. Stockbridge had offered an asylum to Stanley in 1820, when its proprietor, a Tory West Indian in need of money, had sold it to a Whig peer, who nominated the future member of the reforming ministry.[4] And Boroughbridge had been sold by the Duke of Newcastle to Burdett for his first entrance into the

---

[1] 3 Hansard, v, 775.

[2] 3 Hansard, v, 430, 634. The alteration of Schedule B was, according to Greville, one of the most important conditions demanded by the "wavering" peers, if they were to pass the bill, Greville, *Memoirs,* ii, 212.

[3] Roebuck, *History of the Whig Ministry,* ii, 241. Strong opposition to Schedule B was voiced in the *Westminster Review,* xv, 163-165.

[4] Saintsbury, *The Earl of Derby,* 9.

Commons.¹ Other typical boroughs disfranchised were
Gatton, belonging to Lord Monson, who had placed it in
the hands of a broker and sold it for twelve hundred
pounds on condition that the member voted Tory, and
Orford and Aldborough which belonged to Lord Hertford
(Thackeray's Marquis of Steyne).²

Of the boroughs which lost one seat the majority were
under the influence of patrons, although not to so great
an extent as in Schedule A. Most of their constituencies
were rather larger and more difficult to control, but not
more than eight or nine were regarded as really open and
independent constituencies. In some, such as Wareham,
Rye, or Midhurst, the electorate numbered no more than
twenty or twenty-five, and belonged absolutely to a
patron.³ With their boundaries enlarged, however, and
a £10 suffrage introduced, the ministers expected that they
would be "opened up" and transformed into representative constituencies. The electorate of some of the
boroughs losing one member, such as Arundel, Great
Grimsby, and Wallingford, was of respectable size, and
partially independent of a proprietor; but such boroughs
had generally been in the habit of selling themselves to
the highest bidder.

The greater number of the pocket boroughs belonged to
Tory patrons, who naturally threw all their political influence against the bill, and especially against the disfranchisement of the small boroughs. But the ministers had
on their side the popular agitation and the power of the
press, which for the moment weakened the control of the
borough proprietors. The Whigs also possessed pocket

¹ Mask, *Pencillings of Politicians*, 216.
² 3 Hansard, v, 123; Croker, *Correspondence and Diaries*, ii, 126.
³ These mentioned belonged to J. Calcraft, Dr. Lamb, and John
Smith, respectively, 3 Hansard, iii, 49, 819-823; Molesworth, *History
of England*, i, 71.

boroughs of their own, and although they were less numerous than those of their opponents, they were sufficient, when thrown into the scale, to determine the success of the bill. Lord Radnor gave up to the government his borough of Downton, where he held ninety-nine out of the one hundred burgages which conferred the vote in this borough, one of them being in the midst of a watercourse. Sir Sanford Graham, the patron of Ludgershall, also gave up his borough.[1] And a wealthy borough patroness, Miss Holmes, through her guardian, Lord Yarborough, who voted their disfranchisement, sacrificed her boroughs in the Isle of Wight, receiving four thousand pounds for this complaisant action. Lord Bath, who stood for reform, gave up Weobly; and the Marquis of Cleveland voted the disfranchisement of Camelford and Ilchester.[2] It was commonly rumoured that the latter, who had been made a marquis because he owned these boroughs, received his title of duke because he gave them up.

But the ministry, although it employed government influence and funds to their fullest extent, was unable to win over many patrons of the condemned boroughs. Of the disfranchised constituencies, each with two votes, there were thirty which cast both against the second reading of the bill. And the ministers received still less support from the proprietors of the boroughs which were to lose one of their seats. The votes of twenty-three of those boroughs were cast solidly against the second reading, and even some of the members for the independent boroughs in Schedule B refused to support the ministerial plan.[3]

The two disfranchising schedules were accordingly carried through with the greatest difficulty and only after long delay, resulting from party tactics. The Tories

[1] 3 Hansard, v, 220; vii, 1394.
[2] Greville, *Memoirs*, ii, 58, 140.
[3] 3 Hansard, iii, 819-823.

made desperate efforts to save at least one of the seats of the boroughs in Schedule A and preserve entirely the representation of those listed in Schedule B. Sir Charles Wetherell and Sir Edward Sugden, supported by the witty and vitriolic ingenuity of Croker, appeared as counsel in behalf of the condemned constituencies, and attempted to bring under discussion the case of each borough selected for disfranchisement. They argued that the bill was one of pains and penalties, and that each borough deserved a fair trial, hoping thus to obstruct and delay the progress of the measure. They began their plan by attempting to save the first borough on the list, which Croker secretly admitted to his patron, Lord Hertford, was not worthy of representation,[1] and made a vigorous effort to have witnesses called to testify to its size and importance. Had this attempt succeeded, each of the disfranchised boroughs would have claimed the same privilege, and months would have been consumed in the process of hearing and judging the right of each constituency to representation. The committee, as the Tories hoped, would probably have broken down under the infliction, and the bill would have been talked out of parliament. The ministers, however, firmly refused to allow a trial to each individual borough; they held their cohorts steadfast, and relying chiefly upon the tact and influence of Althorp, who possessed the admiration and confidence of all parties, succeeded in passing the schedules unchanged.[2]

As might have been expected, charges of gerrymander-

---

[1] Croker, *Correspondence and Diaries,* ii, 141.

[2] Sir Henry Harding said: "It was Althorp carried the Bill. Once in answer to a most able and argumentative speech of Croker, he rose and observed that he had made some calculations which he considered as entirely conclusive in refutation . . . but he had mislaid them, so that he could only say that if the House would be guided by his advice they would reject the amendment, which they did," Le Marchant, *Althorp,* 400.

ing and the arrangement of the schedules so as to preserve intact the great Whig strongholds, were frequent
and unrestrained. Both outside of the House and in the
debates, the Tories asserted and believed that the bill had
been framed by the ministers with a view to party purposes, and they adduced numerous individual instances in
proof of the assertion. They claimed that Russell's mistake in confounding the limits of parish and borough had
not been unintentional; and that in the case of the Whig
boroughs he had counted in both parish and borough,
while in the case of the Tory boroughs the narrow borough
limits had been strictly preserved. As a result the Whig
boroughs appeared larger and more important than those
of the Tories and less deserving of disfranchisement.[1]
Calne, Tavistock, and Knaresborough, which were all
Whig strongholds and not disfranchised, were special
objects of attack.[2] The first, which belonged to the
Marquis of Lansdowne, was called the "key to the arch"
of party electoral influence that the Whigs were building
up; and the Radical Hunt joined the Tories in their
attack on this constituency, declaring in a characteristic
outburst that Calne was "the most degraded and rotten-
est, stinkingest, skulkingest of boroughs."[3] The fact
that this borough possessed only eighteen electors in 1831
and only one hundred and ninety-one votes after the Reform Act had widened the franchise, certainly laid it open
to attack.[4] Tavistock since the early eighteenth century
had been completely under the control of the Duke of Bedford,[5] while Knaresborough belonged absolutely to the
Duke of Devonshire;[6] but each of these boroughs had a

[1] 3 Hansard, iii, 1399-1402.
[2] 3 Hansard, ii, 1185.
[3] 3 Hansard, ii, 1209.
[4] *Parliamentary Papers*, 1831, nos. 201, 204.
[5] 3 Hansard, iv, 331.
[6] Greville, *Memoirs*, ii, 79.

population of about five thousand, and it was expected that
the electorate would be so increased by the new suffrage
that their character as nomination boroughs would be lost.
But Wycombe in Buckinghamshire, on the other hand,
which was small and to all appearances deserved disfranchisement, was saved and left under the absolute control of
the Whig Carringtons.[1]

The Whigs were accused also of playing for their party
interest by the alteration of borough boundaries. Villages
were included within or excluded from the borough areas
in such a way, it was claimed, as to further Whig influence
in elections. The village of Littlehampton, which was
entirely under the control of the Duke of Norfolk, was
thus included in the borough of Arundel, and its inclusion
made Arundel practically a nomination borough under
Howard influence. Everyone in the borough believed that
the alteration in the boundary was made for party purposes.[2] In the same way Totnes, through the inclusion of
a suburb across the Dart, was brought under the control
of the Duke of Somerset; and Whitehaven was given to
the Earl of Lonsdale.[3]

Accusations of such a type were naturally to be expected
and should in part be regarded as party weapons, and
yet the impression was without question strong at the
time, and continued later, that the Whigs often used the
advantage of their position rather for their own profit

1 Fowler, *Country Life*, 46.

2 3 Hansard, xiii, 540. In the same way the Treasury borough
of Harwich, having less than 4000 inhabitants, was given an extra
parish, which allowed the borough to retain both of its seats, 3
Hansard, xcvii, 899.

3 Russell, *Recollections*, 89; *Speeches*, 68; 3 Hansard, xii, 962.
The Radicals also claimed that the number of boroughs in Schedule
B was reduced from 47 to 30 in order that the Whig borough of
Tavistock might be saved, Roebuck, *History of the Whig Ministry*,
ii, 242.

than for the best representation of the people. Certainly, the story told by Lord Malmesbury, that he had heard Ellice and Durham discussing how "to cook the schedules and the new franchise" so as to get rid of local Tory interests, was generally credited.[1] And Disraeli was able to say in his speech at Aylesbury in 1855: "Everybody now considers that there was in the concoction of that bill a greater number of jobs than was ever concocted before . . . its nominal object was to improve the representation of the people, its great substantial object was the consolidation of Whig power."[2]

On the other hand, there are numerous instances of Tory boroughs, many of them small, which were left untouched by the bill. Thus Marlborough was completely under the influence of Lord Aylesbury; its corporation was composed of the steward, butler, footmen, and other dependents of the family; its mayor in 1831 was the lord's political agent; and even after the electorate was increased Marlborough continued to be a Tory nomination borough.[3] And yet it was not disfranchised by the Whigs. Bridgnorth, in Shropshire, was also left undisturbed, although it had barely four thousand inhabitants and was described as a Tory pocket borough long after the Reform Act.[4] Accordingly it may be said that a strong prima facie case of wholesale gerrymandering cannot be made out against the Whig ministers. Their opportunity for using the

---

[1] Saintsbury, *Earl of Derby*, 21.

[2] Walpole, *Life of Russell*, ii, 296. And Stanley, speaking a generation later, said: "A good deal may be done in the case of boroughs . . . in the way of grouping and of extending boundaries to swamp a hostile constituency, or to save a friendly interest. . . . Even in the Reform Bill of 1832 there was, if I do not mistake greatly, some arrangements of that kind, of which the less said the better."

[3] Dod, *Parliamentary Companion*, 1835.

[4] Bridges, *Reminiscences of a Country Politician*, 16.

schedules for party purposes was less complete than might
be supposed, owing to the fact that many boroughs under
Tory influence, such as Newark, were too large to be
within the scope of the disfranchising clauses.[1]

The enfranchising clauses, and Schedules C and D,
which determined what towns should receive representation
for the first time, were passed with less of acrimonious discussion. In Schedule C were included twenty-two towns,
chiefly in the northern and metropolitan districts, which
were, for the first time, to send two members apiece to
Westminster.[2] Schedule D contained twenty-one towns,
which were to return a single member apiece. Most of
these towns also were situated in the northern industrial
districts.[3]

The chief objection to the towns included in Schedule C
arose out of the increase in metropolitan representation.
Many of the more moderate members considered that with
members from London City, Westminster, and Southwark,
and the four county seats, the metropolis had already quite
enough. Even Hobhouse was of this opinion.[4] Peel believed that the increase in metropolitan seats was the
weakest part of the Whig plan of enfranchisement, and
pointed out that, as a result of the preponderance thus
bestowed, London would occupy in England the perni-

[1] The Duke of Newcastle controlled Newark and the Marquis of
Londonderry Durham City, Morley, *Gladstone*, i, 89, 287; Smith,
Life of Bright, i, 61, 66.

[2] Of the new double-seated boroughs, 5 were in the metropolis:
Tower Hamlets, Finsbury, Marylebone, Lambeth, and Greenwich.
Lancashire received 4, and Yorkshire, 4.

[3] Lancashire received 5, Yorkshire, 3, and Durham, 2. For the
geographical aspect of the redistribution of borough seats, see
Appendix, No. 3. It will be seen that of the 143 disfranchised
borough seats, the southeastern and the southwestern districts lost
105. Of the 65 new borough seats, 45 went to the metropolitan,
northwestern, and northern districts.

[4] Broughton, *Recollections*, iv, 128.

cious position held by Paris in France.[1] King William also disapproved strongly of the increase of metropolitan borough seats, preferring that whatever members were added should be assigned to the county of Middlesex. His feeling was chiefly actuated by the fear that the members for the thickly populated districts of the metropolis would be too strongly imbued with radical if not ultra-democratic ideas. Grey, however, believed that the restrictions attaching to the new franchise would prevent the new metropolitan constituencies from assuming too radical a character.[2]

But nearly all the Tories and in particular those who, like the Marquis of Chandos, represented the sentiments of the agriculturists, were convinced that the metropolitan voters would return Radical members of the lowest class. On the 28th of February, 1832, they made a great effort under the leadership of Lord George Bentinck, to persuade the moderates to refuse extra representation to the metropolitan districts, and thus to render the bill more palatable to the Lords, and avoid a creation of peers. The attempt was, however, defeated by a majority of eighty.[3] In the Lords, the objections to the metropolitan boroughs were met by a long and successful speech of Durham, based on statistics furnished by Francis Place.[4] To the other two-member boroughs now enfranchised little objection appeared. Brighton alone drew forth the protests of the Tories, who complained that it would represent merely "toffy, lemonade, and jelly shops," and

---

[1] 3 Hansard, iii, 1622; Broughton, *Recollections,* iv, 128.

[2] Grey, *Correspondence with King William IV,* i, 423.

[3] Broughton, *Recollections,* iv, 187.

[4] Reid, *Life of Durham,* i, 294; Wallas, *Place,* 324. The surrender of the new metropolitan seats was one of the conditions at first laid down by the moderate peers in return for their support of the bill, Greville, *Memoirs,* ii, 212.

obviously feared the Whig proclivities of the numerous tradespeople established there.[1]

The discussion of Schedule D, which named the new boroughs that were to receive a single seat apiece, also gave rise to some bitterness. It was only after a long struggle that the ministers agreed to recognize the new economic development of Glamorgan by granting a seat to Merthyr Tydvil towards the end of the third reading.[2] This was a concession to the industrial interests. The new seat for Frome, a small town in Somerset, was a concession to the demands of the Southwest.[3] Other towns in Schedule D were subjected to bitter criticism. The Tories objected to Chatham, which because of the government interest would be practically a Treasury borough, and to Cheltenham, whose prosperity largely depended on the trade brought by valetudinarians and young ladies' schools, and whose representation would be, as the Tories said, that of the "circulating library." They also opposed Huddersfield and Whitehaven, on the ground that they would be as completely nomination constituencies as any in Schedule A.[4]

But the warmest discussion arose over the Durham boroughs, in which case it was frankly stated that the Whigs were working for the interests of Lord Durham and themselves.[5] Durham was a Whig county and the Tories complained that the new boroughs were as thick there as the unreformed constituencies had been in Cornwall or Wiltshire. And it is true that the ministers planned to grant representation to four new boroughs lying within a radius of ten miles; and although they

[1] 3 Hansard, x, 1119.
[2] 3 Hansard, xi, 207, 228-233.
[3] 3 Hansard, v, 840.
[4] 3 Hansard, v, 897, 1071; x, 1121, 1155.
[5] 3 Hansard, xiii, 114.

gave up one of these, the three new boroughs of Gateshead, Tynemouth, and South Shields, with the old boroughs of Newcastle and Sunderland, all in the same district and all opposed to Tory interests, furnished some excuse for Tory innuendoes. Althorp explained this conglomeration as due to the importance of the shipping interests, but the Tories persisted in seeing something sinister in it.[1] They demanded that Gateshead, which was merely a suburb of Newcastle, and South Shields, which was unimportant from the point of view of population or taxes, should be merged in Newcastle.[2] Ministerial arguments, however, or their party organization, triumphed, and the Durham boroughs received their representation.

Of the one hundred and forty-three seats made available by the disfranchisement of the small boroughs, sixty-five were thus assigned to the industrial towns. Of the remainder, sixty-five were assigned to the counties, and their distribution determined by Schedule F of the bill.[3] Twenty-six counties were divided, each part constituting for parliamentary purposes a county in itself; Yorkshire was split into its three ridings, two members being returned for each, instead of four for the whole county, and the Isle of Wight was separated from Hampshire and given a single member. Seven other counties, where agricultural interests predominated, were given three members instead of two, in order to balance the increase of manufacturing representation. And three Welsh counties, Glamorgan, Carmarthen, and Denbigh, received an extra seat.[4]

Both Tories and Radicals opposed the division of

---

[1] 3 Hansard, v, 848; x, 1145.
[2] 3 Hansard, x, 1264.
[3] The remaining 13 seats were assigned to Scotland and Ireland.
[4] 3 Hansard, v, 1234. For the geographical aspect of the assignment of county seats, see Appendix, No. 3.

counties, though for different reasons. The Tories feared
that all small divisions in which great towns were situated
would be controlled by town interests, and that the members would be returned by the town freeholders and not
by the landholders of the country districts. The Radicals,
on the other hand, feared the power of the landholder in a
small rural division. Under the old system, when the
county constituencies were extremely large, a single landlord could not hope to control the whole constituency;
but after division it might easily happen that the estates
of one man would be almost coincident with the entire
constituency.[1] The Tories themselves realized that in the
case of Whig estates their own power in some counties
would be threatened. It was for this reason that they
objected strongly to the division of Lincoln, claiming
that the northern section, Lindsay, would be a close nomination constituency belonging to Lord Yarborough.
When this was carried over their heads they were so angry
that they walked out of the House in a body.[2] They also
complained that the Isle of Wight would be a Treasury
nomination county, to which the Whigs replied that since
South Hampshire, because of the dockyards, was under
government control, the Isle of Wight was actually gaining freedom by its separation.[3]

The chief Tory attack was directed against the division
of Northumberland, Durham, Northampton, Worcester,
and Cumberland. The opposition showed that these counties, which were receiving two new seats apiece, were

---

[1] 3 Hansard, vii, 276.

[2] 3 Hansard, ix, 822; Broughton, *Recollections,* iv, 161.

[3] 3 Hansard, vi, 145. Peel objected to the division of counties
because he thought that it would injure their public spirit, and
"their common feeling would be ruined," *Ibid.,* v, 1233. An eventu-
ality that the Tories perceived and feared was that the division
would do away with the differences between counties and boroughs,
Ibid., v, 1242.

smaller than any of the others in the same category and
even than some of those which were given but one, and
that if the original standard of two hundred thousand
population had been adopted by the ministers they would
not have gained so much extra representation. And they
also added in the same breath that it was significant that
these five counties were those where the influence of Grey,
Durham, Althorp, Althorp's brother, and Graham, was respectively paramount. And they insisted that these counties had been made to appear larger than they actually
were by including the town population in their statistics.[1]
In the case of these counties, as in that of others, the
Tories adopted the Radical principle of regular proportion
of members to population, and led by Croker showed by
elaborate statistics the electoral anomalies that the
ministers were about to inaugurate.

Russell, however, refused to admit the validity of any
of the objections to the division of the counties. It was
easier, he said, to elect two men than four, and the smaller
the constituency the less the expense of a county election,
so that it would be possible to diminish treating and that
form of bribery which went on under the guise of conveyance and agency.[2] But he did not consider that the
divisions need be mathematically equal, nor that the proportion of members to population should be uniform.
And the basis of the division was never made completely
clear by the ministers. The Tories believed to the end
that the divisions were made according to Whig interests or to chance, in spite of Durham's claim that they
were as far as possible based upon a division of industrial
interests.[3] In any event, the complaints of the opposition

---

[1] 3 Hansard, vii, 327.
[2] 3 Hansard, ix, 1003.
[3] 3 Hansard, xii, 1389.

were fruitless and the plans of the ministers were invariably supported by the majority in the Commons.

No change was made by the ministers in the representation of Oxford and Cambridge. It was generally taken for granted that the universities should continue to return two members each, and there seems to have been no opposition to their privilege. University representation had hitherto been justified upon the ground that without it the interests of learning would suffer. On this occasion Althorp introduced a new plea, and one which since then has been of significance both in the support of and the attack upon university representation: "It was deemed expedient," said the chancellor of the exchequer, "that Oxford and Cambridge should possess their present elective system as a means of protecting the interests of the Established Church." Outside of England the representation of universities was extended by restoring to Trinity College, Dublin, its former right to elect two members; an attempt to enfranchise Edinburgh and Glasgow was, however, defeated.[1]

The success of the Whig ministers in carrying out their plan of redistribution as a whole was very striking. They were able to put into effect their original ideas far more completely than in the case of voting rights, and were forced to grant to the great landholders no compensation comparable to that which resulted from the Chandos clause. The tentative and often illogical character of the redistribution is the more significant. The details of the disfranchising schedules led in many cases to injustice and inconsistency, and in their opposition to Schedule B, which deprived thirty boroughs of one seat, the Tories had much logic on their side. In the case of the enfranchising schedules, also, it is often difficult to understand

[1] Porritt, "Barriers against British Democracy," in *Political Science Quarterly*, xxvi, No. 1, 17-18.

why the claims of certain towns were disregarded, when others were granted representatives.

The ministers, however, were not attempting to substitute a system of even and regular distribution in place of the numerical anomalies which they had partly destroyed. They wielded the weapon of disfranchisement for the purpose of eliminating nomination, rather than with any desire to apportion representatives according to population. The principle of equal electoral districts was abhorrent to them, although they desired that each class of property should have its fair representation. The legerdemain which they practised in constructing and altering the details of the schedules certainly arouses our distrust, as it did that of their contemporaries; but as Roebuck said, if they had been invariably severely honest, their own party would have deserted them.

Looking at the redistribution from the standpoint of nomination, and viewing it in combination with the opening of the close boroughs, we can see that it was as drastic as the ideas of the age would permit. Nomination was not destroyed, but under the new system it could never play the rôle in government that it had assumed before 1832. Moreover, while the recognition of the industrial towns was accompanied with the disavowal of the representation of numbers as a principle, it was nevertheless a notable step in the development of democratic electoral institutions.

But in this case, as in that of the qualification clauses, the importance of the reform lies not so much in the legislation itself, as in the fact that the redistribution marks the beginning of a series of changes. This significant aspect of the first step was grasped less clearly by the Whigs than it was by their opponents; for the foresight of the Radicals was sharpened by their hopes, and that

of the Tories by their apprehensions.[1]   As Place said,
Wellington and the other Tories were like the schoolboy in
the nursery rhyme who disliked to begin the alphabet,
because,

> "If I say A, I must say B,
> And so go on to C and D,
> And so at once no end I see,
> If I but once say A, B, C."

[1] The accuracy of the Tory forebodings is exemplified in one of
Baring's speeches: "If it [reform] once were carried into effect,
they might have a king by name with less influence than a president
of the United States; and a House of Lords so intimidated that they
would lose the whole of that wholesome influence to which their rank,
their wealth, and their inheritance so justly entitled them.   When
the peerage had once lost its influence then would a democracy
decidedly prevail," 3 Hansard, iv, 1287.

CHAPTER IV

EFFECTS OF REFORM UPON CONSTITUENCY AND PARTY

Numerical effect of the Reform Act—Number of new voters in counties—The tenant electors—Their support given to the Conservative party—Effect of borough freeholder vote in counties—Disappointment of the Liberals—Effect of reformed franchises upon the borough electorate—Gradual elimination of ancient right voters—Such voters generally support Liberal party—Their corruption—Weakening of working class electoral power by the Reform Act—Labour vote generally cast for Liberal party—Effect of the new franchises on nomination in boroughs—Electoral power of patrons lessened by the increase in number of voters—Advantage won by the Liberal party—Effects of the redistribution—Electoral power of the South lessened—Increase in area of the boroughs—Effect of redistribution on nomination—Advantage won by the Liberal party—The new boroughs generally Liberal—General character of the effects of reform—Continued power of the aristocracy.

THE foresight of those who predicted that the importance of the Reform Act lay in its ultimate rather than in its immediate effects, was largely justified by the number of electors registered in 1832 under the reformed qualifications. The legislation of that year, it was soon realized, would not increase the total electorate nearly as much as had been generally anticipated by either the friends or the foes of parliamentary reform. The Tories, we may remind ourselves, had constantly, if vaguely, dilated upon the enormous constituencies that would result from the Whig measure; and Russell represented the mass of Whig opinion when he calculated that the whole electorate of England and Wales would be approximately

doubled. But after the first registration, it was seen that
the net increase in the number of voters was only slightly
more than two hundred thousand, representing a gain of
only about fifty per cent over the pre-reform electorate.
The change wrought in the size of the electorate by the
act of 1832 was thus by no means commensurate with the
acrimony of the conflict.[1]

In the counties the reformed electorate was composed in
greater part of those voting under unreformed qualifications, and in not a few constituencies the electorate was
almost entirely unaffected by the reform.[2] Of the new
voters, the copyholders and leaseholders, whose enfranchisement had aroused so much opposition because of their
alleged dependent condition, were of very little importance in any constituency. They represented altogether
only a tenth of the county electorate, and with the exception of some eight constituencies their influence was
trifling. Even in the division where they were relatively
most numerous (Huntingdon) they comprised less than a
sixth of the voters.[3]

[1] Grey had estimated that there would be 115 boroughs with from
300 to 500 voters; 68 with from 500 to 1000; 20 with from 1000 to
5000; and 12 with more than 5000, 3 Hansard, xii, 19. As a matter
of fact he underestimated the number of very small and of large
boroughs. There were after the Reform Act, 30 boroughs with less
than 300 voters; only 42 with from 300 to 500; 60 with from 500 to
1000; 56 with from 1000 to 5000; and 12 with more than 5000,
Parliamentary Papers, 1833, no. 189. For the numerical effect of
the first Reform Act, see Appendix, No. 1.

[2] *Parliamentary Papers*, 1866, no. 3736. The freeholders voting
on the old qualification represented 70 per cent of the reformed
electorate; the tenants-at-will, 20 per cent; and the copyholders and
leaseholders together, about 10 per cent. In South Stafford the
freeholders formed 90 per cent of the voters; in Hampshire, 80 per
cent; in North Nottinghamshire, of 4000 registered electors, all but
800 were freeholders.

[3] In Cambridge, South Durham, South and North Essex, North
Northamptonshire, North Hampshire, Huntington, West Norfolk, the
copyholders and leaseholders formed between 10 and 15 per cent of

On the other hand, the tenants-at-will, offspring of the much-discussed Chandos clause, were of the first importance in certain constituencies, although they composed less than a quarter of the aggregate county electorate. In Merioneth they outnumbered the freeholders; and in Anglesea, Northumberland, and West Cornwall they were in a majority when they combined with the other new electors. In twenty-three divisions the proportion of voters registered under the tenant qualification approached a third or more of the constituency. For the most part the tenant electors, like the copyholders and leaseholders, were most numerous in the agricultural counties, where the land was held in large estates. In the industrial divisions the freeholders generally formed the mass of the electorate.[1]

It will not be forgotten that the tenant-at-will qualification was introduced by a Tory and carried by the combined efforts of Tory and Whig squires in the Commons. The ministers and the urban representatives had opposed it in the debates, seeing in it a manœuvre calculated to increase the electoral strength of the Conservatives, and also fearing that it would bring the county constituencies more completely than before under the control of the landed aristocracy.

Such forebodings were justified in large measure by the elections of the years that succeeded the introduction of the new qualification. In the twenty-three divisions where the tenant electors were of numerical importance, the

the voters. But in North Leicester only 9 were registered altogether; in the two divisions of Kent, 25; and in South Cheshire, 1. In six of the twelve Welsh counties no voters of this class were entered on the electoral lists, *Parliamentary Papers,* 1866, no. 3736.

[1] As in South Stafford and North Nottinghamshire; although it is true that in the non-industrial divisions of East Kent and East Worcester the proportion of freeholders was also large, *Parliamentary Papers,* 1866, no. 3736.

electoral advantage of the Conservatives was indubitable. During the generation that elapsed between the first and second Reform Acts more than two-thirds of the seats in these divisions were carried by the Conservatives. In a single hotly contested election, such as that of 1841, Conservative strength was still more plainly demonstrated: out of forty-six seats the Liberals were able to carry only nine. On the other hand, in the counties where the tenant electors were few, the advantage lay with the Liberals, who carried between half and two-thirds of the elections.[1]

It is true that in some divisions where the proportion of voters qualified by the tenant franchise was large, the Liberals held complete control. In West Cornwall there was no contested election between 1832 and 1865, and but one Conservative was chosen, who held his seat for a few months only. In Anglesea and East Cumberland the Liberal sway was acknowledged at the poll without a break or a contest. But such carefully preserved county constituencies were more frequently to be found in the possession of the Tories. In West Cumberland, North Shropshire, East Suffolk, Westmoreland, Montgomery, and Merioneth, a Liberal candidate was rarely proposed and never elected. And in other counties where the tenant electors were numerous, such as South Warwick, South Devon, Monmouth, and South Nottingham, a Liberal could win his seat only in the most favourable circumstances.

[1] The divisions where the tenant electors were numerous were East and West Cumberland, West Cornwall, North and South Devon, North Lancashire, both divisions of Lincoln, Monmouth, North Northumberland, South Nottingham, both divisions of Shropshire, West Somerset, both divisions of Suffolk, South Warwick, Westmoreland, the three divisions of Yorkshire, Montgomery, Merioneth, and Anglesea, *Parliamentary Papers,* 1866, no. 3736. The statistics on the results of elections in this chapter are based upon an analysis of McCalmont, *Parliamentary Poll Book.*

The control of the great landowners in the divisions characterized by a large tenant electorate, was thus very complete, and the sway of the aristocratic families, whether Whig or Tory, remained practically unbroken. The power of the landed classes over the tenant voters is brought into sharper relief when we note their failure to control consistently the divisions where the freeholders were most numerous. In general, the latter tended toward the Liberal side; but in none of them was there the steady succession of victories for one party that is to be found where the tenants were able effectually to influence the election.[1]

Except for the proposal to qualify the tenants-at-will, the most debated question arising in the discussion of the county voting rights had been the place of the freeholders in represented boroughs. The Tories had vigorously opposed the proposal, ultimately adopted, that the freeholders should vote in the county divisions, fearing lest the Whig townsmen should swamp the county constituencies. But that fear proved to be far less justified by events than were the doubts of the Liberals as to the influence of the Tories on the tenant voters. In the counties which included within their boundaries the largest town population, the Conservatives more than held their own. Amongst those counties South Lancashire and North Warwick were especially notable.[2] But in South Lancashire, during the

[1] Even in North Durham and South Stafford, which were naturally strong Liberal divisions, one seat was held by a Conservative from 1837 to 1852.

[2] *Parliamentary Papers*, 1832, no. 357, "Report on the Divisions of Counties and Boroughs." In South Lancashire were located Liverpool, Manchester, Salford, Bolton, and Oldham, containing an aggregate population of some six hundred thousand townspeople. In North Warwick were Birmingham and Coventry with a population of nearly two hundred thousand.

period between the first two Reform Acts, the Liberals carried only ten seats while the Conservatives carried twelve. In South Warwick, which was the particular division alluded to in the debates of 1831, the vanity of Tory fears was made still more manifest, for the Liberal freeholders of Birmingham, so far from swamping the county, had the pleasure of seeing their candidates elected only on the rarest occasions. In the entire period of thirty-three years South Warwick elected only two Liberals as against eighteen Conservative members.[1]

In East Surrey and North Durham also, there were numerous freeholders dwelling in the towns and supposed to be ready to support urban interests, and who were generally expected to influence elections in favour of the Liberals.[2] It is true that the proportion of Liberal victories at the polls was far larger than that secured by the Conservatives in these divisions. But they were naturally Liberal constituencies, and the defeats of the Conservatives can hardly be ascribed to the votes of the borough freeholder. The Liberals proved quite as successful in South Durham, where the town population was a negligible factor, as they were in the northern division of the same county; and they were almost as successful in West Surrey, where there were no borough freeholders, as in the neighbouring division of East Surrey. In North Derby, where there were no represented boroughs and few town freeholders, the Liberals carried every election until the second Reform Act. In the southern division of Derby, where it was expected that the town freeholder vote

---

[1] McCalmont, *Parliamentary Poll Book*, 302, 303.

[2] *Parliamentary Papers*, 1832, no. 357, "Report on the Divisions of Counties and Boroughs." In East Surrey were located Lambeth and Southwark, containing about three hundred thousand townspeople; in North Durham were Sunderland, Gateshead, South Shields, and Durham City, containing approximately eighty thousand.

of Derby borough, which was of the most pronounced Liberal character, would ensure equal success, the Conservatives carried twelve seats to their opponents' seven.[1]

Thus the county qualifications introduced in 1832 were apparently favourable rather to the Conservatives than to the Liberals. In twenty-three constituencies, where the tenants-at-will were capable of turning the balance of an election, the sway of the landlords over the tenant electors resulted in a large proportion of Conservative victories, although in a few of these divisions Liberal supremacy was uncontested. When the aristocracy chose to exert their power to its full extent, as in the bitter conflict of 1841, Conservative strength in these constituencies was still greater. Even in cases where the Liberals had looked to the town freeholder as a factor which would offset in part this new element of Conservative power, the control of the Conservatives remained unbroken. To a large extent the complaint of the Liberals that in the counties the landed aristocracy, and especially the Tories, would gain by the Reform Act, was realized in fact.

In the boroughs, as in the counties, the act of 1832 increased the electorate by about fifty per cent. But whereas in the counties the mass of the reformed constituency was made up of old voters, in the boroughs the new occupation franchise provided the major part of the electors. Between an half and two-thirds of the borough electorate after 1832 was composed of those voting under the new £10 qualification.[2] And inasmuch as nearly everyone who held an ancient right preferred it to the new, we

---

[1] McCalmont, *Parliamentary Poll Book,* 76, 77.

[2] Freemen on borough register 63,481
Other ancient right voters 44,738
£10 householders 174,181

Parliamentary Papers, 1833, no. 189; 1866, no. 3626.

may assume that the greater number of the £10 house-holders were absolutely new voters. Thus while the actual net increase in the number of voters in the boroughs was no greater than in the counties, the alteration effected by the act of 1832 was far more complete in the former than in the latter. In the counties, moreover, no disfranchise-ment resulted from the Reform Act; but in the boroughs the enforcement of residence, as a preliminary qualifica-tion, wiped out nearly half of the old voters.[1] It was said that the constituency of Leicester was reduced by seven thousand voters, and that of Westminster by more than three thousand; in many of the smaller boroughs more than three-quarters of the old electorate disappeared.[2]

Of the two hundred boroughs in England and Wales that were represented after the Reform Act, there re-mained one hundred and forty-nine in which ancient right qualifications were exercised; and of the two hundred and eighty thousand borough voters, about forty per cent were registered on the same terms. In many boroughs, natur-ally, these electors formed a small minority; but in a few they comprised the bulk of the electorate. The freemen were by far the most numerous of the ancient right voters, representing between a fifth and a quarter of the entire borough constituency. In forty-eight boroughs the free-men formed a third of the total number of registered voters; in sixteen they had a large majority; while in towns like Beverly, Bridgnorth, and Maldon, they consti-

---

[1] The borough electorate before the Reform Act was estimated at 188,000; after the Reform Act the ancient right voters numbered 108,000, *Parliamentary Papers,* 1866, no. 3626; Lambert, "Parliamen-tary Franchises, Past and Present," in *Nineteenth Century,* December, 1889, 951 (citing an unpublished paper of statistics on the number of borough voters before the Reform Act).

[2] *Parliamentary Papers,* 1831, nos. 201, 204; 1831-1832, no. 112; 1866, no. 3626; Lambert, *op. cit.*

tuted more than five-sixths of the electors.[1] Of the other ancient rights, the scot and lot was exercised in forty-one boroughs, and in many of the smaller ones was the only qualification under which the voters were registered.[2] Besides the freemen there were altogether some forty thousand ancient right electors on the register in 1833.

While the composition of the county electorate remained practically unchanged between 1832 and 1865, that of the borough was radically altered during this period, as a result of the gradual obliteration of the ancient right franchises. The Reform Act provided that with the exception of the freeman qualification, the ancient franchises were to expire with the lives of those exercising them. There was thus, as time went on, a steady decrease in the number of those qualified by such ancient rights; by 1865 all but eight thousand of the scot and lot voters, potwallers, and burgage holders had disappeared. These relics of pre-reform days were at that time scattered through sixty boroughs. In most cases they were rather of electoral interest than importance, although in Haverford West the scot and lot voters formed more than a quarter of the electorate, and in Newark they were nearly as strong; in Lichfield also the burgage holders formed a quarter of the constituency.[3]

[1] Carlisle,	1,209 freemen out of 1,512 electors.	
Coventry,	2,756 freemen out of 3,285 electors.	
Beverly,	865 freemen out of 1,011 electors.	
Maldon,	699 freemen out of 716 electors.	
York,	2,342 freemen out of 2,873 electors.	

Parliamentary Papers, 1866, no. 3626.

[2] It is probable, however, that many of the returns confused the £10 electors with the scot and lot voters.

[3] There were seven boroughs where the old inhabitant householders still exercised the suffrage: Ashburton, Bedford, Cirencester, Guildford, Hertford, Northampton, Preston. In Honiton and Taunton potwallers still voted, *Parliamentary Papers,* 1866, no. 3626.

The freemen, who decreased in numbers from sixty to forty thousand during the generation that followed the Reform Act, were still to be found in ninety-one boroughs in 1865. In twenty-five they held the balance of power, and in ten, by combination with other ancient right electors, they were in the majority.[1] In Coventry four-fifths of the voters were freemen, and in Lancaster there were more than a thousand in a registered constituency of fourteen hundred. Thus, by concentration, the representative strength of the freemen in 1865 was greater than might be supposed from their total number. Although they formed less than a twelfth of the total constituency, they controlled ten boroughs absolutely and could often determine the fate of an election in fifteen others. But even so their practical weight in the electoral system of the country was not great.

The final effect of the Reform Act on the borough electorate was clearly far more extensive than at first appeared. During the elections that immediately succeeded 1832 the ancient right electors could exercise enormous influence; at the end of the period they were in a small minority; for while, by 1865, the new voters had increased from sixty to ninety per cent of the total electorate, the ancient right voters decreased by half, and their electoral influence was confined to about an eighth of all the represented boroughs. This process of gradual elimination was exactly what the ministers of 1832 looked forward to; and if their wishes had been followed, the freemen, as well as the other classes, would have disappeared and the diminution of ancient right electors would have been still more extensive.

It is interesting to note that while the Tories opposed

[1] In Beverly, Coventry, Exeter, Haverfordwest, Lancaster, Newcastle-under-Lyme, Norwich, Stafford, York, *Parliamentary Papers,* 1866, no. 3626.

the disfranchisement of the ancient right voter and did actually secure the perpetuity of the freeman qualification, they did so to their own electoral disadvantage. Their defence of ancient rights resulted largely from the assumption that the freemen were their natural allies, capable of resisting the power of the new voters, who, they feared, were likely to prove "low dissenting Whigs."[1] But their expectations were destined to disappointment, for the proportion of Liberal members in the boroughs where the freemen were in a majority was larger than that of Conservative. In sixteen boroughs where, during the period between the Reform Acts, the ancient right voters formed at least half the electorate, the Liberals carried one hundred and ninety-five seats to one hundred and forty-eight won by their rivals. And in the election of 1841, the year of Tory victory, the Liberals carried seventeen of the thirty-one seats in these boroughs. The alliance between the Conservative party and the ancient franchises, even if it existed, was thus not of great electoral advantage to the former.

Russell's objection to the pre-reform qualifications on the ground that they resulted in a corrupt electorate, was borne out, to a large extent, by the reports of bribery committees during the years that followed the Reform Act. In the sixteen boroughs where ancient right electors were most numerous, there were sixteen elections voided for bribery between 1832 and 1854, a far larger proportion than obtained for the boroughs in general. In the end, three of these boroughs were absolutely disfranchised for corrupt practices, and the same penalty was dealt out to the freemen of a fourth. Later several of the others fur-

---

[1] Peel believed that the Whigs desired to disfranchise the freemen because of their Tory affiliations, thus agreeing with Gladstone's later assertion, Croker, *Correspondence and Diaries*, ii, 180; 3 Hansard, clxxx, 1137.

nished examples of the most flagrant corruption brought
to light after 1832.[1]

The electoral strength of the working classes in the
borough constituencies was naturally weakened by the
qualification clauses of the Reform Act. It was decreased
absolutely by the disfranchisement of ancient right voters
when residence was enforced, and relatively still more by
the introduction of the £10 qualification. It is impossible
to determine the exact proportion of electors who belonged
to the working classes before 1832. From statistics presented to the House of Commons in 1865, it appears that
in that year more than half of the freemen were of the
artisan class. Probably the same or even a larger proportion may have existed in pre-reform days. Gladstone
estimated that before 1832 the working classes formed the
majority in sixty-five boroughs, which together returned
one hundred and thirty members.[2] If that is so, they were
weakened enormously by the disfranchisement of the eighty
thousand ancient right voters that took place in 1832.
The relative importance of the working class in elections
was lessened by the fact that the large majority of the new
electors was in all probability of the middle class.[3] Instead
of forming more than half of the aggregate borough
electorate, the artisans after 1832 were outnumbered more
than two to one.

In forty-seven boroughs, after the reform, approxi-

1 Beverly, Lancaster, and Reigate were disfranchised absolutely,
and the freemen of Yarmouth met the same fate, *Parliamentary
Papers*, 1867, nos. 3777, 3774, 3775; 1870, nos. c. 15, 310.

2 3 Hansard, clxxxii, 1137-1138; *Parliamentary Papers*, 1866, no.
3626.

3 It appeared that about 15 per cent of the £10 occupiers belonged
to the artisan class. Thus before the Reform Act the working
classes would have had 100,000 voters to the 81,000 of the upper
and middle classes; but after 1832 they had only 85,000 electors to
the 193,000 of the upper and middle classes, 3 Hansard, clxxxii, 39;
Parliamentary Papers, 1866, no. 3626.

mately a third or more of the electorate was made up of
the working classes; and in many of these the proportion
of artisan voters amounted to nearly fifty per cent. These
boroughs were for the most part freemen constituencies, or
towns where the government had large works. In the
centres of textile manufactures the proportion of working
class voters was small.[1] On the other hand, in some of the
metropolitan boroughs the proportion of working class
voters ran from a third to a half. In eight boroughs the
artisans had an absolute majority on the electoral
register. In one of these, Coventry, nearly seventy per cent
of the constituency belonged to the labouring class; but
in the other seven the workers had only a bare majority.[2]

According to Gladstone, the working classes after 1832
affiliated for the most part with the Conservative side;[3] but
this generalization is scarcely borne out by the facts. An
analysis of elections between 1832 and 1865, in the constituencies where working class electors could, by reason
of their numbers, largely determine the fate of a candidate,
shows that the Liberals more than held their own. In the
forty-seven boroughs where the proportion of artisan
electors rose to thirty per cent or over, five hundred and
seventy-four seats were carried by the Liberals between
1832 and 1865, to three hundred and fourteen won by the
Conservatives. In the eight boroughs where there was an
absolute majority of working class votes the proportion
of Liberal victories was quite as high.[4] Hence, whatever

[1] 3 Hansard, clxxxii, 860. A manufacturer of Lancashire asserted
that of his 5000 employees there were only 69 voters. In Halifax
only 1 in 10 of the electors belonged to the artisan class; in Leeds,
1 in 14.

[2] The eight boroughs were Coventry, Stafford, Maldon, Newcastle-
under-Lyme, Beverly, Pembroke, St. Ives, Greenwich, *Parliamentary
Papers*, 1866, no. 3626.

[3] 3 Hansard, clxxxii, 1137.

[4] McCalmont, *Parliamentary Poll Book, passim.*

might be said as to the party affiliations of the artisans, it could not fairly be argued that their tendencies were strongly Conservative. Some of the boroughs with a large working class electorate were consistently Liberal. This was the case in Coventry, as well as in Chester, Devonport, Hythe, and the metropolitan boroughs of Greenwich and Lambeth. On the other hand, none of the working class boroughs were so faithful as this to the Tory cause, although some of them, such as Tamworth, Reigate, Cardiff, and Pembroke, deserted the Conservatives only after 1841, under the leadership of Peel.

It is clear that the reform in borough voting rights effected by the act of 1832 was not entirely to the advantage of the democratic element. By imposing a term of residence upon the freemen, as well as by abolishing the other forms of ancient rights, it diminished the electoral power of the working classes; at the same time it weakened their strength relatively by the introduction of the £10 qualification. If the tendency of the act was in this respect undemocratic, however, in another respect it was certainly opposed to the aristocracy, for it struck a direct blow at the electoral power of the landowners and plutocrats which they exercised through the proprietorship of boroughs and the system of nomination. The destruction of that power was the chief design of the Whig ministers and the increase of votes, resultant upon the new borough franchise, proved an effective instrument for the liberation of many of the close boroughs.[1]

There were in 1832 about half a hundred boroughs capable of providing a moderate number of electors, but where the right of vote had been so restricted as to vest electoral control in a few persons or in a single individual. In many other boroughs the right of nomination was often recognized as belonging to one or two patrons, whose

[1] *Supra,* Chap. II.

designation of a member almost invariably met with compliance, although the electors preserved a semblance of independence for the sake of the financial profit which might thereby accrue. Such boroughs, which were of moderate size, must be distinguished from the type of village which had insufficient population for the legal minimum of three hundred, and many of which were absolutely disfranchised. The boroughs under discussion were in many cases towns of some importance, and it was expected that as a result of the new franchise they would produce a large number of voters. Most of them were in the South.[1]

The introduction of the £10 qualification increased materially the electorate in nearly all of these boroughs. It is true that in some of them the reformed electorate fell far below the minimum standard set by the ministers, and towns like Reigate, Thetford, and Calne had even less than two hundred voters apiece. But in others the "opening" process was startling. Portsmouth gained twelve hundred electors and the constituency of Bath rose from twenty-nine voters to nearly twenty-nine hundred. And the aggregate number of voters in the boroughs of this type was rather more than decupled: the average number of electors rose from less than thirty-eight to over three hundred and eighty.[2]

The control of the borough patron was enormously weakened by such increase in the number of electors. In

---

[1] *Parliamentary Papers,* 1831, nos. 201, 204; 1831-1832, no. 112; Oldfield, *Representative History, passim.* In Cornwall there were 5 boroughs where the voting rights were of such a restricted nature before 1832 that the inhabitants had to content themselves with the rôle of onlookers when the elections recurred; in Hampshire there were 6 of this type, in Wiltshire, 7, and in Sussex and Devonshire, 5 apiece. There were only 11 such boroughs north of the Thames and Severn.

[2] *Parliamentary Papers,* 1831, nos. 201, 204; 1866, no. 3626.

a constituency like Thirsk, where of the fifty burgages
which conferred a vote before 1832, forty-nine had been
held by Sir R. Frankland, the election had been merely a
formality. But when the constituency was increased to
two hundred and fifty electors the patron's influence became largely moral. At Knaresborough, before 1832,
the Duke of Devonshire held all the property upon which
the twenty-eight electors based their qualifications. He
had been wont to send his servitors, to whom the burgages
were temporarily conveyed, to vote for his candidate; the
latter did not even consider it worth while to appear at
the election, and some old pauper was chaired by way of
proxy. But after the Reform Act such absolute power
of nomination was lost in a constituency of some three
hundred voters. At Westbury, Horsham, Petersfield,
Midhurst, and in other boroughs, the single obligation
resting on the patron at elections before 1832 had been
that his attorney should bring down in his green bag the
deeds for the burgages, so that the nominal electors might
prove their qualifications. Such simplicity of control was
henceforth impossible and other methods had to be sought.[1]

Naturally much of the moral influence over elections
which came from many years of control, remained to the
patrons. Though nomination in its original simplicity was
out of the question after the Reform Act, so much property
was held by the former patron in many boroughs that
large numbers of the electors, being tenants, had to vote
according to the landlord's wishes or find themselves
harassed if not evicted. In at least seventy boroughs,
after 1832, such positive influence had invariably to be
reckoned with.[2] To exercise their power effectively, however, the patrons had to employ harsher methods than
those used in the days of absolute domination. The intimi-

1 Oldfield, *Representative History*, v, 146, 302, 335.
2 Dod, *Parliamentary Companion, passim*.

dation or purchase of a hundred tenants, to whom the
right of free choice had supposedly been granted, was a
more difficult and dangerous process than to supply a
score of retainers with burgages on the day of election.
Such intimidation was, however, a necessity if votes were
to be controlled; and it was because of the check which the
opening of the close boroughs placed upon nomination
that for a generation after 1832 the elimination of corrupt
influence was considered a vital necessity by those endeavouring to render the legislation of that year effective.

The blow struck at nomination by the introduction of
the £10 electors into the close boroughs, affected the balance of parties immediately and decisively. Of the forty-
seven boroughs referred to, more than half had been
reckoned as the safest of Tory strongholds. During the
two decades previous to the Reform Act, twenty-eight
had been held by Tory patrons and had almost invariably
sent members to swell the Tory majority. Only twelve
had been held by Whig proprietors, and seven were shared
or doubtful. The "opening" of these boroughs threw the
great majority of them over to the Liberal side. From
1832 till 1867 there were only twelve that were carried
more often by Conservatives than by their rivals. In eight
of the forty-seven the Conservatives failed to secure a
single seat between the two Reform Acts, while there was
but one in which the Liberals were totally excluded. Of
the members elected in these boroughs during that period
nearly two-thirds were Liberals.[1] Thus the Conservatives
had not merely lost their controlling interest in these close
boroughs, but were forced to recognize a Liberal domina-

---

[1] Of 766 members chosen in these constituencies, 496 were Liberals.
No Conservatives were elected in Tavistock, Tiverton, Liskeard,
Banbury, Calne, Richmond, Malmesbury. No Liberal was elected
in Christchurch, McCalmont, *Parliamentary Poll Book, passim.*

tion that was almost as complete as that which they themselves had formerly possessed.

Considering generally the reformed qualification clauses of 1832, we see that their effect varied in counties and boroughs, both in extent and in character. In the county constituencies the total electorate was increased in the same ratio as in boroughs; but the new electors formed only a third of the electorate, and except in a few divisions the old electors were in the vast majority. In so far as the change was influential it redounded to the advantage of the Conservatives. Naturally strong in the counties, they could hail the new tenants-at-will as welcome and necessary reinforcements. Nor was this Conservative advantage offset by the county votes of the borough freeholder, whose influence on elections was apparently greatly exaggerated in the reform debates.

In boroughs, the character of the electorate was far more radically altered. Immediately after the Reform Act the old electors constituted less than half of the total borough constituency, and a generation later only a bare ten per cent. This disfranchisement of the ancient right voters was the more important in that it carried with it the exclusion of most of the working class voters, who had probably formed the major part of the electorate before 1832. On the other hand a decided move was made against the power of the aristocracy by the opening up of the close boroughs and the breaking of the absolutism of the borough patrons.

The enormous party advantage won by the Liberals in the reformed borough franchise more than offset the Conservative gain in the county qualifications. That the disfranchisement of the ancient right voter and the artisan was not a Liberal loss is indicated by the general preference shown for Liberal candidates in boroughs where the former were numerous. By the "opening" of the close boroughs not merely was an ancient source of Tory strength destroyed, but constituencies were formed that were destined to display marked Liberal tendencies.

The apparent effect of the new qualifications was to throw complete control of elections into the hands of the middle class. On the one hand the strength of the purely democratic element, which had been manifested through the ancient voting rights, was weakened; while on the other, the power of the aristocracy was attacked by the liberation of the close boroughs. It must be remembered, however, that the new middle class electors did not secure the control that was predicted for them and which historians have often taken for granted. Although they were nominally in power in most of the boroughs, without the fear of working class competition or the domination of a regular patron, they often possessed no more real power than the burgage holders who preceded them. As we shall see, the disposal of the suffrages bestowed in 1832 was by no means invariably in the hands of those who possessed the legal voting qualifications; some votes were controlled by the registration lawyers, who knew how to make and unmake qualifications; others were bought with cash or refreshment; still others were disposed of through the influence of property over dependence and landlord over tenant.

In its immediate effects the redistribution of seats was far more notable than the reform of voting rights. In a number of ways it began the correction of some of the features of the unreformed system which seem most anomalous to modern eyes. It lessened to some extent the enormous majority of burgesses over county members, thus acknowledging the right of the more populous districts to more complete representation. It also started the movement for equalizing the representation of the South and the North, which culminated in 1885 when the industrial centres of Lancashire and Yorkshire obtained electoral power in proportion to their wealth and numbers. Each process was begun, of course, unconsciously and with almost complete uncertainty of the direction which was being taken.[1] A still more important effect of the redistribution was the blow which it struck at the system of nomination, by disfranchising the small boroughs.

The transfer of seats from boroughs to counties in 1832 was extensive, although it left the burgesses still in a large majority. Of the one hundred and forty-three seats taken from the small boroughs, thirteen were given to Scotland and Ireland, and sixty-five distributed among the industrial towns of England. The remainder went to the counties.[2] Thus, so far as the seats of England and Wales were concerned, there was a net loss of seventy-eight burgesses and a gain of sixty-five county members.

The geographical aspect of the redistribution is still more striking, and the enormous preponderance of the South in the Commons distinctly lessened. We have seen that practically all the disfranchisement applied to southern constituencies. The boroughs of the Southeast, Kent, Sussex, Surrey, and Hampshire, lost thirty-six members, and those of the Southwest, Wiltshire, Dorset, Somerset, Devon, and Cornwall, sixty-nine. More than two-thirds of the seats withdrawn came from south of the Thames and the Severn. The new constituencies, on the other hand, were generally situated to the north of these rivers, only

[1] In the debates of 1831 the question of apportionment of members according to population came up at frequent intervals. But the Whigs always denied that the Reform Act was a step in this direction; while the Tories, in their vague and sinister warnings, guessed rather than foresaw the significance of the movement. The geographical aspect of the matter was hardly mentioned.

[2] The total number of members in the House of Commons thus remained unchanged and the principle of Gascoyne's amendment was accepted, *supra,* Chap. II.

forty-five of the one hundred and thirty new members coming from southern counties or boroughs. The Midlands received seventeen and the North and Northwest forty-seven.[1] During the period between the first two Reform Acts this process continued. When in 1844 and in 1852 four seats were made available by the disfranchisement of Sudbury and St. Albans, one was given to the town of Birkenhead in Cheshire, and the others distributed between the divisions of Lancashire and the West Riding of Yorkshire.

Notwithstanding such correction, the advantage of the boroughs and of the South in representation was still overwhelming before the passing of the Reform Act of 1867. The number of burgesses was twice that of the county members. On the geographical side, there were only thirty-nine members representing the counties that lay north of a line drawn from the Wash to the Severn; while to the south of such a line there were one hundred and twenty-three. Of the burgesses, eighty-six came from the northern half and two hundred and forty-eight from the southern. The counties along the southern coastboard sent to Westminster a third of all the burgesses representing England and Wales; while the border counties of the North and the North Riding furnished only twenty-nine burgesses, or an eleventh of the whole.

A decided step toward the assimilation of county and borough constituencies was made in 1832 by the increase in area of many of the boroughs. In a number of cases this had been done in order to bring the population of the boroughs up to the required minimum. Wallingford, which before the Reform Act had included less than half a square mile, now took in twenty-five square miles. Wareham became a large rural area of forty-seven square miles, and Stroud in Gloucester saw its boundaries laid out to

[1] See Appendix, No. 3.

include sixty-one square miles. Similar enlargements were made in the case of many of the small Cornish boroughs, as well as of many in Hampshire and Sussex. The four great rural boroughs, East Retford, Cricklade, Aylesbury, and New Shoreham, enlarged in the first place to prevent corruption, preserved their boundaries, and were larger than several of the counties. Cricklade formed more than a quarter of the total area of Wiltshire, and Aylesbury about a fifth of Buckinghamshire. Shoreham included one hundred and twenty-five square miles, extending straight from the Channel across Sussex to the Surrey boundary. Before the Reform Act of 1832, the total area included in borough constituencies of England and Wales had not exceeded five hundred square miles. As a result of the enlargement of boundaries it was increased to nearly twenty-five hundred.[1]

In the minds of the ministers, who were less concerned with the correction of numerical and geographical anomalies, the most valuable effect of the redistribution was that which it exercised upon the power of the borough patron. Schedule A was important, not so much because it corrected irregularity of distribution, as because it lopped off the tentacles of the nomination octopus. In the boroughs that lost one member, the power of the patron was diminished by half, even if he continued to control the borough; and, as we saw, nomination was largely destroyed in these boroughs by the introduction of the new £10 qualification. The disfranchisement thus tended strongly to render the constituencies more independent.

Notwithstanding Tory presages, most of the new boroughs were free from any dominating influence. It is true that in Chatham and Devonport, governmental control was supposed to be established, and Whitehaven did prove to be under Lonsdale's influence. But in Brighton,

1 *Parliamentary Papers*, 1883, no. 321.

where treasury interests were supposed to be assured because it had been a royal residence, the king's officers were defeated in 1832 and two Radicals elected. The large industrial boroughs of the type of Manchester, Birmingham, and Leeds, were almost entirely free, except from the influence of party associations and electoral attorneys. The effect of the creation of new county divisions was sometimes to increase the power of the landlords; but that power had been so firmly established in the first instance that no marked change was apparent. Before the Reform Act the two parties often split the county seats between them; afterwards they were apt each to take a division.[1]

From the party point of view the redistribution was of the greatest assistance to the Liberals. This advantage was not won, as the Tories had feared, through the division of the counties. It is true that the division of Durham gave the Liberals two more members than they otherwise would have had. But the division of the other Liberal counties resulted rather to the advantage of the Tories, as in most of them, during the succeeding generation, either the two parties divided the seats, or the balance turned in favour of the Conservatives. But the redistribution of the borough seats, on the other hand, was of the greatest value to the Liberal party.

The disfranchisement of the fifty-six boroughs contained in Schedule A struck Conservative power even more directly than had the opening up of the close boroughs. Of these victims of reform, twenty-eight were Tory strongholds, and their extinction meant a loss of fifty-six members to their party in the House of Commons. Of the remaining twenty-eight, a majority were controlled by patrons who in ordinary legislation had supported the Tories. Even under pressure of ministerial and Whig

---

[1] Dod, *Parliamentary Companion*, 1832; McCalmont, *Parliamentary Poll Book, passim.*

funds, only half of the members for these boroughs voted in favour of reform.[1] In Schedule B the loss of the Tories was not so marked, but it was far greater than that of the Whigs. Of the thirty boroughs which lost one member each, thirteen were regularly Tory, eight Whig, and nine doubtful. By disfranchisement the Conservatives were thus deprived of sixty-nine seats, while the Liberals lost only eight that they could invariably have counted upon.[2]

The electoral advantage of the Whigs was still further increased by the distribution of new seats. Most of the latter were allotted to the large industrial towns, where the £10 constituency proved to be strongly Liberal in its sympathies. The new metropolitan boroughs were opposed to the Conservatives almost without exception. In Tower Hamlets and Lambeth not a single Conservative was elected between 1832 and 1867; in Finsbury and Marylebone, during these years, a Conservative was elected but once in each constituency, and in Greenwich but two were chosen. Of the one hundred and ten members elected in these boroughs between the two Reform Acts, all but four were Liberals.

In the new two-member boroughs in Lancashire, seventy-one Liberals were elected as against thirteen Conservatives between 1832 and 1867; Manchester did not choose a single Conservative. For the Yorkshire boroughs that returned two members each for the first time, seventy-four Liberals were elected and but twelve of the opposing party; Sheffield, like Manchester, refused to elect a Conservative. In Birmingham nineteen Liberals and one Conservative were returned, and in Wolverhampton all of the twenty were Liberals. Of the four hundred and sixty-nine members chosen in the boroughs of Schedule C, there

[1] For the enormous influence wielded by the Whigs, see Greville, *Memoirs*, ii, 133; Roebuck, *History of the Whig Ministry*, ii, 162.
[2] Oldfield, *Representative History*, *passim*.

were only sixty-two Conservatives. Thus eighty-six per cent of the elections in these new constituencies were carried by the Liberals.

In the new boroughs returning one member, the advantage of the Liberals was not so great, but was still very marked. In eight of the twenty boroughs, no Conservative member was elected between 1832 and 1867, and there were only three where the advantage was not with the Liberals.[1] Of a total of two hundred and sixteen members, one hundred and sixty-three, or about three-quarters, were Liberals. When we remember that the proportion of Liberal members chosen in all constituencies in England and Wales during these years was only fifty-two per cent, we can easily appreciate the advantage gained by that party through the enfranchisement of the new industrial towns.

The immediate results of the redistribution of 1832 were naturally more striking than those proceeding from the application of the qualification clauses. The latter did not greatly affect the county electorate, and the alteration in the character of the borough constituency was largely gradual. So far as the effect on nomination was concerned, the opening of the close boroughs was not so complete as the absolute disfranchisement, which killed the system altogether in the boroughs of Schedule A that no longer had any representation. In the redistribution, moreover, are to be noted such democratic tendencies as manifested themselves in the Reform Act. The disfranchisement of the working classes which resulted from the qualification clauses, made that part of the legislation a purely middle class measure. But the redistribution, by its attack on the proprietors of boroughs, and by its en-

[1] Ashton-under-Lyne, Berwick, Salford, Kendal, Gateshead, South Shields, Huddersfield, Merthyr Tydvil, McCalmont, *Parliamentary Poll Book, passim.*

franchisement of the industrial towns and their large population, took a decided step in the democratic direction.

So far as regards the balance of parties the Liberals would have gained even without redistribution. The opening up of the close boroughs far more than offset the advantage won by the Conservatives through the new county qualifications. But the great gain of the Liberals was through the redistribution of seats. The disfranchisement of the rotten boroughs eliminated the most powerful of Tory factors, and the newly enfranchised towns became the mainstay of Liberal strength during the generation that succeeded the passing of the Reform Act. But while the conditions which had guaranteed Tory supremacy were thus altered, Tory power was by no means annihilated. Notwithstanding the destruction of Tory nomination boroughs and the formation of many constituencies destined for Liberal control, the Conservatives, strong in the counties, were able in many of the boroughs of moderate size to wage the contest on almost equal terms.[1]

The immediate political effects of the Reform Act thus proved less striking than many had anticipated. Both the king and the ministers overrated the changes that would take place, and attached too little importance to the strength of the old influences by which the House of Commons was formerly returned. The ministers believed that the power of the Tories was annihilated through the destruction of their nomination boroughs, and considered that the Radicals and the rising tide of democracy were the chief dangers of the future.[2] Inspired by this apprehension, the Whig ministers left many bulwarks of aris-

[1] In the old boroughs not marked by a freeman electorate, the proportion of Liberal victories from 1832 to 1865 was 52 per cent, McCalmont, *Parliamentary Poll Book*.

[2] Cf. Roebuck, *History of the Whig Ministry*, ii, 409.

tocratic control by which the Conservatives were destined to profit.

But in their fear of the Radical danger which might rise from the new enfranchisement, the Whigs made a miscalculation. As Roebuck said, the battle of the thirty years that followed the Reform Act was destined to be not between the Whigs, representing aristocracy and wealth on the one hand, and violent democracy on the other; but rather between the two types of wealth and property: the landed proprietors and the manufacturing capitalists.[1] In either case wealth and property remained in control. The old influences by which the House of Commons had been elected still retained much of their importance, and while the system of nomination was broken, it was by no means destroyed. Moreover the control of the two aristocratic parties was maintained in nearly all of the older constituencies and some of the new, in part by the manipulation of the registration system, in part by the exercise of corrupt influence.[2] These aspects of the electoral system after 1832 form the subject of the chapters that follow.

[1] This fact determined Grote's retirement in 1841, as he did not see the use of sustaining "Whig conservatism against Tory conservatism," Kent, *The English Radicals*, 347. From the point of view of those who desired that the electors should have actual control, there was a distinction rather than a difference between Whigs and Tories.

[2] Cf. Russell's speech made in 1839, in which he admits that the provisions of the Reform Act were so perverted and abused that the enfranchisement was often more nominal than real. He called attention to the fact that the free exercise of the franchise was often prevented because of the determination of the upper classes to keep power in their own hands. Peel, also, was of the same opinion, 3 Hansard, xlvii, 1349, 1359.

CHAPTER V

REGISTRATION: THE CREATION OF VOTES

Function of electoral registration—No such system in general
operation before 1832—Necessity of registration recognized by
framers of Reform Act—Details of the registration system—The
overseers and their duties—Compilation of the lists—Claims and
objections—Revision of the lists—The revising barristers—Failure
of the system—Disfranchisement of qualified persons—Attempts
at reform—The act of 1843—It proves unsatisfactory—The
creation of votes—Faggot votes—Party activity—The registration
associations—The Anti-Corn Law League—Its success in Yorkshire—Impurity of electoral lists—Duplicate voters—Resulting
power of party agents.

THE scope of the Reform Act was not confined to the
definition of electoral qualifications and the redistribution of seats; it also introduced a series of regulations which had for their purpose the supervision and
control of the franchise conferred in 1832. These regulations made up the system of electoral registration, and
their practical effect upon the actual operation of the
franchise can hardly be overestimated. Registration is
the process which transforms the potential into the actual
voter. A person is legally possessed of the right to vote,
if he holds a certain qualification; but before he may
exercise that right and cast his vote, he is required to
prove his qualification and have his name entered upon the
electoral lists.

In modern eyes such electoral lists, which form conclusive evidence of the right to vote, seem an almost inherent part of any representative system, and necessary to

its successful operation. It is an essential corollary to
the suffrage that, once the qualifications have been defined,
the law should see to it that all duly qualified persons
have proper facilities for obtaining the insertion of their
names on the register; and also that all bona fide voters
are protected by such checks as will prevent the registration of fraudulent or unqualified claimants. The franchise is merely an academic definition if it does not create
the actual as well as the theoretical power of voting; a
purely platonic privilege if those upon whom the law is not
supposed to confer the vote succeed in exercising the
suffrage.

In England no form of registration was in existence
before 1832. The unreformed representative system had
found no necessity for the compilation of regular lists of
voters, and it is almost impossible today to find reliable
documents stating the number and the qualifications of
voters previous to the first Reform Act. It was, therefore, a totally new departure when the act of 1832 provided that to the exercise of the electoral franchise, the
registration of the elector and of his qualification must
be in all cases a condition precedent and indispensable.[1]

The necessity for registration of electors before 1832
was less compelling. Few of the borough constituencies
were large, and most were extremely small; the electors
and the value of their qualifications were well known. In
the days when contested elections were eagerly anticipated,
as stockholders look forward to their dividends, and when
a vote was worth anywhere from two to fifteen pounds,
all the town looked on to see how each elector cast his
vote; there was little difficulty in detecting an impostor,
and personation was comparatively rare.

In the counties, where the number of electors was often
large, a self-made system of registration had grown up,

[1] 2 & 3 Will. IV, c. 45, sec. 26.

designed to prevent personation and secure the rights of the bona fide elector. In many of the counties the land commissioners made out lists of the tax-paying free-holders and the elector carried to the poll the receipt for the payment of his land tax as proof of his qualification. This system, however, never worked satisfactorily. It caused delay at the poll; the receipt was apt to be lost or abstracted by zealous opponents about the hustings; and in any case the receipt was not decisive proof of qualifi-cation, since many freeholders were exempt from taxation and therefore had no receipt to show, even though they were well-qualified electors.

Both in boroughs and counties the absence of regular lists furnished opportunities for sharp practices and con-ferred great power upon the returning officer in charge of the election. He could at the last moment accept or dis-qualify any claimant, and this power, apparently, was exercised as suited either his politics or his pocket. Thus in 1768 Lowther is said to have "nobbled the sheriff, who rejected a large number of voters on the ground that the land-tax lists, which were the registers of voters, were signed by only two of the Commissioners and not by three" as the law required.[1]

In 1788 an act was passed by parliament establishing an elaborate system of registration, which may be con-sidered the parent of that devised in 1832.[2] The system of the latter year, however, was a posthumous child, for the act of 1788 was almost immediately repealed. During the twelve months in which it was in force its operation gave rise to many complaints, both of expense and inconven-ience, and it seems to have been practically inoperative; we read of only one hundred persons registered in all of

[1] Ferguson, *History of Cumberland*, 168 (cited by Porritt, *The Unreformed House of Commons*, i, 26).
[2] 28 Geo. III, c. 36.

Lancashire.[1] After this abortive attempt at a uniform system of registration, there was a return, in counties, to the land commissioners' lists, while in boroughs no register was compiled. This state of affairs lasted until the Reform Act.

But in 1831 the small committee which drew up the Reform Bill, included in their first draft the stipulation that no one should vote unless he had been registered in his constituency in the autumn preceding the election; and they framed elaborate machinery for the compilation of electoral lists. The author of the registration system thus devised was Sir James Graham, and it appears that his object was not so much to prevent fraud or to secure the rights of the bona fide electors, as to decrease the expense of elections.[2]. The same point was later emphasized in the debates in the House of Commons: the Whigs pointed out that under the old system the poll was necessarily protracted to allow the verification of the electors' claims to vote, and that the voter was at the expense of proving his identity and qualification. A preliminary verification would not only shorten the poll and prevent disorder, but would also lessen the cost of elections. They spoke of the prevention of personation as merely a minor advantage.[3]

In general, the Tories opposed the introduction of a registration system, although they centred their attacks chiefly upon its details. Sir Charles Wetherell insisted that, so far from lessening the cost of elections, registration would increase the expense, would perpetuate party feeling from year to year, and would lead to an infinity of petty lawsuits; the necessity of being registered, he claimed, was in itself an imposition on the rights of the

[1] 3 Hansard, xiv, 1289.
[2] Reid, *Life of Durham*, i, 237.
[3] 3 Hansard, vi, 1051-1055.

people.[1] Others objected that registration would throw
the country into far greater confusion than the election
itself; that it had been tried once before and had failed;
that it was now unnecessary, inasmuch as an automatic
register existed in the rate-books. The system was also
opposed with considerable justice and foresight on the
ground that it would play into the hands of the party
political associations.[2]

Notwithstanding such opposition, which in the main
partook of the nature of party tactics, the machinery of
registration was adopted by the House with but slight
amendments; and as then organized forms essentially the
basis of registration procedure as it operates in England
today.

The system is as follows. For the purposes of registration the existing parish officers and districts were
utilized. The advisability of creating a new officer, a
single competent registration authority in each county
and borough, was considered. By placing at his disposal
sufficient funds and an adequate staff, who should devote
all their time and energies to the business in hand, a simple and efficient system might have been attained. But
while the ministers recognized that the creation of a
special registration official might lessen complexities and
result in greater immediate efficiency, they believed that
not only would this plan entail considerable expense, but
that the appointment of such an official could not be
vested in any department without thereby exposing that
department to local and political jealousy. One of the
great objections to registration was that it would open
the way to party tricks, and the feeling finally prevailed
that the existing parish organization was not only more
satisfactory, because the people were accustomed to it,

<hr>

1 3 Hansard, vi, 1057.
2 3 Hansard, x, 83-93.

but would also be less liable to political bias than any new corps of officials. As a later investigating committee reported, it was thought better to utilize some existing machinery that would entail less additional outlay and give rise to less local opposition, than to adopt a new organization even with the advantage of greater symmetry and efficiency. "They were content with that which was likely to be in practice more acceptable, rather than attempt that which would be theoretically most perfect."[1]

The officers upon whom the system depended were the overseers of the poor, and to them was given the charge of seeing that all who had the right to vote received fair opportunity of placing their names on the register.[2] These local officials of township and parish already performed duties which demanded such information as the making up of the electoral lists would require. They had the compiling of the rate-books under their charge, and therefore knew who were resident in the parish and what were the rated values of all houses. With very slight extra effort such officials would be able to make complete lists of all who, by the value of their qualifications, should be registered as electors; and because of their intimate knowledge of all persons in the parish they would be able to handle effectively all fraudulent or insufficient claims.

In the counties registration proceedings began each year on the 20th of June, when the overseers published a

[1] *Parliamentary Papers*, 1868-1869, no. 294, "Report of the Select Committee on Registration," vii.

[2] The overseers of the poor were formerly appointed yearly in parishes under the Poor Relief Act of 1601 (43 Eliz., c. 2), and in townships, under the Poor Relief Act of 1662 (14 Car. II, c. 12), by the justices of the peace from among the substantial householders. This system continued until 1894 when the Local Government Act of that year (56 & 57 Vict., c. 7), transferred their appointment to the parish council or parish meeting in counties, and to the town council in boroughs. So far as regards registration, the words "overseers of the poor" include "all persons who by virtue of any office or appoint-

notice calling upon all persons who were duly qualified to send in a notification of their claim. This claim was a condition precedent and indispensable to the insertion of a name on the list. The process in counties differed from that in boroughs in this respect: in counties no claimant could be registered until he had proved his qualification, while in boroughs the rate-book was held to be prima facie evidence of the qualification. But once entered upon the list the county elector was not forced to make any subsequent claim, for unless some objection were raised his name stood over from year to year. All voters who had changed their qualification or residence were forced, however, to send in a new claim. This requirement was insisted upon, even though the description of the former qualification that appeared upon the register might be equally applicable to the new.[1]

Before the last day of July, the overseers compiled from the claims sent in and from the existing register a list of voters for the ensuing year. They must enter upon the list every claim recorded, but if they had reason to doubt the claimant's qualification they might mark his name "objected." These lists were kept open for inspection, partly that claimants might see whether their claims were impugned and partly that others, if they so desired, might enter objection. Any elector or claimant might formally "object" to the qualification of any person listed. In all cases of objection, notice must be sent to the overseer and to the claimant concerned before the 25th of August. Private persons might object to those already objected to by the overseer and, as it happened, very often did so, thereby providing against the with-

---

ment shall execute the duties of the overseers of the poor, by whatever name or title such persons shall be called, and in whatsoever manner they may be appointed," 2 & 3 Will. IV, c. 45.

[1] "Burton v. Grey," 5 *Common Bench Reports*, 7.

drawal of objections on the part of the overseer.[1] The objections need not specify exactly the ground of the objection and the flaw in the qualification. If the claimant failed to appear to defend his claim against the objection, his name was summarily expunged. The list of objections was published during the first fortnight in September.

While this complicated process was going on in the counties, an equally tangled skein was being spun in the boroughs. The county elector, as we saw, was forced to make claim if he had a new qualification or if he was to be registered for the first time. But once upon the register and unopposed, he might remain without further effort; if no objections were subsequently raised, he was not called upon to substantiate his claim or give himself further trouble about his vote.[2] In boroughs, on the other hand, although the prospective elector need not bother to make a claim in the first place, he must have paid his rates up to the beginning of the registration period. By the 20th of July the assessors and collectors of taxes made out and gave to the overseers a list of all persons who, by reason of their being in arrears, were prevented from exercising the franchise. With the help of these lists and the information drawn from the rate-books and copies of the tax assessments, the overseers made out preliminary lists of all who appeared entitled to vote, with the exception of the freemen; lists of the latter were prepared by the town clerk.

In the boroughs the lists of all prospective voters was published on the last day of July. All persons who were

[1] *Parliamentary Papers,* 1846, no. 451, "Minutes of Evidence," §§ 5303-5305.

[2] With a clear title the county qualification was considered preferable, since it entailed less trouble in the long run than the borough qualification, *Parliamentary Papers,* 1846, no. 451, "Minutes of Evidence," §§ 3710-3711.

omitted from these lists and claimed adequate qualifications might give notice of their claims to the overseers, and a list of such claimants was also made out and published. As in the counties, the name of any person inserted in the lists might be objected to by any elector, due notice being given both to the claimant and to the overseer. A list of the persons objected to was published and like the other lists was kept for inspection and sale.

After the preliminary lists were thus compiled and the objections entered, the process in counties and boroughs was identical. The lists were handed over to the clerical officials, the clerks of the peace in counties and the town clerks in boroughs, and copies made out for the courts constituted to revise the lists. For the preliminary compilation a well-known local authority had seemed advisable; for the settling of claims and the hearing of objections extra-local officials, trained in the law and less likely to be biased by local prejudices, were appointed. These officials were specially chosen barristers, who held courts for the revision of the lists in all counties, divisions of counties, and boroughs. In the case of Middlesex and the metropolitan boroughs these revising barristers were appointed by the Lord Chief Justice; for the other constituencies they were chosen by the senior judge in the Commissions of Assize. Some latitude was allowed the judge in deciding how many barristers were necessary for quick and smooth revision.[1] The barristers might not be members of parliament nor hold any office of profit under the crown.

The barristers' courts for the revision of the lists sat annually from the middle of September to the last of

[1] In 1843 the number of revising barristers was set at 71, and at the present day the number is fixed at 97, by an Order in Council under section 3 of the Revising Barristers Act, 1873 (36 & 37 Vict., c. 70).

October, three days' notice being posted in some conspicuous place in the constituency.[1] At the opening of the revision court, the barristers were furnished with all the lists of voters, claimants, and objections. The attendance of the overseers and the town clerks was required and they provided the barristers with all the information that lay in their power to give. The barristers then proceeded to make the necessary corrections in the lists, as seemed to them just, upon hearing the evidence offered by claimants and objectors. If any person whose name had not been listed could prove that his qualification was adequate and that he had complied with all the necessary requirements of the law as regarded residence, payment of rates, and due notice, his name might be inserted. Power of objection to these late claimants was granted to any elector. The barristers then proceeded to expunge from the list the names of all those who were shown to have died during the year and of those whose qualification was proved insufficient, or who had failed to comply with the stated conditions of residence or payment of rates. If there appeared upon the list the name of any person proved to have been guilty of bribery, treating, or the exercise of undue influence, or against whom judgment in any penal action for such offenses had been obtained, the name was struck off.[2]

The barristers demanded that the qualification, as set forth in the claim, should be exactly specified: where the name of the claimant, his residence, or his property, was insufficiently or inaccurately described, even though merely a clerical error in an initial or the street number were involved, the claimant was liable to lose his chance of

[1] Revising barristers must now hold their courts between September 8 and October 12 (51 & 52 Vict., c. 10, sec. 6).

[2] *Parliamentary Papers*, 1864, no. 203, "Minutes of Evidence," § 14.

insertion upon the register. No change in the qualification as stated could be made after the case reached the barristers' court. Where, for example, a claimant was shown not to possess sufficient title to the freehold vote that he originally claimed, he could not later claim to be registered upon proof of a copyhold or leasehold qualification.[1]

In the case of objections, the objector must appear in court in person or by agent, to support the objection; in case of his non-appearance the name of the person objected to was retained. It was also retained if the claimant succeeded in proving that, by the 20th of July, he was in possession of a sufficient qualification and had complied with all the conditions imposed by law. If the claimant objected to failed to prove his qualification, or if he did not appear to support his claim, his name was expunged forthwith. Clearly the weight given to objections was enormous. No matter how unequivocal the claimant's title, if objection were made he was put to the expense and bother of proving his qualification; and if by any reason he failed to appear in court, he lost his vote.

---

[1] Even at the present day a revising barrister can only amend an insufficient description of the qualification; he cannot alter the description of another qualification (Lord Esher in "Plant v. Potts," 1891, 1 *Queen's Bench Reports*, N. S., 261-262). For instance in the case of "Friend v. Towers," in 1882, the name of the voter was shown to be on the occupiers' list and the nature of the qualification stated to be a "house." On objection it was found that the clear yearly value of the property was less than £10, but the claimant proved that he had occupied the house as tenant during the whole of the qualifying period, so as to constitute a qualification under the act of 1867. The revising barrister amended the entry by adding the word "dwelling" to the word "house," and was sustained by the courts (10 *Queen's Bench,* 87). But when a barrister, on proof that a claimant possessed a leasehold, but not a freehold as stated, and substituted the former, it was held unanimously by the Court of Appeal that he had no such power (1 *Queen's Bench Reports,* N. S., 256).

After the final revision of the lists they were sent to the clerks of the peace in counties and the town clerks in boroughs, copied into books, and copies of the latter sent to the sheriffs and returning officers. The books thus compiled formed the register of voters for the succeeding year. These registers were considered evidence of the elector's franchise, and at the time of election there was no further inquiry, except as to the identity of the voter, the continuance of his qualification, and whether or not he had voted before at the same election. Persons excluded from the register by the revising barrister might tender their votes and such tender was to be recorded. In case of a petition after the election, the correctness of the register was put in question before a committee of the House of Commons, and might be amended.

It was too much to expect, perhaps, that this system, contrived in haste and with no similar institution before it as a model, should meet with immediate success. English political institutions are in general of great age; they have been slowly evolved through actual experiment and use, and adapted little by little to political necessities. Their growth has been so slow that the people have had time to adapt themselves to the system. The complexities and ramifications of the new registration system were not the only hindrance to success; the very fact that the whole idea of registration was new, made it impossible that the system should operate satisfactorily at once. The two main functions of the system were these: to bring upon the register the names of the duly qualified with a minimum of friction and expense; and to prevent the registration of those not entitled to a vote. In both respects the provisions of the system, as above described, fell far short of their object.

The chief cause of the failure of the system to bring upon the register all who were qualified to be electors, was generally agreed to be the apathy of the prospective voters themselves. This indifference to the suffrage was a matter of common talk only three years after the passing of the Reform Act.[1] Mere legislation was not sufficient by itself to change the habits and the ideas of the people, who failed to appreciate the advisability of registration. "They had always voted without being registered," a contemporary article says, "and did not see why they should have anything of the kind to do now."[2] The system was not designed with a view to this popular indifference, for the legislators had believed that the number of voters after the Reform Act would be over-large rather than over-small; hence the weight given to objections and the difficulties thrown in the claimant's path. Russell admitted this in 1840, when he said that the system of 1832 imposed too many restrictions, in the fear that the country would be inundated with voters.[3] Brougham summarized the gist of the whole difficulty with the lucid brevity that sometimes belonged to him: "The voter did not care for his vote and if left to himself would not go to register it."[4]

The first eleven years that followed the passing of the Reform Act were spent in attempts to discover exactly what was wrong. According to a statement made by Russell in 1834, the chief evils in the system were the laxness of the overseers, who failed to compile complete preliminary lists, the shilling payment made upon registration, which deterred many of the poorer electors, and the opportunities opened up for the presentation of frivolous and vexatious objections.[5] To meet these evils a bill was

[1] *Parliamentary Papers,* 1835, no. 547, "Minutes of Evidence," § 644.

[2] *Edinburgh Review,* lvi, 545.

[3] 3 Hansard, liii, 1201.

[4] 3 Hansard, lxviii, 1093.

[5] 3 Hansard, xxiv, 342.

introduced in that year, of rather a homœopathic character, the chief provision in which was that the shilling fee should be exacted only at the first registration. The bill died, as did a similar one in 1835. The two following years saw bills of the same character introduced, which provided that the person objecting on slight grounds or with vexatious intent, should be liable to costs. These bills passed the House of Commons but were either thrown out or rendered futile by the Lords, the Tories in each House firmly opposing any change of this nature in the system.

In 1839 the discovery was made that the provision requiring each elector to swear that he had not left the property which formed his qualification, led to the disfranchisement of many who had removed to property of even greater value. Consequently a bill was brought in with the approval of the government and so framed as to allow the person who had moved, to retain his vote between registrations and to vote if an election should come up. The assertion was made that in a constituency of two thousand electors there were, on an average, two hundred removals each year. Not more than ten of the persons who changed their residence actually left town, and the change was, in general, to a property of a greater value, but according to the law all were disfranchised.[1] Duncombe said that in Weymouth, where there were five hundred voters, fifty on each side were annually affected by removals, and it was stated that a fifth of the entire electorate of Manchester was thus disqualified.[2] This state of affairs opened up an excellent opportunity for personation, and the necessity of investigating the character of removals when an election petition was presented caused the government enormous expense. A member of an elec-

---

[1] 3 Hansard, xlviii, 994; xlix, 471.
[2] 3 Hansard, lxiii, 1589, 1592-1594.

tion committee stated that half the time of an election
committee was spent in looking into the cases of electors
who had moved.[1] On the other hand, many felt that the
suggestion incorporated in the bill was dangerous.
Nearly all the Tories opposed the suggestion that a man
be allowed to keep his vote for the year after removal,
partly on the ground that it was contrary to the principles of the Reform Act, and partly because they believed that it would reintroduce out-voting and lead to
bribery.[2] The bill passed the Commons, but was thrown
out by the Lords. A similar bill that was brought
forward in 1842 was killed almost without delay.

In the meantime Lord John Russell was advocating a
general reform of the registration system, and in 1840
and 1841 introduced two measures, each of which failed
to secure the approval of parliament. But finally, in
1843, an act was passed under Tory guidance, which
remodelled registration in several of its more important
details, and which forms the real basis of the existing
system. The bill was introduced by Sir James Graham,
the father of the original system, and had for its object
the settlement of the chief difficulties that had been experienced. In order that the overseers should have no excuse for failing to make out the preliminary lists in time
for inspection, the bill provided that the clerk of the
peace,[3] in counties, and the town clerk, in boroughs,
should issue a precept to each overseer directing him to
prepare each year the alphabetical list of the persons
entitled to vote on the 31st of July.[4] The precept was to

[1] 3 Hansard, lxiii, 1594.

[2] 3 Hansard, xlix, 997.

[3] Now the "Clerk of the County Council," under the Local Government Act of 1888, (51 & 52 Vict., c. 41, sec. 83).

[4] "The precept is a form of instruction to overseers informing
them of the nature of their duties in the county registration, and
how to discharge them," Rogers, *Elections*, i, 242.

be accompanied by various forms to be filled out by the claimants, and in the case of counties by a copy of the parish register.[1] As early as 1834 the laxness of the overseers had been pointed out as one of the chief reasons for the incomplete character of the preliminary lists, and it was hoped that these new provisions would make it easier for the claimant to bring his name upon the register.

In order that the wholesale disqualification that had resulted from failure to pay rates in time might be mitigated, the law of 1832 was altered to the advantage of the ratepayer. As the law had stood, a person must have paid all his rates and taxes up to the time of making his claim. The new act allowed him three months' leeway, stipulating that rates and taxes due up to April 6 were to be paid at the time of making claim. Moreover, the overseers must give notice, warning all ratepayers by June 20, that their rates must be paid up if they intended to register.[2]

Another reason for the failure of the system to bring on the lists the names of all those who were duly qualified, had been the number of frivolous and vexatious objections. Many of the non-resident county voters had allowed themselves to be disqualified on entirely insufficient grounds, because of their unwillingness to spend time and money in attending the revising courts. To prevent such disqualification, power was given to the revising barrister to order that costs should be paid by any person whose objections seemed unwarranted.

It was hoped that these changes would tend towards more complete lists, but greater care was taken at the same time that the names of unqualified persons should

---

[1] 6 & 7 Vict., c. 18, sec. 3, 10; *Parliamentary Papers,* 1864, no. 0.39, "Minutes of Evidence," § 6; *Ibid.,* 1868-1869, no. 294, "Report of the Select Committee on Registration."

[2] 6 & 7 Vict., c. 18, sec. 11.

not be entered on the electoral register. The overseers were to publish lists of all persons disqualified by non-payment of rates or by reason of corrupt or illegal practices, in order to furnish definite data for the revising barristers in their task of expunging such names from the register. Moreover, the act provided greater facilities for bona fide objections by allowing them to be served by post as well as in person. When the notice of the objection was sent through the post, a duplicate of the notice was given to the objector by the postmaster. This duplicate was conclusive evidence of the service of objection, and the person objected to was supposed to have been as duly notified as though the notice had been left at his house or delivered into his hands.[1]

To meet the complaint that the revising barristers were too often young men of slight experience who rendered conflicting decisions, the act provided that hereafter the barristers were to be of at least three years' standing. Another complaint was that the number of revising barristers was too great. The more there were, the greater was the variety of their opinions as to what constituted a qualification. A claimant was accepted by a revising barrister one year, only to be rejected by the latter's colleague the

---

[1] It must be delivered "duly directed and in duplicate to the postmaster of any post-office where money orders are received or paid, within such hours as shall have been previously given notice of in such post-office, and under such regulation with respect to the registration of such letters, and the fee to be paid for such registration. . . . The postmaster shall compare the said notice and the duplicate, and on being satisfied that they are alike in their address and contents, shall forward one of them to its address by post and shall return the other to the party bringing the same, duly stamped with the stamp of the said post-office," 6 & 7 Vict., c. 18, sec. 100; *Parliamentary Papers*, 1846, no. 451, "Report of the Select Committee on County Registration," iv; 7 Manning & Grainger, 29; 14 *Law Reports, Common Pleas*, 54; 15 *Law Reports, Common Pleas*, 43; 2 *Common Bench Reports*, 45.

next, and many persons were deterred from claiming by the feeling of uncertainty which naturally resulted.[1] This complaint was met by reducing the number of barristers from about one hundred and forty to seventy-one.

The act effected a still more important change by allowing an appeal from the decisions of the barristers to the Court of Common Pleas, instead of to the House. Appeal was to be granted on questions of law but not of fact; it was left to the barrister to decide whether the point of law in question was material to the case, and he need allow it only when he considered it reasonable and proper that such appeal should be entertained.[2] Both Russell in the Commons and Campbell in the Lords objected to this appeal to the Court of Common Pleas, insisting that by it the ultimate sovereignty of the House of Commons over elections was destroyed, and the practical control of the franchise transferred to officials and courts.[3]

The act of 1843 was passed with little difficulty and was in general regarded as a non-partisan measure. Some complaints were heard voicing the impression that it would result in a restriction of popular rights, and that it was so constructed as to favour the party interests of the Tories.[4] But the common impression of the day was

[1] 3 Hansard, liii, 1202.

[2] 6 & 7 Vict., c. 18, sec. 42-46; *Parliamentary Papers*, 1868-1869, no. 294, "Report of the Select Committee on Registration," xix; *Ibid.*, "Minutes of Evidence," §§ 540-719. An appeal pending did not affect the right of voting and no decision after an election was to affect the results of that election. For various cases of appeal, showing what were considered matters of law and what of fact, see MacKenzie and Lushington, *Registration Manual*, 411-438. For a brief summary of the process of registration under the act of 1843, see *Parliamentary Papers*, 1846, no. 451, "Report of the Select Committee on County Registration," iii.

[3] 3 Hansard, lxviii, 330, 754, 1099.

[4] 3 Hansard, lxviii, 1100.

that the changes in the system would not affect registration conditions to a very serious extent. As a matter of fact it soon appeared that the defects of the system had by no means disappeared, and popular dissatisfaction with its operation became continually more acute. The general apathy and indifference of the prospective electors was not disturbed by the increased diligence of the overseers; the people continued to show that they cared little for their rights and privileges.[1] To bring them to the performance of the duties necessary for registration, they had to be roused by some agency outside of the system, and the greater part of the claims were brought forward through the activity of political associations, or individuals working for party interests.

Moreover, the act of 1843 did little or nothing to lessen the complexities of the system, which offered to electoral agents numerous opportunities for sharp practices; the chance of disfranchising an opponent or obtaining a vote for a non-qualified friend, through chicanery, was too obvious and alluring to be resisted. The granting of costs for vexatious objections proved so innocuous that the raising of objections on wholly unjustifiable grounds soon became a party weapon that was utilized with impunity as well as with success. On the other hand, many facilities for unfair and often fraudulent claims were still offered. The register, therefore, was neither complete nor pure. In 1846 complaints on these scores were so numerous that an inquiry was ordered and a parliamentary committee appointed.[2]

One of the chief complaints advanced was the loophole

[1] *Parliamentary Papers*, 1846, no. 451, "Minutes of Evidence," *passim*.
[2] 3 Hansard, lxxxiv, 929. The committee was composed of Newdegate, Craven Berkeley, Adderly, Colborne, Viscount Sandon, Wood, Wortley, Butler, Walpole, Villiers, Hinde, Parker, Bankes, Milner Gibson, Walsh.

left open by the two acts for the creation of votes on either a freehold or leasehold qualification. The splitting of freeholds so as to create faggot votes, as they were called, was an ancient device of electoral agents that dated back to the first Stuarts.[1] The broad electoral possibilities of the practice had been utilized with skill and party profit until 1696, when the so-called Splitting Act,[2] passed with the intention of preventing the creation of faggot votes, succeeded in curtailing somewhat the growth of artificial qualifications. Introduced by Lord Somers, the act declared that "more than one voice should not be heard to vote for the same tenement." But the courts interpreted the intention of the act loosely and the creation of votes continued to a greater or less extent. In 1831, during the debates on the Reform Bill, Baring told how votes were made by splitting freeholds, and prophesied that the same practice would be extended to the new leasehold qualification; he showed how he himself might easily create two hundred county voters by means of the slightest change in their leases.[3] Other persons of electoral experience pointed out that there might be three voters for each leasehold qualification: the owner would have a vote, the original lessee, and the sub-occupying lessee as well.[4] Certain clauses were proposed in order to mark a difference between real and created qualifications, but no adequate steps were taken in 1832 to prevent the creation of votes.

Nor did the courts make any attempt to restrict the manufacture of qualifications. They still held that the act of 1696 applied to none but cases that were flagrantly fraudulent, and when instances came up before them of

[1] *Calendar of State Papers, Domestic,* 1628-1629, 6.
[2] 7 & 8 Will. III, c. 25.
[3] 3 Hansard, vi, 305-307.
[4] 3 Hansard, ix, 1108-1111.

granting rent charges of 40s. or of splitting property into small freeholds of that value, they held, in at least two cases,[1] that such divisions, although made for the express purpose of multiplying voices in elections, were not within the meaning of the Splitting Act.[2] Thus any large proprietor, if he chose to set aside a portion of his estates to the value of a thousand pounds a year, might at once create five hundred voters. Land of the estate would simply be cut up into lots, each of which would be sold as a freehold to the prospective voter. After the conveyance, the original proprietor might, if he chose to retain actual possession, take back a lease of the lots at a rental of 40s. each. The persons to whom the title was thus conveyed became 40s. freeholders and were fully qualified electors. The original proprietor, on the other hand, was still in actual possession.[3]

Numerous illustrations of such practices during the twenty years that followed the Reform Act might be cited. In 1846 the Crosslands, manufacturers near Huddersfield, sold to thirty-five persons some cottages within the precincts of their own mills. On the very day that the conveyance was signed, they took back a lease of each of the thirty-five cottages for 40s. a year apiece.[4] At Ripon numerous cow-houses were erected for a lady, just within the seven-mile limits of the borough. These

---

[1] In the cases of "Alexander v. Newman" and "Newton v. Hargreaves," X *Jurist,* 313, 317.

[2] "A conveyance made in completion of a bona fide contract of sale," it was declared, "where the money passes from the buyer to the seller and the possession also from the seller to the buyer, and where there is no secret reservation or trust on the part of the seller, is not voided by reason of the object of the purchaser or the seller being to multiply voices at an election," X *Jurist,* 313.

[3] *Parliamentary Papers,* 1846, no. 451, "Report of the Select Committee on County Registration."

[4] *Parliamentary Papers,* 1846, no. 451, "Minutes of Evidence," §§ 4873-4876.

were conveyed to prospective voters and immediately leased back for 40s. apiece. These cow-house voters won an unenviable notoriety during the early forties.[1] At Leeds a pigsty of four stones set upright, together with land of sufficient value, gave votes to three different persons. At Buckingham the Duke, who held five thousand of the eighteen thousand acres included in the borough, covered his property with buildings of small value and was said to hold Buckingham under his control entirely through created votes.[2] At Barnsley, in the West Riding of Yorkshire, fifty persons were on the register as qualified by a single factory.[3]

Under such conditions, election agents were not slow to make the most of their opportunities, and party machinery was set to work in order to stimulate those who already possessed a qualification to make claim for it, as well as to create qualifications in the manner above described. From the first days of the new registration system the party leaders and the whips realized the importance of this factor in electoral campaigns. Durham urged Grey not to dissolve parliament in 1832 until the Whigs learned the complexities and the opportunities of the system.[4] Peel said in 1837: "The battle of the Constitution will be fought in the registration court"; and in the following year expressed himself with still greater emphasis: "There is a perfectly new element of political power—namely the registration of voters, a more powerful one than either the sovereign or the House of Commons. That party is strongest, in point of fact, which has the existing registration in its favour. It is a dormant instrument, but a most

---

[1] 3 Hansard, xxiii, 1; *Parliamentary Papers,* 1846, no. 451, "Minutes of Evidence," § 3491.

[2] 3 Hansard, xxii, 723.

[3] 3 Hansard, xcii, 402.

[4] Reid, *Life of Durham,* i, 311.

powerful one, in its tacit and preventative operation. Registration will govern the disposal of offices and determine the policy of party attacks, and the power of this new element will go on increasing, as its secret strength becomes known and is more fully developed. We shall soon have, I have no doubt, a regular systematic organization of it. Where this is to end I know not, but substantial power will be in the Registry Courts, and there the contest will be decided."[1]

It was in full consciousness of the importance of the matter, therefore, that both parties began to organize associations to win qualifications for their adherents and to make sure that all their qualified friends became registered electors. Party activities along these lines were such that Duncombe could say in 1836, "Organized bodies from one end of the kingdom to the other are employed in the business of registration."[2] The "Liberal and Whig Association" was formed in London, while the Tory "Loyal and Constitutional Association" in Marylebone was soon followed by the larger and more important "Conservative Association."[3] The counties followed the lead of the metropolis, and in 1840 party organizations were active in all the more important constituencies. The Liberals were especially energetic in Yorkshire, the Conservatives in Lancashire. In the latter county the associations were divided into two categories: in the one were included the gentlemen, in the other, the workmen. The latter type was generally called a "Conservative Operatives Society."[4]

---

[1] Peel to Arbuthnot, November 8, 1838, Parker, *Life of Peel,* ii, 368.

[2] 3 Hansard, xxxii, 1169.

[3] *Parliamentary Papers,* 1835, no. 547, "Report of the Select Committee on Bribery," 423; *Ibid.,* 1846, no. 451, "Minutes of Evidence," § 4901.

[4] Ostrogorski, *Democracy and Parties,* ii, 150.

With the advent of the Anti-Corn Law League, registration activities, and especially the creation of qualifications, began to be carried through on a grander scale. The League began its attack upon the register in 1843 and from the first this was one of its chief objects and formed one of the main items on its expense account.[1] In 1844 an agent of the League appeared in the revising courts to support the small freehold claims lately created, and in the following year free-trade agents were in evidence in most of the towns of the West Riding of Yorkshire, where opportunities for the creation of freehold qualifications were most obvious.[2] An officer of the League admitted in 1846 that at least two thousand freehold votes had been manufactured in Yorkshire for the purpose of winning that county to free trade, and that, too, within the space of twelve months.[3]

The importance of this electoral method appears when we note that the creation of only fourteen hundred votes would have been more than sufficient to turn the fate of an election in Yorkshire. Nor was it necessary that any of these electors who owed their votes to created qualifications should be resident in the county or have any interest there with the exception of their freehold, which perhaps they had never seen.[4] The Liberal victory of 1846 in the West Riding, which the formerly successful Conservatives were too weak to contest, was attributed to created votes, which had resulted from the exertions of the Anti-Corn

[1] *Parliamentary Papers,* 1846, no. 451, "Minutes of Evidence," §§ 3326, 3269.

[2] *Parliamentary Papers,* 1846, no. 451, "Minutes of Evidence," §§ 4734-4737.

[3] *Parliamentary Papers,* 1846, no. 451, "Minutes of Evidence," § 4990.

[4] *Parliamentary Papers,* 1846, no. 451, "Minutes of Evidence," §§ 4839-4891.

Law League.[1]   A glance at the register shows the enormous advance made by the Liberals during the years which
followed the operations of the League;[2] many of the new
electors were said to be outvoters, of exactly the type
that has aroused the wrath of the Liberal party in recent
years.   The same opportunity for the creation of votes
was open to any other association, if it chose for its field of
action a similarly large district.   Although the efforts
of the party associations in other counties were attended
by less striking results, it was calculated that about
half a million pounds was spent, in 1846, in purchasing
property for the creation of qualifications.[3]

In the majority of cases the freeholds were in all probability paid for by the new electors and not by the League
or the party association; but the qualification was acquired
avowedly for the purpose of assisting one party or the
other, and the association afforded the utmost aid, through
its agents, in facilitating negotiations and purchases.
Articles in the journal of the League advertised that assistance would be given in securing freeholds; and many thousands of letters were sent from its offices announcing that

[1] The standard histories and biographies have little to say about
this phase of the League's activity.   In Morley's *Cobden*, the registration movement is hardly mentioned.   In Ashworth's *Recollections
of Cobden and the League*, the county registration movement is
touched upon but described in a distinctly favourable light.   Students
of the evidence presented before the committee of 1846 will find it
difficult not to agree with their report, in which the methods of the
League are looked at askance; even a free trader like Villiers, who
served on the committee, did not protest against the strictures made
upon his friends' conduct.

[2]

	Cons.	Lib.
1842	1822	1752
1843	1333	1560
1844	1228	1310
1845	1245	3210

[3] *Parliamentary Papers*, 1846, no. 451, "Minutes of Evidence,"
§ 3491.

all those who lacked a qualification and desired to vote for free trade, might be furnished with a county vote on application.[1] In many cases, sums were paid into the treasury of the League and collected into funds, upon which the agents of the League might draw when any opportunity of creating a new qualification presented itself.[2] All the associations, Conservative as well as Liberal, were actively concerned in these operations, but there seems no doubt that the free-trade society excelled, especially in the North. The central Conservative organization attempted to inject similar spirit into the provincial associations affiliated with it, but it is impossible to trace out so clearly the effects of its operations upon the register.[3]

The control of the registers, thus vested in party organizations, tended to make the electoral lists impure. The strength of the party, which resulted in a certain district from the wholesale creation of votes, allowed the permanent insertion of the name of a person who had no real qualification whatever. The party in power would take care, after registering a claimant, to provide that no objection to his name should be carried through successfully. In many constituencies there were numerous instances of voters registered year after year on purely fictitious or fraudulent qualifications, or perhaps indulging in the common practice of personation; in any case they were safely protected by the skill of the agents or lawyers employed by the party.

Instances of such fraud were not rare. In North Stafford thirty-eight freeholders had been registered for many

[1] *Parliamentary Papers,* 1846, no. 451, "Minutes of Evidence," §§ 3077-3086.

[2] *Parliamentary Papers,* 1846, no. 451, "Report of the Select Committee on County Registration," iv.

[3] *Parliamentary Papers,* 1846, no. 451, "Report of the Select Committee on County Registration," iii.

years as qualified by a certain piece of land. The predominating strength of their party in the district saved
them from objection during this period; when an objection
was at last served, and their title was brought before the
court of revision, they admitted that no title had ever
been conveyed to them, and that they were merely
squatters.[1] It was reported to the House that there were
five hundred and eighteen fictitious voters of such a kind
in a single constituency.[2] The land-agent of the Earl of
Warwick used to supply persons with fictitious receipts
for rent, armed with which they could safely make their
claim and become registered electors.[3]

Personation, or voting under the name of another, was
facilitated by the careless manner in which the register
was kept up to date; often there were left on it the names
of voters who had been dead four or five years. In one
instance, after the widow of a voter affirmed that her
husband had been dead for eight years, the vote cast in his
name by a pseudo-elector and supported by the agent of
the party in power, was not refused.[4] In the election of
1841 at Walsall, the Anti-Corn Law League safely polled
nine dead men, three of whom were understood to have
been firm protectionists.[5]

Personation also thrived upon the fact that the name of
the elector might appear upon the register several times,
for as many qualifications as he possessed. If he changed
his residence and made a new claim for the new property,
his name was listed twice, unless special action were taken
by the overseers. This special action was the exception

[1] *Parliamentary Papers*, 1846, no. 451, "Minutes of Evidence,"
§ 3285.
[2] 3 Hansard, xxiv, 343.
[3] H. Evans, *Sir Randall Cremer* (London, 1909), 49.
[4] *Parliamentary Papers*, 1846, no. 451, "Minutes of Evidence,"
§ 3288; see also §§ 3097, 3271, 3353.
[5] 3 Hansard, lvi, 323.

rather than the rule, and the registers were replete with these so-called duplicate voters. In Wiltshire, a man was registered sixteen times, one in Stafford twelve times, and one in Gloucester nine times.[1] If the person thus registered died or removed to another constituency, and, as generally happened, his name was struck off but once, the list immediately became impure; in any event an excellent opportunity for personation was opened. In a single township in South Lancashire there were five hundred and forty names registered for properties, and only four hundred and twenty-five electors.[2]

As an instance of the unreliable condition of the register, the constituency of South Cheshire furnished a clear example. In half of the districts, represented by about four thousand voters, the names of thirty-six persons who had died the previous year were listed; forty electors had sold the freeholds for which they stood registered; fifty-three who had left their farms entirely were still on the lists as £50 tenants; and one hundred and fourteen who had changed their residence were still registered for their former freehold property.[3]

The failure of the registration system to provide pure and bona fide electoral lists was fully admitted in the report of the committee of 1846.[4] So far as the county constituencies were concerned the actual voters were clearly in many cases not those whom it had been the intention of the legislators of 1832 to enfranchise. The complications of the system, the red tape involved in the process,

---

[1] *Parliamentary Papers,* 1846, no. 451, "Minutes of Evidence," § 3303.

[2] *Parliamentary Papers,* 1846, no. 451, "Minutes of Evidence," § 3276.

[3] *Parliamentary Papers,* 1846, no. 451, "Minutes of Evidence," § 3280.

[4] *Parliamentary Papers,* 1846, no. 451, "Report of the Select Committee on County Registration," ii.

the withdrawal of the state from the functions which
naturally belonged to it, not merely invited but forced the
supervision of party agents and associations. Under the
conditions and especially because of the apathy of the
prospective electors, party action alone was capable of
producing an electorate of even respectable size. Naturally, from the activities of the party associations there
resulted a biased and coloured enfranchisement, since
efforts were made to bring only political friends upon the
register. And with the supremacy of a party in any one
district there resulted a large number of fictitious and
fraudulent voters.

It might have been expected that the increase in the
total electorate resulting from such creation of votes
would have been great. The admissions of the electoral
agents themselves, whether of the Liberal or the Conservative party, show that in many instances qualifications were
manufactured wholesale. And certainly in some constituencies there did result an abnormal increase. The additions to the electorate were, however, irregular and vari-
able, depending as they did upon the activity of the local
association. Moreover, in certain districts, such additions
were more than offset by an equally determined movement
in the reverse direction. While the associations were
working to increase the number of electors friendly to their
party, they endeavoured at the same time to disqualify
their opponents. In many constituencies it proved easier
to destroy than to create. Such party disfranchisement,
as well as other causes leading to disqualification, will be
considered in the ensuing chapter. A study of the
conditions makes it plain that there was an essential
difference between a qualification and a vote, and that,
as Russell himself admitted, the franchise was often
rendered in large measure illusory.

CHAPTER VI

REGISTRATION: METHODS AND CAUSES OF DISQUALIFICATION

Organized disfranchisement—The system of objections—Activities of the Anti-Corn Law League—Frivolous and vexatious objections—Post service of objections—Walpole's bill of 1847—Is defeated—Rate-paying requirements—Disfranchising effects—Evans' bill of 1848—Attitude of parties—After amendment by Lords becomes law—The compound occupiers—Their names not upon the rate-books—Their disfranchisement—Clay's act of 1851—Its failure—Continued disfranchisement of compound occupiers—Investigation of 1864—Pessimistic report—Remedial proposals—The act of 1865—Summary of effects of registration law on the electorate—Restricted the operation of the franchise—Electoral power placed in hands of party agents.

THE preceding chapter has dealt with the opportunities afforded by the registration system for the creation of votes, whether upon manufactured qualifications, or by means of truly fraudulent methods. The ensuing pages are chiefly concerned with the reverse process: the destruction of votes. It mattered little to the party agent whether he enfranchised a friend or excluded an opponent; if he might do both, so much the more was gained. The framers of the system had foreseen that the enfranchising process must result inevitably. Although they had failed to realize the possibility of the wholesale creation of faggot votes, they had perceived the opportunity furnished for the manufacture of questionable claims, and to prevent such claims they had instituted the system of objections. But they did not foresee that by instituting this system they were placing an equally efficient weapon of destruction in the hands of the party associations. At the moment that they hindered the party in the over-enthusiastic enfranchisement of a friend, they assisted it in the disqualification of an opponent.

The system of objections gave the party managers ample opportunity for striking off many hostile votes. Notices could be sent out in the hope that in some cases the objections would prove valid, and that in others the claimants with good qualifications would fail to appear in the revising court to defend them. In either event the vote of an opponent would be destroyed. The Liberals, apparently, were the first to perceive the value of the system of objections from the party point of view. Almost immediately after the passing of the Reform Act, notices of objection were served on Conservative electors by an organization known as the "Reformers' Registration Committee." It was a purely political manœuvre, for the objections were sent out wholesale, regardless of the worth of the qualifications attacked. Retaliation was speedily begun by the Tories and carried to great lengths, especially in Warwickshire, where the "Loyal and Constitutional Association" was organized and sent out objections in large numbers with the purpose of disqualifying opponents.[1]

In all the actively political counties there soon appeared party associations which claimed to do good by removing from the register the names of the persons who were not really qualified.[2] This object, which may have been originally sincere, rapidly degenerated into a means of

[1] *Parliamentary Papers*, 1846, no. 451, "Minutes of Evidence," §§ 625-634.

[2] In Leicester, the "Political Union and Reform Society" and the "Leicestershire Conservative Society," *Parliamentary Papers*, no. 451, "Minutes of Evidence," § 2302. In Stafford, the "Conservative Association," *Ibid.*, § 1076. In Warwick, besides those mentioned above, the "Warwickshire Association for the Protection of Agriculture," *Ibid.*, § 418. In the West Riding, the "Conservative" and

harassing political opponents, and, if the chance of disqualifying legitimate claimants failed, causing them at least worry and expense.[1]

As early as 1834 the number of persons disqualified by such methods was large. In Leeds the names of five hundred and eleven Liberals and two hundred and sixty-eight Conservatives were struck from the lists as the result of objections. There were only one hundred and twenty-three successful claims in that year from both parties at Leeds, so that the net result of the mutual squabbles of Conservatives and Liberals was to disfranchise six hundred and fifty-six electors.[2] Similar conditions existed in many other constituencies. Walpole, who in the following years had long experience as a revising barrister, said later that "hundreds of voters were yearly objected to, not for the purpose of testing the validity of their qualifications, but for party considerations."[3]

With the advent of the Anti-Corn Law League, this means of disqualifying members of the opposing party became systematized. Agents of the League were sent out to every county of doubtful political colour. They made inquiries, frequently from door to door, as to the political opinions of persons upon the register; the information thus gained was transmitted to the central office at Manchester. The office drew up lists of Conservatives in whose statement of qualification some technical flaw appeared, and lists of those who were not considered likely to defend their claim from an objection. The office also compiled lists of

the "Whig" Associations, *Ibid.*, § 5380. In London, the "Central Protective Society," *Ibid.*, § 5380. There were numerous smaller associations, the Liberal organizations generally under the ægis of the Anti-Corn Law League.

[1] *Parliamentary Papers,* 1846, no. 451, "Minutes of Evidence," § 2302.

[2] *Times,* October 16, 1834.

[3] 3 Hansard, xcii, 390.

Liberals whose qualifications were loosely described and who might stand in need of legal assistance in the support of their claims. The solicitors of the League, after they had convened and discussed their campaign, were sent forth to the revision courts, where they reclaimed for all the Liberals whose qualifications stood in need of amendment, and objected to every Conservative whenever opportunity offered. They confessed to bringing a great many objections to persons who had perfectly good qualifications.[1] The number of objections raised, consequent upon the operations of the League and retaliatory societies, was enormous. Out of some eight thousand registered electors in South Cheshire, between two and three thousand found their qualifications objected to in 1845. In North Stafford, objections to a fifth of the voters were brought forward, and in North Cheshire and Buckinghamshire the proportion of objections was nearly as large.[2] The great number of objections was defended by the free traders, and especially by Bright, who pointed out that there were 1276 different roads to the county franchise, and that if the register under such complicated circumstances were to be kept pure, there must necessarily be many objections.[3] With less plausibility he attempted to show that the greater part of the objections were justified. In this belief, however, the investigating committee disagreed with him.[4]

Without question, the system of registration, as constructed by the acts of 1832 and 1843 demanded some party action of this sort. There was no body constituted

[1] *Parliamentary Papers*, 1846, no. 451, "Minutes of Evidence," § 3329. This testimony was given by Mr. George Wilson, chairman of the League.

[2] *Parliamentary Papers*, 1846, no. 451, "Minutes of Evidence," §§ 3327, 4070.

[3] 3 Hansard, xcii, 399.

[4] 3 Hansard, xcii, 400.

by the state to remedy impurities on the register, and such a remedy must perforce be applied by a partial or antagonistic society. Without objections emanating from political organizations, there would have been no effective check whatever upon fraudulent claims; there was no way of getting rid of a bad vote, except by testing it before the revising barrister. The real complaint was not directed against the bona fide objections, but against the large number of those which were merely frivolous and vexatious. These were advanced simply in the hope that the person objected to, even though he held a good qualification, would fail to appear before the court and would lose his vote; or if such striking success were lacking, he would be at least annoyed and harassed.[1] Walpole, who because of his practical experience and because he had served on the investigating committee was listened to with attention, said that the system stood in need of immediate reform in this respect: "A mere man of straw should not be allowed to cast his objections far and wide, not because he has any reason to suppose that the voter's qualification is a bad or doubtful one, but rather in the hope that out of the hundreds against whom he directs his darts haphazard, some may be unable or unwilling to support their votes, and their names will be struck off for non-attendance." "The House," he goes on to say, "has no conception of the vexation and annoyance, the trouble and expense, to which some of the best and most undoubted voters are put . . . no conception of the reckless, thoughtless, and indiscriminate manner in which objections are taken, or how much the electors stand in need of an improved system in order that they may be protected in their undoubted rights and privileges."[2]

[1] *Parliamentary Papers,* 1846, no. 451, "Report of the Select Committee," iv.

[2] 3 Hansard, xcii, 396.

The provision of the act of 1843 which allowed post service of objections facilitated those that were designed to be vexatious. The duplicate signed by the postmaster, we noted above, gave conclusive proof of service. In many cases defective postal arrangements or clever management so delayed the notice of objection that the claimant objected to was not warned in time to appear. Thus in 1845, on the last day permitted by law for the service of objections many thousands were posted in Manchester.[1] So great was their bulk and so carefully the time of posting planned, that they could not be despatched for several days; a large proportion did not reach their destination until long after the date contemplated by the law, and in some cases not until after the day set for public notification of objections.[2] Many of these objections were directed against persons of undoubted qualifications, men of large property in land and houses, and tenants of large farms; the chance was not small that after receiving such tardy notice they would not be able to appear to defend their votes in the court. And, as a matter of fact, numerous unquestionable qualifications were erased from the register because of the non-appearance of the electors.[3]

Nor was this a solitary instance. Some years later

[1] According to the Manchester postmaster, there were posted in the three last days allowed by the law, upwards of 23,000 notices, including the duplicate notices to overseers and occupying tenants. Piles of objections were brought in at the last moment, so that the whole office force worked day and night to get rid of them. Even thus the office was not cleared for some time afterwards, *Parliamentary Papers*, 1846, no. 451, "Report of the Select Committee," iv.

[2] *Parliamentary Papers*, 1846, no. 451, "Minutes of Evidence," §§ 1397-1575.

[3] *Parliamentary Papers*, 1846, no. 451, "Minutes of Evidence," § 4. The exact proportion of the objections directed against good qualifications in this case does not appear from the conflicting evidence; it must, however, have been large.

much the same sort of thing occurred in Surrey, where more than a hundred electors failed to receive their notices of objection. As the objectors had their receipt duplicates, the electors were all disfranchised by the revising barrister.[1] The courts held that such service of objection was perfectly valid, even though owing to accident the notice arrived too late to warn the claimant, since it was the intention of the statute to substitute delivery at the post-office for delivery at the place of abode.[2]

The act of 1843 theoretically gave protection from vexatious objections by allowing the revising barrister power to grant costs when the objection appeared unreasonable or directed with vexatious intent. But in practice this provision had little effect. Party agents were rarely held liable for costs, even when the ground for advancing the objection was of the slightest. If there was any technical or inconsiderable deficiency in the description of the claimant's qualification, this was generally brought up by the agent as fair excuse for an objection, and the barrister generally was willing to consider the technical mistake as justification for refusing costs.[3]

The agents soon learned that they need fear no costs for protesting the qualifications of perfectly bona fide voters. The party agent would run over the lists, and whenever he found the qualification of an opponent imperfectly described, would send in an objection. If the protested elector did not appear at the court, his name was expunged. If he came and proved his qualification, the technical or clerical error allowed the agent to escape

[1] 3 Hansard, cxxx, 1194-1201.

[2] "Hicton v. Antrobus," 2 *Common Bench Reports,* 82; 1 Lutwyche, *Registration Cases,* 363; "Hornsby v. Robson," 1 *Common Bench Reports,* N. S., 63; Keene and Grant, *Registration Cases,* 66.

[3] *Parliamentary Papers,* 1846, no. 451, "Minutes of Evidence," §§ 809-811.

without costs.[1] Thus if the number of an elector's house was set down as "5" instead of "3," or if his name was entered as "John J. Jones," instead of "John K. Jones," the objector was not generally called upon to pay damages. In almost every case the revising barristers laid down the rule that no costs should ever be allowed when an amendment, however trifling, was admitted in the description. The elector, who might have come a long distance, was thus precluded from obtaining any compensation for his loss of time, or for the trouble taken in sustaining his vote.[2]

Sometimes the agents avoided payment of costs by inducing an impecunious elector to present the objection. Thus, even if costs were granted by the barrister, it would be impossible for the outraged claimant to collect them. Walpole said that the majority of the objectors were men of no station or substance, merely the hired tools of the party agents, who were thus escaping the consequences of their own tricks.[3] Other ways were discovered for making objections on slight grounds without the danger of costs. When a large number of notices of objection were to be presented, the legal objector could hand them over to an assistant who would sign the principal's name. These notices would not be considered valid in the eyes of the law; but, if made under the stress of circumstances, the signing of them was not regarded as a definite forgery or

[1] *Parliamentary Papers,* 1846, no. 451, "Minutes of Evidence," § 808. An instance of this occurred in Leigh, Lancashire, where numerous substantial freeholders were objected to in 1845. Some of them appeared in the court, established their qualifications, and were refused costs because of trifling deficiencies in the description of their qualification. Others did not appear and their names were struck off the lists although their qualifications were generally considered to be ample.

[2] 3 Hansard, xcii, 390.

[3] *Parliamentary Papers,* 1846, no. 451, "Report of the Select Committee," v.

even as a misdemeanour.[1] But their invalidity would be
considered a reason for not granting costs to the claimant
who appeared to defend his vote. On the other hand if the
claimant did not appear, the invalidity of the objections
would not come to light, and he would lose his vote. A
case of this kind came up in Birmingham, where we read
that four hundred out of seven hundred and ten notices
purporting to come from the same person were forgeries.
When the protested electors proved their claims, they
asked for costs, but were refused by the barrister on the
ground that as the legal notices and objections were not
signed by the legal objector, they were in point of fact no
objections at all.[2] Objectors could also withdraw when
they found that the claimant intended to come forward in
his defence, thus escaping costs, although causing the
claimant infinite trouble and worry. The courts were
sometimes crowded with claimants who had no remedy,
because the objector had not appeared.[3]

The report of the committee of 1846 laid great emphasis
on the very real obstructions which lay in the path of a
person desirous of transforming a potential qualification
into an actual vote. After weighing much evidence the
committee reported that the evil of vexatious objections,
employed to disqualify or harass political opponents, was
more widespread and affected the register to a far greater
extent that was commonly supposed. The whole tenor of
the report vindicated the opinions of Walpole and Russell
that the franchises granted in 1832 were in many respects
illusory and would continue to be so, unless radical im-

---

[1] "Hinton v. Hinton," 7 Manning and Grainger, *Reports,* 163;
14 *Law Reports, Common Pleas,* 58; "Toms v. Cuming," 7 Manning
and Grainger, 88; 14 *Law Journal Reports, Common Pleas,* 67.

[2] *Parliamentary Papers,* 1846, no. 451, "Minutes of Evidence,"
§ 4.

[3] 3 Hansard, xcii, 391; *Parliamentary Papers,* 1846, no. 451,
"Minutes of Evidence," § 3943.

provements were made in the registration system.[1] Further guarantees were accordingly desired from parliament for ensuring the protection and encouragement of legitimate claimants, and at the same time removing the facilities open to persons who were not really qualified.[2]

As a result of these recommendations, a bill was introduced in 1847 by Walpole, designed to prevent wholesale objections, to purify the lists, and to force the objector to specify something more than a technical defect in the qualification.[3] The measure provided that a claimant might strictly prove his qualification, definitely and formally, and, henceforth, so long as he retained the same qualification, remain on the register, immune from objection. Moreover, the objector was to specify the grounds upon which his objection was based, whether on merit or on a technicality. In the case of an objection based upon a technicality the claimant need not attend the revising court, but might make a declaration before a magistrate, which would allow the revising barrister to correct the description in the absence of the claimant. Objectors were also to make a deposit when entering the objection, which was to be used in the payment of costs if the barrister saw fit. The bill also provided for the elimination of double entries and duplicate voters by forcing each elector whose name appeared more than once upon the lists, to make choice of his determining qualification.[4]

Walpole's bill made no attempt at restricting the creation of faggot votes; apparently he, with the rest of the committee, believed that the registration system acted chiefly in the direction of disfranchisement, and that it

[1] 3 Hansard, xlvii, 1350.
[2] *Parliamentary Papers*, 1846, no. 451, "Report of the Select Committee," ii.
[3] 3 Hansard, xci, 745.
[4] 3 Hansard, xcii, 392-394.

was advisable to bring all the legally qualified persons upon the lists, before attempting to limit enfranchisement. The bill also left the overseers as the chief working officials of the system. The report of the committee of 1846 had stated that it might be preferable to have the registers made up by public officers specially trained and paid for the purpose. But Walpole believed that "the presence of the local overseers was absolutely essential for the purposes of revision. They were the only impartial persons who knew anything certain of the different voters, or who could inform the revising barristers whether voters were resident or had changed their residences, or whether their houses were properly described; and this was information which must constantly be brought under the immediate notice of the revising barristers."[1]

The second reading of Walpole's bill was carried without opposition and met with the hearty approval of the Liberal front bench. But it never reached the committee stage, and was withdrawn, with the excuse that the session was too near its close.[2] Nor was it reintroduced during the following years, and the conditions brought to light in 1846 were left peacefully untouched.

The operation of the registration system evoked complaints in other respects. The necessity of having all rates and taxes paid up by the time of claiming tended to bar many persons from the register. The fact, too, that numerous occupiers had their rates compounded and paid for them by the owners, kept their names off the rate-books, and made it difficult for them to prove their claim. In the first case, obviously, it was the individual's own fault if he were kept from registering because he was in arrears. In the case of those whose rates were paid by their landlords and whose names were not upon the rate-book, it

---

[1] 3 Hansard, xcii, 395.
[2] 3 Hansard, xcii, 389, 398.

was clearly the duty of the state to provide a simple process by which to make the necessary claims. At all events there seems little question but that many persons were deprived of the franchise which had been promised in 1832, because of the rate-paying requirements.

The Reform Act of 1832, as we noted, enacted that no occupier could be registered, unless he had been rated to the poor-rate and actually had paid that rate as well as the assessed taxes for the fiscal year ending July 6; the last day for payment was July 20.[1] From the first, complaints were frequent that the number of those disqualified by this clause would be large. In 1832 numerous petitions were presented to the House of Commons asking that the time for payment be extended; in fact a motion, which failed of success, was made to such effect.[2] The complaints emanated chiefly from Marylebone, Westminster, and the more populous boroughs, where it was asserted there would be wholesale disfranchisement. Francis Place, who made inquiries after July 20, discovered amongst his numerous friends very few ratepayers who had qualified themselves. To mitigate the effect of the law, Althorp was said to have given the metropolitan overseers a hint to stretch a point and accept late payment; with the result that enormous enfranchising power was placed in the hands of the overseers, which, it was claimed, assisted the electoral fortunes of the Whigs.[3] Most of the complaints, however, resulted from the fact that the King's assent to the act of 1832 was given so late as to leave very little time before the date of payment. The inconvenience caused would not, it was supposed, recur when the registration system was in full operation.

[1] 2 & 3 Will. IV, c. 45, sec. 27.
[2] 3 Hansard, xiv, 253, 354, 1230, 1286.
[3] Wallas, *Life of Place*, 324.

But dissatisfaction was prevalent during the following years, and the Radicals protested that the enfranchisement of 1832 was in large part a nullity, because of the rate-paying proviso. Duncombe asserted in 1836 that the constituency had been thereby cut down to "a most alarming and unforeseen extent." He showed that the electorate in London had increased, not by ninety-five thousand, as Russell had promised, but only by forty-four thousand. Not merely was it difficult for the electors to keep track of all their taxes and see that they were paid up; the tax-collectors themselves tricked the voters into not paying, in order that they might be disfranchised.[1] Hume argued along the same lines, and said that in one parish alone five hundred electors had been disfranchised. Duncombe's motion for the abolition of payment of rates as a prerequisite of registration was nevertheless lost.[2]

Four years later Russell planned to loosen the restriction and proposed to abolish the payment of taxes as a condition of registration and to require that the rates should be paid up only to the January preceding registration.[3] Russell's bill, however, failed to become law, and the act of 1843 changed the rate-paying clauses only so far as to allow three months for payment. According to the act, the fiscal year was to end in April instead of July, and rates and taxes due in April need not be paid up before July 20. In 1846 the matter was reintroduced by DeLacy Evans, who obtained leave for the introduction of a bill that extended the time allowed for payment by six months. He failed to carry it beyond the second reading, and bills for the abolition of the rate-paying clauses were thrown out during the session of 1847.[4] But in 1848 Evans suc-

[1] 3 Hansard, xxxii, 1169-1171.
[2] 3 Hansard, xxxii, 1172.
[3] 3 Hansard, liii, 1206.
[4] 3 Hansard, lxxxvii, 909; xc, 406; xciv, 314.

ceeded in carrying through the Commons a measure that provided that the fiscal year should end in October instead of April. Rates payable in October were to be paid as previously by July 20. In other words nine months instead of three were to be allowed the elector to settle his rates and taxes.

Evans' proposal gave rise to long debates and was in the end amended by the Lords. From those debates there stands forth clearly the fact that the suffrage depended largely on conditions which the reformers did not understand and circumstances which they had not foreseen. It was not to be denied that large numbers were disqualified, either because in their indifference to the suffrage they would not take the trouble to keep their rates paid up, or because of the opportunity given tax-collectors and overseers to disfranchise voters for party purposes.[1]   In Marylebone twelve hundred electors were disfranchised because the tax-collector died and no substitute was appointed.[2]   Another year thirteen hundred persons in the same borough were disfranchised by failure to keep out of arrears. In two parishes in Westminster six hundred and eighty-four persons were disfranchised for non-payment; that this was due to carelessness and not indigence was shown by the fact that all but one paid up later.[3]   Williams said that in one borough more than two thousand had been disqualified as a result of their oversight in not paying.[4]   It was estimated that, altogether, one hundred and fifty thousand electors were annually disfranchised from this cause. There was, moreover, the complaint that the freemen did not have to pay the rates for registration, nor did the county voters. Why, it was asked, should there be

1 3 Hansard, xciv, 428.
2 3 Hansard, xc, 408.
3 3 Hansard, lxxxvii, 909.
4 3 Hansard, xc, 428.

this unfair distinction?[1] The Radical point of view was expressed by Wakley, who said "that it was a mere pretence
to say that the people had a £10 franchise conferred on
them, when such a trick was played as to place the restrictions on it which were imposed by the rate-paying
clauses."[2]

One of the worst effects of these clauses, doubtless, was
the opportunity opened up for bribery. There were in
Cambridge and Bristol and elsewhere, associations for the
express purpose of paying the rates of electors. Escott
asserted that there were whole boroughs which were entirely swayed at election time by the corrupt payment of
rates.[3] Disraeli complained that his defeat at Wycombe
in 1832 was due to the fact that his agent had not paid
the voters' rates and that his supporters were not registered.[4] This payment of rates for poor clients had in
many places been a matter of simple charity, entirely
unconnected with political manœuvres. It was on that
account the more dangerous, as the mixture of bribery and
charity made it extremely difficult to distinguish and to
prove corrupt intent.[5]

Evans' proposal to lengthen the period of payment was
but a half step in the eyes of the Radicals. Their real
desire was the abolition of the rate-paying clauses. Duncombe went so far as to assert that they were unconstitu-
tional in principle; for they reversed the principle that
no man shall be taxed who has not consented, seeing that
they declared that a man should be taxed and pay the

[1] 3 Hansard, xc, 424, 428; xcviii, 1140.
[2] 3 Hansard, xc, 424.
[3] 3 Hansard, xc, 410, 429.
[4] Monypenny, *Life of Disraeli*, i, 220.
[5] A purely gratuitous payment of rates by a stranger, however,
even if made without corrupt intent, would, if proved, destroy the
voter's qualification for the year, 10 Adolphus and Ellis, 66.

tax, before he could exercise the power leading to consent.[1] The Liberal leaders, however, would admit of no abolition, affirming the ancient constitutionality of rate-paying and showing that the payment of rates was the certificate and assurance of the fitness of the voter. In fact in 1846 Russell opposed even the extension of the period of payment. If the elector neglected to pay, he had no fair excuse; if he was unable to pay he was not fitted for the vote. In 1847, however, the ministry approved the extension provided for in Evans' bill.[2]

The bill was, however, opposed by the Conservatives, chiefly because it tended towards the extension of the franchise. Evans had said frankly that such was his object, although he believed that it should be attained through an improvement of the existing system rather than by a radical change of franchise. The alleged grounds of Conservative opposition were that it was the electors' own fault if they were disfranchised for non-payment of rates. Moreover, they asserted that most of the electors in arrears wilfully delayed the payment of their rates in order to escape the necessity of registration, voluntarily disfranchising themselves to avoid the risk of being forced to vote against their convictions.[3] Notwithstanding such opposition from the Conservatives, the bill was carried in the Lords, but not before it was amended to the effect that the time allowed for paying rates should be a period of six months instead of nine as proposed. Henceforth the elector must have paid on July 20 all rates and taxes due on the 5th of the preceding January.[4] The Radicals protested against the Lords' amendment, and in 1852 Evans made another attempt to extend fur-

[1] 3 Hansard, xc, 407.
[2] 3 Hansard, xc, 417-418; xcix, 986.
[3] 3 Hansard, xciv, 318.
[4] 11 & 12 Vict., c. 90.

ther the time allowed for payment.   But it was opposed
successfully by the government, on the ground that six
months' leeway was ample.[1]

The other aspect of the registration which caused great
dissatisfaction because of the resulting disfranchisement,
related to the occupiers whose rates were paid by their
landlords and whose names were not entered in the rate-
book.   The disqualification of those who failed to pay
their rates in time was in a measure their own fault.   But
the disfranchisement of the so-called compound householder resulted largely from deficiencies in the system
itself.   Few took the trouble to understand the case of
the compound householders, yet upon its arrangement
depended the enfranchisement of a large body of persons
who might fairly claim that they were entitled to voting
rights.

One of the conditions essential in practice to the winning
of the franchise was that the names of the prospective
electors in boroughs should be on the rate-books.   These
books were the basis of the borough register and furnished
the overseers with the information necessary for the compilation of the preliminary electoral lists.   But in many of
the large parishes, and especially in those of the metropolis, there were local acts which empowered the parish
officers to compound with the landlords for the payment
of the rates.   A deduction of twenty or twenty-five per
cent was allowed when the rate was compounded, so that
the owner of fifty or a hundred small houses derived no
small profit by calling on his tenants to pay him the full
rate in their rent, while he had a discount in paying it
over to the parish.   Naturally it was convenient for the
parish to be saved the trouble of collecting from the small
occupiers.   Such occupiers were known as compound
occupiers or householders.   In general the houses for which

[1] 3 Hansard, cxxiii, 1147.

the rates were compounded and paid by the landlord ranged in annual value from ten to eighteen pounds.[1]

In such cases the only name that appeared upon the rate-book was that of the landlord who paid the compounded rate. The names of the occupiers were not entered; and the overseers had no right to send to the revising barristers for registration the names of occupiers which did not appear upon the rate-book. It is true that the Reform Act had provided for the electoral registration of the compound occupiers to a certain extent, by allowing the householder whose name was omitted from the rate-book to make a special claim for insertion, on tendering payment of the rate himself. If the overseer then failed to place his name on the book, the claimant was nevertheless to be considered to have fulfilled all the necessary steps, and might insist that his name be placed upon the electoral register. But the Court of Common Pleas decided that each new rate must be paid by the occupier, and each occupier must put in his claim and tender after every fresh rate. As there were very often four, and sometimes six, new rates in a year, the result was practical disfranchisement for the compound occupier. There were few who for the sake of a political privilege, would put in a claim to the franchise four or five times annually; and especially was this true of the poorer classes, who had little time to spend upon red tape.

The difficulty was naturally felt most keenly in the more populous boroughs, where the bulk of the £10 electors lived in houses that were under the operation of the compounding acts, and the rates for which were paid by the landlords. In Tower Hamlets sixteen thousand householders were said to be thus disfranchised: about as many, in other words, as were registered. In one parish there were three thousand persons who were in reality entitled

[1] 3 Hansard, cvii, 988; cxiii, 188.

to be placed upon the electoral register, but of these only three hundred, who belonged to a franchise association, had made claim.[1] In other boroughs the proportion of compounders excluded from the suffrage was said to be almost as large, although the figures in general rest upon estimates.[2] But the wide disfranchisement resulting from the custom of composition was denied by none. Russell on the one side and Graham on the other, admitted the need of some remedy.[3]

As early as 1836 Duncombe, who took a very great and constant interest in the practical operation of the franchises, proposed that all £10 occupiers whose rates were compounded and paid for them, should be placed upon the register without making claim.[4] Such a suggestion was however scouted. According to the courts the intention of the Reform Act was that there should be "some payment by the party's own hand," in order that the corrupt payment of rates for an elector might be avoided.[5] And neither the ministers nor the front opposition bench desired to change the act of 1832 in this respect. A decade later, however, the possibility of facilitating the claims of the compounders was discussed and soon taken up in earnest.

In 1849 the member for Tower Hamlets, Sir William Clay, explained the practical disfranchising effect of the provision which forced the compound occupier to make a new claim for each new rate. He suggested that in future the compounder should be forced to claim but once, and that so long as he held the same qualification, he need not make further claim for any new rates. The Liberals

[1] 3 Hansard, cvii, 989.
[2] 3 Hansard, cxv, 902.
[3] 3 Hansard, cvii, 992.
[4] 3 Hansard, xxxiii, 472.
[5] "Regina v. Bridgnorth," 10 Adolphus and Ellis, 66.

approved of the suggestion, provided that guarantees were given that the claimant was personally liable for the full rate and had actually paid it. Notwithstanding the lack of opposition, it was not until 1851 that the bill was transformed into law.[1] An attempt to facilitate the claims of the compounders still further, by allowing them to pay only the compounded rate, was at first opposed by Russell as contrary to the spirit of the Reform Act.[2] The act as passed, however, declared that the compounder, claiming and paying the rate himself, in order to bring his name on the electoral list, should be allowed to pay the reduced or commuted rate.[3]

The problem of facilitating the registration of the £10 occupiers whose rates were compounded, was not however settled by the act of 1851. The compounders did not except in the rarest cases avail themselves of the new facilities for making claims, and in the opinion of contemporaries the act remained to all intents and purposes a dead letter. Gladstone asserted in 1867 that during the sixteen years which followed Clay's act, there were not five hundred voters registered who had been enfranchised by an individual compliance with its conditions. Of the compound householders registered, he went on to say, practically all were placed on the lists, not as a result of their paying the rate and making special claim, but by benevolent or actively political parish officers, in frank defiance of the conditions and stipulations required by the law.[4]

Gladstone's statement, which went uncontradicted, was supported by the reports of the parish and vestry clerks. It appeared that in some parishes the overseers took the

1 14 & 15 Vict., c. 14.

2 3 Hansard, cxv, 907.

3 3 Hansard, cxv, 907.

4 3 Hansard, clxxxvii, 302. For a contemporary estimate of the effect of Clay's act, see Cox, *History of the Reform Bills of 1866 and 1867.*

trouble to enter the names of the occupiers whose rates were paid by the landlord, even when the occupier himself did not claim a qualification. In the majority of cases, however, the tenant was left to take the initiative, and in such cases practically no claims were made and no compounders registered. Thus in the parish of St. Giles, Camberwell, out of 4921 occupiers of £10 tenements of which the rates were compounded, there were only five electors. In Rotherhithe, there were six compound householders registered out of a total of 1426. In All Saints, Poplar, twenty-three out of 4052 compounders had the right of suffrage. The vestry clerk in the latter parish believed that if all who were qualified would make claim, the number of electors of all kinds would be trebled. But practically none of them cared to undergo the bother or the expense of carrying through their claim.[1]

On the other hand, in the rare parishes where the overseers took the trouble of entering the names of the £10 compound occupiers on the list, often the entire mass of those who were qualified were also registered. In St. George, Southwark, and St. Mary Magdalen, Bermondsey, the names of all compound householders were ascertained by a house to house visit, and placed upon the register. In the latter parish out of 4300 £10 occupiers whose rates were paid by the landlord, all but one hundred and thirty were on the electoral list. Often the overseers of one parish took the pains to list the compounders, while those of a neighbouring parish did not, although both parishes were in the same constituency. In Clerkenwell all occupiers, whether they paid their own

---

[1] "The usual reply," the report reads, "when I inform the claimants that they will have to attend the revising barrister's court is, 'Oh! I am not going to lose my time by going there. If you cannot put me on the register I shall not trouble myself any further,'" *Parliamentary Papers*, 1866, no. 3626, "Electoral Returns, 1865-1866."

rates or whether they were paid by the owner, were entered on the register; we read, however, that in the adjacent Holborn, "no compound occupier has hitherto been placed on the register."[1]

The stipulation that all whose rates were compounded must make claim and themselves pay the rate before registration, thus continued to lead, not merely to disfranchisement, but to extreme irregularity in the operation of the franchise. In some constituencies the occupier was absolutely disqualified because his name was not on the rate-book and he failed to make his claim. In others the overseers took the matter into their own hands and the consequent enfranchisement was large. Uniformity with respect to the registration of the compound occupiers was wholly lacking. It was left to the caprice of the parish officers whether a constituency should or should not be doubled or trebled. Since the occupiers of £10 tenements whose rates were compounded by the owners, represented nearly a sixth of all the £10 householders, the importance of the question was obviously not inconsiderable.[2]

The extent of the disfranchisement was naturally largest in the metropolitan constituencies, where nearly all the tenements ranging in value from ten to eighteen pounds had their rates compounded. In these constituencies only slightly more than a fifth of the compound occupiers were entered on the register. Of all the compound householders in England and Wales who might

---

[1] *Parliamentary Papers*, 1866, no. 3626, "Electoral Returns, 1865-1866." In Birmingham 3,000 compounders were enfranchised by the overseers, who on their own authority, and without any claim being made, entered them on the register, *Parliamentary Papers*, 1867, no. 305.

[2] There were in 1867, 644,522 occupiers of tenements at or above a £10 rental; of these from 94,000 to 95,000 were compound householders; the statistics differ slightly, *Parliamentary Papers*, 1867, nos. 136, 305.

have become electors, there were only slightly more than a third who actually obtained the suffrage. Of the entire body of £10 householders before the second Reform Act, more than ten per cent were disfranchised because their landlords paid their rates, and the householders were unwilling or unable to make claim.[1]

No legislative action was taken between 1851 and 1867 to remedy such extensive disqualification, although prominent members on both sides of the House called attention to the anomaly which diminished the electorate of one constituency, while that of its neighbour was extended. Walpole insisted that the electoral qualification ought not to be affected by the hap of payment by landlord or of tenant, and Bright advocated some means of bringing the names of all tenants upon the rate-book.[2] Gladstone also showed the bearing and the importance of the question: "Besides your actual constituency, you have an immense and what I may call potential constituency in a great many towns, consisting of persons who are kept off the register simply by the fact that they do not pay the rate, which the landlord pays for them, but who might claim to be put upon it at any period. I confess I think it undesirable to have a large number of persons, who might at any moment under the influence of some local motive, or from passion or temporary excitement, be brought upon the register and thereby suddenly alter the character of the electoral body. Whatever may be the character of the constituency, be it large or small, it is desirable that the character should be marked and permanent and not subject to sudden and violent changes.[3]

[1] Total number of householders at or above ten pounds, 644,522
Total number of compounders not on electoral lists,   70,116
    Parliamentary Papers, 1867, nos. 136, 305.
[2] 3 Hansard, clvi, 2066; clvii, 907.
[3] 3 Hansard, clviii, 635.

No attention, however, was paid to such complaints, and even Russell, who was in general interested in the practical working of the franchise, failed to touch the question in his Reform Bill of 1860. Gladstone, however, proposed a simple remedy in 1866, namely, the abolition of the rate-paying clauses, and the required insertion of every compound householder in the rate-book. The failure of his bill opened the way in the following year for a more drastic solution, which cut the knot by enacting the abolition of the system of composition of rates altogether. The enfranchisement of 1867 resulted in large part, indeed, from the removal of the electoral disabilities which hung on the compound householder.

During the eighteen years which followed the failure of Walpole's bill of 1847, no attempt was made to change the machinery of the registration system. The numerous complaints of wholesale disqualification which resulted from the action of the party organizations, led, however, in 1864 to the appointment of another investigating committee.[1] The inquiry was confined to the county constituencies, and the report showed that registration conditions were hardly more satisfactory there than in boroughs. The committee declared, after an examination of many witnesses, that the electoral lists were impure and defective; and that in so far as these evils were remedied by the system of objections, the process was attended with annoyance and expense to the claimants, regardless of the value of their qualifications.[2] The facilities for placing or continuing upon the register the names of unquali-

[1] *Parliamentary Papers,* 1864, no. 203, "Report of the Select Committee, appointed to inquire into the system of registration of county voters," ii.

[2] *Parliamentary Papers,* 1864, no. 203, "Report of the Select Committee on registration of county voters," iii; "Minutes of Evidence," §§ 31, 322, 773, 1027-1028, 1828, 1391.

fied persons still afforded a ready means of enfranchisement, especially in large constituencies. They were still
utilized in full by unscrupulous agents.[1] And it was
still a matter of complaint that persons who were possessed of undoubted qualifications might be called upon
each year to substantiate their claim and prove the
correctness of their franchise in every particular.[2]

The chief cause of dissatisfaction was the organized
employment of objections by the party agents, who ven-
tured them continually in all the constituencies, on the
chance that the person objected to would be unable or
unwilling to attend the court and take up the challenge.
The objector was not obliged to specify exactly the
grounds upon which he supported his objection, and the
elector came to court entirely in the dark as to what part
of his qualification was to be attacked and might lose a
vote to which he was absolutely entitled, simply from lack
of sufficient preparation of his case.[3] The power of imposing costs which had been granted to the revising barristers to prevent such practices, failed to guard ade-
quately the rights of the electors from the manœuvres of
the agents. There was apparently no uniform principle
for the imposition of costs, and all the witnesses agreed

[1] *Parliamentary Papers,* 1864, no. 203, "Minutes of Evidence,"
§§ 570, 804-811, 1660, 1815, 2330.

[2] *Parliamentary Papers,* 1864, no. 203, "Minutes of Evidence,"
§§ 31, 581, 816, 1027, 1056, 1252.

[3] Lord Arundel, son of the Duke of Norfolk, held as qualification
a freehold rent charge upon his father's property, which was objected
to in a general and indefinite manner. His solicitors were obliged
to come down from London to Arundel with a whole box full of
deeds, for it was impossible for them to know to what point the
objections related. As the revising barrister pointed out in discussing
the system, it might have been to the Christian name of the late duke,
or it might have been to the actual merits of the qualification, or
the registering of it, *Parliamentary Papers,* 1864, no. 203, "Minutes
of Evidence," § 1996. See also *Ibid.,* §§ 1957, 2537.

that some alteration in the extent or the application of
the remedy was demanded. In general the revising barrister desired that the court should be conducted with
facility and ease. If no costs were given to either side,
his work was accomplished quickly and with absence of
friction. The moment that he granted costs he raised
questions which were fought fiercely on both sides to the
irritation of all concerned.[1] And even when imposed, the
maximum amount of costs was pitifully insignificant, and
failed to serve as a deterrent for the future.[2]

To remedy the unfair facility afforded for the insertion of the claimant's name upon the register, suggestion
was made that every new claimant should be required to
prove, or at least to give prima facie evidence, of his right
to be registered. On the other hand as a provision against
frivolous and vexatious objections, every objector who
failed to strike from the register the name objected to, or
to correct the claim in some substantial point, was to be
necessarily subjected to costs.[3] Many feared, it is true,
that the first suggestion would materially increase the
difficulty of registering new claimants, most of whom,
when not guided by the party associations, had always
displayed extreme apathy in claiming the suffrage. On
the other hand, so long as the purity and correctness of
the register was left dependent upon the diligence of individual objectors, it was neither just nor politic to render
the law of costs such as might deter or materially discourage persons from objecting. New claims and objec-

[1] *Parliamentary Papers*, 1864, no. 203, "Minutes of Evidence,"
§§ 1452-1455.

[2] *Parliamentary Papers*, 1864, no. 203, "Minutes of Evidence,"
§§ 2013, 2314-2340, 1957.

[3] *Parliamentary Papers*, 1864, no. 203, "Report of Select Committee on registration of county voters," iii.

tions were both desirable; the problem was to prevent the parties from manipulating either in an equivocal fashion.[1]

The committee of 1864 expressed themselves in favour of forcing objectors to specify their grounds of objection; they also believed that costs should invariably follow a failure to prove an objection, except when unusual circumstances arose that might justify the revising barrister in withholding them. But the point chiefly discussed by the committee was the possibility of purifying and completing the county register, by rendering the compilation of the preliminary lists less dependent upon the care of private individuals or the activity of political agents. It was, after all, the committee believed, a matter which concerned the state itself, and the process from the beginning ought to be in the hands of official rather than party agents.

The committee believed that the simplest means for depriving the political associations of their power would be to eliminate the necessity of claiming in counties. It was the apathy of the prospective voter that gave the electoral agents their opportunity; and if the names of the freeholders could be entered upon the preliminary lists by state officials, as were those of the occupiers in boroughs, the county registration would be far less dependent upon individual or party efforts. The committee suggested, accordingly, that state officials be appointed in counties to study valuation lists and rate-books, and make out preliminary electoral lists of all freeholders whose qualifications were sufficient. They recognized that the task would not be easy, because of the size of the constituencies, but they believed that the improvement upon the existing system would be vast. It is curious to note the optimism with which this plan for saving the free-

[1] *Parliamentary Papers,* 1864, no. 203, "Report of Select Committee on registration of county voters," iv.

holders from their own apathy was regarded, and the certainty of the belief that by it the illegitimate action of the party associations would be curtailed. It was in the eyes of the committee the universal panacea for all the evils apparent in the county registration system.[1]

The exposure of the defects in registration made in 1864, led to the introduction of a remedial bill in the following session, which was rapidly transformed into law.[2] The scheme of official registration for counties, however, was not adopted and the provisions of the act were merely palliative. The complaint that electors might be brought to the revising court without knowledge of the exact point upon which the objection was founded, was met by the enactment that notice of objection was not to be valid without specific statement of the ground of objection. The penalties attendant upon frivolous or vexatious objections were increased; every separate ground for objection was to be considered as a separate objection, and when objections appeared to be unreasonable a fine was to be imposed for each ground of objection; and this, even if the name of the claimant was expunged upon some other ground. Provision was also made that costs might be awarded up to the amount of five pounds, instead of only

[1] The plan was to be "the means of adding to the register numbers of qualified people who now remain unregistered; it was to provide for the correctness of entries, while in great measure removing the occasion for vexatious and speculative objections; and although the vigilance of party agents will still be requisite to insure a pure and complete register, their action will be confined to the legitimate occupation of assisting in registering their own friends and resisting the registration of those opponents whom they have reason to suppose not entitled to the franchise," *Parliamentary Papers,* 1864, no. 203, "Report of Select Committee on registration of county voters," vi. Their judgment was not entirely at fault, as is proved by the smoother operation of registration in counties since the introduction of the county occupation franchise, and the compilation of lists without claim.

[2] 3 Hansard, clxxvii, 1363; clxxix, 98.

twenty shillings as before. No state organization was set up for compiling preliminary lists in counties as they were in boroughs, so that the making of claims was left, as before, to private individuals and political associations.[1]

This act of 1865 was followed so closely by the alteration of 1867 in the electoral qualifications, that the effects traceable to it may be considered in conjunction with the operation of the new franchises. The establishment of an occupation franchise in counties led naturally to an introduction of the borough system for that class of voter, allowing the occupation electors to come upon the register without claiming. In this way the assimilation of county and borough registration, only possible upon the assimilation of the county and borough franchises, was begun.

It is impossible to state numerically the effects of the intricacies of the registration system upon the electorate of England and Wales between the first two Reform Acts. The opportunity which allowed the creation of qualifications, sometimes in large numbers, was offset by the various causes which resulted in disqualification of many persons who might fairly have claimed a vote. It is easy to see that in some constituencies creation outweighed disqualification, as in the West Riding during the early forties. In others, as in Tower Hamlets, the converse was true. For counties there is no document which allows the student to estimate the net result. In boroughs it is possible to compare the number of £10 occupiers in residence, with the actual number of electors. The proportion varied greatly. In some of the more important towns a large number of those who possessed qualifications, failed to become registered. Thus, in Coventry, out of twenty-one hundred £10 occupiers, there were only a thousand on the electoral list; in Liverpool, also, less

[1] 28 & 29 Vict., c. 36.

than a half of the forty-five thousand persons who had
the right to claim, actually obtained the suffrage. In
Tower Hamlets only thirty-four thousand out of seventy-
five thousand £10 householders were registered.[1]

On the other hand, the few available statistics show that
by 1865 very few potential electors in the smaller boroughs
were disqualified. Especially in those small boroughs
where the system of composition was not in force, the
extent of disfranchisement was less than one might de-
duce from the remarks of the numerous witnesses examined.[2] But altogether the number of total disqualifica-
tions resulting from the requirements of registration was
by no means inconsiderable. There were in the boroughs
of England and Wales, before the second Reform Act,
some six hundred thousand male occupiers at a rental of
£10 or more; of these only four hundred thousand were
registered electors.[3] The enfranchisement of 1832 was
thus limited, in boroughs at least, to sixty per cent of its
face value. In counties the proportion of those excluded
might be estimated as nearly as large. The disqualification resulting from the rate-paying clauses did not hold
in counties, and the county qualification was more simple
to create. On the other hand it was necessary to make a

[1] The reasons for the failure of so large a proportion of the
occupiers to register in Liverpool, was stated in the report to be the
non-payment of rates and the large number of names struck off
the register on account of non-attendance at the revising court when
objections were made. In Tower Hamlets the disqualification was
due to the composition of rates and the unwillingness on the part
of the occupiers to make claim, *Parliamentary Papers,* 1866, no. 3626,
"Electoral Returns, 1865-1866," 162, note.

[2] The figures, however, were not invariably trustworthy; in some
of the constituencies the number of electors given as voting on a
£10 qualification, was greater than the number of £10 occupiers,
Parliamentary Papers, 1866, no. 3626, "Electoral Returns, 1865-
1866," 161, 162.

[3] *Parliamentary Papers,* 1866, no. 3626, "Electoral Returns, 1865-
1866," 54.

claim, and the apathy of the county voters in this respect is well attested. Moreover it was especially in counties that the weapon of objection was most widely in use.

Obviously the disqualification of a third or a quarter of the persons who might have been expected to exercise the suffrage, resulted largely from their own indifference. Freeholders in counties, and compound householders in boroughs, had it within their power to secure the vote if they cared to make the effort of claiming. But when the popular excitement which had accompanied the legislation of 1832 had passed away, interest in the vote also died. The franchise had perhaps been demanded in the hope of economic benefit, or rather from pure excitement than from any appreciation of the suffrage in itself. The process of registration, long and troublesome, was too much bother; the privilege of voting was not worth the pains. And again it must be remembered that even when the individual made a real effort to bring his name upon the list, the legal technicalities were such as often to nullify his rights, especially if he were too poor to employ expert legal counsel.

Hence the system of registration, in its earlier stages at least, restricted the operation of the franchise, which was by no means liberal even in theory. Moreover it tended to obscure the real will of the nominal electors in that it offered a means to the election agents and the party associations for the making and unmaking of qualifications. By the organized system of objections on the one hand and the manufacture of faggot votes on the other, the party committee either destroyed or controlled a large proportion of the suffrages supposedly conferred in 1832. To assert without qualification that the suffrage belonged after 1832 to this class or to that, is to disregard the fact that far fewer new votes were conferred than might have been expected, and that many of those votes belonged in fact to the upper few who pulled the strings of party organization. The control of the suffrage by means of the registration system naturally brings us to that more effective and widespread method of exerting influence through bribery and corruption.

CHAPTER VII

ELECTORAL MORALITY BEFORE 1854

Electoral corruption under the unreformed system—Attempts made to check it—Their failure—Effect of Reform Act on corruption—Extent of corruption after 1832—Bribery at Stafford, Leicester, Liverpool, and elsewhere—Direct purchase of votes—Indirect bribery—Loans, payment of rates, head-money—Intimidation—Exclusive dealing—Treating—Number of elections voided because of corruption—Constant increase—General attitude towards electoral corruption—Control of elections by upper classes through corruption.

IT is obvious that the act of 1832 was not completely effective in its attack upon the abuses of the old electoral system. The disfranchisement of many small boroughs and the widening of the suffrage, it is true, did check the system of nomination to a large extent, and the control of boroughs by the classes of birth and wealth became more indirect. But we have seen how deficiencies in the registration system robbed the people of much of that electoral independence which they had been led to expect. The tricks of election agents and the complexities of registration law combined to restrict or distort the enfranchisement of 1832, and protect the electoral power of the aristocracy. A far greater barrier to the complete independence of the voters, however, was the system of bribery and intimidation, which assumed such proportions after 1832 that in many constituencies the popular interests were no better represented than in the days of direct nomination.

Venality and corruption in English elections date from the time when the acquisition of seats in the House of

Commons first became an object of ambition to men of birth and wealth. In the small nomination boroughs the use of money was not general before 1832 since it was unnecessary; the power of the patron was so complete that the few votes cast could be secured without bribery. But in the larger boroughs, where there was something like an independent electorate, that independence was regarded merely as an opportunity for selling the vote to the highest bidder. The "annual dinner and septennial bribe" were taken as just perquisites, and the freemen in boroughs looked to contested elections as shareholders in great monopolies look to their extra dividends.

The more blatant instances of corruption under the old system have often been described.[1] At Shoreham the "Christian Club" held its meetings only for the purpose of deciding to whom the suffrages of the electors should be sold; Sudbury openly advertised for a purchaser; the electors of Grampound boasted that they received three hundred guineas apiece for their votes. Naturally, all the less direct means of corruption were also freely employed. If the freeholder in the county refused to vote according to the wishes of the local squire, his house might be blown up, and his disfranchisement thus procured.[2] Electors would run up large bills between elections, which the candidates were expected to settle when they entered upon their canvass.[3] In a large constituency, such as Westminster, treating was an effectual means of corruption, with disastrous effect upon the sobriety of the city.[4]

The most striking instances, perhaps, of wholesale cor-

[1] An excellent description of electoral conditions under the unreformed system is to be found in Grego, *Elections in England*, as well as in Porritt, *The Unreformed House of Commons;* see also an article in the *Temple Bar*, xv, 189.

[2] Russell, *Recollections*, 35.

[3] 3 Hansard, ii, 1210.

[4] Wallas, *Life of Place*, 131.

ruption occurred immediately before the passing of the act of 1832. At Liverpool we read that in 1830 a hundred thousand pounds was spent in bribing the electors. The price of votes varied from fifteen to one hundred pounds apiece, and rose and fell like stock as the demand increased or slackened.[1] Three pilots, who arrived from sea on the last morning, each received one hundred and fifty pounds for their votes. Placards were posted which publicly called upon electors to attend and receive their money.[2] At Hertford, in 1826, Duncombe was able to secure his election only, as he admits, "by bribing handsomely."[3] Corruption at Evesham was so great in 1830 that a motion was made for its disfranchisement; this was prevented partly on the ground of the impending general reform, but chiefly because the borough was considered no more guilty than many others.[4] In the boroughs of Shoreham, Cricklade, Aylesbury, and East Retford, electoral corruption was such that they were thrown into the surrounding hundreds in the hope of swamping the dishonest element of the electorate.

Attempts had been made to check corruption from the first days of parliament, when an act of Edward I ordered that all elections be held in perfect freedom, and all through the fifteenth and sixteenth centuries declarations

[1] As each man voted he received a ticket, furnished with which he went to the committee, handed the ticket through a hole in the wall, and received the stipulated sum of money through another hole. Both the reformers and their opponents were equally involved, Greville, *Memoirs*, ii, 79.

[2] 3 Hansard, xiv, 1291.

[3] *Life of Duncombe*, i, 97.

[4] 3 Hansard, ii, 628. The general feeling was that bribery was not an act involving moral turpitude. The electors certainly manifested no shame at receiving a bribe; one of Sheridan's constituents said to him: "Oh, sir, things cannot go on this way; there must be a reform. We poor electors are not paid properly at all," *Life of Duncombe*, i, 108.

were issued against bribery.[1] Such declarations were
vague and platonic, as was the anti-bribery legislation of
the later Stuarts, and it was not until 1696 that an act
was passed which declared definitely in what corrupt
practices consisted, and settled definite penalties upon
offenders.[2] This Treating Act was the basis of all efforts
that were later made to prevent bribery until 1854. It
declared that any candidate who gave money, meat,
drink, or entertainment to an elector in order to procure
his own election, was to be disqualified and the election
declared void. Thirty years later, in 1726, the so-called
Bribery Act enacted that there should be a bribery oath
for all electors, and that any candidate convicted in a
court of law should not merely lose his seat, but should
also be ineligible for reëlection; the guilty voter was to
be fined £500.[3] Indirect corruption was attacked in 1809,
when an act of that year declared that any promise of
office or employment should disqualify the candidate and
void the election;[4] and shortly previous to the Reform
Act a law was passed to the effect that no person employed
by the candidate in any capacity might be deemed capable
of voting, and his vote if cast was to be considered void.[5]

By these successive measures there had grown up a sort
of system for the prevention of corrupt practices at elections, which had, however, done little towards attaining
the ideal laid down in the conventional preamble to all the
bribery acts; the latter remained in many respects futile.
Prosecutions under the act of 1726 were rare and convictions were still less frequent. Many elections, it is true,

[1] 3 Edward I, c. 5; 7 Henry IV, c. 15; 11 Henry IV, c. 1;
6 Henry VI, c. 4; 8 Henry VI, c. 7; 23 Henry VI, c. 14; *Parliamentary History*, i, 765.

[2] 7 & 8 Will. III, c. 4.

[3] 2 George II, c. 24.

[4] 49 George III, c. 118.

[5] 7 & 8 George IV, c. 37.

were voided under the Treating Act of 1696; but it was necessary that a petition should be first presented and many circumstances tended to hinder the presentation of petitions so that numberless cases of the most blatant bribery went unpunished.

The importance of attacking the system of corrupt practices was fully recognized by the Whigs in 1831 and they framed their bill in certain respects with this end in view. The disfranchisement of non-resident voters in boroughs was largely the result of their desire to exclude the most corrupt element in the electorate. The opportunity for the bribery of non-residents had always been excellent; since they were simply paid travelling expenses at a rate which made their travels extremely good business operations. Non-resident electors of Sudbury, which is fifty-six miles from London, were given a shilling a mile, so that an elector in London was paid for his trip to Sudbury as though he were going to Edinburgh, and his food and drink was thrown in.[1] Indirect bribery of such a sort was enormously diminished by the Reform Act. The Whigs also believed that by the disfranchisement of the ancient right voters they were striking at the corrupt part of the electorate, and were confident that the new £10 electors would prove themselves honest in the trust confided to them.

The Whigs did not succeed, however, in disfranchising the freemen, nor were they altogether correct in the confidence placed in the £10 householders. The new county voters were also dependent for the most part. And the destruction of the system of nomination, in so far as it went, tended rather to increase bribery and intimidation. Before 1832 the great lords had, with few exceptions, complete control of the small boroughs; where a corpora-

[1] 3 Hansard, ii, 1328; *Parliamentary Papers*, 1835, no. 547, Appendix, pt. iv, 2310.

tion had controlled a borough the corruption had been confined to a very small class, who managed the sale of the borough through an agent for a fixed price, according to an ancient, hereditary, systematic, and well-known plan. But after the Reform Act the patrons lost their control to a large extent and must strain every nerve to influence the election; where they had before commanded, now they must buy. The close boroughs had been opened and instead of a corrupt corporation there was a numerous electorate, composed often of persons whose circumstances laid them open to temptation. The corrupt were thus increased to hundreds and thousands.[1] Another effect of the act of 1832 was to increase the bitterness of party strife and to redress the balance of party strength. In many boroughs where there had been no hope for one party before 1832, now there was an equipoise, which could be turned by a small number. It was inevitable[2] that money should be used for this purpose; bribery subsists upon contested elections, and the proportion of such elections increased immediately upon the passing of the Reform Act. The registration system, also, opened a door to bribery, for it showed to the candidate and the agent exactly how the lists stood and just where and how much it was necessary to bribe.

With such added inducements to corrupt practices it would have required very stalwart and independent voters to withstand the advances of the election agents, and such adjectives could not be applied to the reformed electorate. The freemen were the same class which had been accustomed to bribery as one of the privileges of their position;

[1] *Prospectus of the Anti-Bribery Society,* 1848.

[2] As in the case of Cambridge, where Sam Long, by controlling 200 electors through bribes, was able to elect whomever he chose after 1840, 3 Hansard, cxxxi, 1024 (giving an epitome of the report of the royal commissioners on Cambridge).

the £10 householders were sometimes more corrupt than
the freemen; and in general they were dependent upon
the good will of the rich, and therefore easily influenced.[1]
The enfranchisement of the leaseholders and tenants-at-
will in counties also furnished an opportunity for intimidation and the exercise of corrupt influence on the part of the
great landholders or their stewards.

Whether corrupt practices actually increased as a
result of the Reform Act or whether, as suggested, they
merely became more notorious because of the nicely balanced state of parties and the outcry of defeated candidates, or whether the political conscience was becoming
more delicate, is doubtful.[2]   But the vast extent of bribery
and corrupt influence after 1832 was generally admitted,
and even those concerned in the passing of the Reform
Act apparently considered that political morality had
suffered from it.   Palmerston said in 1839: "I speak it
with shame and sorrow, but I verily believe that the extent
to which bribery and corruption was carried at the last
election, has exceeded anything that has ever been stated
within these walls."[3]   And a writer in the *Westminster
Review* a decade later wrote: "Bribery is such that the
representative system is utterly defeated.   If corrupt
practices are not restrained the Reform Bill will prove
worse than a nonentity, it will be a curse."[4]   And other
instances of the same kind show that the effect of the
Reform Act in this respect was generally regarded as
unfortunate.[5]

[1] In St. Albans the royal commissioners found that 270 out of
the 354 householders who voted in 1841 were bribed; and only 31
out of 63 freemen; 64 out of 66 scot and lot voters were bribed,
3 Hansard, cxx, 971.

[2] 3 Hansard, xl, 1172.

[3] 3 Hansard, xcviii, 1437.

[4] *Westminster Review,* xxv, 485.

[5] 3 Hansard, xv, 1026; xxxviii, 1458; *Parliamentary Papers,* 1835,
no. 547, "Minutes of Evidence," §§ 853-859, 881, 884.

The extent to which direct bribery was carried is shown by the report of an investigating committee appointed in 1835.[1] The form in which payments were made, as well as the price brought by votes, varied in the different boroughs; but the custom of selling votes was well-nigh universal in all the boroughs where landlord influence was insufficient and where elections were contested. In Stafford, towards the close of the poll and when the election was hotly contested, fourteen pounds was paid for a vote. Here the voters polled in alphabetical order according to their surnames. Those at the head of the alphabet naturally received but little. As the election progressed, if it was hard fought, the price of votes rose. If it was decided by the first day's polling, those in the middle of the alphabet received the highest price and those at the end, their votes not being needed, would have nothing at all. But if the polling lasted two days, the names which began with an S or a W were of the greatest value. This form of voting, which also existed at Newcastle-under-Lyme, always lent itself with the greatest facility to corrupt practices.[2]

Bribery in Stafford had been extensive under the old system owing to the large number of freemen,[3] but after the Reform Act it was found that the new electors were almost equally corrupt; in the first reformed election, 850 voters in an electorate of a thousand received bribes

[1] *Parliamentary Papers,* 1835, no. 547, "Report from the Select Committee appointed to consider the most effectual means of preventing bribery, corruption, and intimidation."

[2] *Parliamentary Papers,* 1835, no. 547, "Minutes of Evidence," §§ 1597-1600.

[3] In 1826 one candidate paid £9,000 and the other, £6,500. In 1830 the successful candidates paid £4,800; the unsuccessful candidate, who received only half as many votes, paid £1,000. In the decade from 1826 to 1836 more than £36,000 poured into Stafford, 3 Hansard, xxxv, 651.

and more than five thousand pounds was expended in corrupt practices.[1] At Bristol large placards were displayed: "Vote for blue—money no object," language equivocal possibly in its terminology, but which left no doubt in the minds of the voters. Bribes were also distributed here in the form of beef, after the election, which as it was employed widely by the Conservative organization, became known as "blue-beef." Seven pounds were given to each Conservative voter in 1832 and fourteen in 1835.[2] At Leicester, as soon as the canvass began, public houses were opened by each party in the various villages near the borough. The voters were collected as soon as possible, generally locked up until the polling, and, according to an election agent, "pretty well corned." When the time arrived carriages were sent from Leicester to bring them to the hustings, "in greater part so drunk that they had difficulty in expressing their choice." Before the poll they received tickets, which were exchanged for money when they had cast their vote. In general one or two pounds was paid for a vote.[3]

At Liverpool, in 1831 and 1832, the bribery was wholesale. More than seventeen hundred freemen were bribed directly in the former and sixteen hundred in the latter year; the average price of a vote was fifteen pounds. Tickets were issued to voters which on their face entitled the bearer to a cask of beer; they were regarded as currency and exchanged at the brewers' for cash. The general impression was that bribery had increased in Liverpool since the Reform Act.[4] In the constituency of Lewes

[1] 3 Hansard, xxvii, 1175.

[2] *Parliamentary Papers,* 1835, no. 547, "Minutes of Evidence," §§ 1598, 6798-6802, 7123; 3 Hansard, lxiv, 370.

[3] *Parliamentary Papers,* 1835, no. 547, "Minutes of Evidence," §§ 1601, 2159.

[4] 3 Hansard, xv, 1020; xxi, 846-856; xxiii, 380.

it was found necessary to put the town in a state of siege at election time, in order to prevent the carrying off and imprisonment of electors. This, with so many crossroads was an expensive job, and in 1837 upwards of five hundred pounds was spent in watching the roads for a week before the election.[1] At Warwick, where the influence of the Earl was lessened by the Reform Act, he found it necessary to send a check for eight thousand pounds to the town clerk, for distribution amongst the electors in his behalf.[2]

During the two decades which succeeded 1832 direct bribery apparently increased as the election agents discovered its possibilities. So extensive was the corruption in the general election of 1841 that the Parliament of that year was generally called the "Bribery Parliament." The widespread assertions of the degradation of electoral morality were confirmed by the report of the special commission sent down to Sudbury. The low grade of political ethics which had made this borough notorious during unreformed days had evidently persisted. When an election was likely to take place every publican opened his house to the town at large. At each public house a large debt was owing for expenses incurred at the previous election; such debts were called "fixtures," and when a candidate came down he was immediately presented with a statement of fixtures; if he paid them he was accepted and stood a fair chance of election, but if not he might as well "pack up and be off."[3] It was stated that if the

[1] *Parliamentary Papers,* 1842, no. 458, "Minutes of Evidence," §§ 1178-1180.

[2] 3 Hansard, xxi, 836-845.

[3] Statement of the Attorney General based upon the report of the royal commissioners on Sudbury, 3 Hansard, lxxvi, 541. See also *Parliamentary Papers,* 1842, no. 176; *Ibid.,* 1843, no. 448, "Minutes of Proceedings and Evidence taken before the Select Committee on Sudbury Election Petitions."

candidate should go down to canvass political opinion seriously as was the custom in pure boroughs he would have been laughed at for his simplicity. He who desired the suffrages of Sudbury needed no political arguments and might go down only the night before the election, provided he was furnished with plenty of money. The commission stated that in 1841 fourteen hundred pounds was expended in direct bribery, and more than twice that sum in treating. Here, as in the almost equally flagrant case of Yarmouth, the supposedly respectable portion of the community countenanced such electoral corruption without compunction; in the latter borough printed defences of bribery were circulated, describing it as an "ancient custom," a "privilege," to which the inhabitants were entitled, and which should be taken as a matter of course.[1]

At St. Albans it appeared that the new £10 voters were more venal than the old electors; the sums paid to them were higher and the system of direct bribery amongst them was more general. Before 1832 the sums spent upon bribery amounted to about one-third of the total expenses of the election; after 1832 they represented about two-thirds. From 1832 to 1852 some twenty-four thousand pounds was spent upon corrupt practices in this borough, although the electorate comprised less than five hundred persons. In 1841 all the electors took the bribery oath, swearing that they had not been tampered with, and yet in this election more than four thousand pounds was distributed in bribes. This election, according to the commissioners, was not an isolated case; there was in the borough a system of corruption of long standing and one steadily continued from election to election.[2]

[1] 3 Hansard, lxix, 1342-1346; xcviii, 599.

[2] *Parliamentary Papers,* 1852, no. 1431, "Report of the Commissioners appointed to inquire into the existence of bribery in the borough of St. Albans."

The commissioners reported that at Maldon bribery was practised in an undisguised and indeed in an ostentatious manner. The bribery oath was worse than useless, since it merely added perjury to the political immorality of the inhabitants. In 1852 this oath was tendered to every voter as he came up to the poll, and was freely taken by all, however recent, open, or unquestionable the bribe.[1] At Barnstaple more than a third of the electorate was proved to have received bribes, notwithstanding the difficulty of establishing absolute proof. The manner of bribery was by lists. The voter was asked if his name was down on the party lists; if he responded that it was, there was a tacit understanding that he should have his share of what money was spent in corruption. At one period, the report says, there appears to have been an apprehension in the minds of some of the electors that no money would be spent, and several of them became alarmed lest the ancient practice of bribery should fall into disuse. They therefore attempted to advertise in the *Times* for a third candidate in the hope of creating a contest. The *Times*, however, refused, as the system of importing a blackmailing candidate for the purpose of bleeding the established parties was fully understood.[2]

At Canterbury the bribery was less direct but equally extensive. Each voter was allowed to name two friends to whom he furnished tickets which allowed them to collect

[1] Statement of the Attorney General, based upon the report of the commissioners for Maldon, 3 Hansard, cxxxi, 1021.

[2] *Parliamentary Papers*, 1854, no. 1704, "Report of the Commissioners appointed to inquire into the existence of corrupt practices in Barnstaple." The ordinary view of the electors was that an uncontested election was hardly fair to the voters; in a small borough in the west of England, a substantial tradesman was asked what sort of an election they had had; "Oh, very bad," was the reply. "Why, you returned your two men." "Yes, but we failed to get a good third man, and without one elections do no good to the town," *Westminster Review*, xlviii, 341.

the money for the elector. The voters were accustomed to meet in the public house and decide at what price their votes should be disposed of; the batch was then sold, one of the voters acting as agent, the chance of discovery being thereby lessened. One family of nine persons was accustomed to receive a hundred pounds at each election, and in the two elections of 1841 their suffrages brought them in two hundred in a single year. From 1841 to 1852, eighteen thousand pounds was spent in bribery in this cathedral city.[1] At Hull a third of the electorate was proved to have been directly bribed in each of the three elections in the decade which followed 1841.[2]

At Cambridge, while the system of corruption was not so widespread, the organization was so perfect that its chief became the absolute political boss of the borough for ten years. During the first four elections after 1832, the new voters remained honest, the result of the elections being invariably in favour of the Liberal candidates, though by a small margin. The Conservatives then organized a system, which was headed by Samuel Long, and which proved capable of controlling the hundred odd voters who could turn the fate of the election. Long mingled with the electors and discovered who might safely be tampered with; he entered the man's name in a book and generally could count upon his vote. The voters bribed here were of the lowest class; in 1852 thirty of the one hundred and eleven who were proved to have received bribes could not sign their names. As a result of Long's system the Conservatives carried every election from 1839 to 1852, with the exception of that of 1847, when the feel-

[1] Statement of the Attorney General, based upon the report of the commissioners on Canterbury, 3 Hansard, cxxxi, 1018; *Parliamentary Papers,* 1853, no. 151.

[2] *Parliamentary Papers,* 1854, no. 1703, "Report of the Commissioners appointed to inquire into the existence of corrupt practices in Hull."

ing over the Corn Law agitation was so intense that there
was no hope for Long, who on this occasion made no
attempt at corruption.[1]

The testimony of election agents, as well as the admissions made by the members themselves in the House of
Commons, indicates that except in the boroughs where
party feeling was exceptionally strong, or where personal
influence controlled the electorate, the result of elections depended very largely upon the amount of money
expended in bribery. It was the regular custom for the
electors to address papers to the candidates asking what
terms would be offered; and the various forms of papers
and tickets issued to authorize the bearer to receive sums
of money in return for his vote were produced in the
House itself. Sir John Pakington told of two boroughs,
each with an electorate of more than a thousand, in which
the majority were accessible to bribes, many of them
wealthy tradespeople and members of the professional
classes; and where seven to thirteen thousand pounds was
expended in direct bribery at each election.[2]

While the direct purchase of votes was the ordinary and,
from the agent's point of view, the most economical method
of controlling elections, the more indirect forms of bribery
were by no means disdained. A variety of means existed
in the different boroughs, differing according to circum-

[1] Statement of the Attorney General, based upon the report of
the commissioners for Cambridge, 3 Hansard, cxxxi, 1024; *Parliamentary Papers,* 1853, no. 185. In 1845 the Liberal candidates had
a comfortable lead, a hundred voters having held back; Long met
them in a public house with a thousand pounds, which was passed
out to them, one by one, through a broken window, and in the last
hour of polling turned the election in favour of the Conservatives.

[2] 3 Hansard, cii, 1044-1045. There appeared in the metropolitan
papers advertisements of electoral agents who promised to do all
the work of electioneering without bothering the candidate, which
meant that he need know nothing of the bribery that went on, *Times,*
July 1, 1848; *Westminster Review,* xlviii, 346.

stances, by which the gratitude of the electors could be obtained and their suffrages secured. In corporation towns the distribution of charities was an efficacious means of winning votes. In Bristol the control of such distribution was vested entirely in the hands of the Conservatives and formed a ready means of influencing the votes of the poorer classes, as were the Christmas gifts distributed by church wardens and vestries.[1] At Coventry the use of Bablake Hospital was granted only to those electors who had voted in the interest of the Liberal Corporation which controlled it. If an impecunious voter applied for assistance from a poor-law board, instead of retailing the size of his family and the misfortunes which had fallen upon his work, he found it more worth while to begin his plea by stating the colour of his politics.[2]

A corrupt loan system was also in general use, and was not considered illegal in most constituencies. Large sums of money were lent electors at Coventry and Maldon, and repayment was not hinted at before the approach of the next election. But woe to the voter if he "ratted" and turned to the other side! In Worcester, in 1835, many attempted to disregard the hold which had been gained on them and voted for the other party, only to find themselves ruined when their large debts were suddenly called in.[3] In Stafford and Ipswich it was the general custom for the election agents to pay the rates and taxes of the voters, and, as we saw, Disraeli complained that he lost his election at Wycombe because his agent failed to pay up the rates of his supporters; at Cambridge and Bristol

[1] *Parliamentary Papers*, 1835, no. 547, "Minutes of Evidence," §§ 1097-1114, 1829-1845, 6425-6428.

[2] *Parliamentary Papers*, 1835, no. 547, "Minutes of Evidence," §§ 1830, 1107-1112, 6829, 6898-6900.

[3] *Parliamentary Papers*, 1835, no. 547, "Minutes of Evidence," §§ 522-530, 2588-2591, 2936-2948.

there were associations for this express purpose.[1] Indirect bribery was also exercised amongst the freemen by paying for their admission to the freedom of the city or borough. Such practices would not come under the provisions of the bribery acts if carried on by the party associations or corporations, and not by the candidate or his agent.[2] In Bristol the Conservative Association was accustomed to assist its members in taking up their freedom, the necessary amount being paid on the day of nomination. In Coventry the admission of poor freemen to their freedom was regularly paid for by both parties.[3]

One of the most frequent forms of corrupt payment and one extremely difficult to prove corrupt, was the distribution of money gifts at the time of election. As there was no bargain between the giver and receiver it did not come under the common interpretation of the term bribe; and it was distributed after the election whether the candidate won or lost and even when there was no opposition. But the effect was certainly to influence the voter corruptly. This gift was known generally as "head-money," and consisted in a presentation of one or two guineas to each elector by the candidate. It was an ancient custom in some boroughs, notably Hull, and was supposed to have originated as a substitute for the election dinner given by the successful candidate; it formed one of the largest items in election expenses, and was accepted by even the well-to-do voters.[4] Of the same type of indirect bribery

[1] *Parliamentary Papers*, 1835, no. 547, "Minutes of Evidence," §§ 1448-1453, 1607-1612; Monypenny, *Life of Disraeli*, i, 220; 3 Hansard, xc, 410.

[2] *Parliamentary Papers*, 1835, no. 547, "Minutes of Evidence," §§ 1138-1139.

[3] *Parliamentary Papers*, 1835, no. 547, "Minutes of Evidence," §§ 1071-1095, 6584-6585, 6788-6795.

[4] 3 Hansard, xxxviii, 1459; xlv, 679, 685; xcviii, 409. In 1841 a single candidate spent £2,500 in head-money at Hull.

was the "market-money" and "basket-money"; the latter
was distributed at Nottingham for weeks before an election, each voter receiving from ten to thirty shillings a
week. In some boroughs the origin of these payments was
shown by the name "dinner-money," which was of the same
character.[1]

The simplest means of indirect bribery was the hiring of
electors to serve on sinecure committees and the payment
of extravagant wages to voters for services which entailed
but little time and effort. At Derby members of nominal
committees received five shillings a day during a period of
a week or more. At Southampton the most desired position was that of messenger, which was a sinecure and
worth five shillings a day; colourmen received from half
a sovereign to a sovereign, and chairmen from a sovereign
to two pounds daily. At Newark, during Gladstone's contest in 1832, a band composed of electors played continually, each of the musicians receiving fifteen shillings a
day.[2]

Besides bribery, direct and indirect, intimidation played
an important part in determining the result of elections;
this was especially true of the larger constituencies and
the counties. The effect of the Reform Act in this respect
was most unsatisfactory; the £10 householders in the
boroughs were largely dependent upon the good will of
the wealthy classes; while in the counties the leaseholders
and tenants-at-will were almost invariably forced to obey
the dictates of their landlords. In all cases the vote of
the tenant was looked upon as the chattel of the landlord,
in which he had the right to deal and of which he might
dispose. His influence was of such a kind as to make it

[1] *Parliamentary Papers,* 1842, no. 250; 3 Hansard, lxiii, 1276-1277;
lxiv, 355; lxv, 676.

[2] 3 Hansard, lxv, 678; xcviii, 409; Morley, *Life of Gladstone,*
i, 93.

difficult to make out a case of corrupt influence against him, but it was clearly understood by the tenantry as well as by the candidate; before the canvass began it was an understood custom to ask permission of the landlord to canvass his tenants,—a permission rarely granted.[1] This electioneering etiquette was infringed by Gladstone when he canvassed Lord Westminster's tenants in Flintshire and provoked bitter complaints from the wounded patrician.[2] And the general feeling with regard to the influence of landlords is shown by the applause of the House of Commons when it was stated that the Marquis of Exeter had taken drastic measures against those tenants who had voted against his interests.

In South Cheshire the landlords brought their tenants to the poll to vote "just like well-drilled soldiers."[3] In South Devon the leaseholders and tenants were shown to be absolutely under the control of their landlord, and many parishes previously enthusiastically Liberal, were brought into the Conservative ranks by the advent of a Tory lord. The defeat of Lord John Russell in 1835 was commonly ascribed to such intimidation.[4] In Denbigh tenants were threatened and turned out for voting con-

---

[1] 3 Hansard, l, 1158; *Parliamentary Papers*, 1835, no. 547, "Minutes of Evidence," § 3978.

[2] "I did think," he wrote, "that interference between a landlord with whose opinions you were acquainted, and his tenants, was not justifiable according to those laws of delicacy and propriety which I considered binding in such cases," Morley, *Life of Gladstone*, i, 239. The attitude of a conscientious steward was that he would not claim votes from freeholders, but that he would not be doing his duty to his landlord if he failed to secure the votes of tenants, 3 Hansard, xlviii, 454.

[3] *Parliamentary Papers*, 1835, no. 547, "Minutes of Evidence," §§ 8951-8953.

[4] *Ibid.*, §§ 2732-2742; 3 Hansard, xxviii, 435. During the election of 1841 for the West Riding, the Duke of Leeds died and the opinions of his successor were uncertain. In the midst of all the bustle of the canvass his lands remained quiet and all wondered in which direction

trary to the landlord's wishes; and in another constituency a peer who feared the hostile vote of his tenantry
brought them all to his castle in the night to prevent
their voting.[1]

In the boroughs the influence of the landlords over their
£10 tenants was equally complete. At Stamford the
Marquis of Exeter turned out Sir George Clerk from his
seat in parliament, and replaced him by Herries through
the influence which he possessed over his tenants who were
householder voters.[2] At Harwich a single individual took
the lease of a large number of £10 houses which he let out,
on the sole condition that the occupiers voted according to
his wishes.[3] At Hertford the Marquis of Salisbury forced
his tenants to sign bonds agreeing to give up their tenements at a fortnight's notice. In contesting the borough
against his influence, Tom Duncombe spent forty thousand pounds chiefly in finding homes for the ejected tenants of the marquis.[4] At Warwick the influence of the
earl over his £10 tenants was exercised so strongly as to
provoke widespread complaints.[5]

the tenantry would turn. One morning a farmer arrived in the
market town and announced, "Well, we have got our orders at last,
we are all to be yellows this time," *Ibid.*, lxiv, 359.

[1] *Parliamentary Papers*, 1835, no. 547, "Minutes of Evidence,"
§§ 3287-3289. The activities of the Whig lords in forcing their
tenants to vote in their interest are shown in an article in the *Leeds
Intelligencer:* "The Duke of Norfolk's agents put on the screw
with unusual severity; Lord Fitzwilliam's did the same; Lord
Thanet's agents made the election a matter of life and death; the
Duke of Devonshire was not a whit behind; Lord Burlington insisted
that promises given to Mr. Wortley should be violated under penalties which the poor tenants understood too well," 3 Hansard, xl.
1139.

[2] 3 Hansard, xciii, 932; *Westminster Review*, li, 146.

[3] 3 Hansard, xcvii, 903; *Parliamentary Papers*, 1847-1848, no. 172.

[4] 3 Hansard, xiv, 1159; *Life of Duncombe*, i, 129.

[5] 3 Hansard, xxv, 1231; *Parliamentary Papers*, 1835, no. 547,
"Minutes of Evidence," §§ 1733-1745. It was easy to exercise
undue influence in such a way that the effect would be as successful

Where the influence of the landlords was less complete, the pressure was put on by the party association. The agents of the association were sent out through the boroughs to discover the private circumstances of the voter and make use of any embarrassment as a club to influence votes. Ledgers were issued for the use of the agents, containing a space for the elector's name, that of his landlord, with the political principles of the latter, for the names of any persons likely to have influence over the voter, such as creditors or persons who had offered him assistance; and finally a space for special circumstances which might give an opportunity for political blackmail, such as debts, mortgages, need of money in trade, commercial relations, and even the most private domestic matters.[1]

In the industrial towns the influence of the master employers over their employees, was generally absolute, especially when trade was dull and jobs scarce. At such times the men invariably voted according to the political

as bribery, and yet it could not be legally proved. The following letter sent by a landlord to his agents shows the ordinary method: "I shall make it a point to know from you (if there are any) the names of all such of my tenants who do not wish to oblige me with their interest, and will not go to vote. Time may come when they may want me to oblige them; we may then fairly toss up our pretensions and strike a balance. If there are any who have refused to oblige me by going, through a pretence of fear, I beg you will ask them again from me, and let me know their answer," *Ibid.*, § 8253.

[1] An example of such election memoranda was read in the House of Commons: "Mr. So-and-so:—see this man, he works for So-and-so; has borrowed money on a bill, see the attorney; is a publican, behindhand with his brewer; has borrowed money on a mortgage, find out the mortgagee," 3 Hansard, lxiv, 367-371. An article in the *Westminster Review* (xxv, 502), describes the methods of operation in the small towns and villages: "The parson, the squire, the neighboring attorney, and the rich old dowager, all belong to the parish political association. They discuss means of putting on the screws; hunt out the circumstances, and ascertain the electors' hopes and fears."

opinion of the head of the factory. When business was
lively and dismissal less serious, the dependence of the
employees was not so marked.[1] The influence of the small
tradesmen over their servants, when the latter happened
to be electors, was complete. There were numerous
instances where workmen were dismissed for voting contrary to their masters' wishes and many cases where servants voted differently at two successive elections when
their masters had changed politics, or when they had
secured a new master of different political opinions.[2]

The influence of the government, the clergy, and the
universities was also exercised so stringently in certain
places as to be considered corrupt. The screws were put
on the tradespeople in such a way that they must follow
the political ideas of the influential class or be ruined.
Where there were great government establishments, as at
Devonport, Plymouth, Portsmouth, or Harwich, the
tradesmen boxed the political compass without scruple;
and the labourers in the dockyards invariably supported
the ministry in power.[3] At Windsor the officers of the
royal household made use of their position so effectually
that the wishes of royalty were generally observed in the
elections. At Chatham the commander of the barracks
promised to ruin tradespeople who voted against the government candidate, and excluded from the barracks all
the slopsellers who controvened his wishes.[4] At Canterbury and in the other cathedral cities, the great influence
of the clergy was corruptly exercised, generally in behalf

[1] *Parliamentary Papers,* 1835, no. 547, "Minutes of Evidence,"
§§ 1196-1212, 2256-2259, 2562-2563, 2886, 4200-4208.

[2] *Parliamentary Papers,* 1835, no. 547, "Minutes of Evidence,"
§§ 114-117, 3110-3113, 6883-6886.

[3] 3 Hansard, cxvii, 895; cxxvi, 1331; *Westminster Review,* xxv,
505. Government influence was also strong at Rochester, Sandwich,
and Plymouth.

[4] 3 Hansard, xvi, 119; xxvi, 1193; xxvii, 204-210.

of the Tories. In the former place an archdeacon discharged his Liberal butcher, and a reverend canon was shown to have gone through his lists of tradespeople, expunging the names of all who had voted for the Liberal candidate.[1] In university towns the college servants always voted in the Conservative interest; and the small tradesmen, if they valued the custom of the college kitchens, must keep their political opinions under proper control. At Cambridge the Vice-Chancellor exercised an almost supreme control over the publicans through his power of licensing the public houses. The lodging-house keepers, too, were under college influence; a lady whose house was filled with undergraduates one year, would find it entirely empty the next, if her husband voted contrary to the wishes of the college dean.[2]

This custom of exclusive dealing was carried on in all the boroughs as a method of influencing the electors. In Birmingham the shopkeepers who voted for the Conservative candidate, found the next morning that a cross had been chalked on their doors and that no customers entered their shops.[3] In Cheshire the printer who for years had received all the official contracts, dared to vote the reform ticket on one occasion and immediately saw his functions transferred to a small but Conservative rival.[4] The party associations drew up lists of tradesmen voters who were to be avoided or patronized, according to the way in which they had voted. At Cambridge this list was classified and

---

[1] 3 Hansard, xxvii, 975.

[2] *Parliamentary Papers*, 1835, no. 547, "Minutes of Evidence," § 89-91, 276.

[3] *Parliamentary Papers*, 1835, no. 547, "Minutes of Evidence," §§ 4118-4119.

[4] *Parliamentary Papers*, 1835, no. 547, "Minutes of Evidence," §§ 3894-3903. And other instances of the same practice, *Ibid.*, §§ 945-948, 3534, 5538, 6674. The corporations of the small boroughs always exercised great influence over the tradesmen, *Ibid.*, §§ 630-634, 679-684, 936-944, 1056-1059.

subdivided according to trades, so that the zealous partisan might see at a glance how he should apportion his custom. Exclusive dealing was openly advocated in many journals as a fair means of electioneering; *Blackwood's Magazine* and the *Quarterly Review*, notably, insisted upon it as a matter of strict political obligation.[1]

As a result of such forms of intimidation, as well as from fear of personal violence often perpetrated by one party or the other at election time,[2] many electors found the franchise less of a privilege than a danger, and voluntarily attempted to disfranchise themselves. Grote said, in 1838: "In numberless cases the franchise is felt and hated as a burden; and if any man doubts this, the bitter experience and the humiliating answers of a canvass will be quite sufficient to teach it to him."[3] Often the elector, caught between the Scylla of his political conscience and the Charybdis of financial interest, would leave town during an election.[4] In Birmingham out of seven thousand electors, a thousand regularly abstained altogether from voting, and the bribery commissioners reported that in

---

[1] 3 Hansard, xxxvii, 13.

[2] Cases of drugging, abduction, and extreme violence were not infrequent, notably at Nottingham, Wigan, and Coventry, 3 Hansard, xxii, 426; xlviii, 829; lxviii, 150. In the latter borough in 1832, a mob of two thousand were said to have been hired as bullies for the Whig interests. They were paid 5s. daily and ordered to "beat the electors soundly and leave them alive, but hardly." One witness said: "Whenever I saw any of them near the booths, I dragged them by the hair . . . we kicked and beat them as long as we liked, and then the constables came and took them away; they dared not interfere before." These statements were accepted as true, but they were made before an empty House, since most of the members were watching the boat race of 1834, and no punitive action was taken.

[3] 3 Hansard, xl, 1141.

[4] *Parliamentary Papers*, 1835, no. 547, "Minutes of Evidence," §§ 118-125, 1745, 3144. It was said to be a common thing to hear an elector remark: "How do you get on in your canvass? We hope you will beat us; but we cannot vote for you," 3 Hansard, xxxvii, 38.

Cambridge two hundred electors took care never to vote, from fear of injuring their interests.[1] There were also instances of tenants going to their landlords or to their friends, begging that their names might be objected to upon registration.[2] The general feeling was expressed by Hume in 1843, when he called the existing franchise a delusion and said that there would never be an adequate number of voters so long as men were liable to be punished for the exercise of the franchise.[3]

Treating was the other form of corrupt influence which exercised an important effect upon the electoral body, and the general impression among election agents was that it had been rather increased by the Reform Act. In certain towns where the amount of money spent in this manner before 1832 ran up to four or five hundred pounds, it rose as high as six or seven thousand after the passing of the act.[4] The public houses in such boroughs were kept open for three or five weeks, generally one for each party, and voters of that colour might enter at any time and order up what they pleased. Of all forms of corruption this was the most difficult to cope with and the most difficult to prove.[5] The bills for food and refreshment run up at the public house by the voters, could be settled months after the candidate had taken his seat in the House of Commons, and none be the wiser. Often these bills would be left for settlement until the next election, and for a new candidate to settle. It was customary, moreover, for the rival

[1] 3 Hansard, c, 1259; cxxxi, 1022 (Statement of the Attorney General, based upon the report of the commissioners for Cambridge).

[2] 3 Hansard, lx, 1158.

[3] 3 Hansard, lxvii, 765.

[4] As in Southampton, where only £480 was spent in 1831, while in 1841 the Whigs spent £3,000 and the Tories £4,000, *Parliamentary Papers*, 1842, no. 239.

[5] *Parliamentary Papers*, 1835, no. 547, "Minutes of Evidence," §§ 431-451, 475-495, 1617, 1626-1629, 2530-2531.

parties to agree that no matter how great the amount of treating, the defeated candidate would not present a petition. Jo Parkes, the most noted and skilful of all agents, stated that such an agreement was regarded as an honourable treaty and that it would be considered a breach of faith for either party to petition.[1]

The amount of treating varied according to the balance of parties and the type of electors. In general the agents considered it cheaper to bribe directly than to expend large sums in treating, but some electors were as easily won by a drink as by a sovereign, while others whose consciences were not completely calloused would accept refreshment or assistance for their family when they would have refused a direct bribe. Treating before the test of the writ was not illegal, and it often went on for months at a time. The effect of wholesale treating on the general morality of the electorate was naturally degrading; the lower classes, and proverbially the freemen, were in a state of intoxication during the entire polling, and the hospitals were filled for weeks afterwards with those recovering from the effects of debauchery or drunken fights.[2]

The extent to which elections after 1832 were controlled by corrupt influence is mirrored to a certain degree by the number of elections that were voided because of the exercise of bribery or other forms of corruption. Between the years 1832 and 1854 there were presented one hundred and thirty petitions alleging undue elections which should be voided because of the bribery and corruption which had

---

[1] 3 Hansard, lxxvi, 541; xcviii, 1439.

[2] Pakington tells of a letter received immediately after an election from a town where "the hospitals were filled with men maimed and bruised and maddened with drink," 3 Hansard, cii, 1044. The items of an inn in a small parish which could have taken care of a portion only of the constituency include 285 glasses of brandy, 302 glasses of gin, 156 glasses of rum, 80 gallons of ale, *Westminster Review*, xlviii, 340.

occurred. And of these elections, two-thirds were actually annulled for such reasons by select committees of the House of Commons. In seventeen other cases, although the election was not voided, because of the impossibility of tracing the corrupt practices directly to the member or his agents, the committee nevertheless discovered the existence of extensive corruption. Thus in more than a hundred cases gross impurity of elections was signalled impressively by parliamentary committees.[1]

It must be remembered that the number of petitions presented is by no means a complete indication of the extent of bribery. Certain boroughs might be corrupt to a great degree and yet no petitions would be presented against the elections. The presentation of a petition demanded a large outlay of capital and unless the chances were extremely good would not be undertaken by the ordinary individual. The petitioner, moreover, must appear with clean hands and where, as often took place, both parties had been guilty of corrupt acts, the defeated candidate dared not petition, no matter how gross the corruption.[2] There was also a species of political blackmail employed to force the withdrawal of a petition after it had been presented and thus prevent the exposure of the corrupt practices. When a petition was presented against the return of a member of one side, another petition would be presented against the return of a member on the other side. Those who understood the secret mechanism of elections knew that this was the best means for compelling a compromise, forcing a withdrawal, and preventing a fair inquiry. In 1842 ten petitions were shown to have thus been paired off against each other. The system was for the Conservative agent to take a letter of withdrawal from the Liberal agent and vice versa; these letters would be

[1] *Parliamentary Papers*, 1866, no. 77.
[2] *Westminster Review*, li, 161.

sent to the Speaker, no more would be heard of the petition, and the existence of corruption would be effectually glossed over.[1]

It was the general opinion amongst members of the House that as a result of this system of election compromises, as well as from the other circumstances which prevented the prosecution of petitions and a searching elucidation of electoral morality, a large portion of the corruption never came before the committees and was never laid bare.[2] In Coventry, where the existence of extensive corruption was generally admitted, not a single petition alleging undue elections on this account was presented from 1832 to 1854. In Maldon, St. Albans, Barnstaple, Liverpool, and Berwick, bribery commissioners and select committees reported that the exercise of corruption had been a matter of general custom; and yet in none of those boroughs had there been a single petition brought before the House before 1852. DeLacy Evans told of large boroughs where bribery and treating were flagrant but where the cases were never brought to light because the guilty candidates had not obtained their seats.

Under such circumstances the number of petitions which did succeed is only partially indicative of the wide extent of electoral corruption. It is also noticeable that, either because of the increase of the evil or the change in the political attitude, the number of voided elections steadily increased. In 1832 there were but three cases in which a committee reported the existence of bribery and annulled the election; in 1835 but one;[3] in the election of 1841 seven towns were shown to have been guilty of extensive corrup-

[1] 3 Hansard, cxxx, 428; *Parliamentary Papers,* 1842, no. 458, "Report of the Select Committee on Election Compromises."

[2] See speeches by DeLacy Evans and Duncombe in 1848 and 1852, 3 Hansard, xcvii, 1139; cxxx, 428.

[3] *Parliamentary Papers,* 1866, no. 77; Hertford, Stafford, Warwick; *Ibid.,* no. 286, Ipswich.

tion, and in 1848, eleven;[1] in 1852 there were twenty-three
cases of void elections where the bribery was traced directly
home to the member or his agent.[2] In all but two cases the
annulled elections had taken place in boroughs, Flintshire
and Huntingdonshire being the only counties where corrupt practices sufficient to unseat the member were proved.[3]
Most of the towns in which corruption was proved were of
moderate size, ranging from seven to fifteen thousand
inhabitants. Contrary to general opinion, the larger constituencies were more often at fault than the smaller.
Within seven years Ipswich, with an electorate of twelve
hundred, had three void elections; Aylesbury, with sixteen
hundred electors, saw its elections annulled three times
within eleven years; while in Hull, where there were nearly
four thousand voters, elections were voided in 1837, 1852,
and 1859. Of the seventy-seven voided elections between
1832 and 1854, twelve were in towns with less than five
hundred electors; twenty-two in towns with an electorate
of more than a thousand; while the remainder, or more
than half, occurred in towns with an electorate of between
five hundred and a thousand.[4] In towns where there was a

---

[1] *Parliamentary Papers,* 1842, nos. 207, 285, 250, 239, 176: Ipswich,
Lyme-Regis, Newcastle-under-Lyme, Southampton, Sudbury; *Ibid.,*
1843, nos. 130, 433: Nottingham, Durham; *Ibid.,* 1847-1848, nos. 220,
194, 156, 727, 382, 212, 172, 200, 737, 381, 296, 95: Aylesbury, Bewdley,
Carlisle, Cheltenham (twice), Derby, Harwich, Horsham, Lancaster,
Leicester, Lincoln, Rye.

[2] *Parliamentary Papers,* 1853, nos. 376, 401, 509, 604, 661, 217, 203,
185, 151, 210, 224, 848, 868, 219, 78, 588, 596, 449, 467, 352, 414, 209,
152, 641, 653, 381, 290, 357, 289, 355, 652, 660: Barnstaple, Berwick,
Blackburn, Bridgnorth, Canterbury, Chatham, Clitheroe, Huddersfield, Hull, Liverpool, Maidstone, Maldon, Peterborough, Plymouth,
Rye, Taunton, Tynemouth, Durham, Derby, Harwich, Knaresborough,
Lancaster, Cambridge.

[3] *Parliamentary Papers,* 1866, no. 77. In North Cheshire, in 1848,
extensive treating was discovered, but in this case the election was
upheld, *Ibid.,* 1847-1848, no. 567.

[4] *Parliamentary Papers,* 1866, no. 77; 3 Hansard, cxxxii, 357.

large freeman electorate, corruption was nearly always notable; there were, in fact, but three of such boroughs where at least one election was not declared void between 1832 and 1854. So far as indicated by the petitions, each of the two great parties was almost equally to blame for the low standard of electoral ethics. Of the seventy-seven void elections there were forty in which Conservative members were unseated because of corrupt practices, and thirty-seven in which the Liberals forfeited their seats for the same cause.[1]

It is almost impossible to overstate the importance or the extent of corrupt practices in England during the generation which succeeded the passing of the Reform Act of 1832. The simple fact of the existence of such practices is indisputable. The number of elections voided for such reasons and the numerous and detailed reports of committees furnish evidence which is borne out by the extraordinary testimony given before those committees by the election agents, as well as by the opinions of the members themselves. After the "bribery election" of 1841, Brougham and Duncombe both spoke of the popular contempt into which the House of Commons had fallen as a result of corrupt elections. The latter asserted his belief that a vast majority of that House were then indebted for their seats to the wholesale system of bribery.[2] In 1834 Russell said: "It must be admitted, on all sides, that the corrupt practices which have prevailed of late at elections, have involved all parties . . . in disgrace, and have tended materially to compromise the character of this House."[3] Another member asserted that "no gentleman who had sat on any election committee could have

[1] *Parliamentary Papers*, 1866, no. 77; McCalmont, *Parliamentary Poll Book, passim.*
[2] 3 Hansard, lx, 71.
[3] 3 Hansard, cxxx, 412.

failed to perceive the extent to which the evil . . . had recently spread." Another witness to the fact that corrupt influence had persisted or increased was Fitzroy Kelly: "the bribery and every species of corruption which prevailed at the last general election, equalled, if they did not exceed, that which had ever been known at any former period of our history."[1]

The extent of corruption was doubtless due in part to the difficulties which lay in the path of its discovery, as well as in the inadequacy of the remedies which had been applied; it was said in the House of Commons that there was no offence within the criminal law of England where the number of offences detected bore so small a proportion to the number actually committed. It was also true of bribery that there was no crime where the number of offences proved and punished bore so small a proportion to the number of offences discovered.[2] The great difficulty, however, was doubtless the general attitude of both the public and the members of parliament towards corrupt practices. The standard of political ethics did not demand purity of elections. As Russell pointed out, the general tendency was to regard bribery as a venial offence, if indeed it were an offence; neither candidate nor agent looked upon it as a crime, and the mass of the people considered it in much the same light as smuggling or poaching. Until a better tone and a more strict regard to the principles of morality sprang up it was useless to hope for rapid improvement.[3]

Amongst the members themselves, the voiding of an election or the light thrown by a parliamentary investigation upon the corrupt management of an election, involved no disgrace. As Jacob Bell said, "bribery was an aris-

[1] 3 Hansard, cxxxii, 340; cxxx, 421.
[2] 3 Hansard, xcviii, 1436.
[3] 3 Hansard, lxiii, 1262.

tocratic, gentlemanly, and respectable offence."[1] To lose
a seat through its discovery was unpleasant and expensive,
but the discovery did not affect one's standing with the
other members. Few of the members preferred to bribe
rather than go through the election in all purity; but they
were informed by their agents that it was necessary for
success; they had perhaps lost an election where they
tried to avoid absolutely any corrupt practices, and the
result had confirmed the warning. In future they did
all that was commonly expected of them if they took care
that whatever bribery that went on was kept from their
own personal cognizance. So long as this experience was
common to a large part of the House and was countenanced by the members, it was useless to try to put a stop
to bribery.

Anyone who will read the evidence given before the committees will be convinced of the extent to which the conscience of the members had been undermined by the advice
of the electoral agents, and the morality of the masses
was largely determined by that of the educated and
wealthy. As a writer of the day pointed out, the notion
of there being any criminality and dishonour in corrupting
wholesale the poor and those liable to temptation was
never once hinted at. The danger of so doing was constantly before the minds of all who were concerned, but the
only point which interested them was the mode of evading
the law and escaping the danger which it threatened.
"Candidates, agents, voters, no matter how exalted or how
degraded their condition, all spoke a similar language,
and exhibited the same utter unconsciousness of any dishonour attaching to the conduct pursued. They desired
to avoid detection, not because the act they were perform-
ing was in their own opinion disgraceful, but simply

[1] 3 Hansard, cxxii, 1311.

because the law affixed a punishment and a disability upon those who performed such acts."[1]

The change in political conditions effected by the Reform Act of 1832 thus tended to nullify, to a certain extent at least, the results which the originators of that act had hoped to obtain. So long as a majority of the House of Commons was returned by the proprietors, a general and widespread system of corruption was unnecessary and accordingly not practised. The aristocracy held their boroughs as part of their estates and returned their members with as little effort as they presented church benefices to their protegés. If a rich man wanted to get into parliament, he had merely to go into the market and buy a borough; in such a case the extent of corruption was comparatively trifling. The amount of wholesale bribery which took place was confined almost altogether to the comparatively few constituencies where the electorate was of an appreciable size. The Reform Act changed the system to a large extent and went far to destroy nomination; in many constituencies the right of electing members was placed in the hands of a comparatively large number of people, and it was necessary for the ambitious rich who desired to buy seats in parliament to purchase, not the borough itself, but the voters. The extent of the immediate positive corruption was thus increased, or at least rendered more widespread.

The Whigs had promised that the effect of the act of 1832 would be to transfer electoral power from the aristocracy and the plutocracy to the hands of those who represented more nearly the respectable mass of the English nation, in broad terms the middle class. This result had not been obtained, at least in its entirety.

[1] For a discussion of the general attitude towards corruption in elections, see an article in the *Westminster Review* for February, 1843 (xxix, 113).

Many of that middle class voluntarily disfranchised themselves in order that they might not offend either their political conscience or the patrons upon whom their fortunes
depended. Many more were practically disfranchised,
in so far as they cast their votes not according to their
own belief, but in the interest of the man who bought or
controlled their suffrage.[1] The system of bribery and
intimidation thus contracted the right of suffrage to a
prodigious degree; and because an appreciable portion of
ostensible voters did not exercise a real, effective, and
untrammelled choice there was a restriction of the franchise within narrow limits. Nomination had lost the
supremacy of its control, but electoral power was not yet
in the hands even of that class to which it had apparently
been assigned by the act of 1832.

[1] Disfranchisement also resulted when the House of Commons
withheld writs from boroughs in which corrupt practices were proved
to have existed. In 1848, 10,122 electors were thus temporarily
disfranchised, 3 Hansard, xcix, 966.

CHAPTER VIII

THE ATTACK UPON CORRUPTION, 1832-1854

Question of corruption continually debated by the Commons—
Failure to impose a remedy—Punitive measures suggested after
1832—Proposals to disfranchise individual boroughs—Failure of
Russell's attempts at reform—The Radicals and the ballot—
Exclusion of the ballot from the Reform Act—Grote's campaign
for the ballot—Failure of the movement—Arguments for and
against the ballot—Difficulties standing in the way of proof of
corruption—Russell's act of 1841—Its effects—Election compromises—The act of 1842—Failure of the legislation—Disfranchisement of Sudbury and St. Albans—The act of 1852—The new
bribery commissions—The act of 1854—Its provisions—Definition
of corrupt practices—Penalties—Election auditors—Significance
of the act of 1854.

THE prevalence, as well as the enormity, of the electoral corruption described in the previous chapter
naturally suggests a query as to what attempts were made
in the direction of purifying political morals and protecting the voter from the temptations to which he was exposed. Judging by the customary attitude of both the
public and the members of parliament toward corruption,
as well as by the continued persistence of the evil, it might
have been inferred that the general indifference to bribery
would be mirrored in the official attitude of the House of
Commons. Such was by no means the case. During the
two decades which followed the Reform Act there are few
subjects so constantly discussed, or in such non-partisan
and apparently sincere tone, as the extinction of corrupt
practices. It was inevitable that at least a show of opposition to electoral corruption should be made. The honour
and dignity of parliament demanded that all possible

effort be instituted to rid elections of this national scandal. And certainly no member, indifferent and callous though he might be in his private opinions, would dare avow openly his approval of, or his patience with, electoral impurity. And there was a semblance of sincerity in the official attempts made against corrupt practices which was not altogether feigned. In the light of these constant efforts the extent and character of corrupt influence is the more striking.

But while the House of Commons as a corporate body was sincerely desirous of eradicating corrupt practices, the members, especially during the period of candidacy, countenanced it. The average member might really prefer a free election; bribery meant expense, and it meant that the skill of the election agent was trusted as more efficacious than the candidate's native powers, an admission that few members liked to make. But there was always a modicum of candidates who preferred to insure their seats by a liberal scattering of gold; in self-protection the others must place themselves in the hands of their agents, thus tacitly accepting, if not approving, corrupt work. Again, while individual members might set their faces firmly against bribery, the series of hotly contested elections which succeeded the Reform Act, invested the political associations with a yearly increasing importance; and the rôle assumed by them in the organization of electoral tactics became more and more extensive. The conscience of corporate bodies is notoriously less tender than that of individuals, and their tactics were not conducive to a high standard of electioneering.

Thus while the members of the House of Commons debated long the subject of electoral bribery and officially set their ban upon it, as candidates and as supporters of their party associations they countenanced it. Actual and effectual legislation resulting from their debates was thus

tardy and in its inception timid. Sincere as they might be
in their protestations, when it came to an actual division
they were slow to destroy the means of electoral organization which had been built up by their agent or their party.
There was, moreover, much honest disapproval of many of
the remedies proposed. New laws, intended to facilitate
the discovery and the punishment of bribery, were often
thrown out because they seemed to infringe upon the
rights and liberties of the individual. Secret voting was
opposed, not merely for party reasons, but from a sincere
disbelief in its efficacy and a distrust of its moral effects.

Various causes thus prevented the initiation of that revolution in legislation which was necessary before corrupt
practices could be eliminated. And the change in public
opinion, yet more important in its effects, was even more
tardy in its arrival. Accordingly, it was not until 1854
that an act was passed which operated even slightly in the
restraint of bribery; and intimidation did not begin to be
checked before 1872. The existent purity of elections,
resulting partly from the most stringent sumptuary laws
and partly from a revolution in public opinion, was not
attained until nearly two political generations after 1832
had passed away.

The difficulty of transforming discussion into legislation was clearly exemplified during the ten years which
followed the passing of the Reform Act of 1832. The
political atmosphere, during the first reformed elections,
was filled with rumours and proofs of the corruption exercised, and the House of Commons was continually busied
with plans both for punishment and prevention. The
traditional method of dealing with corruption, where it
was so extensive as to demand something more than the
mere voidance of the election, had been to suspend either
permanently or temporarily the writ of the offending
borough or to swamp the votes of the corrupt electors by

an increase in the size of the constituency. The latter remedy had been applied when the corrupt voters of East Retford saw their franchise granted to the surrounding hundreds. Such diminutive nibbles at bit-by-bit reform were attempted in the more flagrant cases of corruption brought to light after 1832.

On more than one occasion a bill was introduced for the disfranchisement of Stafford, where more than half of the £10 householders were shown to have been bribed.[1] Whatever opposition to this measure arose in the House of Commons was confined to a demand that the constituency be enlarged. It was claimed that there was not an old borough in the kingdom which could stand the test of strict inquiry and that improvement could be gained only through the infusion of new blood.[2] The majority in the Commons persisted in their preference for absolute disfranchisement, but the bill was thrown out by the Lords and in 1837 a new writ was voted.[3]

A bill was likewise introduced for the disfranchisement of the Liverpool freemen, who in the election of 1830 had sold their votes frankly and altogether realized something like thirty thousand pounds as the result of their electoral corruption. This measure was opposed on the ground that the wealthy freemen were quite as much to blame as their poorer colleagues and that the former would be able to vote in future under the £10 qualification so that no improvement would be effected; many objected also that parliament had no right to confound the innocent with the guilty in such wholesale disfranchisement and that only those individuals who had been actually proved guilty of corruption should lose their votes.[4] In the House of Lords

---

[1] 3 Hansard, xxi, 237; xxviii, 208.
[2] *Ibid.*, xxi, 1173; xxii, 449.
[3] *Ibid.*, xxvii, 1184; xxxv, 650; xxxvi, 453.
[4] *Ibid.*, xxii, 104, 468.

these arguments proved more efficacious than in the Commons, supported as they were by the plea of Wharncliffe that the Reform Act had closed a political era and that a reformed Parliament had no right to punish acts committed in unreformed elections. The bill was accordingly vetoed by the Peers although it had passed the Commons by a majority of two to one.[1]

In the cases of Hertford and Warwick, bills were passed in the lower House for the extension of the boundaries of these constituencies and the increase of their electorate.[2] These bills were opposed by Peel and the Conservatives on rather indefinite grounds, but doubtless under the impression that a Whig gerrymander was being attempted, for both boroughs were regarded as Tory strongholds.[3] The Lords lost no time in throwing out both of the bills and the Commons were able to inflict no penalty beyond the temporary suspension of the Hertford and Warwick writs.[4]

While these bills for the punishment of individual boroughs were under discussion, more general measures, embodying improvements in the existing electoral laws, were also considered. All of the changes suggested were slight and none succeeded in winning the acceptance of both Houses. Immediately after the Reform Act a bill introduced under the auspices of Russell, provided that the period of a fortnight, allowed for the presentation of petitions, should be extended; greater facility was thus to be afforded for the discovery and punishment of corrupt practices. Passed by the Commons it was thrown out by the upper House.[5] In 1834 a bill for the general consolidation of all former bribery acts was stillborn.[6]

---

1 3 Hansard, xxii, 479; xxiii, 369.

2 Ibid., xxii, 83, 102; xxiii, 111.

3 Ibid., xxii, 453.

4 Ibid., xxv, 1035.

5 Ibid., xiv, 962, 1290, 1302.

6 Ibid., xxi, 1057.

In the same year Russell introduced a bill to provide for a more satisfactory and a more effective tribunal of inquiry. He proposed that when corruption was indicated in any borough a special committee should be chosen by lot and reduced to numerical efficiency by the Speaker. Special legislation was then to be based on the report of the committee.[1] The House of Lords, however, objected to the power given the lower House by this measure and amended it so as to divide the power of investigation between both Houses. According to their amendment, the Commons were to communicate the existence of bribery to the Lords and with the consent of the latter a joint address was to be issued to the sovereign; the crown should then appoint a commission composed of a judge and members of both Houses, upon whose report punitive legislation should be founded. Russell, however, objected to the amended plan, and especially to the judge, who had the power of rejecting evidence. It resulted that the Lords' amendments were not accepted and the bill was dropped.[2]

In 1835 and the two following years, bills were introduced for the prevention of intimidation, and for an alteration in the law of evidence which might enable committees to force both candidates and agents to testify on oath.[3] In each case, however, the measure was killed in one House or the other. Interest in the subject had not lapsed and the general debates on corrupt practices were hot in their crimination, but confidence in the efficacy of piecemeal legislation of this sort had died out, and in considering the details of these measures the House of Commons was counted out on more than one occasion.[4]

All of these latter measures directed against corrupt

[1] 3 Hansard, xxi, 1390; xxii, 610.
[2] *Ibid.*, xxv, 579, 1020.
[3] *Ibid.*, xxvi, 1170; xxxv, 1275; xxxvii, 71.
[4] *Ibid.*, xxxv, 1211, 1239.

practices were of similar character. They evinced great timidity on the part of both Liberals and Conservatives, and seated distrust for any plan which might involve a real change in the electoral system. They were all directed towards slight alterations in the means for the discovery of corruption. Such discovery depended upon the presentation of a petition against the return, and such petitions resulted from individual initiative. To assist this individual effort and to increase facilities for the exposure of corruption was as far as these bills were designed to go. Their action, moreover, was confined to the period which followed the election. No attempt was made to alter electoral procedure with a view to a removal of the circumstances which laid the voter open to bribery. In such respects the electoral system, as determined by the Reform Act, was faithfully respected. All the legislation proposed by Liberals and Conservatives in these years was inquisitorial and punitive, not preventive.

The Radicals, however, and an increasing number of the more liberal Whigs, contended that if corruption was to be eliminated, the efforts of the legislators could not be confined to an improvement in the method of discovery and punishment. Steps must be taken which would prevent corrupt practices in the first place, by rendering them useless. And some means must be found for the protection of the voter from intimidation, that form of corrupt influence which it was almost impossible to prove after the act, and which invariably escaped punishment. Such a remedy, the Radicals asserted, was to be found only in the substitution of secret for open voting; by secret voting alone could bribery and intimidation be stopped, because under the system of secret voting the wealthy and influential would be unable to discover the exact results of either their threats or their financial outlay.

The system of secret voting, or the ballot as it was called, had for more than half a century formed one of the chief points in the program of Radical reform. On all sides it was believed that its introduction would change the manner of taking the poll so essentially that the result would be little less than a revolution in the whole electoral system. According to the ancient system, on the day fixed for the nomination of the candidates a platform was raised, called the hustings, upon which sat the election officials as well as the candidates themselves. The meeting was held in the open, or in a public hall, and was made a festival for the town or countryside, who mixed indiscriminately with the electors. Silence was proclaimed and the writ read by the returning officer, who also announced the penalties prescribed for acts of corruption or bribery. Each of the candidates was then proposed by one elector and seconded by another, and each in turn addressed the crowd.

The scene which followed is familiar to all from the brush of Hogarth and the pen of Dickens. Confusion, blows, applause, groans, clapping of hands, hisses, were all mingled with the strains of the rival bands and combined to drown out the electoral speeches. If the election was uncontested, the number of candidates not exceeding the number of seats, the candidates were declared elected by acclamation. If several were contesting the seats, the returning officer called upon the electors to display their preference by a show of hands. All the township being present, and many raising their hands who had no right to vote, the defeated candidate might call for a poll, where the real electors could be distinguished from the fictitious. The poll took place generally two or three days after the nomination. Each elector voted in public for his candidate and record of his vote was kept in the poll-book. In a hotly contested election in a large pre-reformed constituency, where none of the candidates retired, the poll lasted often for several weeks. The electors were rarely in a hurry, for treating was unceasing and the price of votes was apt to rise as the election continued; but in 1832 polling was confined to one day in boroughs, and a few years later in counties as well. The state of the poll was declared from time to time showing the relative position of the candidates. Operations were closed by the returning officer, the votes were added and the final result announced.

The substitution of the ballot for this system of open voting would obviously alter the character of elections very greatly; the extent of the changes which would result was admitted both by the supporters and the opponents of the plan, differing though they might on their character. So radical was the change that, if it was to come, it should logically have been included in the Reform Bill. The Whigs had succeeded, however, in smothering the question by promising, or hinting at, a fair discussion of the merits of the ballot later; and the Radicals, in order not to endanger the bill, had not pressed the point. During the discussions of the sub-committee which drew up the first plan of reform, the advisability of including the ballot came up and it actually formed part of the first scheme presented to the cabinet. This was chiefly owing to the efforts of Lord Durham who stood as sponsor for it; the other members of the committee accepted it, not because they loved it but as a concession to the more democratic Liberals who would object to the £20 qualification in boroughs, which the committee then had in mind.[1] When that qualification was lowered to £10, the ballot was

---

[1] *Life of Grote*, 76; Russell, *Recollections*, 69-70; Parker, *Life of Graham*, 101; Grey, *Correspondence with King William IV*, i, 114. Graham later denied that he had ever supported it, 3 Hansard, lxiv, 402.

accordingly struck out from the government's plan of reform.

The disappointment of the extreme reformers was commensurate with the extent of their hopes. By the 22d of March, 1831, there were presented to the House two hundred and eighty petitions from widely scattered constituencies, praying for the ballot; and it was hoped in many quarters that the ministers might be willing to accept it.[1] Orator Hunt constantly pressed for it, and Warburton and Hobhouse believed that it would be absolutely necessary in reformed constituencies.[2] On the other hand, many reformers opposed it, chiefly on the ground that it would inaugurate the era of complete democracy, and almost invariably calling to witness its failure both in classic and recent times. Corruption in America was specially invoked as clear proof of the ballot's inefficacy against bribery, if indeed it was not a main factor in such corruption.[3] Russell, speaking for the government, insisted that although the ballot might favour the conscientious voter, it afforded a cover to fraud, deceit, and treachery; it prevented the operation of that beneficial influence which was exercised over the poorer voters, and it rendered the voting classes irresponsible.[4] The government, however, acknowledged the importance of the question and asked only that the Reform Bill should be first passed before the merits of the ballot were freely discussed. The Radicals, hopelessly outnumbered by both reformers and Tories, and unwilling to harass the government, allowed the matter to drop.

After the passing of the act, however, the promise of the Whigs was remembered and the question was resumed and

[1] 3 Hansard, iii, 797.
[2] *Ibid.*, ii, 8, 12.
[3] *Ibid.*, ii, 10, 26, 347.
[4] *Ibid.*, xii, 1084.

debated with far greater intensity and feeling than had yet been displayed. In several of the most important constituencies the ballot was advocated on the hustings by the successful candidates. In the city of London, George Grote, who insisted that the Reform Act would never have a fair trial until the ballot was introduced, was triumphantly elected at the head of the poll, with more votes than had ever been cast for any London candidate.[1] At Manchester, Mark Phillips, who also included the ballot in his platform, was likewise returned at the head of the poll.[2] The enthusiasm with which Durham's speeches at Glasgow and Newcastle were received showed the popular appreciation of his arguments in favour of secret voting.[3] Even Lord Melbourne was said to be looking upon the ballot with no great disfavour.[4] At Wycombe the ballot found a warm advocate in Disraeli, who was now seeking his first entrance into parliament. It was, he said, a measure in full consonance with Tory principles and had formed part of the Tory scheme of the preceding century. The borough constituency, as determined by the Reform Act, he believed to be essentially and purposely a "dissenting and a low Whig constituency," under the influence of the principal employers of labour; the ballot was the sole instrument for extrication from such difficulties. In this case, however, as at Marylebone in 1833, his advocacy of secret voting failed to win the coveted seat for the future prime minister.[5] It is interesting to note that the young Gladstone was equally emphatic in his opposition to the ballot. Basing his objections on historical rather than contemporary political grounds, he

1 *Life of Grote*, 71, 74.
2 Smith, *Life of Bright*, i, 124.
3 Reid, *Life of Durham*, i, 404.
2 *Ibid.*, ii, 112.
5 Monypenny, *Life of Disraeli*, i, 217, 222, 225.

"discharges a fusillade from Roman history against the bare idea of vote by ballot, quotes Cicero as its determined enemy and ascribes to secret suffrage the fall of the republic."[1]

In the House of Commons the fight for the ballot, as the single effective remedy for corruption and particularly for electoral intimidation, was led by Grote. His maiden speech, delivered in a full House, was on this subject and the success of his *début* furnished an impetus to the ballot movement which was felt in all parts of the kingdom. Hobhouse, although he was at this time opposed to the measure, admitted that there was no logical answer to Grote's arguments and said that this speech was one of the best two he had ever heard in the House of Commons, in which opinion Abercromby concurred.[2] Although Grote's motion for leave to introduce a bill was lost, he was supported by more than a hundred members; this division indicates the advance made by the ballot inasmuch as three years before there had been but twenty-one votes in favour of its introduction into the single corrupt constituency of East Retford.[3] During the following years the Radicals made great efforts in the country at large to familiarize the people with the idea of vote by ballot, as well as to impress them with its practicability. They organized a "Ballot Union" and constructed and distributed hundreds of model ballot boxes; many converts were gained, Grote tells us, as a result of the exhibition of boxes and voting cards.[4]

The strength of the movement for the ballot is roughly

---

[1] Morley, *Life of Gladstone*, i, 99.

[2] *Life of Grote*, 83, 84; Broughton, *Recollections*, v, 57. Hobhouse had supported the ballot in 1831, but after being a party to the carrying of the Reform Bill did not feel at liberty to vote for any essential change.

[3] 3 Hansard, xlviii, 453.

[4] *Life of Grote*, 109, 125.

indicated by the increasing number of its adherents in the
divisions which took place on Grote's annual motion for
leave to introduce a bill. In 1835, one hundred and forty-
four voted for it, a gain of forty-one over the number of
its supporters in 1833. Although only eighty-eight
entered the lobby with Grote in 1836, in the two following
years there were one hundred and fifty-three and one hundred and ninety-eight respectively. In 1839, two hundred
and sixteen members voted for the ballot.[1] In 1838,
although the Whigs strove vigorously to make a stout
show against the ballot, the popular pressure of the electoral body on the Commons was strong; two members of
the government voted for it,[2] and even those who opposed
it most fiercely, acknowledged that numerous converts
had been made as a result of the bribery and intimidation
prevalent in the election of 1837.[3] In 1839 the cabinet
stated that it was regarded as an open question and
Macaulay, George Grey, and Ellice all cast their votes
for it.[4]

On each of these occasions, however, no matter how
large the absolute number of those in favour, the majority
against the ballot in the House of Commons was impressive and the hope of overcoming the combination of Whig
and Tory conservatives seemed slight. Grote himself became discouraged by the impossibility of winning definite
support from the Whigs, who officially maintained the
declaration of war against further reform of the electoral
system. In 1839, the year in which he secured the greatest
number of supporters, he brought his motion forward not
so much from any hope of success, as because some members wished for the opportunity of voting in favour of it in

1 3 Hansard, xxviii, 471; xxvii, 67; xl, 1221; xlviii, 453, 504.
2 Robert Steuart and Sir Hussey Vivian, *Life of Grote*, 125.
3 3 Hansard, xl, 1170.
4 *Ibid.*, xlviii, 504.

order to satisfy their constituents. The flatness of the debate itself was incontestable.[1] So hopeless was the prospect that in 1841, foreseeing the triumph of the Tories and the rout of the Radicals, Grote determined to give up the struggle.

With his retirement from parliament, the ballot lost its most capable advocate, and it was almost a generation before the question of secret voting reëntered the circle of practical politics. It was kept before the country by the agitation of the Chartists, but their advocacy of the ballot tended, on the whole, to discredit it in the eyes of the influential members of parliament and doubtless postponed its ultimate acceptance. It is true that soon after Grote's retirement the attempt to introduce a Ballot Bill once more became the subject of annual discussion in the Commons, but the life which had been imparted to the propaganda by Grote was departed.

The arguments advanced for and against the introduction of the ballot, during the annual debates on the subject, were of an unvarying character; necessarily the logic of the matter was soon exhausted. These arguments gilded over the basic difference in attitude of the two sides, which, however sincere, was largely determined by conditions of social circumstance and party affiliation. The conservative Whigs and Tories, now that the electoral power of the landowners and wealthy classes had been lessened by the attack on direct nomination, were not inclined to destroy that power entirely by making the new electors completely independent. The moral influence exercised over the electors by those in a higher station of life was, in their eyes, too valuable a characteristic of the constitution to be lost. Bribery and illegal influence were doubtless deplorable but in cutting out these vices care must be taken to maintain what they considered fair,

[1] *Life of Grote,* 131.

legitimate, and traditional influence. The ballot, if effective, would excise both the evil and the good. A less
drastic remedy must be applied.

The more liberal Whigs and the Radicals maintained,
on the other hand, that in receiving the suffrage the elector
was invested with a substantive and independent character; he must be dealt with as a voluntary and independent agent, capable of discharging an office of trust. All
constraint must be eliminated. The amount of bribery
and illegal influence far outbalanced that of the desirable
and legitimate influence, if indeed such a thing existed.
Corrupt influence could be destroyed only by making it
useless, through concealment of the vote; the desirable
moral ascendancy of the upper classes, if it sprang from
a legitimate source, would not be destroyed. At bottom,
the difference in standpoint between the two sides is still
more sharply cut. The Conservatives desired that electoral
power should remain in the hands of the propertied class.
The Radicals wanted that power in the hands of the middle
class.

In arguing for the ballot, its supporters pointed out
that the extent of bribery and intimidation was such as to
make the suffrage granted by the Reform Act a delusion.
They contended that the Reform Bill as finally passed
stood in far greater need of secret voting than the original plan, for the enfranchisement of the £50 renters in
counties and the reduction of the borough qualification
from £20 to £10 had placed the franchise in the hands of
those who were the most dependent of all upon property
and capital. Under the existing system the vote of these
classes was the property of the landlord and the manufacturer.[1] It might, indeed, be claimed that the elector
ought to give his vote under a feeling of responsibility to
the public and that this feeling would be lessened, if not

1 3 Hansard, xxviii, 423; xl, 1143.

destroyed, by voting in secret. But this theory assumed an inaccurate view of the elector's position and duty; the law presumed him qualified and only asked his opinion; he could not be held accountable to his neighbours. The existing system, while it rendered him responsible to an imaginary public, as a matter of fact made him responsible to a private person.

As to legitimate influence exercised on electors, the Radicals asked what that meant. Influence that was really legitimate was useless. If influence coincided with the elector's own opinion, it was superfluous; if contrary to it, it was pernicious. Again, it might be argued that the ballot would enable electors to break their election promises and would induce deceit and treachery. But ought such promises to be kept? The voter has no right, the Radicals insisted, to promise his vote, and treachery to an election agent is no more criminal than treachery to one's conscience: "The sole intent and purpose of the elective franchise is that he may deliver his free and indifferent suffrage at the poll."[1]

The opponents of the ballot avoided political theory for the most part and laid stress upon the practical results of secret voting, which they distrusted. They refused to believe that complete secrecy could be secured and contended that even if the vote were not disclosed, intimidation would be exercised to prevent the elector from voting at all.[2] Stanley and Russell felt that the ballot would actually increase bribery because no scrutiny of votes could be held after the election and it would be impossible to prove the offence.[3] Numerous instances of the corruption supposed to result from secret voting in France and America were adduced, and letters from citizens of the

[1] 3 Hansard, xxviii, 381, 398.
[2] *Ibid.*, xxxvii, 65.
[3] *Ibid.*, xxviii, 449-453. Peel agreed, 464.

United States were read in which the evil results of secret voting upon corruption were described.[1] Peel objected that the ballot was at variance with the institutions of the country, inasmuch as publicity was the keynote of the constitution; in this point he was supported by the mass of the Tories, most of whom stigmatized secret suffrage as un-English and accordingly unmanly. He believed also that the ballot would lead to lying and dishonesty. Other opponents spoke to this effect in no measured terms: "it would afford protection to none but skulking cowards; the voter would be led to conceal his real intentions and give his vote in contradiction to his word;" it would incite fraud; the morality of the people would be injured.[2]

Almost the sole theoretical argument advanced by the opponents of the ballot lay in their estimate of the character of the franchise. If the franchise were a trust, and as such it had been treated in the act of 1832, it entailed a responsibility. The responsible exercise of the franchise and secret voting were incompatible, since the public and the non-electors were entitled to full knowledge and observation of the manner in which this trust was carried out by each individual voter.[3]

At bottom, however, the real objection to the ballot was expressed by Peel when he told Hobhouse that it would take away that influence over the vote which preserved the representative system from being of too democratic a

---

[1] A letter from Washington said: "I have not found an eminent lawyer or statesman in this country, who does not, as regards England, lean to the conservative side more or less. Federalists, Nullifiers, Whigs, and Jacksonians all agree in saying: for Heaven's sake take care of what you are about in England. We know the practical effects of vote by ballot. . . . I send you this information having been brought up a good Whig, but I verily believe had I come here a Radical I should have returned to England a Tory," 3 Hansard, xxviii, 457.

[2] *Ibid.*, xxvi, 1174; xxviii, 414.

[3] *Ibid.*, xl, 1174; *Westminster Review*, xxix, 509.

character.[1] This basic objection was openly enunciated by Russell in the House of Commons; the ballot, he said, would necessarily lead to other and more democratic changes, which were desired by neither of the ruling parties.[2] Electoral conditions prevalent after the Reform Act prevented the operation of even that modicum of democratic influence the existence of which was ostensibly permitted by that act. This fact was realized and approved by those who had carried through the first reform legislation, and they felt it was better to maintain such conditions, even at the expense of the scandal of corruption. The ballot would radically alter these electoral conditions and the democratic flood would be let in.[3]

The refusal of the two chief parties to accept the drastic reform of secret voting threw on them the burden of discovering other remedies for the existent corruption. Casting aside the discussion of preventive methods, there was a return to the attempts at penal legislation, which confessedly in the minds of many was the sole method of destroying the evil, while preserving the good of the electoral system.[4] In 1841 a measure was introduced by Russell, which, after being shorn of most of its clauses by the Peers, was passed with the intention of facilitating the proof of bribery. In the following year further legislation was directed against the concealment of corrupt practices; and in 1852 extraordinary power for the appointment of commissions of inquiry was created.[5]

[1] In this opinion Hobhouse concurred, Broughton, *Recollections,* v, 120.

[2] 3 Hansard, xl, 1192.

[3] The prophecies of the sinister results of the ballot take the reader back irresistibly to the debates of 1831. The specific fear in the minds of many was the repeal of the corn laws, 3 Hansard, xlviii, 452.

[4] *Ibid.,* xxxvii, 65.

[5] 4 & 5 Vict., c. 57; 5 & 6 Vict., c. 102; 15 & 16 Vict., c. 57.

Three great difficulties standing in the way of the proof of bribery made the legislation of these years necessary. The offer of a bribe, unless acceptance on the part of the voter were proved, could not be prosecuted except as a misdemeanour.[1] When an agent proposed a sum of money to an elector for voting in favour of a certain candidate, no charge of corruption could be successfully brought, unless it were clearly proved that the money had been received. On the other hand, an offer to sell his vote made by an elector did not constitute bribery unless it were shown that the candidate or his agent accepted such offer.[2] In the second place, there was no functionary to see that the penalties inflicted upon voters convicted of corrupt practices were duly carried into effect. Finally, in all cases where bribery was charged, the court required that the accuser should prove the party bribing to be the agent of the candidate before it permitted further investigation. To void an election it must be shown that the corruption was committed by the authority of the candidate or his agent, so that the mode of procedure was first to ascertain the criminal and then to prove that the crime had been committed. Bribery might have prevailed to the most shameful and notorious extent, the returns affected by it and the constituency defrauded of its rights; but unless the corruption could be brought home to the sitting member, there was no redress, beyond the punishment of one or two electors, by no means the most guilty of the parties concerned.[3]

It was this last defect in the bribery law which Russell attempted to remedy by his act of 1841. As passed in the Commons, it provided that the candidates, agents, attor-

[1] *Parliamentary Papers*, 1835, no. 547, "Minutes of Evidence," §§ 7-21, 367, 370.
[2] 2 O'Malley and Hardcastle, 21.
[3] *Westminster Review*, xxv, 490.

neys, and all persons implicated could be compelled to testify, although indemnity might be extended to witnesses.
It also provided that when petitions alleging corrupt
practices were tried, evidence of bribery was to be given on
the whole matter before proving agency. The inquiry
then might follow as to whether the party bribing was or
was not an agent of the candidate. In the Lords,
Brougham opposed the first clauses strongly, pointing out
that the indemnity granted to witnesses might be extended
to all the parties implicated, so that by calling a candidate
or agent as witness, an attorney could exempt him from
punishment and the intent of the law would be nullified.[1]
The bill, as passed by the Lords, accordingly contained
only the preamble and the clause which allowed proof of
bribery before agency was shown.[2]

The effect of this single clause was immediate and startling. But instead of rendering the election agents more
fearful of the consequences which might follow wholesale
bribery and thus inducing purer electioneering, it merely
sharpened their wits to devise means for the concealment
of corrupt practices. The election of 1841 was hard
fought and notable for the corruption employed. Both
parties understood the importance of the contest and both
were unscrupulous as to the means taken to insure success.[3]
The candidates and their agents on both sides, in their
eager desire to win, failed to heed the change which had
been made in the bribery law and never calculated the
consequences which would follow from it. These consequences were quickly manifest when the election trials
began. The accusing party in each case began by
laying before the committee evidence of a wholesale
and systematic plan of bribery; when this was made

[1] 3 Hansard, lviii, 1560.

[2] *Ibid.*, lviii, 1594.

[3] *Westminster Review*, xxxix, 114.

out, the committees were not slow in coming to the
conclusion that the persons by whom it was committed
were in reality agents of the candidates for whom the
votes were purchased. Election after election was declared void and a general panic among all parties followed.

It was early in May, 1842, that the effect of the new
law was demonstrated. Suddenly there went abroad
rumours of various arrangements hastily concluded between certain members against whom petitions had been
presented, and the parties who claimed their seats. The
truth of these rumours was speedily demonstrated. Petitions were withdrawn, trials brought to a close, and
bribery investigations blocked. The explanation of these
manœuvres was to be found in the belief of each party,
that it was better to compromise their cases than to
scandalize the nation by an exposure of the extent to
which bribery had been carried. The Liberal and Conservative committees, which sat at the Reform and Carlton
Clubs, soon realized that they were waging a mutually
useless war, spending money only for the benefit of the
lawyers concerned, and bringing discredit upon their
party methods. The Tory majority was too large to be
affected by the decisions of the committees, and the accusations of bribery on both sides were nearly equal, so that
no gain would result to either party by persevering in
their petitions.

This equality afforded a ready means of compromise:
compromise in two ways. In certain cases, wherein the
result of an election might be doubtful or the trial expensive to both sides, one seat of the two was given up; the
petition was dropped, and one of the members petitioned
against applied for the Chiltern Hundreds, resigning his
seat. One of the petitioners was then allowed to stand
unopposed. Such corrupt compromises were definitely

proved in the six boroughs of Bridport, Reading, Harwich, Penryn and Falmouth, Nottingham, and Lewes.[1] Another mode of compromise, of a more wholesale description, acquired the technical name of "swopping." The case of the Conservatives might be hopeless in the approaching trial for corruption in one borough, while in another case the Liberals were certain of defeat. The managers on one side said to those on the other, "We will give you this, if you will give us that." Acceptance was signified, all petitions were dropped, and further exposure of corrupt practices prevented.[2]

This systematic method of concealment, which seems to have been approved, if not actually devised, by the central committee of each party,[3] was brought to light by Roebuck in the House of Commons; the explanation of the persons implicated was so unsatisfactory as to lead to the appointment of a committee of investigation.[4] Some attempt was made to stifle further inquiry, into which Palmerston foolishly allowed himself to be drawn. Peel, on the other hand, was shrewd enough to avoid the popular odium cast on the system by urging the most thorough investigation. Supported by the prime minister and led by the outspoken Roebuck, the committee probed to the

[1] *Parliamentary Papers,* 1842, no. 458, "Report from the Select Committee on election compromises." The documents in which are contained the terms of compromise are set forth in full in the report.

[2] This practice of swopping was not investigated by the committee but seems to have been a matter of common talk in 1842, *Westminster Review,* xxxix, 118.

[3] The evidence on this point is chiefly negative; but the replies to certain questions indicate that contributions to the campaign funds of the members who made the compromises came from the central committees and that these committees were in close touch with the proceedings, *Parliamentary Papers,* 1842, no. 458, pp. 9, 59; "Minutes of Evidence," §§ 727-729.

[4] *Parliamentary Papers,* 1842, no. 458.

depths this systematic hushing up of corrupt practices. By the frankness of their report, rectifying legislation was made inevitable.[1]

This legislation was embodied in an act passed in 1842, which attempted to frustrate such organized devices of party convenience directed as they were against the public weal. In future, where charges of bribery were brought and abandoned, the election committee was to have the power of inquiring further into the matter. If it were shown that the cause of the withdrawal was a compromise, agents and candidates might be examined and the investigation continued at the discretion of the committee. The act also attempted to check treating and indirect bribery; treating before the test of the writ or after the return was to be considered as equivalent to bribery and the payment of head-money was to be regarded in the same light.[2] It is obvious that the act was not framed to effect a vital change in electioneering methods or to effectively disclose corrupt practices. No power was given the election committee to go down to the guilty borough and take evidence, and loopholes were left by which valuable witnesses might disappear.[3] Witnesses on examination could refuse to give evidence if it tended to incriminate themselves and committees were destined to find many of their paths of investigation blocked by this privilege; the agents and attorneys naturally shared such

[1] Fullest details of the bribery committed by both parties and the circumstances leading up to the compromises are given in the report, *Parliamentary Papers,* 1842, no. 458.

[2] 3 Hansard, lxv, 1061; 5 & 6 Vict., c. 102.

[3] The suggestion that a royal commission be appointed for investigation upon the spot was successfully opposed, 3 Hansard, lxv, 716. During the following years the Commons spent much time and effort in bringing before the bar of the House recalcitrant witnesses; the latter were always apt to disappear when their evidence was essential to complete proof.

immunity with the accused members.[1] It was proposed
that a more competent tribunal of inquiry than a committee of the House should be created, but Russell, who
had charge of the bill, refused to allow jurisdiction over
elections to pass to the courts.[2]

In so far as the prevention of wholesale bribery was
concerned, neither the act of 1841 or that of 1842 was
effective; the sole result was simply that more petitions
were presented and more elections voided. That election
agents were deterred by fear from the commission of
corrupt practices does not appear. Indeed, the corruption prevalent in the election of 1847 created the more
scandal in that the excuse of an unusually hot contest
was lacking. Peel, in 1848, admitted frankly that both
acts were a disappointment. That of 1841 was valuable
when once a petition was presented, but in the majority of
corrupt boroughs the defeated party was itself guilty or
lacked funds for prosecution and no petition was brought
forward. The existing law, in his opinion, was insufficient,
not because its provisions were not stringent enough, but
because its operation depended entirely upon the presentation of a petition. The variety of circumstances which
deterred possible petitioners was so great as to minimize
all chance of the detection and punishment of bribery.[3]
The act of 1842, directed against corrupt compromises,
had for its practical effect merely the alteration of the
time when the compromise was made. It was still possible
to agree before election that in case a petition was pre-

[1] The clause which forced testimony in answer to all questions
was struck out in committee. Peel said, "Though truth might
occasionally be elicited . . . yet it was at the expense of great
principles, and when parties were compelled to criminate themselves
it became a question whether a great temptation was not held out
to perjury," 3 Hansard, lxv, 725.

[2] *Ibid.*, lxv, 1491.

[3] *Ibid.*, cii, 1041.

sented it should be compromised. "We see," said Peel, "that notwithstanding the penalties threatened these usages continue to prevail."[1]

During the decade which followed the passing of these acts there was a return to the penal legislation directed against individual boroughs where corruption was shown to be habitual and flagrant. The electoral condition of Sudbury in 1841 led to the recommendation that it be disfranchised absolutely.[2] In two successive sessions a bill of disfranchisement passed by the Commons was thrown out by the Lords, who failed to secure the incontestable evidence laid before the lower House. But in 1844, after an abortive attempt to throw the borough into the hundreds, the Lords passed the bill of disfranchisement. This step in the punishment of corruption was followed up in 1852 when a similar penalty was meted out to St. Albans; electoral practices were here of such a character that even Lord Verulam, who held the chief influence in the borough, considered it impossible to oppose disfranchisement and was sorry for the counsel who tried to do so.[3] As a result of the corrupt election of 1847 at Yarmouth, the committee recommended the disfranchisement of the freemen, amongst whom bribery had been most prevalent; the recommendation was carried into effect and the brevity of discussion testifies to the increasing feeling against bribery.[4] Less drastic measures were applied to other corrupt boroughs; where the bribery was less flagrant, or where the constituency was protected by government influence, suspension of the writ for the session was deemed sufficient penalty. In some cases, how-

[1] 3 Hansard, xcix, 340; cii, 1043.

[2] *Parliamentary Papers*, 1842, no. 176; 3 Hansard, lxii, 473; lxiii, 343; lxvi, 207; lxix, 491.

[3] 3 Hansard, cxx, 977.

[4] *Parliamentary Papers*, 1847-1848, no. 143, "Report of Yarmouth election committee."

ever, the issuance of the writ was postponed for a longer period.[1]

The extensive corruption practised in the election of 1847 led to a consideration of more general measures. Public opinion was roused to a lukewarm degree of disgust at the failure of legislation to cope with the evil, and the Commons felt bound to continue their efforts.[2] In 1849, Sir John Pakington, emphasizing the futility of purely penal measures and yet hesitating to go so far as the ballot, introduced a bill which demanded a solemn oath of electoral purity from all candidates. In his eyes prevention was the sole cure and what better means of prevention, he asked, could be found than an oath of honour taken by the candidate? The bill, which was seriously discussed by the Commons, was thrown out by the Lords.[3]

The chief efforts of the Commons were, as in earlier years, directed towards better facilities for discovering corruption. The difficulty of determining the real extent of the evil was demonstrated in the trial of every petition. As in the case of registration, the process was largely left to individual effort; the petitioner proved so much corruption as would convict his adversary and then stopped; it was more than could be expected of him that, merely to perform a national duty, he should go to all the expense of further action after his own end was attained. Thus inquiry into what was a public grievance was confined to

[1] The withholding of the writ often led to party recriminations and accusations of gerrymandering. Thus in 1848 the Whigs were accused of urging the issuance of the writ for Derby, where two Whigs had been elected for twenty years, while they opposed the Horsham writ because of the danger of a Tory victory, 3 Hansard, xcix, 344.

[2] The pressure of public opinion had led to the formation of an anti-bribery society which issued pamphlets and encouraged investigations, *Westminster Review*, xlviii, 335.

[3] 3 Hansard, cvii, 1116.

personal and private interests.[1] The election committees, also, were apt to content themselves with taking only enough evidence to invalidate the return; composed of members of the House, they were in general rather delicate in their attempts not to trace the bribery directly to the member petitioned against, in order to give him a chance to stand for another constituency.[2] Moreover, even if they desired to ascertain the extent to which corruption prevailed, as soon as they had determined the title to the seat and corrected the return, their functions were at an end; they had no jurisdiction vested in them to pursue the inquiry.[3] Again, as soon as it became evident that corrupt practices were likely to be proved, an almost automatic combination was formed between the agents of both parties and the electors of the borough, with the object of concealing the true extent of the bribery. The candidate, the agent, and the persons who received the bribe, were all interested in the concealment of the facts and it was to their mutual advantage that the matter should be hushed up. This, according to Peel, was the great difficulty of investigation and this was the explanation of that inevitable absence of witnesses whenever the committee was approaching the kernel of the truth.[4]

With these conditions in view, a bill was introduced in 1848, reviving the proposition that the Commons be given power to appoint a select committee for the purpose of determining whether corruption in any borough was such as to warrant a local investigation; if the committee discovered traces of corruption a commission was to be appointed whose duty it should be to probe the matter to

---

1 3 Hansard, cxx, 969.

2 *Ibid.*, xcvii, 902.

3 *Ibid.*, ci, 481.

4 Lansdowne agreed with Peel, 3 Hansard, lxiii, 1272; cxxii, 563. See also lxi, lxii of Hansard for numerous instances of the difficulties the House had with recalcitrant witnesses.

its depths. The Lords threw out this bill as unconstitu-
tional.[1] In 1852, however, a special act was passed by
both Houses appointing a commission for inquiry at St.
Albans, and the success of this particular measure was
such that in the same year a bill was introduced, designed
to convert the particular into a general measure, applicable in all cases. According to this bill, if the House of
Commons considered the indications of bribery such as to
demand further inquiry, it was to have the power of issuing
an address to the crown, praying for the appointment of
commissioners, who were to go down to the borough; all
persons implicated might be forced to testify on oath, but
indemnity could be granted to witnesses at the discretion
of the commissioners. There would thus be held over every
borough the prospect of an investigation on the spot, not
confined to the events of one election, but going back, if
necessary, to exhibit the general state of the constituency
during a number of years.[2]

In the discussions of the Lords, the Conservatives
objected to the wide powers granted the lower House in
this bill, and Derby was able to embody the provision
that there be some safeguard to prevent the Commons
from exercising such power arbitrarily. The principle of
the bill was, however, accepted. As amended in the upper
House, the act provided that the concurrence of the Lords
must be obtained, before an address could be issued to the
crown, thus dividing the power between both Houses.
Russell objected to the proposed participation of the
Lords, on the ground that two preliminary inquiries would
thus be necessary, so that time would be lost and the efficiency of the act reduced. But the Tories in the Commons supported the amendment, and it was finally

[1] 3 Hansard, c. 470, 715; ci, 307, 480.
[2] Ibid., cxxii, 563.

accepted.[1] The new law was immediately put into operation and in 1853, after conferences between the Houses, joint addresses were issued, praying for the appointment of royal commissioners in the cases of six boroughs. In the case of but one borough did the Lords fail to concur with the Commons in their desire for a commission.[2]

It is to the credit of both parties and particularly to that of Russell that efforts to disclose conditions of corruption increased with their success. The disclosures made by the new commissioners of investigation and the large number of voided elections in the trials of 1853, spurred the Commons on to new remedies. The ballot, which had once more resumed its rôle as subject of annual motions, was invariably refused.[3] Schemes for the giving of votes by voting papers, where secrecy was not required, also received slight attention.[4] But during 1853 and 1854 measures were discussed for the better discovery of corruption by a scrutiny of the candidates' expenses, as well as for the stricter interpretation of the bribery laws by clear definition of corrupt practices. An attempt along such lines was made in 1853 by Spencer Walpole, who laid down in definite terms the exact meaning and full extent of the offences which his bill aimed at preventing.[5]

[1] 3 Hansard, cxxii, 904, 1301; 15 & 16 Vict., c. 57.

[2] Commissioners were appointed for Barnstaple, Cambridge, Canterbury, Hull, Maldon, and Tynemouth. The case in which no agreement was reached was that of Clitheroe, 3 Hansard, cxxv, cxxvi, *passim;* cxvii, 211.

[3] In 1848 and 1851 resolutions in favour of the ballot were carried by Berkeley in a thin House, by a small majority. In 1854 he received 157 votes but the majority against him was nearly 40. Enthusiasm for the ballot was not intense in the Commons; even Duncombe said he did not believe that it would prove as effectual as some supposed. He, with other Radicals, believed that large constituencies and frequent elections would be a more effectual cure, 3 Hansard, c, 1268; cxviii, 356; cxxxiv, 114; cxxx, 437.

[4] *Ibid.*, cxxviii, 1410; cxxix, 268.

[5] *Ibid.*, cxxix, 1699.

The measure was dropped after the second reading, but in the following year, Russell, from the opposite side of the House, presented a similar proposal, which after brief discussion was transformed into the Corrupt Practices Act of 1854.[1]

The most important characteristics of this enactment were the exact definition of the various kinds of corrupt practices, and the creation of election auditors whose duty it should be to receive and scrutinize all accounts payable by the candidate. Corrupt payments could no longer be made without danger of immediate detection when the statement of expenses was presented for audit. Nor could the candidate hope to escape the judgment of an election committee because of the doubtful meaning of the law. The act was thus in line with the previous policy of the House of seeking better methods of discovery and more effective means for bringing the offender to task, rather than some method of prevention in the first instance. Fear of detection and of punishment was still considered the most efficient deterrent from the commission of corrupt practices.

The act of 1854 gave the first exact and complete definition of bribery. Its provisions covered, so far as was humanly possible, the cases, both direct and indirect, of this offence, which had been brought to light in the trial of election petitions. Any person was guilty of bribery who gave, lent, or promised any money or valuable consideration to a voter in order to induce him to vote or refrain from voting. Bribery also included the performance of such acts after the election, on account of the person's having voted or refrained from voting. The offer or gift of any office or employment with the intent of influencing his vote, was also bribery. On the receiver's side, a voter was guilty of bribery if he accepted or contracted for any

[1] 17 & 18 Vict., c. 102.

money, gift, loan, or employment for himself in return
for voting or agreeing to vote. Thus both the giver and
the acceptor were to be equally guilty, if convicted of the
offence. Bribery was and always had been a criminal
offence at common law, but the statutory definition was
now so far-reaching that it included nearly every possible
case of bribery imaginable. Almost the only kind of
bribery that was not defined in the act was that involved
in corrupt wagers. But votes given under the influence
of such wagers had, as far back as 1835, been held void
by election committees.[1]

In assigning penalties, the act of 1854 continued the law
that any candidate guilty of bribery by himself or his
agent, should be incapable of being elected, or of taking
his seat in the House of Commons during the Parliament
then in existence.[2] The voter, if proved guilty of bribery,
was liable to prosecution for a misdemeanour and a fine
of ten pounds, and his vote was cast out as well. The
enormous pecuniary penalty which had been attached
formerly to a conviction thus disappeared. Russell
believed that it was ridiculous to force a poor elector, who
received five shillings for his vote, to pay five hundred
pounds. The result of the enormous penalty had been that

---

[1] Knapp and Ombler, *Cases of Controverted Elections*, 146, 196,
225: Monmouth, Windsor, and Worcester, 1835.

[2] The House has never exercised this species of authority, upon
the ground of corrupt practice at an election to any Parliament
except that actually sitting; since 1724 it does not seem to have been
exercised at all. In 1700 four members were expelled from the
House for corrupt practices at an election to the Parliament then
sitting; another somewhat similar case, arising out of a corrupt
compromise of an election petition, occurred in 1724. In 1870 it
was brought before the notice of parliament that several of its
members had been reported guilty of corrupt practices. The committee appointed to look into the law, upon finding that none of
these members were alleged to have been guilty of any corrupt
practice in connection with the Parliament then sitting, declined to
take any action, *Parliamentary Papers*, 1870, no. 302.

it was never applied in practice. But he believed that guilty electors should be permanently struck from the register so that they might never vote again. He would also have been glad to render guilty candidates perpetually incapable of election.[1]

The definition of and the penalties for treating were also clearly laid down. Any person who provided, or paid wholly or in part the expense of providing, any meat, drink, or entertainment for the purpose of influencing a vote, was to be held guilty of this offence; every elector who accepted such entertainment on account of voting or refraining from voting was also guilty. The penalty for single cases of treating was not, under the act of 1854, such as to vitiate the election. The guilty candidate was liable to a fine of fifty pounds; in the case of an elector, his vote, if given, was to be void and cast out.

Before 1854 the bribery laws had been entirely silent as to the offence of intimidation or undue influence. The act of that year defined undue influence for the first time, as the making use of, or threatening, any force or restraint, or in any manner practising intimidation upon a person in order to influence his vote. Abduction, or any fraudulent device or contrivance which might interfere with the free franchise of the voter, was placed in the same category. The penalty was to be a fine of fifty pounds and the liability of undergoing prosecution for a misdemeanour. Notwithstanding the breadth of the definition and the amount of the penalty, the opinion was general in 1854 that intimidation would hardly be checked by this clause, and experience was to prove the justice of such fears.[2]

The act said nothing about the effect of general bribery, treating, or undue influence. But according to the com-

[1] 3 Hansard, cxxx, 414.
[2] *Ibid.*, cxxx, 426, 427, 431.

mon law, if such acts of corruption were so prevalent as to prevent a true election, the return would be considered void; and this was so, even though it could not be proved that the candidate, or any agent of his, was responsible for such corruption. In the language of the jurists the prevalence of corrupt practices, "quite apart from acts of members or their agents, would vitiate an election, because it would show that there was no pure or free choice in the matter,—that what occurred was a sham and not a reality."[1]

The most important creation of the act of 1854 was the system of election auditors. Direct bribery through money had always been the most frequent and the most efficacious of the various modes of electoral corruption. The ease with which it was employed had been the greater in that the law left to the care of the candidate all the expenses relative to elections. Such large sums were expended for legitimate purposes that it was easy to scatter extra payments here and there for the purpose of corruption. To prevent such covering up of bribery it was enacted that the accounts of the candidates should be published item by item; it would thus be made clear for what purposes the money had been expended. With this

---

[1] In the following years elections were voided on several occasions for general corruption where it was not brought home to the candidate or agent: for bribery at Lichfield in 1869; for treating at Bradford in the same year; for undue influence at South Meath in 1892. "If there were general bribery, no matter from what fund or by what person, and although the sitting member and his agents had nothing to do with it, it would defeat an election on the ground that it was not proceeding pure and free as an election ought to be, but that it was corrupted and vitiated by an influence which, coming from no matter what quarter, had defeated it and had shown it to be abortive," per Willes, J. Undue influence "prevailing generally was sufficient to avoid the election without any proof of agency whatever," per O'Brien, J., O'Malley and Hardcastle, *Decisions of the Judges for the Trial of Election Petitions*, i, 26; iv, 132.

end in view, the returning officers were to appoint auditors of election expenses. All persons, agents as well as others, who had bills or claims upon any candidate, were to send them in within one month after the declaration of the election. Otherwise they were barred of their right to recover. The bills were handed over to the election auditors for payment, and no payment was to be made except through them. Accounts of all expenses were to be kept by the auditors and might be freely inspected, and abstracts of such accounts were to be published. The candidates should, at the time of their nomination, notify the auditors of the names of all agents, and provisions were made for bringing the auditors into close touch with all the election proceedings.

The effect of twenty years of discussion and legislation against corrupt practices was, perhaps, more striking than might have been expected when we consider that it was not until 1841 that any act at all was passed, and not until 1852 and 1854 that measures of completeness and force were carried through. Considering the general tone of public opinion, which still regarded electoral corruption as a rather venial offence, it is almost surprising that this moral disease was palliated so far as it was by legislative remedies. The effects of the acts of 1852 and 1854 are certainly traceable and apparently salutary. We have it on the authority of an investigating committee, that six years after the passing of the latter act direct bribery had diminished.[1] And it is certainly true that, although the facilities for the detection of corruption had been improved, there were but nine returns voided for bribery in 1857, whereas in 1852 there had been twenty-three. In the election of 1859 there was but one member

[1] *Parliamentary Papers,* 1860, no. 329, "Report from the committee appointed to inquire into the operation and effect of the Act of 1854."

unseated on this account, and the amount of bribery proved in this case was insufficient to warrant a special investigation.[1]

On the other hand, the improvement in electoral conditions was merely relative. The reports of committees during the following years are filled with detailed accounts of varied corruption. If the extent of direct bribery had been limited, the wits of the agents were sharpened to find other methods, less easily detected, for corruptly influencing the suffrages of the electors.[2] Intimidation, in particular, was very slightly affected by the legislation of 1854; and there is little doubt that during the next fifteen years this form of corrupt influence played an important rôle in all elections, especially in counties, where bribery was less rampant.[3]

But although the act of 1854 failed to eliminate corrupt influence, it laid the basis for future legislation that was destined to prove more effective. The exact definition of corrupt offences was a great step in the purification of electoral methods, and all that was lacking was machinery for carrying the penalties into effect. The scrutiny of election accounts, although it became a mockery because of the incapacity of the official auditors, pointed the way to a sumptuary restriction of election expenses that was to be of great value. In these two respects the act prepared the way for the successful provisions of 1883. On the other hand the legislation of 1854 failed in two particulars: it made no attempt to prevent bribery by rendering it useless, nor did it impose any real check upon undue

[1] *Parliamentary Papers,* 1866, no. 77.

[2] *Parliamentary Papers,* 1860, no. 329. And see reports of select committees trying election cases and the minutes of evidence published annually in the *Parliamentary Papers.*

[3] *Parliamentary Papers,* 1870, no. 115, "Report from committee appointed to inquire into the present modes of conducting parliamentary and municipal elections."

influence; and it left the old cumbrous system of election committees, whose failure to detect and punish electoral misconduct had been so obvious. It was not until 1868 that the jurisdiction over election trials was given to the judges, and only in 1872 that the introduction of secret voting helped to lessen the effectiveness of corruption. Another element, indeed, was necessary before complete elimination of the evil could be secured: a change in public opinion was essential, without which, legislation, whether of an inquisitorial, penal, or preventive character, was bound to be largely ineffective.

CHAPTER IX

THE BEGINNINGS OF DEMOCRATIC SUFFRAGE: THE REFORM ACT OF 1867

Growing desire for more liberal franchise—The Radical and Chartist movements—Weakness of reform movement in House of Commons—The Liberal recognition of need for further franchise reform—Russell's Reform Bills of 1852, 1854, 1860—Disraeli's Reform Bill of 1859—Difference between the Liberal and Conservative proposals—Gladstone's bill of 1866—The £7 franchise in boroughs—Abolition of rate-paying requirements—Probable effects of the bill—Opposition in the Commons—Robert Lowe and the "Adullamites"—Methods of opposition—Resignation of the Liberals—Disraeli's bill of 1867—Household suffrage in boroughs—Restrictions—The dual vote—Probable effect of the original bill—The Liberal opposition—Question of personal payment of rates—The compound occupiers—Abolition of composition—Effects of this amendment—Removal of other restrictions—The new county franchise—Borough freeholders in counties—Contemporary opinion on the act as passed—The Reform Act of 1867 incomplete.

T HE extent of corrupt practices and the failure of parliament to assure freedom of elections operated, without question, as a very serious barrier to the development of an electoral democracy. The opinions of the voters were stifled either by gold or by fear, and the wealthy classes were able to maintain their domination at the polls to a large degree. This fact was clearly perceived by the keener spirits, and it was not merely to obliterate a cause of national scandal, but also to assure the rights of the voters, that Russell endeavoured to purify methods of electioneering. Many others, also, realized that because of corruption as well as through the complexities of the registration system an appreciable portion of the electorate was disfranchised.

But to a large number of those who desired a democratic electoral system it seemed lost effort to tinker with the details of the existing system. In their opinion the simplest and most direct road was the extension of the franchise. With a larger electorate bribery would be difficult, if not impossible, and intimidation would automatically disappear. The chicanery by which registration lawyers destroyed or created qualifications would be useless, for the constituency would be too large to be affected by such methods. If the people were to have an influential voice in elections, a democratic franchise was the first and possibly the only essential.

The suffrage qualifications established in 1832 remained unaltered for a generation, despite the frequent and sometimes determined attempts made in the hope of rendering their character more popular. Efforts to widen the franchise and increase the constituency emanated generally from one of two sources. The parliamentary Radicals, looking at the borough qualification of 1832 as merely the first step, agitated for a simple household qualification; with them some of the Liberals gradually joined, who, if they did not go so far, believed that the £10 value required in boroughs should be reduced, and that the county franchise should be more nearly assimilated to the borough. This movement sprang chiefly from the middle class.

The working classes also demanded a wider qualification, organizing however a distinct movement. Disappointed in the result of the Reform Act, and alienated from those who had passed it, especially because of their Irish and poor-law policy,[1] they drew up a plan for the thorough recast-

[1] See the publications of the artisans, in particular *The Working Man's Friend,* for the bitter enmity of the working classes towards the Whigs, especially Althorp and Stanley. The labourers also

ing of the representative system, which developed into the
People's Charter. Although the character of the Chartist
movement was in the main social,[1] and the question of the
franchise was but one of many reforms, the unconditional
demand for universal manhood suffrage was perhaps the
most obvious factor in the agitation. Between the middle
and working class movements, there stood a third element
demanding reform of the franchise, which hoped to reconcile the similar and yet divergent aims of each.

Whether successful pressure could have been brought
upon the legislating body had the demands for reform
been coördinated, is doubtful.[2] The hostility existing between the two sections of reformers, which, on the side
of the working classes at least, was bitter in the extreme,
precluded such coöperation. The mutual misunderstand-
ing was doubtless in part one of terminology merely. The
working classes believed that "household suffrage" was a
totally inadequate measure of compromise and covered a
hypocritical design for their betrayal, as had the £10
qualification of 1832. On the other hand the Chartists
speedily rendered the term "universal suffrage" hateful
to the middle class politicians.[3] Divided at bottom upon
their ultimate object as well as upon the method of agitation, the mutual distrust of class was brought to a head
by the movement for corn-law repeal. The Chartists "saw

complained that municipal reform was solely for the benefit of the
middle classes, *Autobiography of Cooper*, 137.

[1] The subordination of the political aspect of the movement is
constantly illustrated in such works as Gammage, *History of the
Chartist Movement;* Holyoake, *Sixty Years of an Agitator's Life*,
and the *Autobiography of Cooper.*

[2] Place thought that there was little chance of success, unless
some accident, as in 1832, should put politics in a revolutionary
position. A well-managed agitation might then create a strong
democratic party, able to exercise pressure upon parliament, Wallas,
Place, 369.

[3] Wallas, *Place*, 390.

the cloven hoof of bourgeois tyranny" in this agitation; the cry of "cheap bread" they insisted, was in reality the forerunner of "low wages," and there should be no alliance with the middle class.[1]

The Radical middle class movement was thus not merely unassisted, but also thwarted by the working class agitators, notwithstanding the similarity of their object so far as the franchise was concerned. In 1841 Roebuck, Thompson, and Hume organized a series of meetings for the reform of the suffrage, beginning with one in Leeds, where the middle class Radicals outnumbered the Chartists. Unfortunately O'Connell, who was regarded by the latter as a renegade, was expected to take the lead, and they invaded the hall, after holding a counter demonstration, and turned the Radical into a Chartist agitation, giving "three terrific groans" for the Irish Radical leader.[2] Again in 1848 when Hume began an agitation for household suffrage, he was opposed by Feargus O'Connor, who warned the "old guard" of Chartism against him; later in the year, O'Connor turned toward the veteran Radical, but it was only when the popularity of the Chartist leader had begun to wane and his forces to divide.[3]

In 1842 an agitation led by Sturge was directed towards compromise and coöperation between middle and working class reformers. Place's suggestion of a slogan of "general suffrage" was passed by in favour of "com-

---

[1] *Autobiography of Cooper*, 137; Kent, *The English Radicals*, 370.

[2] Gammage, *History of the Chartist Movement*, 191-192, 194. It is true that the "People's Petition" was presented to the House of Commons by Duncombe, in 1842, and that he later joined the "National Chartist Association," and worked with O'Connor. But this did not result in anything like a union between Radical and Chartist forces, *Life of Duncombe*, i, 308.

[3] A public meeting of Hume's party was held at the London Tavern, May 16, 1848, and a Chartist leader, T. Clark, attended; later there was a meeting of the "Household Suffrage Association" at Drury Lane, attended by Chartists. But active coöperation was

plete suffrage," which gave the name to the union organized.[1] A "People's Bill of Rights" was drawn up, including the six points of the Charter. The leaders were in general opposed to O'Connor and were regarded as "more respectable" by the rank and file of the Chartists.[2] Their failure in the attempt at conciliation is therefore easily comprehended.

The movement for widening the voting qualification was thus of too disunited a character to exercise strong pressure upon the House of Commons. Both of the ruling parties were avowedly determined to abide by the electoral settlement of 1832, and many politicians were disinclined even to render their legal rights to the nominal electors by reform of registration or the stringent prevention of bribery. Their determination was strengthened, for the moment at least, by the violent character which the Chartist movement assumed in 1848. Moreover, the reformers in parliament were themselves divided. DeLacy Evans believed in the increase of the constituency, but regarded the perfection of the registration system, rather than a change in the qualification, as the preliminary step. Cobden had perfect faith in the people and would risk universal suffrage. But Bright was opposed to any violent change and looked upon household suffrage as the final point of safety; in his eyes redistribution was the more crying necessity.[3] Some of the older Radicals were inclined not to push the question of alteration in the franchise until the opportunity of so doing should come up naturally.[4]

never instituted, Gammage, *History of the Chartist Movement*, 326, 332, 348.

[1] Gammage, *History of the Chartist Movement*, 241; Wallas, *Place*, 390.

[2] *Autobiography of Cooper*, 220, 228.

[3] Kent, *The English Radicals*, 381; 3 Hansard, xcviii, 1141.

[4] Place wrote to Hume, February 10, 1840: "There is at present

It resulted that the efforts made in the House of Commons before 1852 in the direction of lowering the voting qualifications of 1832, were spasmodic and supported only by a small minority; they were obviously directed not so much in the hope of success as with the object of inducing discussion. In 1839 an amendment to the address, which called for further reform of the franchise, was wittily assailed by Peel and extinguished by Russell.[1] In the same session Fleetwood asked leave for a bill providing for the introduction of the £10 qualification in counties; such a measure was not, he claimed, an alteration or even an extension of the reformed electoral system, but rather a logical coördination along the lines laid down in 1832. He looked to the Conservatives for support, hoping that the subservience of the £50 tenants would lead that party to expect still greater support from the small occupiers in counties. Peel, however, was satisfied with existing conditions in the counties, and rested on the finality of the Reform Act. Russell emphasized the necessity of giving effect to the existing franchises before attempting any alteration in the qualification.[2] Fleetwood's motion was lost by a large majority, as were the proposals of Crawford in 1843 and 1844, which included universal manhood suffrage.[3] A suggestion of the Marquis of Normanby that the electoral franchise be given to all persons paying the income tax, received slight attention, and even the pro-

no possibility of doing good to the working people or anybody else by any proposal for reform in Parliament. The working people are not in a condition to join in any scheme of the sort, nor will they be so for some time to come," Wallas, *Place*, 388.

[1] Parker, *Life of Peel*, ii, 382. The Whigs were rather upset at this time by the radical attitude of some of their friends, notably by the *Morning Chronicle*, which declared for further reform, Broughton, *Recollections*, v, 183.

[2] 3 Hansard, xlvii, 1347-1374.

[3] Fleetwood's motion was lost, 81-207; against that of Crawford there was a majority of 70 in a thin House. In 1844 an attempt was

posal of George Grey that the working classes might be allowed an annual assembly in which to draw up petitions and express grievances, was negatived without a division.[1]

A decided step in the direction of franchise reform was, however, taken in 1848. This is not to be discerned in the division list of the House of Commons, but rather in the altered attitude of Lord John Russell. After the failure of the element of force, as typified by Chartism, Hume brought forward a resolution to the effect that the existing discontent resulted from the fact that the population, property, and industry of the nation were not fairly represented; he therefore again advocated, with the ballot and equal electoral districts, a household franchise. In the long debate which followed he emphasized the exclusion of five-sixths of the male adults from the suffrage, the unevenness of the franchises, as well as their complexity. He was supported by Cobden, who claimed to voice middle class opinion, and bitterly opposed by O'Connor, who stigmatized household suffrage as the "nostrum of reform."

Russell opposed the suggested franchise as one which would exclude many adult males and was thus illogical, while he believed it would render the representative system dangerously democratic. But in his objection he made the momentous statement that the time for some reform was near, if not at hand. For the first time one of the leaders of the Liberal party thus departed from the doctrine of "finality," reiterated by them in the debates of 1831 and reaffirmed by Althorp, Stanley, and Russell in 1833. Admitting that the Reform Act was capable of improvement, Russell asked merely that the Commons

made to stop supplies until the franchise was amended, in which Bright, Cobden, Villiers, and Duncombe joined, 3 Hansard, xlvii, 1374; lxix, 529; lxxiii, 467; lxxiv, 1134.

[1] 3 Hansard, xlix, 993; lxxix, 934.

await less troublous times for the consideration of the kind
of reform that should appear most desirable.[1]

The effect of this change of attitude on the part of the
Liberal leader cannot be traced immediately. In 1849
and 1850 Hume was defeated by a large majority in his
attempt at bringing in a measure providing for a household qualification. Locke King also failed, though by a
narrower margin, to introduce a bill for the assimilation
of the county and borough qualification.[2] But at a
moment well chosen for combining disaffected Liberals in
1851, the latter reformer succeeded in gaining leave to
present a measure granting the electoral franchise to all
£10 occupiers in counties. The Liberal ministry who
opposed were put in a minority on the motion, and although the second reading of the bill was lost, a distinct
pledge was drawn from Russell that the government would
present a plan of franchise reform early in the following
session.[3]

With Russell's Reform Bill of 1852 a new period in the
development of the franchise began. During the twenty
years which followed the act of 1832, the leaders of both
the ruling parties had suppressed all efforts designed to
alter the qualifications. It was considered treachery
towards those who had collaborated in passing the great
act to harbour any suspicion of its inadequacy, at least
so far as the franchise was concerned. But after 1852 the
ministers themselves began to consider the possibilities of
change and extension; even the Conservatives ceded and
brought forward reform of their own. The quiet pressure from without, the reflex action of Chartism, the ad-

---

[1] 3 Hansard, xcix, 879-966; c, 156-229. And see Molesworth,
England, ii, 297-302, for an epitome of the debate. Hume's motion
was lost, 84-351.

[2] The votes on these motions were respectively, 83-268; 96-242;
100-159, 3 Hansard, cv, 1156; cix, 137-218; cxii, 1146-1184.

[3] 3 Hansard, cxiv, 850; cxv, 910, 940.

mission of Radicals to the cabinet, assisted the movement
in parliament. Delayed by foreign affairs, by the apathy
of some ministers, and the absolute dislike of others,
progress was slow;[1] but with the death of Palmerston in
1865 and even without the impetus of popular pressure
from the country at large, the question of franchise reform
again became the paramount issue.

Of the four bills that were brought in by ministries
from 1852 to 1860 and that proposed alteration in the
electoral qualifications, three were the handiwork of the
veteran reformer Russell.[2] The principle of alteration
was similar in each of the three. In the boroughs the
value of the property required to form the franchise was
to be reduced from £10 to £6. In the counties the franchise was to be given to all £10 occupiers.[3] An attempt

[1] The bill of 1852 was not pressed because of the change of
ministry, which took place in that year. That of 1854 might have
passed, according to Russell, had it not been for the Crimean war.
It was discussed amicably in the cabinet in 1853, notwithstanding
Palmerston's resignation, which was withdrawn. But in 1854,
although Aberdeen and Graham were averse to postponement,
Palmerston opposed its continuation, and Gladstone and Molesworth
wanted to give it up for the rest of the year; Russell himself
admitted that parliament as a whole was in favour of postponement.
Russell, *Recollections,* 272; Morley, *Gladstone,* i, 490, 648; Walpole,
Life of Russell, ii, 206. The bill of 1859 was generally opposed by
the Liberals and thrown out on the second reading. That of 1860
was defeated largely through the veiled hostility of Palmerston and
the popular indifference. Russell himself gave the appearance of
lack of earnestness; in 1854 he had been unable to conceal his
emotion when forced to give up the bill; in 1860 he hardly attempted
to conceal his indifference. On one occasion the House was within
an ace of being counted out during a debate on this bill. Greville
said that everybody was sick of the subject, 3 Hansard, clxxxviii,
2016, Walpole, *Life of Russell,* ii, 331; Greville, *Memoirs,* viii, 313.

[2] Those of 1852, 1854, and 1860. That of 1859 was introduced
by the Conservatives. Russell was certainly the active spirit behind
the Liberal measures, supported in 1854 by Aberdeen and Gladstone,
3 Hansard, clxxxii, 93; Morley, *Gladstone,* i, 490, 648.

[3] For the bill of 1852, see 3 Hansard, cxix, 252, 502; for that of

to vary the character of the borough electorate was made in the measure of 1854 by the introduction of what came to be called fancy franchises. An income of £10 from certain dividends, the payment of 40s. in direct taxes, deposits of three years' standing in a savings bank, as well as an academic degree from a university, might qualify the claimant. But the main principle of all three bills was the preservation of the old property franchise reduced in value.[1]

The Conservative measure of 1859, on the other hand, purposed to increase the town constituency, not by lowering the borough qualification, but through the operation of "fancy franchises" similar to those of the bill of 1854. The £10 borough franchise was retained, but persons who had funded property worth £10 yearly, £60 in the savings bank, or £20 pensions in the naval, military, or civil services, graduates of the universities, and members of the learned professions, were all to be qualified. The chief characteristic of this Conservative Reform Bill and the main source of increase in the prospective electorate was the extension of these qualifications, as well as the old £10 occupation franchise, to counties. The proposed reduction thus affected the county constituencies solely. The Con-

---

1854, *Ibid.,* cxxx, 491; cxxxi, 277; cxxxii, 836; for that of 1860, *Ibid.,* clvi, 2050; clvii, 839, 1030, 1793, 2141, Appendix; clviii, 137, 229, 336, 564, 1951; clix, 26, 225.

[1] Except in the bill of 1852 where a £20 tenant-at-will qualification was suggested; in 1860 the £10 qualification must include a residence or building of the annual value of £5. In 1852 the borough qualification was set at £5. Both in that year and in 1854 the value of the property was to be "rateable"; it is curious to note that Disraeli objected strongly to the rating test, because of the inequalities prevalent in different parishes, 3 Hansard, clii, 983. In 1860 Russell returned to the determination of the value of the qualification by taking the rental as the criterion, acknowledging the great variety in the proportions of a rating franchise to the true value of the tenement.

servatives were also minded to redress their old grievance of 1832 by excluding the town freeholders from county votes; according to this plan, freeholders were to vote in the place where they resided, or, if their qualifications were real property, in the place in which it was situated. Many freeholders would thus be transferred from the county to the borough registers.[1]

The main issue between Liberals and Conservatives in their alteration of the qualifications was thus the manner of increasing the borough electorate. The former held by the principle of determining electoral fitness by a single property qualification, but one demanding less property than had been required in 1832; their principle was what came to be called "vertical extension." The Conservatives, on the other hand, sought to vary the electorate by introducing new and different tests, and increase the constituency by means of "lateral extension." The chief complaint, indeed, made by Disraeli against the Liberal plan of reduction was that it would result in too homogeneous a class of voters. The weakness of the £10 electorate, he felt, was that it was a class electorate; the £6 constituency would have the same fault, with the danger of ultra-democratic tendencies superadded. In his opinion the counteraction of the class legislation which had existed since 1832 was not to be sought in transferring power to another class, but rather by securing a counterpoise in a variety of franchises.[2]

In response to the complaint that the working classes would be excluded unless the principle of vertical exten-

[1] For the bill of 1859, see 3 Hansard, cliii, 388, 531, 692, 825, 915, 1044, 1157, and Appendix.

[2] "What has been the object of our legislative labours for many years past but to put an end to a class legislation which was much complained of? But you are now proposing to establish a class legislation which may well be viewed with apprehension," 3 Hansard, clviii, 844.

sion was adopted, Stanley replied that the Conservatives wished to admit them to the suffrage, but desired that they should prove their fitness in each case. The test should be the possession of property of a recognized value or some special proof of frugality and worth. The question was whether "they should be admitted indiscriminately, the ignorant with the educated, the idle with the industrious, the man who spends as well as the man who saves."[1] The Conservatives thus advanced against the £6 franchise in boroughs objections similar to those which had arisen in 1831 to the £10 franchise; the predominating opinions of the resulting constituency would be identical. "It certainly would be most injudicious, not to say intolerable," said Disraeli, "when we are guarding ourselves against the predominance of a territorial aristocracy, that we should reform Parliament by securing the predominance of a household democracy."[2]

The Liberals, on the other hand, insisted that the time for lowering the qualification in boroughs had arrived. Even Palmerston admitted that while some property test was essential, that which existed already might be safely reduced. Russell pointed to the increased knowledge and capacity of the working classes and insisted that the £10 limit excluded far too large a number of capable and independent persons.[3] It was, in fact, on Russell's amendment, to the effect that the Conservative extension in boroughs was insufficient, that the bill of 1859 was thrown out.[4]

[1] 3 Hansard, cliii, 413. Stanley believed that the savings bank franchise, the £20 franchise, and £10 funded income franchise would provide for all worthy and frugal artisans.

[2] 3 Hansard, cliii, 388-482, 1231.

[3] 3 Hansard, cliii, 396, 877.

[4] 3 Hansard, cliii, 1257. Henley and Walpole, who seceded from the Conservative cabinet in 1859, chiefly because they disliked the assimilation of county and borough suffrage, both advocated warmly the reduction of the borough qualification, 3 Hansard, clii, 1058; cliii, 771, 1218; clxxxii, 1954.

On the question of the town freeholder, the issue between Conservatives and Liberals was clean cut as it had been in 1831. Russell complained that the alteration proposed by Disraeli allowing freeholders to vote in boroughs would subvert freeholder rights which had existed for centuries, and entirely alter the character of the county constituencies. Bright also argued against the exclusion of the town freeholder from the county register; the freeholder was the most independent of county electors, Bright asserted, and his removal would throw the counties still more into the hands of those who were most easily intimidated, and put them completely under the control of the landlords.[1] On the question of the county qualification both Liberals and Conservatives advocated a reduction, and, so far as the occupation franchise was concerned, to the same value. The Conservatives designed a counterpoise by the introduction of their fancy franchises. The assimilation of county and borough franchise proposed by Disraeli was distasteful to the Liberals and especially obnoxious to a section of the Conservative party itself.[2]

With the failure of Russell's attempt at reform in 1860, the movement for change in the electoral qualifications rested immobile for six years.[3] Probably at no time during the period which succeeded the act of 1832, had the

[1] 3 Hansard, cliii, 775.

[2] For a description of the bill brought in by Bright in 1858, see Molesworth, *History of England*, iii, 132. The franchise was to be given to all persons paying rates, and to £10 lodgers in boroughs, and to £10 occupiers in counties.

[3] In 1861 Baines obtained leave to introduce a bill for the reduction of the borough qualification and Locke King for that of the county; both bills were, however, speedily thrown out, 3 Hansard, clxi, 586, 655; clxii, 351. Similarly in 1864 and 1865 Baines introduced his so-called "single-barrelled" franchise bill, which was thrown out on the second reading in each session; these bills provided for the reduction of the borough franchise to £6, 3 Hansard, clxxv, 302-347; clxxvii, 559; clxxviii, 1372, 1613.

question of alteration in the electoral system been so completely submerged.[1] The preservation of peace, the reduction of taxation, the freedom given to the employment of capital, and most of all the enormous popularity of Palmerston, who was known to be satisfied with the status quo, all tended to postpone any mooting of new franchises. In the election address of Disraeli as well as in that of Palmerston, in 1865, no mention was made of electoral changes. Notwithstanding the efforts of Bright, who insisted that reform was the question of the hour and ought to be so treated, as well as the vague persiflage on the same subject which emanated from both Liberal and Conservative candidates, the issue in the electoral campaign of 1865 was at no time so much reform as confidence in Palmerston. His death, however, in the autumn of 1865 changed, not the attitude of the nation, but the policy of the government, and in the session of 1866 a new measure of reform was introduced by the Liberals.

In this measure voting qualifications in boroughs were to be reduced from £10 to £7; a higher property value

[1] "For the present, the question of Parliamentary Reform (using the phrase in its popular sense) is completely withdrawn from public discussion. No democratic eloquence, no pertinacity of popular agitation could make it just now an active influence," *Westminster Review*, lxxviii, 62. And in November, 1860, Gladstone wrote to Graham, "We live in unreforming times," Morley, *Gladstone*, ii, 37. Even after Palmerston's death, Gladstone told Denison that there was no strong feeling for reform among his constituents, *Grey Papers*, October 22, 1865, cited in Morley, *Gladstone*, ii, 198. Even the introduction of the bill of 1866 failed to rouse parliament from its indifference, and at the time of his resignation Russell confessed to the Queen the "general apathy of the South of England," Argyll, *Memoirs*, ii, 230; Walpole, *Life of Russell*, ii, 415. During the debates of 1866, *Punch* issued a cartoon representing John Bull, his wife, and his dog each endeavouring to read speeches on reform, and each dropping to sleep before the end of the sentence was reached.

was thus demanded than that required in Russell's bill of
1860. The principle of reduction rested not on any logical difference between a £6 and £7 qualification, but
rather on the prospective increase in the electorate. Gladstone, who was chiefly responsible for the bill, computed
that a £6 franchise would add two hundred and forty odd
thousand new electors, of whom all would be artisans.
The working classes, with the former electors of that
category and the compounders who would be enfranchised,
would thus be in a clear majority of the whole constituency.[1] Such was not the intention of the government,
although Gladstone refused to admit that the alteration
would be attended with any real danger. The number of
new borough voters which it was deemed advisable to
enfranchise was placed at about two hundred thousand.
The £7 qualification would admit approximately one hundred and forty-five thousand, while sixty thousand more
were to be qualified through a lodger franchise and by
means of alterations in the registration system.

The qualification which the Liberals proposed at the
same time for all persons occupying lodgings of the
annual value of £10 was not expected to enfranchise a
numerous constituency; such electors, moreover, would be
chiefly of the middle class, because the operation of claiming every year, as Gladstone foresaw, was bound to be

---

[1] Gladstone estimated that under a £6 franchise the artisans
would be represented thus:

242,000 new artisan voters.
 60,000 artisan compounders.
126,000 old artisan voters.
_____
428,000 artisan voters.

Total,

The estimate of the borough constituency as increased was put at
816,000, 3 Hansard, clxxxii, 52. See also *Parliamentary Papers,*
1866, no. 170.

extremely burdensome to the working classes.[1] But a suggested reform in registration requirements was expected to bring a large number of new electors on the lists and meet the complaints prevalent since 1832, that many persons actually possessed of a sufficient property qualification were excluded from the franchise. Gladstone proposed to follow the oft-refused suggestion of Duncombe and abolish the rate-paying clauses entirely. As we have seen, many persons were disfranchised, either because they failed to pay their rates in time, or because the rates were paid for them by the landlord.[2] According to his bill, all qualified occupiers might be registered, even though they had not themselves paid rates. The names of all occupiers whose rates were compounded for, should be placed in the rate-book and thence transferred to the preliminary electoral lists. Gladstone computed that, besides the electors qualified by the £7 franchise, this alteration in registration requirements together with the lodger qualification would enfranchise some sixty thousand new electors.[3]

The government also planned to grant the suffrage to depositors in savings banks. The Liberals argued that the possession of £50 thriftily saved furnished as good a qualification as land, and was also without complications. There were some eighty-seven thousand of such depositors in England and Wales; but many of them would have other qualifications and the bother of making the required

[1] 3 Hansard, clxxxii, 48.

[2] For a discussion of this point, see Homersham Cox, *The Reform Bills of 1866 and 1867*, 32-35. Tinged with a strong Liberal bias, a mass of valuable information has here been collected.

[3] See *supra*, Chap. VI. Without such alteration in the law of registration the reduction of the qualification from £10 to £7 would have had small effect, since most of the rates of the £7 occupiers were paid by the landlords, *Parliamentary Papers*, 1867-1868, no. 11.

annual claim would cut down the number.[1] The savings bank franchise was designed to operate in counties as well as in boroughs, as was the lodger qualification as well. The £50 tenant qualification in counties was to be reduced to £14, greater caution being displayed in 1866 than Russell had shown in 1860 when he proposed a £10 tenant franchise. Moreover, the rights of copyholders and lease-holders in represented towns were assimilated to those of freeholders; henceforth they might vote in counties pro-vided they could not be registered for their property in the borough where it was situated.[2]

The net result of Gladstone's enfranchisement would probably have been to increase the total constituency by about four hundred thousand electors. The proportion-ate increase would thus have been about forty per cent, and would have affected the county electorate to a slightly less extent than it would that of the boroughs. In the latter the new voters would have been composed almost entirely of the working classes; two-thirds would have been formed by the £7 householders and the remainder those enfranchised by the abolition of the rate-paying clauses and by the lodger and savings bank qualifications. In counties the £14 tenants, whose number was estimated at about one hundred and seventy thousand, would not, strictly speaking, belong to the working classes. As a result the proportion of artisans in the total prospective electorate would be increased from an eighth to slightly

---

[1] 3 Hansard, clxxxii, 32.

[2] The act of 1832 had allowed the freeholder to vote in counties provided that he could not be registered himself in the borough on the qualification in question (*supra*, Chap. II). But the leaseholder or copyholder in the represented borough was excluded from the county list if his property conferred on him or on anyone else a borough qualification. The effect of Gladstone's proposal would have been to increase the number of plural voters.

less than a quarter.[1] The Liberal measure of 1866 thus provided, even on paper, for a smaller proportionate increase of the electorate than did the act of 1832 in fact; and it would have still left the middle class in the majority even in the boroughs.

Notwithstanding the comparative slightness of the proposed alteration the new qualifications were bitterly assailed, not only by the Conservatives but by a section of the Liberals themselves. It was, indeed, the strenuous opposition of some forty of the latter, termed by Bright the "Adullamites," who generally acted under the brilliant leadership of Robert Lowe, that determined the failure of the government measure.[2] According to the Liberal leader in the Commons, Lowe was so superstitiously enamoured of the old £10 franchise that he was thrown into a temper of general hostility to the government which did not recognize its finality and sagacity. Following the example of the Tories of 1831 he refused absolutely to admit the necessity of any reform, and could not see "why the con-

---

[1]

Borough electorate, 1865,	514,000	New electors (£7), .	144,000
		Compounders, etc., .	60,000
County electorate, 1865,	542,000	New county electors,	172,000
		Depositors, lodgers, etc.,	24,000
Total electorate, 1865,	1,056,000	Total new electorate,	400,000

Total prospective electorate, . 1,456,000
Of these, artisan voters enfranchised, . . 200,000
Of these, artisan voters already on lists, . 126,000
Total number of prospective artisan electors, 326,000

The working classes would thus have formed 40 per cent of the borough electorate and about 23 per cent of the total electorate, *Parliamentary Papers,* 1866, nos. 3626, 170, 335.

[2] Gladstone wrote later that Lowe "really supplied the whole brains of the opposition. So effective were his speeches that during this year, and this year only, he had such a command of the House as has never in my recollection been surpassed," Morley, *Gladstone,* ii, 201.

stitution which we have lived so long under, might not be left to us for a little longer."[1]

Lowe's objections to the proposed alteration in the franchise were also based on an outspoken distrust of the new borough electors. He, with others, complained that the bill proposed to reincarnate under a different guise the potwallers with their corruption and the freemen who had been disfranchised for bribery.[2] According to him, the suffrage was about to be granted to the class which had invariably shown itself least capable of worthy response to its responsibilities. "If you want venality, ignorance, drunkenness," said he in an outburst which became notorious, "if you want impulsive, unreflecting, and violent people, where do you look for them in the constituencies? Do you go to the top or the bottom? . . . The effect [of the reduction in the franchise] will manifestly be to add a large number of persons to our constituency of the class from which, if there is to be anything wrong going on, we may naturally expect to find it."[3]

Another of the "Cave of Adullam," Horsman, supported by Lowe and the Tories, insisted that the principle of vertical extension of the franchise was based on that of government by numbers, which had always been anathema to Whigs as well as to Tories; there could be no final resting place at £7, no settlement until the logical limit

[1] 3 Hansard, clxxxii, 144. Lowe considered that, because of the rise in wages as well as in rental values, all the workmen worthy of the vote had already secured it under the existing qualification; in this he was supported by Grosvenor, who asserted a "silent change" which had been working to transform the character of the constituencies in favour of the artisans, *Ibid.*, clxxxii, 146, 1160. Lowe also argued that it was unnecessary to disturb the constitution in order to reward the working classes for their good behaviour: "You should not argue the reform question as if the franchise were a boon, of which you should make equal distribution," *Ibid.*, 154.

[2] 3 Hansard, clxxxii, 1208, 1316.

[3] 3 Hansard, clxxxii, 147.

of household or manhood suffrage was reached. The arguments for Gladstone's £7 franchise, like those for Bright's household suffrage, were good for nothing at all, or they were good for universal suffrage.[1] The old Tory objection to the homogeneous character of the electorate was revived; a £7 qualification, they said, was a blind and indiscriminate test, a brick and mortar franchise. Bulwer-Lytton even proposed to remedy this defect by introducing different franchises for different boroughs, according as their characteristics differed.[2] Others objected that the capacity of the working classes for the suffrage was not germane to the discussion; the right of vote was, and always must be, based upon property; the theory of fitness would necessarily lead to a social and political revolution.[3]

The Liberal arguments in favour of the proposed borough franchise rested chiefly on the advisability of increase in the electorate and on the character of the class they proposed to admit. Gladstone showed that in the constituencies of municipal boroughs the artisans had long been in the majority with no resulting antagonism of class or danger to property. Moreover the persons who would be qualified by the £7 franchise were the cream of the artisan class; such a qualification indicated a far larger income than that possessed by the peasant or the poor day-labourer.[4] Mill emphasized the fact that in many

[1] 3 Hansard, clxxxii, 1810, 1844, 2092.

[2] 3 Hansard, clxxxii, 1241, 1790.

[3] 3 Hansard, clxxxii, 1932. As in 1832 the Tories quoted the Bible against the reform of the franchise. They also brought up the point (the reverse of that of 1832 when they feared the abolition of the corn laws), that all democracies were protectionist and the "fair jewel of free-trade" would be lost, *Ibid.*, 1934, 2106. Disraeli was in general rather vague, but confessed that he considered the addition of 400,000 new voters likely to "Americanize" the constitution and produce calamities and disasters, *Ibid.*, clxxxiii, 111.

[4] 3 Hansard, clxxxii, 52, 1136. Gladstone's warmth in defence of the artisans often lured him into exordiums which drew forth the

boroughs a large proportion of the £10 electors belonged to the working classes and yet their electoral conduct had been so impeccable that no one had suspected their identity.　Moreover, under the proposed franchises, the diffusion of artisan electors among the various constituencies would render them practically unable to choose their own representatives except in rare cases, and under exceptionably favourable circumstances.[1]

Attempts, direct and indirect, were made in the hope of attenuating the suggested reduction of the qualifications, or of forcing the government to throw up their measure. Walpole, who had resigned in 1859 because of the assimilation of county and borough franchise that was proposed in the Conservative bill of that year, now fought the approximate assimilation which would result from a £14 qualification in counties.　In offering an amendment which would have raised the county franchise to £20, he based his arguments, as before, on the necessity of maintaining a wide distinction between the county and borough constituencies.[2]　Disraeli supported his former colleague, notwith-

---

sneers of his vexed and amused opponents. "Do not regard the workmen as you would the forces of an invading army," he said, "are they not our fellow-Christians, our own flesh and blood?" *Ibid.*, clxxxii, 873. Gladstone's assumption that his plans were under the special patronage of God always irritated the Tories and sometimes the Radicals. Labouchere is said to have remarked: "I don't object to his playing with three cards up his sleeve, but I do object to his saying that God Almighty put them there." Gladstone's casuistic skill in drawing the conclusions he desired from different premises was illustrated by the fact that in 1864, before electoral statistics were secured, he estimated the proportion of artisan voters in boroughs at 7 per cent and argued that therefore the franchise should be extended. When in 1866 it was discovered that 26 per cent of the electorate were artisans, he argued that the fact that there were so many of them and they had been so well behaved was good reason for giving the franchise to more.

1 3 Hansard, clxxxii, 1256.
2 3 Hansard, clxxxiii, 2077.

standing the fact that this point had been the occasion of their earlier separation, and although he had himself urged a still lower franchise for counties. His reasons were diametrically opposed to those of Walpole, inasmuch as he contended that the chief condition of a £10 franchise in counties was that the borough qualification should not be less than £10.[1] Walpole's amendment was lost.[2]

Indirect attempts were also made to raise the qualification in both counties and boroughs, and it was the success of one of these attempts that led to the resignation of the Liberal government. In determining the value of the qualification Gladstone had followed the example of the Whigs in 1832 and of Disraeli in 1859 by making use of the gross estimated rental of the property. This rental was entered in the rate-book, and, according to the Liberals, provided a far more certain criterion than the rateable value of the property.[3] The deductions made for the purpose of establishing a rate varied widely in different constituencies, and depended largely upon local usage, so that the test of a rateable value must necessarily have been uneven. It was such variation from constituency to constituency, and even from street to street in the same borough, as well as the fact that the rental represented more nearly the capacity of the tenant, that induced the government to discard their original plan of a rating test and employ that which had always been in use.[4]

[1] 3 Hansard, clxxxiii, 2116.

[2] 283-297, 3 Hansard, clxxxiii, 2126.

[3] The gross estimated rental is "the rent at which the hereditaments might reasonably be expected to let from year to year, free from all the usual tenants' rates and taxes and tithe commutation rent charge, if any," 25 & 26 Vict., c. 103. Rateable value is computed from gross estimated rental by making various deductions. In some parishes the rateable value was taken at 10 per cent less than the estimated rental, while in others the deduction amounted to 35 per cent, Cox, *Reform Bills of 1866 and 1867*, 70.

[4] 3 Hansard, clxxxiv, 190.

The opponents of the bill, however, saw in this matter an opportunity of harassing the government and possibly of forcing them to drop their measure. They argued that since the rate-book was the basis of the register it was natural to make use of the rateable value of the property as the standard. Such a change in the criterion of property value as was implied by the proposal for a rating franchise, would have obviously raised the qualification of voters, for property rated at £7, possessed in general an £8 rental value or even more. As Gladstone clearly demonstrated, it would also render the franchise extremely uneven.[1] It was the defeat of the government on this point that proved the occasion of their resignation. A motion made by Ward Hunt that the value of the property in the counties should be determined by the rate and not by the estimated rental, was defeated. But a similar amendment of Lord Dunkellin providing for a rating franchise in boroughs was carried against the government by a majority of eleven. The issue in itself was narrow and the ministers had not intended to treat it as a vital question. But the debate of the evening covered the whole range of the bill, and the prospect of adjusting the rateable value to the figure of rental proposed, as well as seeing the whole plan through committee, appeared so difficult that after a week's deliberation the cabinet resigned.[2]

[1] Disraeli supported the amendments, although he had proposed the test of rental value in 1859, discarding rating for the same reasons as those advanced by the Liberals in 1866. But he claimed that since 1859 there had been a marked advance towards effecting an equalization of rating throughout the different parishes, 3 Hansard, clxxxiv, 197.

[2] Apparently many of the members were confused by the use of the abbreviated terms "rental" and "rateable," and assumed that Gladstone did not propose to use the rate-book as the basis of registration. Morley and Walpole in their biographies of the Liberal leaders assert that the amendment of Dunkellin was not in itself

The failure of the bill of 1866 opened the way for a new and ultimately more radical plan of franchise reform. The working classes, which before 1866 had displayed little desire or enthusiasm for the suffrage, speedily manifested their unwillingness to see it snatched from them, when once proposed. The new Conservative ministry, led by Derby, were forced not merely to bring in a measure of their own, but to make it finally of a far more complete character. The plan was Disraeli's and, as his chief opponent prophesied, was tortuous and complex.[1] Failing to secure the adhesion of the House to his first scheme of proceeding by resolution, the Chancellor of the Exchequer submitted to a Conservative meeting two plans: one embodied the principle of household suffrage in boroughs, counterpoised by a double vote granted to the upper classes, and various other safeguards; the other, a £6 franchise based on rateable value. The general sense of the Conservative party inclined to the latter. But its tentative introduction in the House was greeted so unfavourably that it became clear that a £6 rating franchise would be acceptable to neither side. Accordingly it was speedily replaced by a measure which from its face

important and that it would have been easy to arrange a rating franchise which would have corresponded to the £7 rental franchise, Morley, *Gladstone,* ii, 207; Walpole, *Life of Russell,* ii, 413. Gladstone himself, however, showed the impossibility of arranging a rating value which would have expressed faithfully the scale of enfranchisement desired, 3 Hansard, clxxxiv, 686. His arguments were borne out by the electoral returns which showed the extreme variation in rating as compared to rental values. The degree of enfranchisement would have depended upon the local custom; and even the total enfranchisement would have been difficult to arrange. A £5 ratal would have enfranchised 86,000 more than a £7 rental, while a £6 ratal would have enfranchised 25,000 less, *Parliamentary Papers,* 1866, no. 170. Russell, it is true, proposed to rehabilitate the clause, but seven of the cabinet disapproved of the attempt, Morley, *Gladstone,* ii, 209.

[1] Gladstone to Brand, October 30, 1866, Morley, *Gladstone,* ii, 223.

value would result in a far wider extension of the franchise.[1]

This measure of reform in the qualifications, which for the moment threatened to break up the ministry,[2] had the popular recommendation of the phrase "household suffrage." As Gladstone admitted, once that phrase had been advertised by the government as its battle-ground, its force was irresistible.[3] According to Disraeli's plan, any man who had occupied a dwelling house for two years, and had been rated to the relief of the poor, and had paid his rates, was to be enfranchised in the boroughs. Those who paid 20s. in direct taxes annually were also to be qualified, and if householders as well, were to enjoy a double vote. The "fancy franchises" of 1859, a university degree, membership in a learned profession, £50 in the savings bank or funds, were also proposed.

Apparently the new borough franchise was the whole-hearted surrender of progressive Toryism to the demands of the Radicals. Disraeli announced that it would bring on the register a million voters. Such an estimate, however, disregards the operation of all those electoral conditions which had greatly hindered enfranchisement after 1832. Of these, one of the most important was that connected with rate-paying clauses, which Disraeli retained and which Gladstone had discarded in the measure of the previous year. It would even appear probable that had the Conservative bill been enacted without amendment, the increase in the electorate would hardly have been greater than that promised by the bill of 1866; the electoral power

[1] Explanation of the Earl of Derby in the House of Lords, 3 Hansard, clxxxv, 1283. See also *Daily Telegraph*, February 26, 1867.

[2] Carnarvon, Peel, and Cranbourne resigned.

[3] "The government bowled us over by the force of the phrase," Morley, *Gladstone*, ii, 225.

of the upper classes on the other hand would have been enormously strengthened.[1]

Disraeli stated that there were two hundred and thirty-seven thousand rated householders as yet unenfranchised, who would all be immediately qualified by his measure.[2] Of these, however, he failed to take into account those who were exempted from paying their rates on account of poverty, who defaulted, or who were disqualified because of the receipt of parochial relief.[3] Through the extension of the period of required residence from one to two years a large number of the poorer classes, who were essentially migratory in their habits, would fail to be registered. From the number of prospective voters must also be deducted the fifteen thousand freemen who were already registered, as well as the occupiers of buildings, such as shops and other tenements which were not dwelling houses. Disraeli later admitted that of the householders who paid their own rates about fifty per cent should be deducted from his first estimate.[4]

For the large number of compound householders who did not pay their own rates, no provision whatever was made in the bill of 1867 as first proposed. Disraeli vaguely promised certain facilities for the insertion of their names on the rate-book, and for the payment of their

[1] See Cox, *Reform Bills of 1866 and 1867*, 108, for a lengthy discussion of the probable effects of the original plan of Disraeli.

[2] There were 245,000 occupiers of tenements under £10 value whose rates were not compounded by the landlords, and 486,000 whose rates were compounded, *Parliamentary Papers,* 1867, no. 136; 3 Hansard, clxxxvi, 13.

[3] On January 1, 1867, 963,000 persons were in receipt of poor relief. Doubtless as many more were assisted during the course of the year. Thus 10 per cent of the population was aided by the parish, and this proportion would be larger amongst the occupiers below the £10 line, "Poor Law Report, 1867-1868," cited by Cox, *Reform Bills of 1866 and 1867,* 109.

[4] 3 Hansard, clxxxvi, 661.

rates. But the failure of Sir William Clay's act had shown that even when the occupier was allowed to pay the compounded rate, few availed themselves.[1] The bill of 1867 offered even less inducement for registration inasmuch as it demanded that the occupier of a tenement under £10 in value should pay the full rate. Of the persons who would be qualified under the "fancy franchises," the greater part were already qualified householders; the depositors in savings banks, university graduates, and the majority of professional men almost invariably lived in houses above £10 in yearly value.[2] Altogether the new voters in boroughs could hardly have exceeded two hundred and forty-five thousand.[3]

On the other hand, the dual vote must have increased enormously the electoral power of the wealthier classes.

[1] *Supra*, Chap. VI.

[2] In 1866 the savings bank depositors, lodgers, and copy- and leaseholders had been estimated at 24,000. The fancy franchises would hardly have enfranchised more.

[3]
Rated householders,	120,000
Compound householders,	100,000
Fancy franchises,	25,000
	245,000

This estimate errs possibly as being too large. Cox, *Reform Bills of 1866 and 1867*, estimates that the addition in boroughs would not have exceeded 144,000. He does not, however, admit the enfranchisement of any compound householders. The proportion of compounders enfranchised before 1867 was about one in four, *Parliamentary Papers*, 1867, no. 305. But the facilities offered to the occupiers below the £10 line were not so favourable, and two years' residence was required; the poorer occupiers were less apt to have the time for making claim. The estimate of rather less than one in four, therefore, seems generous. The county franchise originally proposed by Disraeli would not have enfranchised more than 180,000, *Parliamentary Papers*, 1866, no. 3626, "Electoral Returns, 1865-1866," 286. The total increase in the electorate in all probability would not have surpassed 400,000. "The aggregate result," Gladstone wrote later, "would be ludicrously small as a measure of enfranchisement," Morley, *Gladstone*, ii, 224.

It is impossible to state how many new votes would have been created by the fundholder, academical and professional franchises.[1] But it was assumed by Disraeli with apparent justice that the persons to be qualified by the payment of 20s. in direct taxes would correspond in number to the £20 householders. There were in 1861 at least two hundred and sixty thousand of them in England and Wales.[2] As they would have a vote for the occupation of the house and another for the payment of the direct tax, the electoral strength of the upper and the upper middle classes in boroughs would have been doubled.[3] Thus at the moment when the working classes were receiving votes through the operation of the limited household suffrage, their new electoral power would be counterbalanced by the votes granted to the classes above the £20 line. The balance of class which existed in the electoral body before 1867 would hardly have been disturbed, or would indeed have turned in favour of the upper middle class.[4]

Thus Disraeli, with all the popular force of the slogan

[1] No statistics were presented to the House of Commons.

[2] *Parliamentary Papers*, 1861, no. 90.

[3] Doubtless many of those thus qualified would not have been registered because of non-residence or through carelessness; but as the number of those paying 20s. in direct taxes had increased since 1861 (Disraeli believed by 23 per cent), the number of prospective dual voters could not have been far from 250,000. There were in 1866, 340,000 occupiers at a rental of £20 or above, *Parliamentary Papers*, 1866, no. 494. Making the average deduction for those not registering there were 245,000 voters above the £20 line.

[4] According to the above calculation the voters before 1867 above and below the £20 line were almost equal in numbers; assuming that all of the 225,000 new voters in boroughs were below the line, the prospective constituency would have about 435,000 votes representing tenements of less than £20, while with the dual vote there would be 490,000 votes of persons above the £20 line. The upper and upper middle classes instead of a majority of 35,000 would have one of 55,000, *Parliamentary Papers*, 1866, nos. 494, 3626. Cox (*Reform Bills of 1866 and 1867*, 119) believed that the proportion of upper class votes would have been still larger.

"household suffrage" behind his bill, planned by means of the rate-paying requirements and the dual vote to preserve the status quo. The Liberals both in and out of parliament were, however, determined that if household suffrage were to be introduced into boroughs, it should be made effective and the reality of the bill should be brought into correspondence with its great professions.[1] Accepting the principle of the measure and signifying his willingness to vote for its second reading, Gladstone enumerated certain vital defects in the proposed borough franchise which must be remedied in committee. The most important of these were the capricious and irregular operation of the franchise, which would result from the variation in the custom of ratepaying, the disqualification of compound householders, the omission of a lodger franchise, and the dual vote.[2]

The Liberals argued with keenness and much justice that in boroughs where the rates were compounded, the increase in the electorate would be insignificant, whereas in those where the system of composition was not in force, the result would be almost residential manhood suffrage. The local vestry, by accepting or discarding the compounding system, might thus determine absolutely the extent of the enfranchisement. In boroughs like Carlisle, where the rates were compounded and the occupiers did not pay their own rates, there would be only four hundred persons qualified as occupiers, while thirty-five hundred householding occupiers would be excluded; in Chippenham twenty would be qualified and seven hundred excluded; in Hull sixty-four would be qualified and twelve thousand excluded. On the other hand, in Sheffield, where the rates were not compounded and the occupiers did pay their own rates, some twenty-eight thousand persons would be quali-

1 Morley, *Gladstone,* ii, 224-225.
2 3 Hansard, clxxxvi, 39, 475-504.

fied; Stoke-upon-Trent would gain fifteen thousand voters; and the electorate of Oldham would increase from three to fourteen thousand. In Thetford, where the compounding acts were not in force, the proportion of electors to population would be one in five; the same proportion throughout England would give a constituency of four millions. The bill would thus create, according to the Liberals, "an extravagant franchise, flooding some towns with thousands of voters and only adding a few in others."[1]

The bill, as introduced, provided practically for a £6 rating franchise in the fifty-eight boroughs where the Small Tenements Act was in operation; for in those places the landlords of houses under £6 rateable value were entered on the rate-books to the exclusion of the tenants. The same effect would have resulted partially in ninety-eight other boroughs which were in part under the compounding act; even in many where the rates were not compounded they were paid by the landlord, and this practice would have proved an effectual bar to true household suffrage. Obviously, if the restriction imposed on the suggested franchise were removed, by enabling tenants whose rates were compounded to bring their names on the rate-book, the constituency would be enormously extended. Lowe perceived this when he said: "The bill has a double aspect and that is the mischief of it. If looked at by the

---

[1] Similarly in Kidderminster, where composition was in force, the proportion of householders enfranchised would be less than one in a thousand of population; in Gateshead, one in 250; while in York it would be one in 10, and in Thirsk, one in 8. In the 171 boroughs where the system of composition was entirely or partly in force, the rate of enfranchisement would have been 8 in a thousand; in the 29 boroughs where there was no composition the proportion would have been 53 in a thousand. The operation of enfranchisement would thus have been more than six times as great in the aggregate in the boroughs where there was no composition, *Parliamentary Papers*, 1866, no. 3626; Cox, *Reform Bills of 1866 and 1867*, 130-131, 137-138.

light of what it will immediately effect, it is not a large measure of enfranchisement, or even one that a timid man might fear. But if we look on it in its potentiality, keeping in view that to which it may lead, it is a measure of the very largest nature."

Not only did the Liberals object to the irregularity of enfranchisement which would result; they also disliked the invidious distinction made between compound householders of the £10 class claiming under Sir William Clay's act, and those now to be given the opportunity of claiming under the act of 1867. The latter were to be required to pay the full rate, while the former need pay only the reduced rate or composition. As the allowance made in composition varied from twenty-five to fifty per cent, the additional financial burden thus thrown on the poorer occupiers was not inconsiderable. According to Gladstone, the compound householder who desired the vote would thus be fined a half or a quarter of the rate, that being the difference between the reduced compound rate and the full rate which he would pay if individually rated.[1] The Liberals also bitterly attacked the residential distinction between the old and the new voters. Occupation was required for but one year only of the £10 householders as a condition precedent to registration; while of the householders of less than £10, two years' residence was to be demanded.[2]

The Conservatives, in the earlier discussions at least, defended both the irregularity of the franchise which resulted from the differences in payment of rates, and the so-called fine imposed upon the claiming compounder. Disraeli asserted that anomalies were the characteristic of the constitution, and that by means of the variations in the local rating acts, exactly that varied representation

[1] 3 Hansard, clxxxvi, 33.
[2] 3 Hansard, clxxxvi, 479.

would be secured, the loss of which had been so deplored. "I always thought," said he, "that what we have been complaining of for years was the dreary monotony of the settlement of 1832, and the too identical character of the constituencies under that act."[1] The Conservatives also insisted that it was only fair that the compounder should pay the full instead of the reduced rate. Karslake, the Solicitor General, contended that it was reasonable to exempt the landlord, who by offering to save the state the bother of collection, had earned the reduction; the occupier, however, performed no such obligation, and when he received the privilege of the suffrage he ought to pay as though he were individually rated. Curiously enough the Conservatives were supported in this discussion by Roebuck, who had so often and so bitterly assailed the rate-paying clauses.[2]

In committee, however, the government was forced to adopt a more conciliatory attitude towards the criticisms directed against the uneven restrictions on the borough franchise. It could hardly be denied that there was a real and effectual hindrance to the enfranchisement of the compound occupiers, not only under the existing system of registration for £10 voters but also under that proposed by Disraeli for householders. The failure of Sir William Clay's act showed that when the name of the occupier was not on the rate-book he would not, except in rare cases, take the trouble to send in his claim. For this Gladstone had brought in a remedy to the effect that the franchise should be made dependent not upon the rating but upon the value of the tenement. No such provision, however, was made by Disraeli in his bills. To facilitate the regis-

---

[1] "We were told again and again that what the country languished for was the variety of franchise they were deprived of by the act of 1832," 3 Hansard, clxxxvi, 659.

[2] 3 Hansard, clxxxvi, 543.

tration of compounders Gladstone brought forward another suggestion: lét a line be fixed for the qualification, at and above which all occupiers should be entered on the rate-book, and have equal facilities for the enjoyment of the suffrage.[1] His suggestion would have rendered uniform the practice of composition for all tenements below the value fixed, and would have provided automatically for the registration of all occupiers of tenements of higher value. Gladstone also gave notice of an amendment providing that the qualifying premises must be of the yearly rateable value of £5 or upwards, but that the claimant might be registered whether he himself or his landlord paid the rate.[2]

Neither of these attempts to fix a line of value for the qualification succeeded. The Radicals disliked the test of value, believing that it would be possible to alter the law of rating so that the household franchise could be made really democratic. In reference to the plan for setting a hard and fast value at which occupiers' names should be entered on the rate-book, Montague Chambers said: "There is something very equivocal to true reformers in this. They think it restrictive." Locke thought it would lessen the number of persons placed on the register, and the hostility of the "tea-room section" of the Liberals to this plan determined Gladstone not to push it.[3] The Conservatives also opposed the suggestion of a £5 franchise without the requirement of the personal payment of rates; they objected generally to the test of value and insisted that the payment of rates by the occupier and not the landlord should be the primary test of a qualification.[4] Radicals,

[1] *Daily Telegraph,* April 6, 1867.
[2] 3 Hansard, clxxxvi, 1338.
[3] *Daily Telegraph,* April 9, 1867.
[4] 3 Hansard, clxxxvi, 1865. As a matter of fact the courts had decided with regard to the £10 franchise that payment of rates by the landlord was to be considered as payment by the occupier, and

"'Tea-roomers," and "Adullamites" voted against the Liberals and the amendment was lost.[1]

Notwithstanding this success of the government in requiring the payment of rates by the occupier and in preventing the test of value, Disraeli was gradually forced to make concessions which tended towards a more democratic measure. He had announced, even before the committee stage, a series of clauses which he believed would greatly facilitate the registration of compound householders.[2] A more vital concession was made in committee to the demands of Gladstone that the compounder under the £10 line should not be fined by the payment of the full rate. An amendment, which it was alleged had been secretly encouraged by Disraeli, was made providing that all occupiers need pay only the reduced rate.[3] To this the government at first denied their approval and the suggestion was vetoed. But almost immediately they acknowledged that the Liberal complaint was just, and might be rectified by allowing the occupier to deduct the full rate, when paid, from his rent.[4] Notwithstanding opposition

was effectual for the purposes of registration, "Cook v. Luckett," 1846, Lutwyche, *Registration Cases,* i, 432.

[1] 289-310. There were 12 Radicals, 8 "Tea-roomers," and 25 "Adullamites" who voted with the government. The vote of the first named was due to their hope of removing restrictions and converting the franchise into one of pure democracy.

[2] The name of the occupier and the rateable value of his tenement were to be entered in the rate-book; every occupier was to send in his claim by post; the overseer in return was to state the amount due, and on payment being made was to enter the name of the occupier as being liable to the rate, 3 Hansard, clxxxvi, 1105. Two years or even three months before, such suggestions would have been accepted as generous.

[3] 3 Hansard, clxxxvii, 12; *Times,* April 13, 1867.

[4] Disraeli said, "It would be disingenuous in me not to acknowledge that this point at an earlier period of the session was placed before the House by the right honourable gentleman [Gladstone] . . . with great powers of argument and illustration . . . I am bound to

based on the argument that the result would be a general rise in rentals,[1] the amendment was carried by the largest majority yet secured by the Conservatives.[2]

This concession was, however, a mere palliative compared to the drastic remedy accepted a week later by the government, with the object of removing the uneven restrictions which would throttle the franchise of the compound householder. Gladstone had sought to establish uniformity in 1866 by requiring the overseers to place the names of compound householders on the electoral lists. An equally simple, but more effective, remedy was now proposed by Hodgkinson, a comparatively obscure member. He suggested that the obvious means for avoiding irregularities in the custom of rate-paying was to insist that the occupier and not the owner should be rated in parliamentary boroughs. In other words he dealt with the occupiers who were disfranchised because their landlord paid their rates, by "annihilating them altogether as compound householders and reviving them in their original character as ordinary ratepayers." In answer to the objection that the collection of rates would be impossible without the facility rendered by composition, he pointed out that in large towns such as Manchester, Stockport, and Oldham the system of composition was not in force and yet the rates were collected without undue difficulty.[3]

To the surprise both of Liberals and of Conservatives, Disraeli showed himself willing to accept this solution.

say that subsequent researches, and the more enlarged information we now possess, justify the conclusion," 3 Hansard, clxxxvii, 18.

[1] Made by Hibbert who had failed to carry the previous amendment that the occupier might claim on payment of the reduced rate, 3 Hansard, clxxxvii, 271.

[2] 322-256, 3 Hansard, clxxxvii, 357. The amendment was retroactive in its operation; it provided for the abolition of the right of £10 occupiers of registering on payment of the reduced rate.

[3] 3 Hansard, clxxxvii, 710.

The supporters of government who had accepted household suffrage on the faith of the limitations imposed by personal payment of the rates, found themselves suddenly committed to a measure virtually far larger than any that Bright himself had sought to impose.[1] The Chancellor of the Exchequer even went so far as to say, "It is the policy of their [Her Majesty's government] own measure, which if they had been masters of the situation, they would have recommended long ago for the adoption of the House."[2] And later at a public dinner Disraeli claimed that the abolition of the compounder was his original solution; impossible at first, as the session went on it became feasible with the education of the party; "the compounder giving up his peculiar position and paying rates for the exercise of the suffrage was the triumph of the principle of the bill."[3] Gladstone accepted the solution ungraciously, regretting the interference with the rating system, but admitting that it provided for a liberal and equal extension of the franchise, instead of what promised to be limited, unequal, equivocal, and dangerous: "I have depre-

[1] It would appear that on the day when the amendment was to be brought forward the supporters of the government were under the impression that it was to be resisted, 3 Hansard, clxxxvii, 184. Gladstone states that he never underwent a stranger emotion of surprise than when, as he entered the House, he learned that Disraeli would support the motion, Morley, *Gladstone*, ii, 226. He also states that the cabinet themselves were not aware of Disraeli's intention, and only knew the probable results from the statistician Lambert afterwards.

[2] 3 Hansard, clxxxvii, 724. On the second reading and only ten days before accepting the amendment, Disraeli had condemned the abrogation of the rating acts, *Ibid.*, clxxxvi, 649; clxxxvii, 354.

[3] *Times*, October 30, 1867. Disraeli, however, attempted to neutralize the effect of the amendment, by proposing that the continuance of the system of composition should be optional. Obviously this would have given to the landlords the power of dictation to their tenants and practically the right to say whether they should or should not be enfranchised; the suggestion was refused.

cated it all along and have assented to it as I would assent
to cut off my leg rather than to lose my life, on the principle of choosing the lesser evil."[1] Lowe, whose bitterness
was unrestrained, did not hesitate to dub the alteration a
Conservative attempt to win the support of Demos.[2]

The vital change was adopted without a division and
without disturbance, as though it had been an affair of
the most trivial importance. By it, however, the bill was
altered so radically as to enfranchise about three times as
many borough electors as were promised by the original
measure. Of the five hundred and seventy thousand compound householders in boroughs, ninety-four thousand
were at or above the £10 line, and four hundred and
seventy eight thousand below it.[3] For these latter the
original bill made no direct provision and it is difficult
to believe that more than a small proportion of them
would have been enfranchised. It is safe to say that
by the change which prevented the payment of rates
by the landlord nearly half a million occupiers were qualified who would otherwise have failed to receive the suffrage.[4] Obviously, by far the larger part of the addition

---

[1] 3 Hansard, clxxxvii, 717; *Daily Telegraph,* June 12, 1867.

[2] "They think that the middle classes have been uniformly hostile
to them, and that something may be gained if they get to a lower
class—that the one will counteract the other. . . . We have two
parties of competition, who like Cleon and the sausage-seller in
Aristophanes, are both bidding for the support of Demos." Sidney
Herbert had prophesied this competition in 1858: "Whatever they
[the Conservatives] propose, our friends must cap. If Derby goes
for universal suffrage, Johnny will produce the women and children,"
Argyll, *Memoirs,* ii, 121.

[3] *Parliamentary Papers,* 1867, no. 136.

[4] Five years after the reform there were 1,200,800 occupiers on
the borough register; of these not more than 500,000 were those
voting under the borough franchise of 1832, and 225,000 those who
would have been enfranchised under the original bill of 1867,
Parliamentary Papers, 1872, no. 343.

made by the amendment was composed of the working classes.

The democratic character of the new borough franchise was further increased by reducing the term of residence required of the new voters from two years to one. Disraeli had confessed that there was at first sight something invidious in having one householder qualification based on one year and another based on a longer term, and he admitted his readiness to consider a change, in committee. The government resisted an amendment of Ayrton embodying such an alteration, citing as precedents for a longer term Russell's bill of 1854, where two and a half years were required, and also the term of residence demanded of municipal burgesses. The reduction was nevertheless carried through.[1] A further step in the democratic direction was marked by the insertion of a lodger franchise which offered the vote to every man who had occupied the same lodgings for the twelvemonth preceding the last day of July. Such lodgings, however, must have formed part of the same dwelling house and must be of a clear yearly value, if let unfurnished, of £10 or upwards. In the Lords, Cairns proposed to raise the requisite value from £10 to £15; but his amendment, at first successful, was reversed by motion of Russell. Derby obviously feared the discontent of the London workingman, who was supposed to profit by the lower qualification.[2] The dual vote, which would have furnished the upper classes with a weighty counterpoise to the new working class element, was surrendered by the Conservatives on the second reading. Disraeli acknowledged that it had been generally opposed,

[1] 3 Hansard, clxxxvi, 1907.

[2] As will be seen, the lodger qualification was little more than a dead letter; only 5000 were thus qualified in 1872, *Parliamentary Papers*, 1872, no. 343.

and that from first to last no one had spoken a single word in its favour.[1]

In contrast to the radical characteristics of the new borough franchise, the reformed county qualification appears almost aristocratic; nor were the original proposals of Disraeli greatly changed during the passage of the bill. The Conservatives had originally planned to enfranchise occupiers of tenements in counties rated at £15 annually, as well as persons qualified under the educational and pecuniary franchises;[2] but the latter were abandoned before the committee stage was reached. The occupation franchise was reduced from £15 to £12 as a compromise with the amendment of Locke King, who suggested £10 as a suitable value. The claimant must have occupied the land or tenement for twelve months, have been rated and paid the rates. By this reduction some thirty-five thousand county electors were enfranchised who would not have possessed the suffrage under the qualification first proposed.[3] Similar Liberal amendments which reduced the copy- and leasehold qualifications from £10 to £5 were either carried in division or accepted by the government.[4]

The Conservatives would doubtless have been pleased to abrogate the provision which allowed the freeholder in

[1] Gladstone had attacked the dual vote bitterly, calling those who were to exercise it, "those favored children of fortune, those select human kings, made of finer clay than the rest of their fellow subjects," 3 Hansard, clxxxvi, 477.

[2] Disraeli's first idea had been to set the qualification at £20, 3 Hansard, clxxxv, 937.

[3] Attempts were made to render the occupier's qualification dependent upon the occupation of a "dwelling house" and later of a "house." But this condition of residence was finally not adopted, 3 Hansard, clxxxvii, 1002, 1151.

[4] The copyhold qualification was raised in the Lords to £10 by a large majority on the motion of Harrowby. But the Commons insisted on the lower franchise.

represented boroughs to vote in the counties, if he could not be registered on his property in the borough. Disraeli had provided in his bill of 1859 that the town freeholder should vote in boroughs and in 1866 had opposed plural voting. He had insisted that the electoral system recoiled from a plurality of votes; "that a man should have only one vote is, I think, the right principle. The law of England recognizes, and I hold nobly, equality . . . of the political citizen who is invested with duties and privileges for the public good."[1] And in 1867 he emphasized the essential difference between town and country and held it to be as illogical that a freeholder in a town should cast a county vote as it would be if an occupier in the county were granted the borough franchise.[2]

The Liberals, however, still believed that the town freeholders were their electoral strength in counties and refused any change.[3] They even attempted to extend to copy- and leaseholders in towns the privilege of the freeholders, by allowing the non-occupying owners of such tenements a county vote, even though their property conferred the borough suffrage on the occupier. It was shown that many who had held tenements in boroughs separately under the value of £10, but collectively above,

[1] 3 Hansard, clxxxiii, 882.

[2] 3 Hansard, clxxxviii, 467.

[3] The Liberal theory in 1867, so opposed to that now in vogue, is put forcefully by Homersham Cox: "The theory of non-intrusion in county representation rests upon an assumption that owners of property in boroughs have no personal interest in the local concerns of counties. But this hypothesis is contrary to fact. . . . There is no borough which does not contribute something to county expenditure. A certain portion of the expenses of the county of Warwick are borne by Birmingham. . . . Obviously, upon questions arising in parliament respecting the affairs of that county, Birmingham has a right to be heard; and if so, the borough has a legitimate interest in seeing that the county is fitly represented," *Reform Bills of 1866 and 1867*, 237-238.

had before 1867 possessed a vote for the county; but in the future their occupying tenants would each obtain a borough vote, so that they themselves would accordingly lose their county franchise.[1] The attempts to remove this distinction between freeholders and copy- and lease-holders, and prevent the disqualification of certain of the latter, were, however, unsuccessful.[2]

It has become an historical platitude to remark upon the curious sequence of events which led to the adoption by a Conservative government of a borough franchise which in 1832, when proposed by Hume and Hunt, had been considered tantamount to anarchy, and even in 1866 was regarded as the quintessence of Radicalism. Previous to 1867, even the more advanced reformers in the House had been averse to household suffrage. Bright himself had dared to tell popular mass meetings that an undesirable "residuum" of the working classes would thereby be admitted to the exercise of the franchise; and Gladstone had held firmly to the principle of drawing a line, below which a portion of the artisans and labourers would be excluded. The characteristic of all the proposals for franchise reform before 1867 was their failure to promise any material alteration in the character of the constituency; Gladstone's £7 electors would after all have differed very slightly from the £10 householder enfranchised in 1832.

Nor was Disraeli's original proposal a greater concession to democracy, except in name. It was, indeed, in one light, a reversion to the pre-reform franchises, and in thorough consonance with Tory principles. In the

---

[1] Under the provision of the act of 1832, which provided that if a copy- or leasehold in a borough conferred the right to vote on the tenant or any other person, it would not serve the owner as a county qualification.

[2] 3 Hansard, clxxxviii, 464, 471.

boroughs where the system of composition was not in force, there would practically have been a resurrection of the old scot and lot voter; the extreme variation in the size of the electorate from one constituency to another would have been reminiscent, to a certain extent, of the old system. The restricted character of the franchise in the boroughs, where practically all rates on houses under £6 value were paid by the owner, would have prevented any breaking through of the democratic flood, and the two-year residential provision would have been another bar to the working classes. At the same time the dual vote would have reinforced the electoral power of the upper middle classes and relatively weakened that of occupiers of houses ranging from £10 to £20 in value. Even the lowering of the occupation franchise in counties might be reckoned as an eminently safe step, since experience had proved the county tenants to be almost wholly under the control of the landlords.

The explanation of governmental complaisance in the removal of the most important of the restrictions placed on the borough franchise in the original bill, if hidden explanation there be, remains yet to be discovered. The reduction of the term of residence and the abolition of the dual vote were plainly forced upon Disraeli by a combination of Liberals, Whigs, and Radicals. But why the Chancellor of the Exchequer was willing to accept so easily Hodgkinson's alteration in the law of rating cannot be clearly demonstrated. It was only a few weeks before that he had dubbed the proposal of such a measure "rash counsel." His position at the moment, in consequence of the defeat of Gladstone's attempt to set a line of value, was more secure than it had been during the whole session.[1]

[1] Gladstone said later, "The government were beyond all doubt, at least for the moment, masters of the situation," Morley, *Gladstone,* ii, 225.

The cabinet itself was surprised at the sudden approval of the radical amendment.

Certain it is that the whole character of the borough franchisè was altered from top to bottom by the change in the law of rating, combined with the shortening of the period of residence and the disappearance of the dual vote. Whether or not Disraeli hoped to preserve these restrictions, and by a back-hand stroke thus prevent the introduction of a democratic suffrage, whether he looked with indifference or secret pleasure on the counterbalancing of the middle classes by the labourers, or whether he was adrift, is not certain. At least he managed to preserve the outward show of consistency, in so far as he had always said that if the borough qualification was to be reduced at all, there was no resting place until household suffrage was reached.[1] And notwithstanding his recent warning against the dangers of a "household democracy," he may have trusted to the restrictive effect of the registration requirements; perhaps he believed that the Conservative registration associations, whose extensive development was already in his mind, would be able to mould the new electorate into acceptable political pliancy.

Whatever may have been the secret opinion of Disraeli on the new democratic franchises, the leading members of both Houses either condemned them absolutely, or indirectly with the faintest of praise. Cranbourne and Lowe, as might have been expected, were unable to contain their wrath and scorn. The former anathematized the acceptance of the Liberal amendments as a "policy of legerdemain"; the latter bewailed the shameful victory won by England over herself. Bright admitted that the franchise was extended to a class to whom the suffrage could be at

---

[1] In saying this he had evidently intended it to be inferred, not that household suffrage was desirable, but that any reduction was unwise.

A Leap in the Dark

the time of no advantage, nor would it be for the good of the country. Gladstone was doubtful; admitted that there was promise for the future, but not unmixed with evils.[1] Even Lord Elcho, speaking for the dissident Liberals, refused to predict the results and was able to excuse the new franchise only on the ground that it was inevitable.[2]

In the Lords, the expressions of condemnation were still stronger. Russell, whose experience qualified him to speak on electoral matters, believed that the change was much for the worse and would have such effect on the House of Commons. Harrowby predicted the destruction of all those social influences which were relied upon to steady government. Shaftesbury insisted that the suffrage was dishonoured by lifting the residuum of society up to the level of the thrifty workingman. Grey declared that the settlement could not be final, while Argyll prophesied the swamping of the constituencies by the mere power of numbers.[3] Almost all predicted an increase of electoral corruption as a result of the extension of the franchise to the classes most open to temptation. Even the members of the government defended the franchise only on the ground that it had been forced on them, and that the best must be made of the matter. And Derby, making use of an expression which had been employed by Palmerston in 1860 and one which had figured in the debates of 1866, characterized the alteration as "a leap in the dark."[4]

[1] Morley, *Gladstone,* ii, 236.

[2] For the general opinions on the franchise in the Commons, see 3 Hansard, clxxxviii, 1526-1614.

[3] Argyll, *Memoirs,* ii, 237-238. For the general opinion of the Lords, see 3 Hansard, clxxxviii, 1774-1872, 1916-2023.

[4] Palmerston made use of the phrase in connection with the £10 county franchise in Russell's bill of 1860. Gladstone's bill of 1866 was on more than one occasion, notably by Horsman, alluded to as "One inviting members to take a leap in the dark," Walpole, *Life*

It is curious to note that the prophetic powers of some of the peers, quickened by their apprehensions, foresaw the removal of the last of the restrictions which still hung upon the borough qualification. According to the act, as passed, it was necessary before registration that the claimant should himself have paid all his rates, and in order that uniformity might be attained we saw that the practice of composition of rates by the landlord was forbidden. As was pointed out by Lord Morley, it was inevitable that the parishes, having experienced the convenience of the composition system, should refuse to accept the arrangement. They would without question agitate for a return to the compounding system, with the proviso that the electoral rights of occupiers should not be affected. The principle of personal payment of rates would then have had its day; the country would be landed in household suffrage pure and simple, the last checks would have melted away. Within two years the accuracy of such predictions was demonstrated by the return to the convenient system of compounding rates and the abrogation of the requirement that the rate must be paid by the occupier himself.[1]

The Reform Act of 1867, like that of 1832, thus "contained no finality." It is undeniable that it marks a very large step in the direction of electoral democracy, and that by adding a great number of new voters it infused a democratic spirit into the parliamentary machine, which had previously been lacking. But, as Lowe perceived, the chief importance of the Reform Act lay in what it promised for the future. The breaking down of the last restric-

---

of Russell, ii, 330, 3 Hansard, clxxxii, 1397, 1850. Similarly Robert Lowe's phrase, "Our masters" in reference to the newly enfranchised working classes (of 1867) was employed by Cranbourne in 1866, 3 Hansard, clxxxii, 876.

[1] 32 & 33 Vict., c. 41; 48 Vict., c. 3.

tion upon household suffrage in boroughs, which came two years after the passing of the act of 1867, was the first of the changes that followed, which were destined to render the franchise democratic all through the country. The very fact that the enfranchisement in boroughs was so complete, made it inevitable that the democratic suffrage would be ultimately extended to counties as well; for it accentuated anomalies of franchise at a moment when opinion was continually becoming less inclined to tolerate anomalies. The consideration of these anomalies, as well as the more immediate results of the second Reform Act, are deserving, perhaps, of some detailed consideration.

CHAPTER X

THE REFORMED ELECTORATE, 1867-1884

THE reform of 1867 has not infrequently been regarded as the departure which first brought democracy into the electoral system, and more than one writer has believed that it sounded the knell of that middle class rule which rested upon the act of 1832. In reality the power of the middle classes between 1832 and 1867, as we have seen, by no means displaced the control which the aristocracy exercised in elections previous to the first reform. And notwithstanding the far-reaching enfranchisement of 1867, the electoral system can hardly be termed essentially democratic before 1884. But the importance of the second reform should not be minimized, even though its results have been sometimes exaggerated. Notwithstanding the very real power which the upper and upper middle classes retained in elections, the effect, numerical and moral, of the act of 1867 was enormous.

The extension of the franchise and the alteration in rate-paying regulations, consummated in 1867, led to an increase in the total electorate of far greater importance, relatively and absolutely, than that of 1832.[1] Especially was this true of boroughs, of which the franchise had been the centre of discussion and where the alteration was the most complete. The regularity of suffrage which followed upon the act of 1867 was another result of almost equal importance. As we have seen, one of the most salient characteristics of the pre-reform system had been the variety of franchises, which resulted in a widely extended electorate in one constituency and a low ratio of voters in its neighbour. The act of 1832, although it introduced an unvarying qualification for boroughs, did not equalize the proportion of electors to population from one constituency to another. That process of equalization was begun by the second Reform Act. Although it failed to place the suffrage on an equal plane in counties and boroughs, it did regularize in each type of constituency the ratio of voters to inhabitants.

The accretion of voters induced by the act of 1867 was naturally greatest in boroughs. Here the number of electors was more than doubled, chiefly because of the new

---

[1] The effect of the act of 1832 was to increase the electorate by 217,000: 40 per cent of the former number of voters. The act of 1867 added 938,000 voters: 88 per cent of the former number of voters, *Parliamentary Papers*, 1866, nos. 3626, 3736, "Electoral Returns"; *Ibid.*, 1868-1869, nos. 418, 419.

householder franchise, although the change in the rate-paying system accounted in part for the increase in the electorate.[1] Of the four main classes of electors, the most numerous were the new householders, of whom there were about seven hundred and fifty thousand on the register. For the first time, the mass of the electorate was qualified by a democratic franchise, and for the first time the working classes were placed in a clear majority. The number of £10 electors increased in some boroughs, through the elimination of the glaring anomalies which had resulted from the uneven operation of the compounding system; but their franchise was in general superseded by the newer and more democratic household qualification. The lodger qualification, which soon disappointed the expectations of the labourers, introduced only some five thousand new electors and proved little else than a name. Of those voting by virtue of ancient rights there still remained forty-three thousand.[2]

The operation of the act differed widely in different boroughs. The average per cent of increase was in general not far from 150; but exceptions were by no means infrequent, especially in the smaller boroughs and in those which had been long represented.[3] In these latter the number of new voters was often very small; in places like Dorchester, Hertford, Newport, and Weymouth the proportion of new electors was only about forty per cent. In others, where the electorate increased notably, the newly enfranchised householders represented only a small

[1]
Number of borough voters, 1866,	.	.	514,026
Number of borough voters, 1871,	.	.	1,210,491
Increase, ...	.	.	696,465
Per cent Increase, . . .	.		134

[2] *Parliamentary Papers,* 1872, no. 343, "Return of the Number of Electors."

[3] Statistics in the succeeding pages are taken from *Parliamentary Papers,* 1868-1869, no. 419, "Return of the Number of Electors."

part of the addition: in Windsor the householders comprised less than a quarter of the entire constituency, and in Dover and Bath similar conditions prevailed; in Brighton barely a ninth of the electorate was made up of householders. In such places the new voters were generally £10 electors, who now obtained the suffrage for the first time by means of the alteration in the conditions of ratepaying.

In the metropolis and some large towns the number of new electors was surprisingly slight. In Finsbury, Lambeth, and Tower Hamlets the increase was very small, even taking into consideration the change in boundaries which was essential for the carving out of two new boroughs.[1] Counting in the electors of the new boroughs, the aggregate electorate of the metropolis gained only sixty-six per cent. Liverpool gained less than ninety per cent by the new franchise, while in Plymouth the new electors represented only a third of the constituency.

But in most of the large industrial towns the operation of the act resulted in very wide enfranchisement. The electorate of Birmingham was tripled and that of Leeds was more than quadrupled. In the Lancashire towns, like Blackburn and Bolton, the number of electors was increased fivefold, and the same was true of Halifax and Stoke-upon-Trent.[2] The electorate was six times as large in Oldham and in South Shields in 1869 as it was in 1866; in Merthyr Tydvil, where the most striking increase took place, the number of voters was more than decupled. Of the small rural boroughs, on the other hand, Woodstock was the only one where the electorate was increased abnormally; here it was more than quadrupled.

---

[1] Westminster and Southwark only gained 6000 voters apiece.

[2] The increase in Manchester and Liverpool was less striking. In the former town the electorate was merely doubled, and in the latter it was not even doubled.

We have noted the fact that a large part of the increase in some boroughs occurred amongst the £10 electors, as a result of the change in the payment of rates. Exactly how important this increase in the number of those voting on the old franchise may have been, the returns do not show exactly. But in Reading and Brighton the £10 electors increased by more than a thousand, in Newcastle-upon-Tyne by two thousand, and in Manchester by nearly three thousand. In Windsor, for the same reason, the number of £10 electors was practically doubled.[1]

The failure of the lodger franchise, supposedly introduced for the benefit of the artisans, was striking. As Gladstone had prophesied, the difficulties and red tape of registration rendered this qualification a practical nullity.[2] There were lodger voters in all but forty-five of the represented boroughs in 1868, but in only ten did they number as many as a hundred.[3] In the metropolitan boroughs alone were they of appreciable importance. It is true that by 1884 they had increased from five to twenty-two thousand. But even then they had no influence in elections outside of London; and even in Westminster, where they were most numerous, they formed but a tenth

[1] In six boroughs those registered on the old franchise vastly outnumbered those registered on the new:

	House-holders	£10 occupiers
Bath, . . .	1,394	3,450
Brighton, . .	944	7,590
Dorchester, . .	187	451
Dover, . .	788	1,758
Maidstone, . .	1,005	2,029
Windsor, . .	452	1,267

[2] In 1868 they numbered only two-fifths of one per cent of the total number of voters.

[3] Bath, Bristol, Chelsea, Finsbury, Lambeth, London, Marylebone, Plymouth, Southampton, Westminster, *Parliamentary Papers*, 1872, no. 343.

of the electorate; in Chelsea they formed only seven per cent of the voters and in Southwark and Finsbury about five per cent.[1]

The persistence of the ancient right voters upon the register was as striking as the absence of lodgers from the register. In general the ancient right electors were important from the antiquarian rather than the numerical aspect; for, although they were to be found in 126 boroughs, in most their numbers were too small to allow them to affect the electoral balance.[2] But in certain boroughs their strength was exceptional; in as many as twenty-eight they composed at least a tenth of the electorate, and in nine they formed a quarter.[3] The liverymen of London were more than half as numerous as all the other classes of voters combined; and the freemen of Coventry could almost hold their own against all those voting under the modern qualifications. By 1884 there had taken place a steady decrease in the numbers of those qualified by ancient rights; but freemen, liverymen, burgage holders, even potwallers, were still to be found exercising their peculiar electoral privileges in more than half of the represented boroughs. The constituencies in which the ancient right voters were sufficiently strong to influence elections, were generally devoted neither to one party nor the other.[4]

The extension of the suffrage was far more restricted in the counties than in the boroughs, the number of voters

[1] *Parliamentary Papers,* 1883, no. 321, "Electoral Returns."

[2] There were nine boroughs in which freeholders were qualified, three containing voting burgage holders, and one (Taunton) with potwallers on the register; in the other 113 the freemen and scot and lot voters were the only ancient right electors, *Parliamentary Papers,* 1872, no. 343.

[3] Bridgnorth, Coventry, Durham, London, Malden, Newcastle-under-Lyme, Norwich, Stafford, York, *Parliamentary Papers,* 1883, no. 321.

[4] *Parliamentary Papers,* 1883, no. 321.

increasing only from 540,000 to 790,000. Of the 250,000 new electors, all but a fifth were registered under the £12 occupation franchise. The reduction of the lease- and copyholder qualification from £10 to £5 was of minor importance.[1] But the new occupation voters formed a quarter of the entire county electorate, and in the industrial divisions more than a third.[2] In West Kent and Mid Surrey they were nearly as numerous as those voting on the ownership qualifications.[3] In the agricultural divisions the occupiers were of small electoral importance as a rule; in some, like Worcester and Wiltshire, they represented only fifteen per cent of the voters, and in West Gloucester only twelve per cent. So that, as might have been expected, it was generally the industrial and manufacturing divisions which profited most by the new county qualification.

The county electorate increased by twenty per cent during the fifteen years which followed the act of 1867, chiefly because of the rapid growth of the occupiers, who gained seventy per cent and in 1883 formed more than a third of all the county voters.[4] In at least ten of the non-rural constituencies the occupiers comprised more

[1] It added less than 56,000 electors, *Parliamentary Papers,* 1868-1869, no. 418.

[2] Such as Chester, East Derby, South Essex, West Kent, Southwest Lancashire, Middlesex, Mid Surrey, *Parliamentary Papers,* 1868-1869, no. 418.

		£12 occupiers	All other qualifications
[3]	West Kent,	4,064	4,764
	Mid Surrey,	5,017	5,548

[4]	£12 occupiers,	356,344
	£50 tenants,	92,934
	Owners (freeholders, leaseholders, etc.),	514,226
	Total,	963,504

Parliamentary Papers, 1883, no. 321.

than half of the electorate, and in such thickly populated divisions as South Essex and Mid Surrey, more than two-thirds. But notwithstanding this increase, the old free-holders still controlled the counties, in contrast to the boroughs where the democratic element, represented by the occupation voters, formed the vast majority. The property qualification which dated back to 1430 still remained the most important of all the county franchises.[1]

The act of 1867, besides increasing the number of voters, resulted in the removal of certain anomalies, which were defended feebly, even by those most enamoured of pre-reform electoral characteristics. It is true that after 1832 variations in the ratio of electors to population were by no means so extreme as in the ratio of members to population. The more flagrant irregularities of the old system were smoothed out by the first Reform Act; no longer were there constituencies like Preston, where the whole male population voted, and others, like Bath, where the suffrage was restricted to a tiny knot of magistrates. But the proportion of electors to population continued to vary widely between 1832 and 1867. It was higher in boroughs than in counties. The latter, although their population was greater by thirty per cent, had only five per cent more voters; in 1865 one man in every twenty-one inhabitants was an elector in the counties, whereas in the boroughs, one man in sixteen was an elector.[2] This difference was accentuated by the act of 1867, which introduced a radical borough franchise, so that by 1869 the ratio of county voters was only half that which obtained in

---

[1] *Parliamentary Papers*, 1883, no. 321.

				Population	Electors
[2]	Counties,	.	.	11,427,755	542,456
	Boroughs,	.	.	8,638,569	514,026

Parliamentary Papers, 1866, nos. 3626, 3736.

the boroughs. In the latter type of constituency the ratio was one in seven; in the former only one in fourteen. But while the discrepancy between the two kinds of franchise was thus emphasized, differences in the ratio of voters from borough to borough, and from county to county largely disappeared.[1]

In counties, before the second Reform Act, the electorate was relatively far greater in the rural and agricultural divisions. In the West Midland constituencies the proportion of electors was distinctly higher than in the industrial Northwest. In the manufacturing and urban divisions of South Lancashire, the ratio of voters was not half so high as in the comparatively rural North Riding of Yorkshire.[2] In Westmoreland, where the industrial and manufacturing element was unimportant, the electorate was large in proportion to population; in North Derby, which represented the industrial type, it was relatively small; in the former there was one voter to eleven inhabitants, in the latter but one to thirty-one. Numerous instances of a similar character might be adduced to illustrate the great extent of the suffrage in the agricultural counties.[3] Indeed, there were few exceptions to the

			Population	Electors
1	Counties,	. .	11,428,632	789,218
	Boroughs,	. .	9,131,034	1,210,491

Parliamentary Papers, 1868-1869, nos. 418, 419.

2 In the North Riding the proportion of electors to population was one in 13; in South Lancashire it was one in 29, Parliamentary Papers, 1866, no. 3736.

3 Cf. the industrial constituency of North Durham, which had a ratio of one in 28, with agricultural Hereford, which had a ratio of one in 14; Radnor (one in 11), with Glamorgan (one in 21); North Stafford (one in 15), with South Stafford (one in 24). Where contiguous constituencies had a different industrial character the advantage of the more agricultural was marked: thus East Cornwall had a ratio of one in 23, while the less agricultural West Cornwall had a ratio of only one in 36, Parliamentary Papers, 1866, no. 3736.

rule that the more industrial the character of a division, the lower was the proportion of electors. In ten constituencies of a distinctly rural type, the ratio of voters was notably greater than in the same number of industrial divisions.[1]

Similar variations were to be found in the case of the borough constituencies, and, almost without exception, it was in the newly enfranchised towns of the manufacturing type that the low ratio of voters occurred. In the boroughs of the Northwest, where the population amounted in the aggregate to more than two millions, there were only one hundred thousand electors; a proportion of one in twenty; in the industrial Midlands, the ratio was one in seventeen, and in Westminster and Tower Hamlets, one in twenty. On the other hand, the proportion of electors in the South Midland boroughs, which were, for the most part, rural constituencies, was one in thirteen;[2] and in the old cathedral cities, with few exceptions, the same ratio was to be found.[3] It was in the old boroughs

---

[1] In the ten manufacturing constituencies of North and South Lancashire, North Cheshire, South Stafford, South Essex, Glamorgan, North Durham, West Riding of Yorkshire, North Derby, the average ratio of voters to population was one in 26. In the rural divisions of West Sussex, Isle of Wight, Oxfordshire, Buckinghamshire, Rutland, Huntingdon, North Wiltshire, Herefordshire, Westmoreland, Radnor, the ratio was one in 17. The constituencies above selected for comparison were by no means the extremes of widely extended and closely restricted suffrage; a list might be compiled which would make the differences existing between the manufacturing and rural constituencies appear far more striking. The constituencies were chosen merely as being of the most typically rural or industrial character, *Victoria County History, passim; Parliamentary Papers,* 1866, no. 3736.

[2] The ratio of electors in the boroughs of the rural Southeast and East was as high as one in 14, *Parliamentary Papers,* 1866, no. 3626.

[3] The city of Oxford, for example, showed a ratio of electors of one in 9, and Lincoln a ratio of one in 11; but the industrial towns of Warrington and Oldham had but one in 34 and one in 40,

of the latter type that the electorate was relatively the largest. A comparison of ten newly enfranchised industrial towns with the same number of cathedral cities, illustrates this fact unequivocally. With an aggregate population of 330,000, the cities had 27,000 electors; the towns on the other hand, with a population of 350,000, had only 12,000 electors. The ratio of electors in the former was thus two and a half times that of the latter.[1] In boroughs, as in counties, the newer elements of industry and commerce thus found it more difficult to express their will through elections before 1867, entirely apart from the number of members returned.

In the larger towns the ratio of electors varied greatly before the second reform, probably because of the uneven operation of the compounding of rates. Thus in Bristol, a tenth of the population were upon the electoral register,

respectively. Comparing near-by boroughs of different industrial character, the advantage of the non-industrial cities is obvious:

	Ratio
{ Exeter,	one in 11
{ Devonport,	one in 22
{ Worcester,	one in 12
{ Dudley,	one in 33
{ Durham,	one in 12
{ Sunderland,	one in 24
{ York,	one in 9
{ South Shields,	one in 29

Parliamentary Papers, 1866, no. 3626.

[1] The cities chosen are Canterbury, Chester, Durham, Exeter, Lincoln, Norwich, Oxford, Winchester, Worcester; in none of these was the ratio of electors lower than in Winchester, where it was one in 15; in all but three it was higher than one in 12. The industrial towns chosen are Bury, Chatham, Gateshead, Kendal, Oldham, Rochdale, Tynemouth, Wakefield, Warrington, Whitehaven; in none of these was the ratio of electors higher than one in 17; and in all but two it was lower than one in 26, *Parliamentary Papers*, 1866, no. 3626.

while in Wolverhampton there was only one man out of every thirty inhabitants who possessed the franchise. In Liverpool, because of registration conditions, the ratio of voters was low, as it was in Leeds and Sheffield. On the other hand, it was comparatively high in Manchester, and the proportion of electors in London city, before 1867, was as high as in most towns after the introduction of household suffrage.[1] With such exceptions, however, the centres of population and industry possessed a comparatively small electorate.

The second Reform Act went far towards removing these inequalities, so that after 1867 the variations in the ratio of electors in each type of constituency were comparatively slight. As we saw, the act resulted in a varying accretion of electors; in some the number of new voters was large, in others small. These variations proved actually of assistance in making for uniformity of suffrage conditions, for the increase was generally slightest in the boroughs where the constituency had been relatively large, and most striking in the industrial constituencies where, before 1867, the proportion of voters to population had been small. The new occupation franchise was, for example, of comparatively slight importance in the county divisions of the South Midlands, while it enfranchised so many new voters in the Northwest that after 1867 the advantage was actually with the latter.[2] In the counties the variations between groups were generally very slight and ranged only from one in thirteen to one in

---

[1] In Liverpool, one in 20; in Sheffield, one in 20; in Leeds, one in 24; in Manchester, one in 15; in London, one in 6. But it should be remembered that a large number of London electors were outvoters.

[2] The ratio of electors in the South Midland county divisions was one in 16; in the Northwestern, one in 15. In rural West Sussex the ratio was one in 14 and in industrial South Lancashire it was one in 15. In the West Riding of Yorkshire the ratio was one in 16,

sixteen. As between individual constituencies the variations were rather more noticeable, but neither so frequent
nor so great as before 1867. Of the twenty county divisions referred to above, the agricultural showed a ratio of
one elector to every twelve inhabitants, and the industrial
one to every fifteen. The relative size of the electorate
had increased forty per cent in the latter and only twenty-
five per cent in the former.

During the fifteen years which elapsed before the third
reform there was a decided relative increase of electors in
many of the industrial divisions. In Middlesex, although
the population gained only by eight per cent, the number
of voters increased by more than fifty per cent. The
ratio of voters rose in South Lancashire, while it actually
fell in rural West Sussex; that of Stafford was higher
than that of Rutland or Buckingham. Thus the formerly
invariable electoral advantage of the agricultural over
the industrial counties was swept away. On the other
hand, some of the divisions in which new industries were
springing up were at a great disadvantage. This was
especially true of the mining divisions; in North Durham
the ratio fell from one in sixteen to one in twenty-two,
and in Glamorgan, from one in twelve to one in seventeen.[1]
So that in 1883 the variations in the proportions of voters
did not rest, as before, upon a distinction between rural
and industrial communities; it was rather a contrast be-

and in rural Buckinghamshire it was one in 15. The following table
illustrates the process of regularization:

	Ratio in 1866	Ratio in 1869
North Cheshire, ...	one in 30	one in 15
Durham, ...	one in 28	one in 16
Huntingdonshire, ...	one in 19	one in 15
Berkshire, ...	one in 19	one in 15

Parliamentary Papers, 1866, no. 3736; *Ibid.*, 1868-1869, no. 418.

[1] *Parliamentary Papers*, 1883, no. 321.

tween those constituencies where the industry had been long established and the population was increasing slowly, and those where a newly developed industry was resulting in a large and sudden increase of population.

The enfranchisement of 1867 tended towards an equalization of suffrage conditions in the boroughs also. The gain of the industrial groups was very striking, so great indeed that the manufacturing towns of the Northwest could show a higher proportion of electors than the rural boroughs of the Southwest.[1] Variations were still to be found between individual boroughs, but the proportionate advantage of the old cathedral cities almost entirely disappeared. Neighbouring constituencies of different industrial types furnished clear illustrations of this fact; and there were not a few in which the ratio of electors before the act was widely different, where in 1868 they were almost identical. Proportionately to population the electorate of Worcester had been three times that of Dudley; but after 1867 it was exactly the same. In York, where the number of electors was doubled by the operation of the act, and in South Shields, where it was increased sevenfold, the proportionate size of the electorate became identical. The ratio of voters in the ten typical cities of the old type was increased only from one in eleven to one in six; in the industrial towns it rose from one in twenty-seven to one in seven.

Variations still occurred in the larger towns, although such variations were always less striking than before the reform. The ratio of electors in Westminster was as low as one in thirteen, hardly greater in Finsbury and Marylebone, and in Liverpool, one in eleven. In Leeds, Birmingham, and Sheffield, on the other hand, it was actually above the average of one in seven. But with

[1] In the Northwest the ratio of electors was one in 7; in the Southwest, one in 8.7, *Parliamentary Papers*, 1868-1869, no. 419.

these exceptions, the proportion of electors in the larger towns departed only slightly from the mean: The low ratio in the metropolitan boroughs and in Liverpool would have been less surprising if it were not for the number of voters in manufacturing towns like Bradford and Rochdale, where manhood suffrage could hardly have produced more electors.[1]

It is a fact, not undeserving of attention, that during the following fifteen years, most of the remaining variations in the ratio of borough voters disappeared. There was a sort of automatic adjustment, which took place without the assistance of any alteration in the law of franchise. In the boroughs where the increase of electors, consequent upon the introduction of household suffrage, was small, there was a steady growth. Thus Liverpool had raised its proportion of voters by 1883 from one in eleven to one in eight, and a similar increase took place in Wolverhampton. On the other hand, the towns where the electorate had been relatively large, were unable to keep the increase of voters abreast of the growth of population. There was thus an automatic approximation to a mean, of which the two towns of Tynemouth and Rochdale furnish an illustration. In 1869 the proportion of voters in the former was one in thirteen, in the latter one

---

[1] The following table illustrates the general evenness of the suffrage, even in boroughs of a different type:

	Ratio
Birmingham,	one in 6
Gateshead,	one in 6
Midhurst,	one in 6
Oldham,	one in 7
Rye,	one in 7
Sheffield,	one in 6
Wakefield,	one in 6

In Bradford the ratio was as high as one in 5, and in Rochdale, one in 4, *Parliamentary Papers*, 1868-1869, no. 419.

in four. By 1883 both were close to the average of one in
seven. And with few exceptions, the proportion of electors
in the boroughs was more regular in 1883 than immediately after the second reform.[1]

The act of 1867 thus did much to wipe out the numerical anomalies which existed between borough and borough
as well as between county and county. But to the more
democratic reformers the measure was nevertheless unsatisfactory because of the partiality shown to boroughs.
It actually increased the difference between the proportion
of electors in counties on the one hand and in boroughs
on the other. Herein lay the complaint of those to whom
electoral anomalies were distasteful alike by sentiment and
policy; and herein is to be found the point which rendered
the "finality" of the measure of 1867 impossible. As we
saw, the numerical effect of that measure had been comparatively slight in the counties, resulting in a voting
increase of only forty per cent, in contrast to the gain
of one hundred and thirty-four per cent made by the
boroughs; so that the latter, although their population
was smaller by two millions than that of the counties, had
one and a half as many electors. And while, after 1867,
the proportion of voters in boroughs was one in seven, in
counties it averaged only about one in fourteen.

This advantage of the borough inhabitants continued
up to the Reform Act of 1884, and in many constituencies
actually increased. In the metropolitan county of Middlesex,[2] it is true, the freeholder and the £12 qualification

---

[1] *Parliamentary Papers,* 1868-1869, no. 419; *Ibid.,* 1883, no. 321.
This regularity was without question due in large part to improvements in the registration system and the abrogation of the stipulation
for the personal payment of rates.

[2] In 1869 the ratio in Middlesex was one in 14, and in the metropolitan boroughs, one in 10; in 1883 the county ratio was one in 10,
the borough ratio one in 9, *Parliamentary Papers,* 1868-1869, no. 419;
Ibid., 1883, no. 321.

operated almost as liberally as did household suffrage. But in other parts the difference between the proportion of voters in counties and boroughs was striking. In Gateshead one man in every five inhabitants was qualified, but in the county of Durham, beyond the borough boundaries, only one in twenty-two were voters. In the city of Oxford the ratio of electors was one in six; in the county it was one in sixteen. Nor were these exceptional anomalies; their frequency was almost regular. Thus in the eastern group of boroughs the proportion of electors was one in six; in the eastern counties one in fifteen. In the South Midland boroughs and counties, the proportions were one in seven and one in sixteen respectively.[1]

Such anomalies would have been of less practical importance if the theoretical distinction between counties and boroughs were maintained in fact. If it had been true that the county constituencies were rural and the boroughs urban, the doctrine that the county franchise represented property and the borough, personality or numbers, would not have seemed so absurd. Nor would a distinction between the two types of franchise have appeared illogical. But the breaking down of the line which separated county and borough seemed to point directly towards that assimilation of franchise which the Whigs of 1832 had avoided and against which Walpole and Henley had protested. Counties like South Lancashire, the West Riding, Essex, Durham, and Glamorgan were imbued with a far more urban character than boroughs like Aylesbury or Cricklade, which were purely rural, and possessed of all the traditional county characteristics. Sentimentally and practically the anomaly was keenly felt by those who were excluded from the franchise, and their complaints were magnified tenfold by their supporters in parliament.

[1] *Parliamentary Papers*, 1868-1869, no. 419; *Ibid.*, 1883, no. 321.

The mass of those who were still deprived of voting rights was composed of the small tradesmen of the towns, the artisans and labourers, especially in the mining districts, and the peasants.[1] The anomaly weighed upon them, because persons whose condition and qualifications were absolutely analogous to their own could vote, and they themselves could not; and the only difference lay in that they lived upon different sides of an imaginary line.[2] The artisan of St. Helens was excluded, while his brother, working in a similar factory at Warrington, five miles to the south, or at Wigan, eight miles to the north, drawing no better pay and living in the same circumstances, was fully qualified. One miner in Morpeth possessed the franchise, but his neighbour, who lived across the street, and outside of the boundary line, did not. The agricultural labourer of Shoreham or East Retford enjoyed the privilege which was withheld from the peasant, no richer or better educated, of Sussex or Nottinghamshire. It was not without logic that the reformers asked how anyone could resist the extension of voting rights to the people of non-represented industrial towns, when such rights were already held by the inhabitants of exactly similar towns; or how it was possible to refuse to the labourers of Rutland the franchise which had already been granted to the rural boroughs, which were quite as extended in area and quite as agricultural in character as the county.[3]

The anomaly was also keenly felt by the working class voter when he changed his residence in search of work. By following the demand for labour it often happened that the artisan or miner removed from one town or district to another, or from one part of a town to another. In the

[1] 3 Hansard, cclxxxv, 108.

[2] This anomaly was brought out with emphasis in 1884 by Gladstone, *Annual Register,* 1884, 89.

[3] 3 Hansard, cclxxxv, 404.

case of the miners especially, such change of residence was necessary and frequent. But if, in so doing, the borough boundary was crossed, the voter's qualification was at once destroyed. In Nottingham, certain voters who moved across the street lost their votes although they received the same wages and paid the same house rent as before. And in the mining districts which surrounded towns like Merthyr Tydvil or Morpeth, the labourers hardly considered it worth while to register if they could, because their vote would almost certainly be lost within a few weeks.[1]

The advantage of the borough inhabitants was thus not merely statistical, but actual. The electoral anomaly affected directly persons who had possessed votes and lost them, as well as others who were excluded from a privilege which seemed to depend entirely upon the hap of location. It was this state of affairs that enabled Gladstone in 1884 to say, "The present position of the franchise is one of greater and grosser anomaly than any in which it has heretofore been placed, because the exclusion of persons of the same class and the same description is more palpable and more pervading than before."[2]

The movement for the removal of this anomaly and the extension of household suffrage to the counties began only five years after the introduction of that suffrage into boroughs. Led by Trevelyan, who brought forward an annual motion for the assimilation of county and borough suffrage, it was received at first with indifferent tolerance by the majority of both parties, and not infrequently debated in an empty House. But after 1873 the Liberals gradually rallied to its defence, and in the session of 1874 household suffrage in counties received the cautious sanction of Hartington. The latter, although he distrusted the political capacity of the agricultural labourers, and

[1] 3 Hansard, cclxxxvi, 933.
[2] 3 Hansard, cclxxxv, 109.

CAD AND CLOD

Mr. Punch. "Well, my lord, you educated your 'party' up to *that*! Don't you think you might educate 'em up to *this*!!!*"

feared that they would be governed by Conservative influence, could not deny the injustice of excluding the poorer classes in counties from the franchise.[1] On the other side, the Conservatives were equally cautious in their opposition, and in one of the first debates Disraeli significantly avoided any direct condemnation of the principle of the motion, at the same time reiterating his professions of confidence in the political capacity of the working classes.[2]

But both Conservative and Liberal leaders agreed that the question was one that should be handled by the government and not by private members, and that it could not be introduced apart from a large measure of redistribution.[3] So long as Disraeli, who disliked the thought of a radical redistribution, remained in power, no change could be expected. In 1880, however, came a general election, and although its chief issue was foreign policy, it was understood that Liberal success would mean the elevation of the reform question to the position of a ministerial measure. The victory of the Liberals at the polls was unequivocal. Largely in consequence of the pledges given, a bill for the extension of the household franchise to counties was introduced by Gladstone in 1884. Before proceeding to a study of this measure it is essential that the effect of franchise upon parties be considered, in order that their attitude on various points raised in discussing the later legislation may be more clearly understood.

Few questions were more warmly discussed at the time than the probable effect of the second Reform Act upon the relative strength of parties. To those who refused

---

[1] "I see no convenience or wisdom in excluding permanently from the franchise any class, unless it can be shown that they are less fully qualified to exercise it wisely than the class we have enfranchised in boroughs," Holland, *Life of the Duke of Devonshire*, i, 155.

[2] *Annual Register*, 1874, 6.

[3] Holland, *Life of the Duke of Devonshire*, i, 155.

to believe in the existence of the Tory workingman, it seemed inevitable that the wide extension of the franchise in boroughs, so long the strongholds of Liberal power, must cripple effectively the Conservative electoral machine. Nor was it to be expected, men argued, that Tory strength could be increased in the counties. Little change would result from the introduction of the £12 franchise; the new qualification would effect only the farmers that were held in the bondage of the landed aristocracy, and the latter would continue to direct county elections. On the other hand many persons looked to the new voters to express their gratitude to the party which had enfranchised them by supporting its candidates at the polls; and many trusted in the foresight of Disraeli and the influence of the Conservative workingmen's associations.

Neither of these beliefs was exactly justified by the event. Although the borough labourers with few exceptions did not voice their appreciation of the Conservative Reform Bill by a warm support of Conservative candidates, that party succeeded in attracting enough electors to maintain the position which it had occupied in boroughs before 1867. The reduction of the county occupation franchise resulted in a more surprising development, for it assured the Conservatives even more complete control in the counties than they had previously secured. In many constituencies where the Liberals had been wont to divide the representation, they were forced to cede absolutely to their opponents.

Statistics, which are proverbially misleading, cannot be relied upon implicitly in discussing the results of the second reform. There followed only three elections in which the effects upon party can be tested, and in many constituencies the full effect of a household franchise was not experienced until the third of those elections. But as a rough indication, the poll-book may serve.[1] From such figures it appears that although the electoral strength of parties was not greatly altered, so far as the change extended it was for the benefit of the Conservatives.

From 1832 to 1867 the advantage in England and Wales had been with the Liberals.[2] That advantage was slight, most of Liberal superiority in parliament coming from Scotland and Ireland. But from 1867 to 1884 the number of seats secured by each party in England and Wales was almost exactly equal; of a total of fourteen hundred seats for which elections were held during those years, three more were secured by Conservatives than by their opponents. The gain thus made by the Conservatives, which is to be reckoned as an advance from forty-six to fifty per cent, lay almost entirely in the counties. The Conservatives had been considered strong indeed before 1867, when they carried sixty-five per cent of the county elections. But from 1868 to 1880, nearly seventy-five per cent of the county seats were held by members of that party.[3] Much of their gain lay in the agricultural counties, and the party was doubtless more closely connected with the landed interest than before; but as will be seen, the Conservative advance in the industrial county divisions, by means of the £12 franchise, was yet more notable. In the boroughs the relative strength of parties remained essentially unchanged.

The gain of the Conservatives in the counties after 1867 is perhaps worthy of closer study. In accordance with

[1] The conclusions reached in the following pages are based upon election statistics taken from McCalmont, *Parliamentary Poll Book*.

[2] During that period the Liberals secured 2300 seats in elections to 1985 won by the Conservatives. The Liberals thus carried 53.6 per cent of the elections.

[3] Between 1832 and 1865 the Conservatives took 926 seats, and the Liberals 520. From 1868 to 1880 the Conservatives took 405 county seats, while the Liberals won only 149.

general expectation, the operation of the Chandos clause of 1832 had strengthened Conservative electoral power. In the constituencies where the tenant farmers were numerous, from 1832 to 1867, the control of the landlords was supreme, and the latter were more often affiliated with the Conservatives than with their opponents. The tenant farmers were naturally most numerous in the agricultural divisions, and their support, combined with that of the freeholders, effectively secured Tory predominance in those constituencies.[1] In the industrial counties, on the other hand, the tenant farmers were in a small minority on the register, and most of the freeholders formed part of the urban element. Their affiliations were in consequence Liberal, and that party had secured a slight majority of the seats in those divisions before 1867.[2]

It was generally assumed that the introduction of the £12 franchise in counties would not benefit the Conservatives, if, indeed, their power was not to be injured by it. In the agricultural divisions, the yeomen, who would be qualified by this franchise, were supposedly of the same general type as the £50 tenants, and the percentage of Conservative seats might fairly be expected to remain almost unchanged. In the industrial divisions, on the other hand, and in those which partook largely of the urban character, the new franchise should logically operate as had the £10 qualification of 1832, and, as was well known, the latter had assured nearly two-thirds of the seats to the Liberals. More than one Tory adherent complained that the compensation offered to the Conservatives in 1832 by the Chandos clause, was wholly lacking in 1867.

[1] The Conservatives carried 779 seats in these divisions before 1867, to 338 taken by the Liberals. The former thus won 77 per cent of the seats.

[2] The Liberals carried 162 seats and the Conservatives, 147.

But in the three elections which followed the second Reform Act, the new county voters proved themselves far more enthusiastic in the Conservative cause than had their predecessors. In the agricultural divisions the yeomen polled almost solidly for that party, and their opponents were able to carry barely a fifth of the seats. In the constituencies where the freeholders were not swamped by the new voters the Liberals maintained their position; but the number of such constituencies was not great. Before the act of 1867 the Conservatives took sixty-seven per cent of the agricultural county seats; afterwards they carried seventy-seven per cent.[1] In the industrial divisions the gain of the Conservatives was yet more striking. The £12 electors in the unrepresented towns, instead of following the example of the £10 borough voters, transformed the Liberal majority in those divisions into a clear minority. Before 1867, and while the urban freeholders held the power in the industrial counties, the Liberals secured fifty-two per cent of the seats; with the advent of the £12 electors they carried only thirty-four per cent.[2]

The Conservatives thus gained no little by the new county franchise. To a large extent the change is doubtless to be explained by the disgust experienced by the middle classes at the growing influence of the Radicals in Liberal councils. In the urban communities the £12 voters could no longer look to the Liberals for middle class legislation, as the £10 electors had done before 1867; Liberal party tendencies appeared to be all in favour of the class below those voters in the social scale. The existence of this attitude is borne out by that fact that in the boroughs where the £10 voters still remained in the majority after 1867, the strength of the Conservatives in-

[1] From 1868 to 1880 the Conservatives carried 313 and the Liberals only 95.

[2] The Conservatives carried 102 and the Liberals, 54.

creased notably. In the agricultural communities the
feeling between the yeomen farmers and the labourers
during this period was at its most acute point, and it was
to the Radicals that the latter looked for support. By
sentiment and by policy the middle class county voters
supported the Conservative candidate, who, notwithstanding the growth of Tory democracy, was not yet inclined
to compete with the Radicals for the alliance of Joseph
Arch and his followers. Nor were the £12 voters desirous
of witnessing the introduction of household suffrage in
counties, a development which, after 1877, was generally
considered to be an inevitable consequence of Liberal
success at the polls.

The effect of the new borough franchise upon party
strength is more difficult of analysis. The county constituencies were mainly of two types—rural and industrial.
But the boroughs differed from each other in an infinity
of forms and individualities, which often defy exact classi-
fication, and boroughs of which the general characteristics were almost identical, were frequently so strongly
affected by the tradition or sentiment of the community,
or by the influence which still rested with the local grandee,
that their party affiliations were of totally different colour.
The influence of the county landlords was largely devoted
to one party, but the landlords who controlled the
boroughs belonged to either. In boroughs, moreover, corruption played an important part; while in counties the
elections, except for intimidation and the payment of
travelling expenses, were comparatively pure. Thus the
normal effects of household suffrage in boroughs were not
experienced, and the results of the new franchise were to
a large extent denatured.

In the sum the relative strength of parties in boroughs
was unaffected by the act of 1867. As before the enfranchisement, the Liberals carried about sixty per cent of

the seats.[1] In certain types of boroughs the Conservatives made very striking gains, which clearly foreshadowed the hold that their party was destined to win over the labourers in the decade which followed the reform of 1884-1885. The most notable point of the Conservative advance lay in the metropolis. Before 1867 this had been the chief stronghold of Liberal strength, and of all parts of the kingdom it was apparently the most secure from all possibility of Tory attack. In the nine elections which succeeded the first reform more than ninety-five per cent of the metropolitan seats were held by Liberals. Of a total of one hundred and seventy-two seats for which elections took place, only seven had been won by Conservatives, and four of these were in the city of London. Although the new franchise still left the control of the metropolitan boroughs with the Liberals, it enabled their opponents to secure a strong minority. In the elections which followed 1867, the Conservatives carried thirty-four per cent of the seats instead of five per cent, as before the second reform.[2]

A similar advance, although less marked, was made by the Conservatives in the industrial towns.[3] In some, such as Ashton and Salford, where they had been totally excluded, they succeeded in carrying the majority of seats under the new franchise. In others, like Portsmouth, where Liberal control had usually been secure, electoral preëminence was transferred to the Conservatives. And

[1] From 1832 to 1865 the Liberals carried 1800 borough seats and the Conservatives, 1049; from 1868 to 1880 the Liberals carried 527 borough seats and the Conservatives, 304. In the earlier period the proportion of Liberal success in boroughs was thus 63.1 per cent; in the latter, 62.6 per cent.

[2] The Conservatives took 19 metropolitan seats; the Liberals, 35.

[3] From 1832 to 1865 the Conservatives took only 25 per cent of the seats in the large industrial towns; from 1868 to 1880 they took over 34 per cent.

even where the latter were still in a minority, the superiority of their opponents was not so overwhelming as before.

The increased electoral strength of the Conservatives in the metropolitan and industrial boroughs apparently justified the prediction of those who trusted to the Tory workingman, and counted upon his gratitude, as well as upon the results of his political "education." And that the householders of 1868 were far more ready to support Disraeli than the £10 electors of 1832 had been to bring Peel into power, cannot be doubted. But the advantage of the Conservatives did not extend into the larger industrial towns. While the percentage of Conservative seats increased in towns of less than a hundred thousand inhabitants, in the ten large centres of industry it remained unchanged. In the former it rose from a quarter to a third; in the latter it remained still a quarter.[1]

Thus, notwithstanding their gain, the Conservatives failed to control the foci of population and industry. In the great industrial towns of the provinces the artisans, like their middle class predecessors, preferred the Liberal candidate in three cases out of four; in the smaller centres of industry and in the metropolis, the Liberal party carried two-thirds of the seats. Moreover, in the boroughs of moderate size, a type characterized by cathedral cities and county towns, the new franchise left unchanged the Liberal supremacy which had been guaranteed by the support of the ten-pounders. In the thirty-four boroughs of this type, the control of the Liberals, under the suffrage of 1832, had been almost as undisputed as in the great industrial centres.[2] In such constituencies the

----

[1] In the ten large towns between 1832 and 1865 the Liberals carried 137 seats to 45 won by the Conservatives; from 1868 to 1880 the Liberals carried 55 to the 17 taken by the Conservatives.

[2] From 1832 to 1865 the Liberals carried 379; the Conservatives, 161.

Liberals more than preserved their advantage after 1867, and the labourers of Gloucester, Salisbury, and York proved less amenable to Conservative organization, and less strongly attracted by the lure of Tory democracy than the artisans of Liverpool or Westminster.[1] Inasmuch as these boroughs returned sixty members, the fact that three-fourths of them were Liberal, is to be reckoned an element of importance in the strength of that party; of far greater weight, indeed, than Liberal supremacy in the large industrial towns.

Of the smallest boroughs, of which there were more than fifty, the forces of Liberals and Conservatives had been, and continued to be, evenly matched.[2] In these constituencies, which were the most easily controlled by local or plutocratic influence, the introduction of household suffrage affected party strength in the slightest degree only. In but four boroughs was there any instance of an electorate formerly devoted to one party, transferring its favour to another, upon the accession of the new voters to power.

But in boroughs of which the population ranged from ten to twenty thousand, frequently of a semi-rural character, the effects of the new franchise can be traced in more definite lines. Liberal strength had always predominated in this type of constituency under the £10 franchise, and the advent of household suffrage increased it. In some towns, like Tiverton or Chipping Wycombe, old Whig pocket boroughs, the seat was assured to the Liberals no matter what the franchise. In Peterborough, Kendal, or Banbury, which were always Liberal, as in

---

[1] From 1868 to 1880 the Liberals carried 131; the Conservatives 49. Before 1867 the Liberal proportion was 71.4 per cent; after 1867 it was 72.7 per cent.

[2] Before 1867 the Liberals carried 48 per cent of these seats; after 1867 they took 47 per cent.

others like Whitehaven (invariably Conservative), no change was effected. But in many, like Newark, Whitby, or Barnstaple, a complete change of front took place, and to the disadvantage of the Conservatives. Before 1867, sixty-two per cent of these seats were in the hands of the Liberals; from 1868 to 1880 their ratio of seats was increased to seventy per cent.[1] Nor was Liberal strength in this quarter to be despised by their opponents, for this category of boroughs, so far as the number of seats was concerned, was strongest of all. It is not beyond the limits of possibility that the value of these smaller boroughs to the Liberal party was in the minds of those who arranged the redistribution of 1885; it may account for Liberal willingness, at that time, to retain boroughs of only ten thousand inhabitants, as it may for Conservative anxiety to disfranchise them.

In the remaining category of boroughs the franchise of 1867 effected a change more striking than any, and one which can hardly have failed to affect the future policy of the Liberals. This category included a type of borough which has already been referred to and which closely approximated that of the county constituencies; of great territorial extent, some of them larger than counties, these boroughs possessed a relatively scattered population, and their interests were essentially of a rural and agricultural character. Such were East Retford, Aylesbury, Cricklade, Shoreham, and others whose boundaries had been extended in 1832 in order to include the number of electors prescribed by the Reform Act. Their value to reformers was not small, especially after 1867, since they afforded an index of the manner in which a household franchise would operate in counties.

Previous to 1867, and under the £10 suffrage such

---

[1] Before 1867 the Liberals carried 416 seats; the Conservatives, 250. After 1867 the former won 144; the latter, only 63.

boroughs had shown themselves inclined to favour the Conservatives. The percentage of Conservative seats had been, indeed, larger in this type of constituency than in any other, with the exception of the agricultural counties. But the effect of household suffrage and the enfranchisement of the rural labourer was to transform this element of Conservative strength into one of weakness. Instead of sixty-three per cent of the seats, the Conservatives were able, after the reform of 1867, to secure but forty-six per cent.[1] At the moment the importance of the change was not great, since the seats were comparatively few in number; but the significance of the Liberal gain could not be denied. If the attitude of the agricultural labourer in the country as a whole might be gauged by that of the agricultural boroughs, it was hardly to be expected that the Liberal leaders would long delay their advocacy of a household suffrage in counties. Nor would the Tories hail that development with sincere delight, notwithstanding their general satisfaction at the result of the act of 1867, and their oft-repeated protestations of confidence in the capacity and integrity of the country labourer.

The effects of the act of 1867 cannot be completely summarized without reference to the redistribution of that and the following year, the results of which were also very slightly in favour of the Conservatives. That redistribution was, however, not extensive and even without it the Conservatives would have benefited by the alteration in the franchise. That fact appears if we summarize the results of the foregoing analysis. The qualifications of 1832 had entrenched the Liberals strongly in the boroughs, although their strength in the counties was lessened by the Chandos clause, which called the tenant farmers into elect-

---

[1] From 1832 to 1865 the Conservatives carried 103 seats and the Liberals only 59; after 1867 and to 1880 the Conservatives carried 25 and the Liberals 29.

oral existence, and thus did something to redress the balance disturbed by the opening of the Tory close boroughs. In 1867 came the other party's turn. The gain of the Liberals in the rural and smaller boroughs was counterbalanced by that of the Conservatives in the metropolis and smaller centres of industry. In the counties the £12 occupier assured the Conservatives greater power than had ever before come to their lot. Where the new voters clearly outnumbered the old the advantage of the Conservatives was overwhelming; and even in the divisions where the freeholders still held the balance, the influx of occupying voters turned the fate of many elections against the Liberals. That the Conservatives might without discouragement look to the workmen in the industrial towns, and that the Liberals had nothing to hope from the yeomen farmers became inexorably clear as election succeeded election.

The advantage of the Conservative party was not, as might be rashly assumed, an implication that old-fashioned Conservative principles had triumphed. The advance of democracy was not stopped by it and it is in the very period that follows the second Reform Act that began the most striking changes experienced by the representative system. It is curious that the change, which is made patent in many directions, should not have been manifested in the composition of the House of Commons. After 1867 as before, the majority of members were still closely connected with the great families of the aristocracy. It is certain that the domination of the aristocracy of land in the Commons was being replaced by that of a plutocracy; this change, which had been under way before 1867, still continued; but that the process was accelerated or even related to the act of 1867 does not appear. Nor did the working class suffrage result in working-class representatives. In the three elections which followed the enfranchisement of householders in boroughs, only three men of the labouring class and directly representative of the interests of that class were sent to Westminster. Candidates like George Howell and Randall Cremer, who might have been expected to poll an overwhelming labour vote, were hopelessly defeated in constituencies where the franchise was extended to all the labourers. Few emulated their example, and the success of Burt in 1874 and of Broadhurst in 1880 stood forth as shining exceptions.[1]

The practical identity of composition of the House of Commons under a restricted and under an extended franchise, appears clearly in a comparison of the English and Welsh members in 1865 and in 1880.[2] In the former year there were one hundred and sixty-five sons or near relations of peers, by birth or marriage; in the latter year there were one hundred and fifty-five, of whom in each case about half were sons. Many of these scions of the aristocracy owed their title to the rapidly made wealth of their relations; but half of them at least were closely connected with the heads of the thirty-one houses, known as the "great governmental families." In 1865 there were seventy-three baronets or sons of baronets in the Commons, and in 1880 there were eighty, for the most part representative of the interests of the landed and county families. More than sixty commoners in each parliament had the gift of one or more church livings. Those directly engaged in the legal profession increased, it is true, after 1867: before that year there were eighty-two barristers and solicitors, who by 1880 had increased to ninety-six.

[1] For a discussion of contemporary opinion upon the chances of workingmen candidates as a result of the act of 1867, see *Spectator*, September 14, 1867. For a popular description of working-class members, see *Harper's*, lxxiii, 505.

[2] The following figures are based upon an analysis constituted from Dod, *Parliamentary Companion*, 1865, 1880.

It is rather surprising that the strength of business in the House grew slowly. In 1865 there were ninety members ostensibly engaged in manufacturing and mercantile operations, while in 1880 there were one hundred and twelve. The power of business, however, does not really appear in the number of those who described themselves as engaged in business pursuits. For both before and after 1867 about three hundred members of the House were concerned in the management of railways or were directors in large or miscellaneous companies.[1] In both 1865 and 1880 there were eighty members who had served in the army or navy, generally as officers in one of the crack regiments; and two hundred and fifty had attended one of the great public schools or had gone up to Oxford or Cambridge.

But to measure the effect of the enfranchisement of 1867 by the electoral gain of the Conservatives, or by the composition of the House of Commons before and after the introduction of the new suffrage, would obviously be illusive. There can be no doubt but that basic changes resulted from the enormous increase in the electorate; these changes were retarded by the unequal distribution of seats, by the complexities of registration, as well as by corrupt electioneering, and were by no means complete until after 1885. But even before the third Reform Act they began to affect radically the relation of constituency to candidate, the attitude of members, and consequently the character of legislation. To exactly define the change accomplished between 1867 and 1885 is not so easy as stating its existence; but its main lines have often been indicated and probably with accuracy.

As Goschen pointed out in the suffrage debate of 1884, that which might naturally have been expected from a vast accession of one class to the franchise actually took place,

[1] *Spectator*, February 17, 1866.

and without delay.[1] The powers of resistance to any popular demand decreased notably both inside and outside the House. Much of this change doubtless resulted from the influence of the new party organizations, whose birth followed naturally the provisions of 1867 and 1872. The relation of member to constituency was radically altered by the growth of the Caucus and the corresponding Conservative associations. Hitherto the choice of candidates and the management of electoral affairs had been in the hands of quite independent and self-nominated local committees, who corresponded when necessary with the party whips, but formed no part of any larger association or federation.[2]

But with the enormous and sudden growth of the electorate, a system of centralization became inevitable; first forced by the necessity of nullifying the effect of the minority clause of 1867, it tended to throw the member wholly into the power of his constituents. It resulted that there sprang up what Hartington called the identification of the House of Commons with the people; this fact, or feeling, fostered the growing idea, dear to Radicals of the old school, that the Commons were not a sovereign assembly, but a body of delegates who could only act in large matters upon special "mandates," granted them by the electorate. Against this idea strong individualities, like Forster's, might strive, and for a time successfully, but the ultimate victory was inevitably with the organization.[3]

This new-found power of the electorate, which is not to be traced in the poll-book or in the composition of the House of Commons, was not slow to prove its force in

[1] 3 Hansard, cclxxxv, 419.

[2] Holland, *Life of the Duke of Devonshire*, i, 244.

[3] Ostrogorski, *Democracy and Parties*, i, 194-204; Holland, *Life of the Duke of Devonshire*, i, 253.

other and more vital directions. It was not to be expected that the balance of power should be changed and the affairs of state placed, at least potentially, at the discretion of a new class, without finding a reflex of such a development in the attitude of members. Both Gladstone and Argyll complained in 1880 that opinion outside of parliament was coming to have more weight than the judgment of the members, or the cabinet itself. No longer were the Liberals capable of withstanding the force of Radical influence.[1]

Upon the Conservatives, the effect of the change was still greater. The act of 1867 was the work of a Conservative government and its first-fruits, the new Conservative electors, must henceforth be considered in formulating party policy. As Goschen pointed out, the Conservative workingman elector was called into existence by the act of the Conservatives; he voted for Conservative candidates; but he coerced Conservative members in a democratic direction.[2] Tory democracy, as Disraeli claimed, might reach back to Bolingbroke, but its application after 1867 resulted from the weakened powers of Conservative resistance. And its force was increased by the new attitude of parties, so bitterly execrated by Lowe, which led both Liberals and Conservatives to promise their readiness to carry out the will of the people, in competition with each other.

Nor was the position of the Commons alone affected. The crisis of 1832 had determined the superiority of the lower over the upper House; it was inevitable that the weakening of the former's independence must affect the recognized functions of the latter. If the mandate of the supreme electorate was to determine the action of the Commons, the Lords could not expect to emancipate them-

1 Morley, *Life of Gladstone,* iii, 4.
2 3 Hansard, cclxxxv, 419.

selves from its control; nay, they were even to be used as a weapon of democracy against the resistance of the Commons. With bitterness and unavailing regret the Whigs recognized the growth of the belief that the proper function of the Lords was to see that the Commons did not act without, or go beyond, the popular mandate. And the Conservatives, accepting the position, frankly announced that the chief duty of the Peers was to force an appeal to the people.[1]

But while these results of the enfranchisement of 1867 began to make themselves felt during the period under consideration, their full effects were by no means clearly manifest until after 1885. The powers of resistance to popular demands had, it is true, been weakened by the introduction of household suffrage, but they were still vigorous. The element of conservatism in both of the chief parties maintained its position and found support in many characteristics of the electoral system, which were all to the disadvantage of democracy. As we saw, the suffrage in counties was still such as to exclude the agricultural labourers as well as the miners and the artisans of the unrepresented towns. The franchise was still based upon privilege, to a large extent, and the county members, chosen by a small minority of the population continued to be strong bulwarks of conservatism. The distribution of electoral power was such that the centres of industry and population were still outvoted by the landed interest, which often more than held its own against the clamour of public opinion. Through the system of registration the local associations and magnates still controlled the making of qualifications, and, until the rise of the caucus, in the interests of the wealthy. The voice of the people was still hushed by means of corrupt influence, and the

[1] 3 Hansard, cclxxxvi, 954; Lowell, *The Government of England*, i, 410.

choice of candidates restricted by the expense involved in an election contest.

In the succeeding chapters I purpose to show how the first limited effects of the suffrage of 1867 were completed and made universal. Partly by the extension of the franchise to the counties, and by a complete revolution in the distribution of electoral power, partly by the surrender of registration to the popular associations, and partly by the elimination of bribery and the forced reduction in election expenses, the process of electoral democratization was largely finished. The buttresses of aristocratic dominion were undermined and a new epoch in constitutional development begun.

CHAPTER XI

The Distribution of Seats and Its Effect upon Electoral Power Before and After 1867

Necessity of redistribution after 1868—The distribution of 1832—First Reform Act did not recognize principle of uniform representation—Advantage of the boroughs in representation—And of the South—Claims of the counties—Disadvantage of the manufacturing districts—Advantage of the landed interest through small boroughs—Absolute and relative electoral strength of the small boroughs—Movement for redistribution—The Chartists—Hume—The *Eclectic Review*—Both Liberals and Conservatives opposed to radical redistribution—Disraeli's theory of representation—His defence of the small boroughs—Supported by Gladstone—Question of redistribution in 1866—Principle of grouping boroughs—Disraeli's proposals of 1867—Extended slightly—Power of landowners little reduced by redistribution of 1867-1868—Borough boundaries—Urban districts not cut out from counties—University representation—The minority provision—Its effects—Attitude of parties towards the redistribution—Effect of the redistribution upon party strength—Anomalies of distribution after 1868—Continually accentuated—Electoral strength of small boroughs and the South—Upper classes profited thereby.

THE suffrage anomalies which persisted in counties and boroughs after 1867, and which were in part actually emphasized by the act of that year, were by no means the sole object of Radical attack. The power which the landed aristocracy exercised in elections certainly depended to a large extent upon the restrictions placed upon county voting rights. But a more important factor in the electoral strength of the landlords was the uneven distribution of seats. Notwithstanding the extent of the redistribution of 1832, there remained numerous small rural boroughs through their control of which the upper

classes continued to return a large majority of the House
of Commons. The agricultural districts of the South
continued to enjoy a representation far exceeding, proportionately to their wealth and population, that of the
industrial Midlands and Northwest. The changes made
in 1868 were slight, and their effects were soon obliterated
by the growth of the industrial districts. Hence, at the
moment when Trevelyan was agitating for the extension
of the suffrage to the counties, there were many who
believed that the more crying necessity was a drastic redistribution, by which the great centres might receive
seats apportioned more fairly in relation to their wealth
and importance.

In the minds of those who had carried the first Reform
Act, the redistribution of seats had been conceived with a
double object. The power of nomination belonging to the
proprietors of the small boroughs was to be weakened, if
not destroyed, by the disfranchisement of the smallest and
least wealthy of the constituencies. In the second place
certain new interests which had developed in the wake of
the industrial revolution and built up centres of commerce
and manufactures, were to be recognized. It was, however, no part of the reformers' plan to so order the distribution of seats that the numerical anomalies, existent
before 1832, should disappear completely; nor were they
inclined to admit that the principle of distribution should
depend upon the population or the wealth of the district
represented. It is true that the ministers in 1832 took
population and taxes as a rough test as to whether a
borough was a nomination constituency, or whether it was
worthy of receiving representation for the first time; but
Whigs agreed with Tories in discarding any idea of
allotting seats in strict proportion to the size or importance of the constituency.

The doctrine of uniform representation or of equal

electoral districts had not been without its advocates. Pitt had brought it forward in 1785, and in 1820 it formed part of the Radical creed and was emphasized as strongly as the principle of household suffrage.[1] In 1831 Durham planned to introduce a bill which embodied the theory of uniform representation, and the application of that theory was evidently considered in the light of a possibility, for Macaulay congratulated the reforming ministers on their refusal to adopt it.[2] Even Howick hinted at the advisability of considering some such plan, and so moderate a member as P. W. Wynn believed that the number of members for a district ought generally to be approximated to the number of inhabitants. Hume, as might have been expected, warmly advocated the distribution of seats in equal electoral districts.[3]

In the redistribution of 1832, however, the test of population and wealth was followed so loosely that the Tories, on the lookout for some pretext for obstruction, were able to spend long hours in expatiating upon the electoral anomalies which were preserved or accentuated by the schedules.[4] It is true that the act of 1832 diminished, in some degree, the electoral preponderance of the South of England over the North, and of the boroughs over the counties; but the measure was a palliative merely, and the advantage of the South and of the boroughs remained striking. The boroughs returned more than twice as many members to Westminster as did the counties; and of the 496 members, a third only came from the rich and thickly populated districts to the north of a line drawn from the Wash to the Severn.

---

[1] 3 Hansard, iii, 226; *Edinburgh Review,* xxxiv, 468.
[2] 3 Hansard, ii, 1191; Russell, *Recollections,* 69.
[3] 3 Hansard, iii, 145; v, 1352; x, 1085.
[4] Croker, especially, laid great stress upon the assertion that the reformers, while they were destroying traditional principles, failed to introduce principles of order and regularity.

The electoral advantage of the boroughs over the counties was still more impressive if considered relatively to their population. The counties, before the second Reform Act, had less than half as many seats as the boroughs, although they exceeded the latter in population by three millions; the proportion of members to inhabitants was hardly more than a third as great in counties as in the boroughs.[1] In the South, the home of the small borough, this disparity was still more striking. Relatively to their population, the boroughs of the Southwest had eight times the representation of the county divisions.[2] And the contrast between individual constituencies was still greater; the eastern division of Cornwall county, containing eight times as many inhabitants as lived in its boroughs, had only half the number of members. In the North, where small boroughs were less numerous, the advantage of the boroughs was not so great; but even there the ratio of members to inhabitants was between three and four times as great in the boroughs as in the counties.[3]

This fact offered to the landowning aristocracy, whose electoral strength was supposed to lie in the counties, some ground for protest against the predominating representative strength of the towns. From the middle of the

	Population	Members	Ratio of members to population
[1] Counties, . . .	11,427,101	162	one to 70,000
Boroughs, . .	8,667,858	334	one to 26,000

Parliamentary Papers, 1866, nos. 3626, 3736. Unless otherwise stated the figures in the following pages are taken from the same sources.

	Population	Members	Ratio of members
[2] Boroughs, . .	512,014	62	one to 8,000
Counties, . .	1,298,251	13	one to 68,000

[3] In individual cases the numerical anomaly was very striking; the boroughs of Ripon and Knaresborough, with an aggregate population of 11,000, had equal representation with the West Riding, which had a population of 888,000.

eighteenth century frequent claims had been advanced for additions to the number of county seats. Chatham and Pitt both advocated the increase of the county members, and were supported by Shelburne and Burke. It was in the spirit of concession to this demand that the new seats were created for the counties in 1832 and, in 1843 and 1846, Croker asked for more.[1] Disraeli, in 1847 and 1852, and Cranbourne, in 1866, pointed out the electoral disadvantage of the counties, demanding a redistribution, and such a rectification of boundaries as would prevent the swamping of agricultural constituencies by the manufacturing element in the unrepresented towns.[2] Additional representation for the counties was judged especially necessary at that time in view of the prospect of the lowering of the franchise and the increase in power which would thereby result to the urban element.

The manufacturers, however, were able to show that the disadvantage of the landed classes was purely theoretical, and depended for its proof upon the fallacy that the agricultural interest lay purely in the county constituencies, and the manufacturing in the boroughs. As a matter of fact, many of the boroughs were as rural in their character and offered as strong support to the squires in elections as the most rural of the county divisions. Disraeli himself admitted that agriculture exercised strong influence through the small boroughs, whose electoral strength, in proportion to their population and even absolutely, was enormous. In the small boroughs the landed interest found a compensating balance which more than countervailed the power of the manufacturing element in the large towns.[3]

The manufacturers pointed out also that many of the

---

[1] Kent, *The English Radicals*, 408.
[2] 3 Hansard, cxx, 1202; clxxxii, 74, 226; clxxxiii, 885.
[3] 3 Hansard, clxxxiii, 885.

county divisions which were at a representative disadvantage, were industrial rather than agricultural in their character. It was true that in the West Riding the boroughs, with a population of half a million, had sixteen members in 1852, although the county divisions, with a population of eight hundred thousand, had but two members. But that fact was no proof of the disadvantage of agriculture, for the county was, in truth, largely of an industrial character; "from Leeds to Bradford there was a continual succession of stacks, not of wheat, but of chimneys."[1]

A comparison of the representation of the agricultural and manufacturing counties shows very plainly the electoral advantage of the former, relatively to their population. In the agricultural divisions of the South Midlands, before the redistribution of 1868, there was a member to every 46,000 inhabitants; in the manufacturing Northwest, on the other hand, there was a county population of more than two millions, represented by only thirteen members: one seat to every 170,000 inhabitants. South Stafford, the centre of the potteries, in the midst of a network of railways, the most industrial of the industrial Midlands, had a population of 260,000 and two members; the neighbouring county, Buckingham, of a purely agricultural character, returned three members, although it contained but 120,000 inhabitants. In South Cheshire, the most rural of the northwestern county divisions, representative strength was proportionately three times that of the industrial West Riding.[2] A succession of similar comparisons indicates the same general conclusion. The average ratio of seats to population in ten

1 3 Hansard, cxx, 1202.

		Population	Members	Ratio of members
2 West Riding,	.	880,994	4	one to 220,000
South Cheshire,	.	160,000	2	one to 80,000

agricultural counties, was four and a half that which prevailed in the same number of manufacturing divisions.[1]

The main strength of the landed interest, however, as indicated by statistics as well as by the Radical attack and the agriculturalist defence, was the number of small boroughs which had survived the disfranchisement of 1832. The extension of their boundaries which had then taken place, naturally transformed many of them into purely rural areas.[2] Although the Radical complaint that they were "decayed and decrepit" villages can hardly be deemed fair, certainly a large number of them represented a mere pin-prick of town in the centre of an extended agricultural district.[3] In certain parts of the country

---

[1] The comparison of contiguous constituencies of different industrial character renders the anomalies more obvious:

{ West Kent,	one member to	138,000 inhabitants
{ West Sussex,	one member to	26,000 inhabitants
{ North Durham,	one member to	84,000 inhabitants
{ Westmoreland,	one member to	24,000 inhabitants
{ Glamorgan,	one member to	71,000 inhabitants
{ Radnor,	one member to	18,000 inhabitants

The twenty agricultural and manufacturing divisions selected for comparison are the same as those chosen in the preceding chapter. In the agricultural divisions the lowest ratio of members to population was to be found in Oxfordshire: one to 41,000. The highest was in Rutland: one to 10,000. The average ratio in the agricultural divisions was one to 32,000. In the manufacturing divisions the lowest ratio of members was in the West Riding: one to 220,000. The highest was in Glamorgan: one to 71,000. The average ratio was one to 143,000. The *Eclectic Review* (xcvii, 99) published statistics comparing certain manufacturing with agricultural divisions from the point of view of total rental as well as of population:

	Population	Rental
6 manuf'ng divisions returning 81 members,	4,886,360	£20,788,551
7 agric'l divisions returning 81 members,	1,290,052	£ 7,407,283

[2] There were 59 boroughs of more than 15 and less than 25 square miles; 47 of more than 25 and less than 40 square miles; and five of more than 45 and less than 80 square miles, 3 Hansard, clxv, 767.

[3] 3 Hansard, clxxxiii, 510.

the small boroughs were to be found in such frequency,
and so late as 1865, as to recall unreformed conditions.
In the South especially, the small boroughs practically
controlled representation, and many of these boroughs
contained less than six hundred voters apiece. Of the boroughs in the southeastern and south-midland groups,
more than half could not show a population of ten thousand, although they were widely extended areas. And
although the proportion of small boroughs was less
striking in the other parts of the country, a half of all
the borough members were returned by towns of less than
fifteen thousand inhabitants.[1]

The absolute representative strength of the small borough was thus by no means small. And in proportion to
the number of persons represented, the electoral power of
the landed interest in the small boroughs far exceeded
that of the manufacturing interests in the large towns.
The great industrial centres of the Northwest, with their
ten thousands, received no more representation than the
thinly populated rural boroughs of the South.[2] And the

---

[1] In the Southwest, out of 38 represented boroughs, 24 were of
less than ten thousand inhabitants, and 15 of seven thousand or
under. Ashburton, Lyme-Regis, and Honiton, each contained barely
three thousand inhabitants; Dartmouth, Totnes, and Wells, each had
but little over four thousand. Twenty-four constituencies among
the southwestern boroughs had an electorate of less than six hundred,
and seven of them had less than three hundred voters apiece. In
the Southwest, 23 of the 62 borough members were returned by the
15 smallest boroughs, which contained less than a sixth of the aggregate borough population of that group. In the Southeast, Arundel
in Sussex contained only 2500 inhabitants. Exclusive of the
metropolitan boroughs, there were in the southern groups 79 represented boroughs, of which 60 had less than fifteen thousand inhabitants. And there were at this time 93 unrepresented townships in
the West Riding, and 111 in Lancashire, with an aggregate population
of 909 thousand, *Parliamentary Papers*, 1866, nos. 3626, 3736; *Eclectic
Review*, xcvii, 99.

[2] In the Southwest and South-Midlands there was a borough
member to every 8000 inhabitants, whereas in the industrial Mid-

relative weakness of the industrial interests before the
second Reform Act appears still more clearly, if we compare individual constituencies. Thus Honiton with about
three thousand inhabitants was equally represented with
Liverpool and its four hundred thousand.[1] Five manufacturing towns with an aggregate population of a million
and a half, sent no more members to the Commons than did
the same number of agricultural boroughs with a population of twenty-two thousand.[2] Moreover, in many of
the towns of the rural type the population had decreased

lands there was but one to every 32,000; and in the Northwest, even
including various small rural boroughs, there was but one to 49,000.
In the metropolitan boroughs the ratio of representation was only
one to 137,000.

[1] Totnes with a population of 4000 and Tower Hamlets with its
650,000 were equally represented. Cf. also:

*Ratio of members
to population*

{ Dudley,	one in 44,975	In Worcester
{ Evesham,	one in 2,640	
{ Bristol,	one in 77,046	In Gloucester
{ Cirencester,	one in 3,168	
{ Norwich,	one in 39,945	In Norfolk
{ Thetford,	one in 2,104	

[2] Liverpool	. . 443,938	Honiton	.	. .	3,301
Manchester	. 357,979	Totnes	.	. .	4,001
Birmingham	. 296,076	Wells	. .	. .	4,648
Leeds	. . 207,165	Marlborough		. .	4,893
Sheffield	. . 185,172	Knaresborough		. .	5,402

Forty rural boroughs with an aggregate population of about 200,000
returned 64 representatives, whereas Birmingham with 300,000
returned only 2 members. The representatives of 51 large towns,
with an aggregate population of more than five millions, could be
offset in a division of the House by the representatives of 66 small
boroughs which had an aggregate population of only 450,000. There
were living in the large towns more than four millions, about half
of the entire borough population of England, and yet that half had
only 34 out of 334 borough seats, *Parliamentary Papers,* 1866, nos.
3626, 3736; 3 Hansard, clxxxviii, 823.

since 1832, whereas in the manufacturing towns the population had increased by more than one hundred and fifty per cent.[1] The anomalies were therefore becoming more striking with the passing of each year.

There was accordingly much justification for the complaint of the Radicals that the redistribution of 1832 had bequeathed too large an influence to the landed interest. In the counties the ratio of seats was far higher in the agricultural than in the manufacturing divisions. The number of small boroughs offered opportunity for the electoral control of the landowners, and the number of seats thus devoted to the agricultural interest was out of all proportion to the number of their inhabitants. Impelled by practical considerations, as well as by their confidence in democratic theory, the Radicals began to urge again the principle that seats should be apportioned according to the population of the constituency represented.

This principle was voiced by the Chartists in their demand for equal electoral districts, but, like other of their points, it was rather lost in the turmoil of their agitation, and the extent to which opinion was influenced is doubtful. But the failure of the Chartist crusade found the Radicals ready and anxious to take up the movement for a more regular distribution of seats. In the House of Commons, Hume, when bringing forward his motion on representation in 1847, argued strongly for a closer relation between population and distribution; and shortly afterwards Bright pointed out with great keenness the importance of a democratic redistribution. In his opinion, the question was far more vital than the much-discussed

[1] Buckingham, Chichester, Cockermouth, Huntington, Knaresborough, Lichfield, Lymington, Marlow, Newport, Poole, Stamford, Totnes, Wells, Windsor, had all decreased in population from 1851 to 1861, *Parliamentary Papers*, 1867, no. 367.

subject of the franchise, and he believed that any bill, no matter what concession it appeared to make on the suffrage question, should be repudiated unless it provided for the extinction of the small boroughs and the transfer of their seats to the towns.[1]

A few years previous to the reopening of the reform question in the Commons, a vigorous campaign for the removal of the more glaring electoral anomalies was begun in the *Eclectic Review*, which provided food for discussion in the country at large. The starting point of this argument, which was carried on for a decade after 1848, was in no sense philosophical; the contention was based entirely upon the practical injustice done to the middle and lower classes by the existing distribution. So long as the absurdities continued which allowed Calne and Midhurst equal power with Liverpool, upper class interests must remain paramount, and were bound to be protected to the detriment of the masses. The middle classes, it was asserted, were excluded absolutely from all direct influence in government as a result of the anomalies; the single means which was left them to express and obtain their will, was popular agitation of the type which had won the victory for free trade. The waste and carelessness of government, which the articles emphasized and declared to be similar to that which had caused the first Reform Bill, was the result of the absolutism of the "ruling legislative class"; such absolutism could be broken down only by a drastic redistribution.[2]

The articles laid stress upon the disproportionate electoral strength of the large and small constituencies, tested both by population and property, and published the gist of current pamphlets which attempted the easy task of throwing into contrast the wealth of the West Riding or

[1] 3 Hansard, clxxxii, 885, 1214.
[2] *Eclectic Review*, lxxxviii, 233; xcv, 227; xcvii, 93; cix, 74.

Birmingham with that of Arundel or Totnes.[1] Exact
electoral symmetry was not demanded; no magic talis-
man lay in perfectly uniform distribution, and inequality
of itself would not be harmful if it did not affect the social
and political progress of the nation. But the existing
system furnished so well fortified a stronghold for the
aristocracy that, in the opinion of the reformers, progress
was impossible; and the equality of the value of a vote
in each constituency was as necessary for the realization of
the nation's welfare as the extension of the franchise.[2]

Approximation to such equality even in the most distant sense was, however, distasteful to both the chief
parties in the House of Commons. The Reform Bill of
1852 included no plan of redistribution whatever, and
the effect of the redistribution proposed in the government bills of the next eight years, would only have affected
numerical anomalies in the slightest degree. The scheme
brought forward in 1854 by Russell was the most complete. Of the smallest boroughs, nineteen were to be disfranchised absolutely, where the electorate fell below three
hundred or the population below five thousand; one seat
was to be taken from thirty-three others, where the
standard was placed at five hundred and ten thousand
respectively. In the bill of 1859, Disraeli proposed a
still more limited plan; no borough was to be absolutely
disfranchised, and only fifteen, with a population not
exceeding six thousand, were to lose one seat. Russell's
bill of 1860 was only slightly more progressive, in that
it proposed to take one member from the twenty-five
boroughs which contained less than seven thousand
inhabitants.[3]

1 Alexander Mackay, *Electoral Districts,* London, 1848.
2 Bright agreed thoroughly that the system was wholly delusive
and that it defrauded the middle class of the power which the act
of 1832 proposed to give them, Smith, *Life of Bright,* ii, 235.
3 3 Hansard, cxxx, 499; clii, 1003; clvi, 2060.

THE HOMOEOPATHIC MINISTER

"You see, Mr. John Bull, large Doses of Reform are bad for your
Constitution. But here is a Globule, or Infinitesimal Bill, which," etc., etc.

While the power of the landed aristocracy would thus
have been left almost unimpaired by the narrow range of
disfranchisement, each of the bills proposed to reaffirm
that power, by giving most of the seats taken from the
small boroughs to the counties. They were all truly conservative measures and provided a fair counterpoise to
the loss which the aristocracy would have undergone
through disfranchisement. Of the sixty-two seats which
would have been available in 1854, forty-six were destined
for the counties; in Disraeli's bill, eight of the fifteen
were for the counties, and in that of the following year
fifteen of the twenty-five. The members who denied, as
well as those who affirmed that distribution of seats should
bear some relation, however distant, to population and
property, all agreed in increasing the number of county
seats. Such different types as Russell, Knightly, Lord
Robert Cecil, and writers in the *North British Review*,
advocated, though for different reasons, the transfer of
seats from the small boroughs to the counties.[1] Disraeli
refused always to admit the relevancy of population to
representation; but he asserted that if it were admitted,
the claim of the counties was undeniable.[2]

But none, with the exception of the small circle of Radicals, desired a wide disfranchisement, and practically all
of the great figures of the House defended the small boroughs as a valuable factor in the electoral system. The
idea of electoral districts, or of distribution based upon
exact equality of population, was bitterly decried by

[1] Russell, because he believed that population should be taken
as a rough-and-ready guide; Cecil, because he insisted that rural
boroughs were generally urban in their sympathies; Knightly, because
he believed that even though the aristocracy could exercise influence
through the small boroughs, the small farmers in the counties
deserved more representatives, 3 Hansard, cxxx, 499; cliii, 477, 578;
North British Review, xxviii, 461.

[2] 3 Hansard, clii, 978.

both parties. Russell believed that only through variety of type of constituency, was the element of moderation and compromise infused into the representative system. Walpole's chief reason for objecting to the assimilation of county and borough suffrage was that such identity would lead to equal electoral districts, an opinion in which Graham concurred.[1] Disraeli based his opposition to a proportionate distribution upon the traditional dislike and fear of granting power to the numerical majority.[2]

The latter was most distinct in his refusal to argue the case upon the question of numerical anomalies. The function of the House, he said, was something more than to represent property and population. If that principle were accepted the House of Commons would be composed of landowners and manufacturers solely; an excellent assembly, but by no means representative of the nation. All the other interests must also be recognized, and constituencies must be provided through which their voice might be heard in the Commons. If Liverpool, with its four hundred thousand, ought to be represented to express the views of that wealthy community, so ought Arundel, with its two thousand, which returned a member to represent the Catholics throughout the kingdom. Population and property were in Disraeli's opinion elements, but by no means the sole elements, deserving of representation. Numbers and property exercised such wide influence through indirect means that they could not expect to snatch the single chance of representation still left to the other interests of the country.[3] This principle of representation of interests and not of numbers, was embodied by Disraeli in his bill of 1859, which disfranchised no borough entirely and recognized new constituencies, not

1 3 Hansard, cxxx, 496; cliii, 769.
2 3 Hansard, clii, 994.
3 3 Hansard, clii, 972-979.

on account of their population, but because in them were to be found distinct interests hitherto unrepresented. In the division of counties, also, the principle of division was not based upon population, but rather upon the separation of interests according as they were industrial or agricultural.[1]

As might have been expected, Disraeli defended the small boroughs warmly, since in his opinion they furnished desirable variety and opened so many avenues to the representation of different interests. Nearly all the eminent personalities in the House of Commons agreed with him. Russell considered the small boroughs necessary for carrying on the government, and felt that they had returned some of the best men sent to parliament in latter years.[2] Such different types as Sidney Herbert, Bulwer-Lytton, Liddell, and Walpole agreed with him on this point. Naturally the hard-shell Tories went still further in their support of the small boroughs, and did not hesitate to claim that the government since 1832 had practically been administered by that part of the representative system which had been unaffected by the first Reform Act.[3] Gladstone's eulogy of the small boroughs, in 1859, and his list of eminent members returned by them, recalled vivid echoes of 1831 and the shades of Croker and Wetherell.[4]

The sole opposition to the small boroughs, except that emanating from Radical quarters, was founded upon dis-

[1] 3 Hansard, clii, 999-1001.
[2] 3 Hansard, clvi, 2059; clvii, 1003; Argyll, *Memoirs,* ii, 132.
[3] 3 Hansard, cliii, 446, 554, 593; Walsh, *The Practical Results of the Reform Act,* 73. Stuart Wortley said that no measure would have a chance of passing which proposed a large disfranchisement of the smaller boroughs; and Gladstone admitted that the plan of 1854 "would have gone to the dogs" because of the extent of disfranchisement, 3 Hansard, cliii, 868, 1053.
[4] 3 Hansard, cliii, 1055-1059.

like of the power of nomination which still remained vested in the chief landowners. This objection, however, was by no means general, and many frankly advocated the small boroughs on this very score. The *North British Review* deplored the growing disappearance of nomination as being the chief reason for the decadence of parliamentary talent.[1]

The general concurrence of the chief political parties upon the question of redistribution was thus established. Numerical anomalies were no evil, and the advantages of small boroughs were unquestioned; Russell, Palmerston, and Graham all approved of Disraeli's ideas; Gladstone did not hesitate to praise his plan of redistribution enthusiastically, and deplored more extensive disfranchisement.[2] The Radicals, it is true, protested against the barrier to democracy which was maintained by the small boroughs. Bright demanded what interest would be left if population and property were removed, and what they did not include; he sneered at the small boroughs as the cities of refuge for the political destitute; Roebuck pointed out that despite himself Disraeli took population as a basis of distribution.[3] These and other ineffectual complaints represented a body of reforming opinion, which was, to all appearances, however, limited to a few of the more active spirits.

With the resurrection of reform in 1866, the question of redistribution immediately assumed a paramount position. Both Radicals and Tories considered it the crux of the situation; the former hoped to use it as a means for increasing the electoral prospects of democracy, while

[1] 3 Hansard, cliii, 538, 749, 921; *North British Review,* xxviii, 463.

[2] He said at this time, "There is no substantial difference of opinion between political parties upon this subject," 3 Hansard, cliii, 1046-1053.

[3] 3 Hansard, clii, 1020, 1028; cliii, 780.

the latter desired to safeguard the property interests threatened by the lowering of the borough franchise.[1] Bright, as before, insisted that as it was a fallacy that the middle classes had been in power after 1832, so the working class suffrage would be nugatory and a weapon without edge or temper, unless the value of a vote was everywhere made equal.[2] The Whigs and Tories, on the other hand, believed that in redistribution lay the solution of the problem as to how the number of electors was to be increased without unduly affecting the influence of property. For this reason, the moderate Liberals were willing to join with the Conservatives in demanding that no extension of the suffrage take place without a redistribution.

In 1866, for the first time, however, the principle of distribution according to population began to be generally advocated in the House, and the belief that the electoral power of the constituencies should be proportionately equal suddenly gained strength. Stanley, in seconding the motion of Lord Grosvenor that redistribution should accompany the change in the franchise, referred to the numerical amomalies in the distribution of seats as a distinct evil.[3] Lord Hobart, too, complained that herein lay the most serious defect of the representative system: "No member of a community can be said to be represented . . . who has not an equal share with each of the rest of the nation in the choice of its rulers."[4]

But Gladstone, while he no longer professed such fervid admiration for the small boroughs as in 1859, did not depart from the principles upon which the redistributions previously proposed had rested; and the representation of

---

[1] 3 Hansard, clxxxiii, 16-17; clxxxii, 1214.
[2] Smith, *Life of Bright*, ii, 235.
[3] 3 Hansard, clxxxii, 1171.
[4] *MacMillan's Magazine,* xiii, 260.

interests and not of numbers was the basis of his scheme of 1866. Like Disraeli, he planned to obtain the seats which must be found for new and growing districts, not by extinguishing, but only by limiting the representation of the small boroughs.[1] Gladstone's limitation, however, rested not on the transfer of one seat from the two-member boroughs, but on the grouping together of the smallest. According to the bill of 1866, all boroughs with a population of less than eight thousand were to be associated in pairs and trios for the election of their members. Geographical convenience naturally played its part in the arrangement, and the result afforded nothing like numerical equality. Such grouping, taken in conjunction with the partial disfranchisement of a few other boroughs, would have rendered forty-five seats available. Of these twenty-six were to go to the counties, five to the larger towns, four to the metropolis, six to towns hitherto unrepresented, and one to the University of London. The remaining seven were to satisfy the claims of Scotland.[2]

Gladstone's plan was thus by no means radical, and would have preserved the influence of the aristocracy by granting the lion's share to the counties. More extensive than that of 1859, it was in no respect conceived in a democratic sense. It was indeed so moderate that Disraeli, casting about for the wherewithal of criticism, was forced to content himself with a rather empty attack on the idea of grouping the small boroughs.[3] Disraeli

1 3 Hansard, clxxxiii, 487.
2 3 Hansard, clxxxiii, 493.
3 3 Hansard, clxxxiii, 886. Disraeli proposed the plan that was adopted with variations in 1885: to unite with the existing boroughs the smaller unrepresented towns, *Ibid.,* 890. Russell was opposed to the plan of grouping the smaller boroughs for he believed that it would destroy local influence and result in compromises and intrigues, and, as Roebuck also feared, would heighten the expenses of agency. Argyll, on the other hand, advocated the plan of grouping, Argyll, *Memoirs,* ii, 132, 321.

objected also to the increased representation of the larger towns proposed by Gladstone, as being a step in the direction of redistribution according to population. Opposition to the plan was, however, for the most part perfunctory, and the question dropped out of sight entirely in the strife which raged over a rating and a rental franchise.

With the failure of the Liberal attempt at reform in 1866 and the introduction of the Conservative Reform Bill of 1867, Disraeli once more was called upon to produce a scheme of redistribution. As might have been expected, that scheme proved to be of the most conservative character. He refused, as before, to argue the case upon the existent anomalies, and once more insisted that the sole reason for change was to supply representation to unrepresented interests and communities.[1] Holding to the principle, that no borough should be absolutely disfranchised because of its small population, he planned to obtain the necessary seats by depriving the smaller two-member towns of one seat. Only in the case of the four boroughs proved guilty of extreme corruption, which were absolutely disfranchised, did he make an exception. The principle of the redistribution, as Derby later admitted, was to carry disfranchisement only so far as was necessary to render available seats for the enfranchisement that was universally demanded.[2] No attempt at uniform representation was hinted at, and the effect of the original proposal would have been to palliate only slightly the numerical anomalies.

This moderate plan, which would have transferred only twenty-seven seats, of which all but three were destined for the counties, was extended in committee. But even as finally enacted the measure of redistribution was of the most limited character, and hardly worthy of the name of

[1] Murdoch, *History of Constitutional Reform,* 253.
[2] Cox, *Reform Bills of 1866 and 1867,* 268.

compromise.[1] The first extension of disfranchisement
resulted from a Liberal amendment, which embodied the
test of population by declaring the loss of one seat for
each two-seated borough of a population of less than ten
thousand in 1861. The motion was resisted by Disraeli,
possibly because he feared to see the empirical criterion of
population so rigidly applied. He expressed the hope
that the committee would not "enter into the sea of
troubles they would find themselves in by the adoption of
this motion." But the amendment was carried, and the
number of boroughs losing one seat thereby increased to
thirty-eight.[2] The Liberals then attempted to carry the
principle of a population test still further, moving that
all boroughs with less than five thousand should be absolutely disfranchised. In support of this motion, Cardwell
showed that the ten boroughs which fell within its range
returned fifteen members and did not contain an aggregate population of forty thousand. This amendment was
rejected and no absolute disfranchisement was enacted in
1867.[3]

In the following year, however, the demands of Scotland
for increased representation could not be denied. The
question was whether they should be met by an increase in
the membership of the House of Commons, or by further
disfranchisement of small English boroughs. The latter
course was warmly advocated by Gladstone; and Disraeli,
admitting that the preservation of the small borough could
no longer be maintained as a necessary principle of the
electoral system, expressed himself as willing to make the
concession. It resulted that seven of the small English
boroughs, each with a population of less than five thou-

---

[1] Cf. Argyll, *Memoirs*, ii, 237.

[2] The amendment, moved by Laing, was carried 306-179, Cox,
Reform Bills of 1866 and 1867, 216.

[3] 3 Hansard, clxxxvii, 1523.

sand, were completely disfranchised. Their seats were given to Scotland, despite the complaints of a large minority, who insisted that if the small boroughs were to be sacrificed, the claims of the English counties and towns were undeniable.[1]

By the disfranchisement of the small boroughs, as finally enacted in 1867 and 1868, fifty-two seats were made available. Of these, ten were obtained by the complete disfranchisement of the seven towns under five thousand in population; thirty-five by the partial disfranchisement of those under ten thousand; and seven by the elimination of the four corrupt boroughs. Of the forty-five seats distributed in England, twenty-five were granted to the counties by assigning three to Lancashire, two to the West Riding, and subdividing ten of the larger counties into three instead of two parts.

The remaining twenty seats were ultimately granted to the large towns and to the University of London. In his original plan Disraeli had not indicated any increased representation for the six largest towns; and notwithstanding their aggregate population of a million and a half, their representation of only twelve seats in the House of Commons was to be left unchanged. But the Liberals, under the leadership of Laing, contended that the large boroughs deserved consideration quite as much as the counties; the comparative inequality previously existing between the latter had been redressed to a certain extent; the same principle should be applied to the former. Disraeli rested upon the old Conservative argument that the boroughs already had much the largest share of power, in proportion to their numbers, and the motion for granting an extra member to the six was at first rejected. But

[1] *Annual Register,* 1868, 22-24. For the debates on redistribution in 1868, see 3 Hansard, cxcii, 435, 840, 954, 1010, 1231, 1892, 1913; cxciii, 363.

the Liberals renewed their efforts so effectively that the
government finally consented to an extra seat for Manchester, Leeds, Birmingham, and Liverpool. Salford and
Merthyr Tydvil also were given each a new seat. Eleven
towns, hitherto unrepresented, were also granted seats,
of which Hackney and Chelsea carved out of the metropolis were to return two members each; the others were
single member constituencies.[1] The final arrangement,
notwithstanding these new borough seats, provided for a
net loss of thirty-three seats for the boroughs, and a clear
gain of twenty-five seats for the counties.[2]

The power of the landowners was in reality but slightly
reduced by the redistribution of 1867. The losses experienced through the disfranchisement of the small boroughs
were, in large part, counterbalanced by the additional
representation granted to the agricultural counties. One
means of bolstering up the electoral strength of the landed
classes was, however, denied them. Disraeli had been able
to persuade the Conservatives to accede to his vast alteration in the franchise largely by his promise to secure a
rectification of county and borough boundaries. The
growth of the large towns had resulted in a gradual inva-
sion of the county constituencies by the urban element, and
the landed interest felt that it ought to be protected
against the adverse electoral influence of those dwelling in
the outskirts of the towns. A rectification of boundaries
which would place this urban element in the boroughs,
where it belonged, was, in the minds of the country
gentry, a measure of simple justice. It was certainly held
out by Disraeli to the country party as one of the chief
safeguards against democracy.

[1] Cox, *Reform Bills of 1866 and 1867*, 219; Murdoch, *History of
Constitutional Reform*, 256; *Saturday Review*, February 22, 1868,
May 30, 1868.
[2] See Appendix, No. 4.

With this in mind, the government appointed commissioners who, after studying the growth of the large towns, recommended the inclusion in the borough area of all that belonged indisputably to the urban element. Notwithstanding protests which had been raised by Bright as to the personnel of the commission, and which resulted in certain changes, it was generally agreed that the report of the commission was animated by party bias in no degree. But the content of the report was by no means satisfactory to the towns affected, and the old Conservative principle of separation of urban and rural elements was fiercely attacked. Bright, especially, opposed the report, largely, it was hinted, because of his personal interest in Birmingham and the neighbouring constituencies. The commissioners, according to the rule they laid down, had planned to add to Birmingham some thirty thousand Radical townsfolk who had hitherto been outside of the borough area. As the *Saturday Review* pointed out, "hearts of the Conservatives in Warwickshire and Worcestershire leapt within them," for those thirty thousand were of the utmost danger to the counties in elections and could not affect the result of elections in Birmingham, which was already Radical. Bright naturally disliked the commissioners' arrangement; his seat was sure in any case and the thirty thousand suburbanites, who were under his influence, might prove a valuable leaven in the county divisions.[1]

The protest of the towns, and of influential Radicals in the House resulted in the rejection of the commissioners' report, and for it was substituted a new scheme, according to which parliamentary boundaries were not to follow urban limits. Both Walpole and Bruce agreed that the county should not be deprived of the urban influence

---

[1] *Saturday Review,* June 13, 1868. And see leading article in the *Times,* June 2, 1868.

since, in their opinion, the best type of constituency was that where the suburban and agricultural elements were combined. They also considered it unwise to weaken the county electorate numerically and overload that of the boroughs. The government was by no means pleased at the rejection of the commissioners' report which suited them practically and theoretically, but they were unable to cope with the combination of Radicals and Liberals which for the moment controlled the House. The old idea of absolute distinction between the urban and the rural in the representative system was thus repudiated. The principle had been weakened, indeed, in 1832 by the enlargement of the boundaries of the small boroughs, and now, for the three elections that followed 1868, the type of electors in many constituencies was by no means homogeneous. Although the actual effect of mixing up a town and country population was not clearly manifested, it was universally believed at the time that it meant a diminution in the electoral strength of the country party.[1]

The redistribution of 1867 and 1868, which pleased the Radicals in its settlement of urban boundaries, was less satisfactory to them in another respect. It will be recalled that the attempt made to grant representation to the Scotch universities in 1832 had failed. But in the plans of redistribution advanced by Russell and Disraeli in 1854 and after, the government, whether Liberal or Conservative, was committed to the enfranchisement of London University. In 1867 the Radicals, especially Bright and Bernal Osborne, were eminent in their attack on university representation. But Disraeli defended the pro-

[1] *Parliamentary Papers,* 1867-1868, no. 311, "Report of the Select Committee on the boundaries of boroughs"; *Ibid.,* no. 3972, "Report of the Boundary Committee"; 3 Hansard, cxci, 196; cxcii, 248; cxciii, 495, 710; *Annual Register,* 1868, 33-36; Cox, *Reform Bills of 1866 and 1867,* 241.

posed enfranchisement on the principle of representation
of interests; he argued that an intellectual element should
be introduced into the House through the members for a
constituency of learned and enlightened men, and that the
House ought to be representative of something more than
material interests. It resulted that London University
received a member, although the plan of the government
for including with it the University of Durham was defeated. At the same time two seats were given to the
Scotch universities.[1]

An innovation carried through in 1867 by those fearful
of the approaching rule of numbers, was the so-called
minority provision. In the three-member constituencies
each elector was to have only two votes, so that by careful
organization a two-fifths minority might gain one seat.
As far back as 1831 the Tories had protested against the
tyranny of the numerical majority, and Praed had voiced
eloquently the rights of the minority. Althorp, however,
opposed the suggested device for minority representation
and it was withdrawn.[2] But in 1854 Russell admitted that
much soreness had resulted from the failure of the system
to represent a numerous minority; he also deprecated the
division of the country into opposed camps of landed and
trading interests. In his bill of 1860 he accordingly proposed the same sort of proportional representation as that
adopted in 1867.[3]

The provision of that year emanated from the Peers
and was frankly regarded by them as a possible "means of
escape from some of the evils connected with the bill."[4]
Carried in the Lords, upon the motion of Cairns, it became

[1] 3 Hansard, clxxxix, 983; Porritt, "Barriers against British
Democracy," in *Political Science Quarterly*, xxvi, no. 1.

[2] 3 Hansard, v, 1359-1369, 1373; ix, 992.

[3] 3 Hansard, cxxx, 498; clxvi, 2062.

[4] 3 Hansard, clxxxix, 546, 935.

the subject of fierce debate in the Commons. The Radicals opposed the minority clause as contrary to democratic principles, while it was strongly endorsed by Lowe, who looked upon this provision as the sole bulwark which remained to protect the constitution from the dangerous tendencies of the new electorate. Favoured by the philosophical Liberals, as well as by the Conservatives, it was ultimately accepted in the Commons. The disgust of the Radicals was profound. Even admitting that it was innocuous, they believed it useless, for they held the minority of one constituency to be the majority of another.[1] Forster objected that it was a Conservative job, since the Conservative minority in the large Liberal constituencies would gain partial representation there, while the Conservatives would retain complete control in the small constituencies. The *Spectator* hoped, however, that the third seat would not go to another party, but to a different shade of the party which held the majority; Labour candidates might thus find a place in Liberal constituencies.[2]

But the effect of the minority clause, as had been expected, was generally to provide a seat for the party hitherto unrepresented. The large Liberal minority in Liverpool was able to return a member, as did the Conservative minority in Manchester.[3] But the most important result of the provision is to be found in the new electoral organizations which it forced. The Liberals of Birmingham realized that if they were to retain the third seat, their votes must be divided economically between the three candidates. To prevent waste of votes, an organization must be built up which could control absolutely the choice of the elector; and each elector must vote invariably as he was told. The success of the Birming-

1 Cox, *Reform Bills of 1866 and 1867*, 270.
2 *Spectator*, September 21, 1867.
3 *Annual Register*, 1868, 172.

ham organization, which soon became known as the Caucus, was unbroken and no Conservative candidate was returned. It was copied in many other constituencies and inaugurated a new era in the development of party electoral machinery, the effect of which upon the representative system has been profound.[1]

The redistribution of 1867 was satisfactory to no class or section of opinion. The Radicals regarded the limited character of the measure not so much with disgust as with contempt; they looked forward frankly to a more sweeping change in the near future, which would equalize the value of a vote in the different constituencies.[2] The Tories, on the other hand, were dissatisfied because the hated principle of numbers had entered, to some extent, into the bill, and because the measure had not succeeded in granting to the counties sufficient representation to counterpoise the new democratic electorate in the boroughs. Moreover, they deplored the failure of the boundary com-

---

[1] Ostrogorski, *Democracy and Parties*, i, 161-163. "The Liberal committee selected candidates for all three seats in view of the impending general election (in 1868). But as each elector could only vote for two candidates, owing to the minority clause, the committee hit upon the following device: by a preliminary canvass the central committee ascertained the exact number of Liberal electors in each ward and the minimum of votes necessary to obtain the majority at the poll, then distributed the three candidates by twos among the electors of the ward, in such fashion that each candidate would only receive the number of votes strictly necessary to obtain the majority at the poll, and the votes over and above this would be given to one of the other two candidates so that each of them should eventually have a majority. . . . Vote as you are told, was the password . . . the immense majority of the electors voted as they were told, and the three Liberal candidates were elected in spite of the restricted voting clause passed for the benefit of minorities." See also, Lowell, *Government of England*, i, 469-471; Langford, *Modern Birmingham*, ii, 362; Ostrogorski, "The Introduction of the Caucus in England," in *Political Science Quarterly*, June, 1893.

[2] "When the time comes the fight will not be about four seats or fourteen either," *Spectator*, July 6, 1867.

missioners to separate the urban from the rural elements. They watched with bitterness and regret the increasing belief that the doom of the small boroughs could not long be postponed; although they still insisted on the value of small constituencies, the Conservatives were forced to admit that since hope had been held out to the large towns, a wide and sweeping redistribution in the democratic sense was inevitable.[1]

Even in the Lords many believed that distribution of electoral power must soon rest primarily upon the principle of population. Halifax complained of the numerical anomalies in tones almost as strong as those of Bright a decade before, and the Duke of Cleveland admitted that the small boroughs, decaying and representing nothing, could not long be maintained beside the large constituencies.[2] That a measure of redistribution to some extent commensurate with the alteration in the franchise ought to have been passed was the general opinion of the moderates, as represented by Russell and de Grey. In their eyes the government scheme unsettled everything without offering any real solution; as Argyll said, it was a "compromise—or rather a mere makeshift."[3] And Derby himself admitted that the plan was thoroughly unsatisfactory. The general feeling that the arrangement was temporary only, resulted in a striking lack of comment; journalists as well as platform orators hardly considered it worth while to discuss the solution of a problem which had been slurred over for the moment, but which must necessarily be settled in the near future.

The disfranchisement, partial and complete, of some of the smaller boroughs, while it weakened the power of the landed aristocracy, affected the Liberal and Conservative

1 3 Hansard, clxxxix, 283-284.
2 3 Hansard, clxxxix, 261-271, 290.
3 3 Hansard, clxxxix, 289-290, 291; Argyll, *Memoirs*, ii, 237.

parties almost equally.[1] Of the seventeen seats taken from the boroughs completely disfranchised, eleven were regarded as regularly Liberal, two as doubtful, and two as rather inclined to the Conservative side.   On the other hand, of the thirty-five boroughs which lost one seat, twenty-one proved Conservative in the elections which took place from 1868 to 1880, and only fourteen were Liberal. So that had these boroughs retained their full representation the Conservatives would have gained seven seats over their opponents. The effect of granting new seats to towns and counties was also almost the same on each party. The Liberals gained by the enfranchisement of the towns, while the Conservatives won an offsetting advantage by the increased strength of the counties.

Notwithstanding the general impression that the redistribution of 1867 was the beginning of a movement which would terminate in allotting seats in mathematical proportion to the population of the constituency, the immediate effects of the measure upon the electoral power of rural and manufacturing constituencies were slight. To a certain extent, it is true, the agricultural divisions of the South lost, while the manufacturing groups of the Midlands and Northwest gained. The southwestern constituencies suffered a net loss of thirteen seats; the south-midland five, and the southeastern four. On the other hand there was a net gain of nine members for the Northwest, of two for the North, and five for the Midlands.[2]

But even with this gain for the industrial constituencies the conditions which prevailed before the passing of the act were not materially altered. In every case the members for the manufacturing county divisions represented a far more numerous population than did those of the agri-

[1] The following figures are taken from McCalmont, *Parliamentary Poll Book.*

[2] See Appendix, No. 4.

cultural. In the South-Midlands the proportion of seats to population was two and a half that of the Northwest.[1] The representation of Rutland was relatively five times that of its manufacturing neighbour, South Essex; and while a member in South Lancashire represented one hundred and fifty thousand inhabitants, one in Cheshire represented about fifty-seven thousand and one in Sussex twenty-six thousand. In the North and in Wales the contrasts in the electoral strength of industrial counties, like Durham or Glamorgan, and the comparatively rural divisions of Westmoreland and Radnor, retained much of the force possessed before 1867.[2]

The increase in population in the manufacturing divisions, which took place between 1867 and 1884, rendered such contrasts still more striking. In the latter year there was in the Southwest a seat for every fifty-five thousand persons and in the South-Midlands the ratio was as high as one to forty-six thousand; in the whole Northwest, on the other hand, there was only one member to every one hundred and fifty thousand. In the three new industrial centres which had grown up,—South Essex, South Wales, and the northeast coast,—the representation was notably inadequate. In North Durham a member represented one hundred and fifty thousand persons, while in Westmoreland there was a seat to every twenty-

		Population	Members	Ratio
[1]	Northwest	2,225,967	20	one in 111,298
	South-Midlands	842,254	18	one in 46,791

		Population	Members	Ratio
[2]	Rutland	21,861	2	one in 10,930
	Essex (South and West)	207,270	4	one in 51,817
	North Durham	169,543	2	one in 84,771
	Westmoreland	48,788	2	one in 24,394
	Glamorgan	143,305	2	one in 71,652
	Radnor	18,305	1	one in 18,305

five thousand. The relative weight of the Lake District in the Commons was thus six times that of the mining and shipping focus of the northeast coast. The textile districts of the Northwest were naturally those where the ratio of seat was low; in South Lancashire it was only a fifth of that of Buckinghamshire.[1]

The two divisions of Warwick offered a striking example of the representative advantage of agriculture in 1884. The southern partook largely of the agricultural character of Oxford, Northampton, and Worcester, by which it was bounded; it was a country little crossed by railway lines, whose arteries of transportation were small canals, whose typical scenery was that of Warwick Park and the reaches of the Avon, whose towns were those of old England—Stratford and Warwick. North Warwick, on the other hand, infected with the spirit of the pottery district, cut by the line of the chief railway to the Northwest, the home of Birmingham and such transportation centres as Rugby and Nuneaton,—this was a typical industrial and commercial district of the new England. But the non-industrial had a member to every fifty-five thousand inhabitants, while the industrial had but one to eighty-five thousand. Other instances might be adduced wherever a typically industrial or agricultural division could be found. An analysis of twenty constituencies brings out the electoral power of agriculture. In the ten typically

		Population	Members	Ratio
[1] South Lancashire	. .	773,111	4	one in 193,277
Buckinghamshire	. .	117,823	3	one in 39,274

Cf. also:

{ Glamorgan	. . .	234,115	2	one in 117,057
{ Radnor	. . .	16,888	1	one in 16,888
{ Monmouth	. . .	166,441	2	one in 83,220
{ Herefordshire	. . .	95,083	3	one in 31,694

Parliamentary Papers, 1883, no. 321.

rural divisions there was a member to every thirty-two
thousand inhabitants; in the industrial the ratio was one
to one hundred and eighteen thousand.[1]

The redistribution of 1867 had thus done little to
render the electoral strength of the industrial interest in
counties commensurate with the enormous increase which
had taken place in its importance. The twenty-five seats
given to the more populous counties had barely sufficed to
palliate for the moment the more glaring inequalities; by
1884 the growth of the manufacturing divisions produced
new anomalies and furnished ample material for the
speeches of those who demanded some approximation
of representation to population. The disproportionate
strength thus given to the landed interest was, however,
small in comparison to that which, as before 1867, they
exercised through the small boroughs.

Notwithstanding the disfranchisement of fifty-two seats
carried out in 1868, the statement then made that England was practically governed by the small boroughs,
could hardly be considered more than slight exaggeration.
As lately as 1884 there were still fifty-six boroughs of less
than ten thousand inhabitants and seventy-three of less
than fifteen thousand. With their eighty-one seats they
were capable of outvoting the thirty-one boroughs which
had each a population of more than one hundred thousand, combined with the West Riding and all Lancashire.
The small rural boroughs, with an aggregate population
of about half a million, were of greater weight in the representative system than the ten millions of the great metropolitan, midland and northern boroughs, and the county
population of the industrial Northwest as well.

[1] There were but three of the industrial counties (Cheshire,
Stafford, Derby) where the ratio of members to population was
higher than one to 100,000. Of the ten rural counties there was only
one (Isle of Wight) where the ratio was lower than one to 40,000.

Practically all the small boroughs were in the South. In the agricultural Southwest eighteen boroughs, each with less than ten thousand inhabitants, were represented at Westminster; of these there were ten of less than seven thousand, and one of less than five thousand. On the other hand, in Marylebone a member represented two hundred thousand inhabitants and in Finsbury one hundred and ninety thousand. The ratio in the great manufacturing towns of the Northwest was almost as low. In Manchester and Birmingham the proportion of members to inhabitants was one to one hundred and thirty thousand. Knaresborough with a population of five thousand had proportionate electoral strength thirty-six times that of Liverpool. Members representing about one hundred thousand inhabitants of the rural boroughs of Cornwall, Devon, and Wiltshire could outvote the representatives of more than two millions from the manufacturing towns of the Midlands, Lancashire, and Yorkshire.[1]

Such uneven distribution of electoral power requires little comment. It is clear that the upper classes profited

[1]

	Population	Members		Population	Members
Barnstaple,	12,494	2	Birmingham,	400,757	3
Bodmin,	6,866	1	Leeds,	309,126	3
Bridport,	6,799	1	Liverpool,	552,245	3
Calne,	5,271	1	Manchester,	393,676	3
Chippenham,	6,776	1	Sheffield,	284,410	2
Devizes,	6,645	1	Wolverhampton,	164,303	2
Launceston,	5,675	1			
Liskeard,	5,591	1		2,104,517	16
Malmesbury,	6,866	1			
Marlborough,	5,180	1			
Tavistock,	6,909	1			
Tiverton,	10,462	2			
Wareham,	6,192	1			
Westbury,	6,014	1			
Weymouth,	13,704	2			
	111,444	18			

greatly by the number of small boroughs and by the electoral disadvantage of the industrial constituencies. The
strength of the aristocracy, indeed, was almost as great
in this respect after the second Reform Act as after the
first. The small value of a vote in the manufacturing
towns affected the influence of the masses most adversely
and tended to nullify the result of the enfranchisement of
1867; as Bright had predicted, household suffrage could
work no revolution so long as the populous constituencies
were deprived of their proportionate number of seats. The
high value of a vote in the small boroughs not merely
operated in favour of aristocratic influence, but prevented
the elimination of bribery; for it made the suffrage so
valuable that the voter could not resist the temptation
which was offered directly as a bribe, or indirectly in one
of the other multifarious forms of corruption.

But the end of this system of distribution was in sight,
and even in 1867 it was becoming obvious that the power
of the aristocracy could not much longer be maintained by
the seats of the small boroughs and the rural constituencies. It was certain that a sweeping distribution could
not be far distant, and as certain that when it came the
approximate equality of a vote in every constituency
would be established. As the keener political minds of the
day perceived, such equality would deprive the upper
classes of much of that influence which they still possessed
in elections, despite the attack on nomination made in
1832 and the democratic borough franchise of 1867.

CHAPTER XII

REGISTRATION AND THE PARTY ASSOCIATIONS, 1865-1885

Practical operation of the franchise largely affected by registration—Disqualification of potential electors—Complexity of process of registration—The rate-paying requirement—Abolition of composition in 1867—Resulting protests—Irregularity of enfranchisement—Abolition of rate-paying requirement by the Liberals—Further removal of restrictions—Case of Morpeth—Continued apathy of prospective claimants—Inefficiency of the overseers—Causes—Difficulties of registration—Lodger voters practically excluded—Power of registration associations—Gained largely through use of objections—Abuse of this system—Attempts to break the power of the associations—Remedial bills defeated—Liberal bill of 1873 carried in Commons—But defeated in Lords—Institution of night courts of revision—Acts of 1878 and 1885—Recognized the party associations—But checked their abuses of the system of registration—Increased facilities for compilation of lists—Regulation of objections—Effects of these changes—Reasons for better operation of registration system—Remaining grounds of dissatisfaction—Development of registration system in its relation to electoral democracy.

THE foregoing chapters have attempted a sketch of the chief electoral anomalies which marked the representative system after 1867. Notwithstanding the step made at that time in the direction of democracy, the control of elections still rested largely in the hands of the upper classes,—in part at least because of those anomalies. The unequal distribution of electoral power deprived the industrial constituencies of the seats to which they believed themselves entitled by their wealth and population. And similar inequalities existed in the extent of the suffrage; in boroughs the proportion of voters was high and in counties it was low. Such irregularities were to be remedied in 1884.

But the extension of the franchise which took place in that year, would have been less effective were it not for the preceding reforms in the registration system. And a study of that system's operation explains, in part, minor anomalies which marred the work of the legislators of 1867. It was because of the restrictions imposed upon the claimant to the franchise, and because of the varying attitude of registration officials, that certain boroughs, such as Rochdale, enjoyed manhood suffrage after 1867, while in neighbouring towns, like Tynemouth or Morpeth, the number of electors was small.[1] Because of registration conditions the lodger franchise remained little else than an academic definition; and it was also by means of the registration system that the control of the franchise was in many constituencies transferred from the local magnate to the party association. The practical importance of registration was thus no less after the second Reform Act than it had been before.

The part played by the registration system in the practical operation of this franchise during the years which followed 1832 has been dwelt upon at length. Many persons, otherwise qualified, had been disfranchised because of failure to meet the residential and rate-paying requirements. The system of claims and objections had thrown control of the franchise into the hands of election agents, who made or unmade votes at will. The apathy of electors and the inertia of government in this respect, were so great that many seats depended upon the skill of election lawyers rather than the political opinions of the voters.

Much of the difficulty had resulted from the complex

[1] In the first borough the proportion of electors to population in 1868 was one in 4; in the second it was one in 13, *Parliamentary Papers*, 1868-1869, no. 418.

nature of the franchises, which made a simple process of registration impossible. The reform legislation of 1867 could not fail to increase such complications. As was pointed out by Brand, all the new franchises were in addition to those already existent; the ancient rights and the £10 qualification still remained in the boroughs, nor was the county rental qualification abrogated by the introduction of the new occupation franchise.[1] Each new qualification meant so much more work for the overseers, so much greater chance for the omission of names from the lists, and so much more opportunity for the party associations in their business of making or unmaking qualifications. The existence of such complications and their unfortunate effect was generally acknowledged by all who took the trouble to understand them. The uncertainty which clouded the exercise of the franchise was further increased by the confusion resulting from the abolition of the composition of rates. Designed to remove all doubt as to who had fulfilled the requirements of law, the clause ·which provided for personal payment of rates threatened to bring on a social crisis without solving the electoral difficulty.

It was this rate-paying problem which was most acute, and the one which was first settled. The principle that every claimant must himself have paid rates before registration had been insisted upon by Disraeli in the debates of 1867, and had in fact formed the chief centre of discussion. This test was looked to by all the anti-reformers as the last dyke against the inrushing democratic flood. Because of the prevalence of composition, under which system rates were paid by the owner and not by the occupier, this restriction would naturally have reduced enormously the number of new voters. But the act of 1867

[1] 3 Hansard, ccvi, 579.

had abolished composition in parliamentary boroughs, so that the restrictive effect of the rate-paying requirement was, to a large extent, mitigated.

But as the more far-sighted had predicted, the interference with social and economic convenience implied by the abolition of composition, aroused a storm of protest all through the country. Composition had enabled the parish authorities to collect rates on small tenements at a minimum of effort, and in many cases where it would have been impossible to obtain the rate from an impecunious occupier. The landlord, who included the rate in his rent, was enabled to make the collection with little difficulty and no more friction than would accompany the ordinary collection of the rent by itself. The occupiers themselves preferred paying once to paying twice; and the abolition of composition proved more expensive to them, since the landlords, even though they no longer paid the rate, refused to lower the rental. The occupiers were thus forced to pay their old rental and the rate in addition, or else give up their tenement.[1]

Immediately upon the passing of the act of 1867 a wave of opposition to personal payment of rates ran through the country. Meetings were held at the larger towns, condemning the abrogation of composition and demanding that it be reauthorized. Threats of violence were freely uttered against any who should attempt to collect rates directly from the occupiers, and the determination to continue the old system was general.[2] In some boroughs the occupiers of small tenements refused, almost without exception, to pay rates; in Hackney there were four thousand more summonses than usual issued for non-payment of rates; in Shoreditch fifteen thousand were issued; in Birmingham twenty-five thousand were issued in October,

1 3 Hansard, cxc, 1561.
2 3 Hansard, cxc, 438, 442, 1894.

1867, and fifteen thousand in May, 1868, for the same reason.[1] It was said that rather than pay the rates directly, hundreds of artisan families were giving up housekeeping and going into lodgings. More significant still, several boroughs in which composition of rates had not existed previously, proceeded to introduce it in defiance of the law during the autumn of 1867.[2]

The government's dilemma was obvious. The parochial machinery all through England was being clogged and very real inconvenience imposed upon the tenants, as well as upon the overseers. The system of composition was in partial continuance in some boroughs notwithstanding the provisions of the act, and as a result, the names of occupiers did not appear in the rate-book nor were they entered upon the electoral lists. But to resign the principle of personal rating would have been a confession on the part of government that their main contention of the previous session was, after all, a point of no vital importance. To surrender their demand that each claimant must have paid his own rates, meant the removal of what was in Tory eyes the last barrier against pure household suffrage.

This was not the only time in Disraeli's career when he adopted the policy of masterly inactivity. Ultimate surrender to the universal protest was inevitable, but such surrender might be postponed or slurred over. Hence when questions were put as to government policy they were evaded.[3] Direct abrogation was, it is true, opposed by Gathorne Hardy; and the government was able to defeat a resolution which proposed that the payment of rates by the owner, under the system of composition, be considered equivalent to payment by the occupier, and that the name

[1] 3 Hansard, cxciv, 317.
[2] 3 Hansard, cxc, 442, 1561.
[3] 3 Hansard, cxc, 730, 795-797.

of every occupier be entered upon the rate-book.[1] But at
the same time the principle of personal payment of rates
was practically surrendered by the Attorney General when
he admitted that payment by the landlord could legally
be considered sufficient for the registration of the
occupier.[2]

It resulted that, during the registration of 1868, the
principle of personal payment was not enforced in many
constituencies. Rates were paid by the landlords, and the
names of the occupiers were placed on the electoral register.[3] In other boroughs such a payment was not recognized as sufficient for qualification, and the claimants
were refused. More than two thousand claimants were
thus disfranchised in Tynemouth by the revising barristers, who held strictly to the necessity of personal payment of rates.[4] In fact, the number of persons enfranchised in 1868 depended to a large extent, in many of the
boroughs, upon the political activities of the lawyers, and
the attitude of the overseers and revising barristers.

In the next session the matter was revived, and one of
the first questions laid before the new Liberal ministry
was the restoration of composition and the repeal of the
rate-paying clauses. Gladstone was at first rather vague
in his statement of intentions, although he admitted the
hardship incurred by the abolition of composition, and
felt the necessity of some remedy.[5] But in 1869, he tested
the feelings of the House by a bill introduced by Goschen,
which would have contrived in circuitous fashion the repeal
of the legislation of 1867; and soon afterwards the
Liberals converted the feint into a direct attack upon the

[1] 3 Hansard, cxc, 1894-1922.
[2] 3 Hansard, cxc, 446.
[3] 3 Hansard, cxc, 1563.
[4] 3 Hansard, cxciv, 326.
[5] 3 Hansard, cxciv, 127, 510.

Conservative principle of personal rating. Nor did any
of the Conservative reformers think it worth while to vin-
dicate their main contention of 1867.   Quietly, and as
though it shrank from any renewal of the old controversy,
parliament enacted that the system of composition might
exist, and should be extended to parliamentary boroughs;
at the same time it provided that the names of all compound occupiers should be entered in the rate-book and
upon the electoral lists.[1]   It was the removal of the last
great restriction upon pure household suffrage.   The
principle or fiction of personal rating, as the *Times* com-
mented, "had served its turn when it provided uneasy consciences with an excuse for supporting household suffrage."[2]   But henceforth the rate-paying clauses lost
much of their force as a bar to enfranchisement.

Other minor restrictions which led to disfranchisement
were removed in particular localities, either by the action
of revising barristers or by supplementary legislation.
An instance of the removal of electoral disabilities imposed
by registration requirements is to be found in Northumberland. Here the miners, like those of Glamorgan, lived
in colliery houses for which they paid rent in no direct
form, and no rates. Even after the legislation of 1869
their names were not entered in the rate-book, since their
status was not considered that of ordinary occupiers who
paid rent.   Only the merest handful of the miners were
registered. In 1872, however, there was formed at Morpeth a "Franchise Association" which aimed at the extension of the suffrage to all such miners, on the ground
that although they paid no direct rent their position was
in reality that of the compound householder. A year of
agitation followed, with the result that in 1873 all the
pitmen claimants were admitted by the revising barristers.

[1] 32 & 33 Vict., c. 41.
[2] *Times*, August 11, 1869.

The increase of electorate in the mining boroughs was large, and in Morpeth alone the constituency leapt at a bound from twenty-six hundred to forty-nine hundred electors.[1]   An interesting result of this enfranchisement was the return to Westminster of Thomas Burt, the first real representative of the labouring classes.   In other constituencies similar restrictions upon the acquisition of the franchise were removed by later enactments.   Of these the most important was that which reduced the stringency of the residential demands.   In future, persons removing from one house to another in the same borough were not to be disqualified on that account.

The abrogation of the principle of personal payment of rates and the loosening of the residential requirements did not, however, remove all the restrictions laid upon the franchise by the system of registration.   The forces which had operated before 1867 in the direction of disfranchisement still persisted.   The natural apathy of prospective electors still tended to mitigate against complete enfranchisement, and was especially notable in the counties, where those qualified by an ownership franchise were forced to make special claim.   The occupiers were saved this necessity under the act of 1867, which provided that the overseers should themselves make out preliminary lists as in boroughs.   There were thus two processes of registration in counties: the one taking its inception from the private initiative of the claimant, the other begun by the overseer. The question arose naturally as to whether it would not be possible to assimilate the law for the two classes and enable owners as well as occupiers to be registered by the action of the overseers.   Such a scheme had in fact been

[1] For a description of the franchise situation at this time in Northumberland, see Watson, *Life of a Great Labour Leader, Thomas Burt,* 124-129.

proposed by Disraeli in 1859, and would have gone far
to assure complete registration of all qualified persons.[1]

A great difficulty, however, stood in the way of such an
alteration of the law. The overseers were well acquainted
with the status of the occupiers of land and tenements;
from them were collected the rates in counties, and the
overseers, in the pursuance of their parochial duties, had
every inducement to preserve an accurate list of all rated
occupiers. But since no rate was ordinarily collected in
counties from the owners, the overseers had no object in
ascertaining and checking the correctness of the list of
owners published in the rate-book. As a matter of fact
that list proved extremely inaccurate as a rule and was
likely to be more misleading than helpful to the overseers,
if they were asked to register owners as well as occupiers.[2]

To ensure accurate registration of owners it would be
necessary to devise some system of division of rates between
owners and occupiers. Then only would the overseers
come to obtain sufficient knowledge of the owners' status
to be able to enter them on the preliminary lists without
claim. But under the existing system it was hopeless to
expect that the overseers would succeed in drawing up
satisfactory lists. The same objection applied to any
scheme for the official registration of ancient right voters.
For them as for the owners, the system of individual claim
appeared strictly necessary.[3]

Even where they had the assistance of the occupiers'
column in the rate-book and their own personal knowledge
of the qualified persons, the work of the overseers in compiling preliminary lists did not escape scathing criticism;

[1] 3 Hansard, clii, 995.

[2] *Parliamentary Papers,* 1870, no. 360, "Minutes of Evidence,"
§§ 519, 993, 1508.

[3] *Parliamentary Papers,* 1870, no. 360, "Minutes of Evidence,"
§§ 577, 1045, 1566-1570, 1977, 2919.

it was often asserted that to their laxness was due primarily the impurity of the electoral register. Their incapacity had been predicted in the debates of 1831, and it was a matter of common complaint in 1846 that they were inefficient in their investigation of fraudulent claims, as well as that they were careless in their omission of many names from the lists.[1] They were defended as the only persons fitted for the performance of registration duties, but dissatisfaction with the character of their work continued, until in 1870 it reached a climax of protest.[2]

Those desirous of becoming electors complained that the overseers formed a fluctuating body, changing almost every year and that they were not really acquainted with the ratepayers of the parish. As a matter of fact, it was asserted, they usually left the making out of lists to the professional rate collectors, who consulted with the election agents of each party, and sent in the names to the overseers for their formal signature. Contrary to general opinion the overseers in most of the rural parishes were unlettered men, shopkeepers and small farmers, since persons of better education, such as magistrates and the professional classes, were generally exempt.[3] Moreover, registration duties came upon the overseers at the moment when they were completely absorbed in the labour of persons engaged or connected with rural pursuits; those duties they frankly regarded as a nuisance, something outside their regular work, so that the work of registration was accordingly badly performed. At times the overseers were affected by political bias, as was natural, and for the exercise of which they possessed unrivalled oppor-

---

[1] *Parliamentary Papers,* 1846, no. 451, "Minutes of Evidence," § 3964.

[2] 3 Hansard, cxci, 1458.

[3] *Parliamentary Papers,* 1870, no. 360, "Minutes of Evidence," §§ 26, 509, 1497, 2467, 2875; 3 Hansard, ccxi, 1247.

tunity. Local parsimony also affected the accuracy of the register; in 1867 it was discovered in Birmingham that extra funds were being spent for the accurate up-keep of the electoral list; the curtailment of the municipal budget which followed resulted in the immediate imperfection of the parliamentary register.[1]

The date set by law for the publication of the register and of objections also afforded excuse for delinquencies, as well as opportunity for politics. The lists, which were ordered to be published on the 1st of August, were supposed to contain the names of persons qualified on the 31st of July. To ascertain whether the occupiers were really resident on one day and to publish the list on the day following, was a feat far transcending the capacity or the energy of the overseers.[2] In practice they necessarily began to make out the lists long before the electoral year was complete, regardless of contingencies that occurred before the last of July which might render the lists inaccurate. There was, moreover, no reasonable interval between the date set for the publication of objections and the date of claim. Persons objected to upon one qualification were thus unable to claim upon another. The overseers, however, were accustomed to give private notice of such objections to their political friends, enabling them to substitute another claim before it was too late. Such secret intimation was naturally withheld from their opponents.[3]

The factor most adverse to the efficiency of the overseers was, perhaps, the lack of sufficient inducement to conscientious labour. They were unpaid officials and

[1] *Parliamentary Papers*, 1868-1869, no. 294, "Minutes of Evidence," §§ 669-670, 681-683, 950-963.

[2] *Parliamentary Papers*, 1868-1869, no. 294, "Minutes of Evidence," §§ 1289, 1301, 1885-1895, 2256, 2354-2360.

[3] *Parliamentary Papers*, 1868-1869, no. 294, "Minutes of Evidence," §§ 1302, 1410, 1895; 3 Hansard, ccxiv, 1953.

unless illegally interested in political tricks, it made little difference to them whether the work was well or ill performed. The act of 1843 had provided for the payment of the bare expenses of registration, but no extra remuneration for the overseers' labours was given them. It was a significant fact that when assistant overseers were employed upon a salary, the process of registration was carried through far more efficiently.[1] Taken all in all, effective performance of such laborious occupation was too much to expect from these unpaid functionaries, who changed office periodically and who possessed neither the knowledge resulting from accumulated experience, nor the inducement of material reward.

One result of the inefficiency of the overseers and the complications of the system was the existence of double entries upon the electoral lists. Before 1867 it was bad enough that a voter's name should be entered for three or four different qualifications; but after the enormous increase of electors in that year the duplicate voters became a source of serious and continual annoyance.[2] Double entries not merely increased the cost of registration but caused much practical inconvenience at elections, and the opportunities thus opened for fraud and personation were

[1] *Parliamentary Papers*, 1870, no. 360, "Minutes of Evidence," §§ 1032, 1331.

[2] The duplicate voters are not to be confused with the plural voters. The former was an elector holding various qualifications in the same constituency, for each of which his name might appear on various electoral lists in that constituency; legally he could vote but once in that constituency; no man had ever the right of voting more than once in the same constituency. The plural voter held qualifications in different constituencies, in each of which he might vote. In the case of county electors the County Electors Act, 1888 (51 & 52 Vict., c. 10, sec. 7), does not prevent a county elector from being registered in several divisions of the same county, but he can vote only once, "Knill v. Towse," 24 *Law Reports, Queen's Bench Division*, 186-697; 59 *Law Journal, Queen's Bench*, 136, 455.

numerous.[1] The number of duplicate voters varied; in some of the county constituencies there were a large number of them; in East Kent ten per cent of the names listed were duplicates; in South Essex there were two hundred and thirty double entries, and in East Cheshire, four hundred and fifty.[2] Naturally the revising barristers protested, but always in vain, since they had no power granted them for the expunging of names without cause being shown.

Complaints of manufactured and fraudulent qualifications were far less numerous than in the early days of registration, and so far as they occurred related to the county ownership franchise. In the boroughs such claims could not be advanced with prospect of success because of the use of the rate-book as the basis of the preliminary lists. In counties a man need not prove his claim absolutely unless he were objected to; in the boroughs, if his name did not appear upon the rate-book he must adduce very clear evidence of his qualification, and this was a dangerous business for the fraudulent claimant and one rarely indulged in.[3] But faggot votes in counties were still created and to such an extent that loud and frequent protests were heard against the ownership qualification which provided the opportunity. But since the faggot votes were not, as in later years, devoted almost solely to the interests of one party, such protests passed unheeded.

The real complaint with the registration system lay not so much with the opportunities given for the creation of votes, but rather with its disqualifying effects. This

[1] *Parliamentary Papers*, 1870, no. 360, "Minutes of Evidence," §§ 1181, 1374, 1456.

[2] *Parliamentary Papers*, 1870, no. 360, "Minutes of Evidence," §§ 669-670, 876-877.

[3] *Parliamentary Papers*, 1868-1869, no. 294, "Minutes of Evidence," § 2031.

was shown most plainly in connection with the new lodger franchise. Gladstone had predicted in 1866 that the lodger vote would never be large because the working classes would not have the time to carry through their claims, and the registers of the years which followed the introduction of this qualification justified his foresight.[1] The difficulties cast in the way of those desiring to gain a vote on the lodger qualification were such that Brand could say in 1871 that this franchise was practically inoperative. In the metropolitan boroughs the number of lodgers was estimated at between two and three hundred thousand; but the number on the electoral register for 1868 was only about fourteen thousand. Apparently the difficulties were so great that most of the few who were registered became discouraged, for in 1872 there were only four thousand registered lodgers in the entire metropolis. In Westminster the proportion of lodgers who were electors dropped from one in four to one in ten, in Southwark only one in every three hundred lodgers was registered, and in North and South Hammersmith, although there were several thousand lodgers, there was only one registered in the former, and four in the latter ward. In the large provincial towns the proportion of lodger voters was similarly small, so that in 1872, outside of London, there were only five thousand lodger voters in all of England and Wales.[2]

The small proportion of persons enfranchised by the lodger qualification is explained in part by the necessity of going to court and making special claim. The franchise

[1] 3 Hansard, clxxxii, 48.

[2] *Parliamentary Papers,* 1868-1869, no. 294, "Minutes of Evidence," §§ 1810-1820, 1838-1839, 1844, 2207. Many of these startling statistics were furnished by John Boyd, who, as chairman of the Chelsea Registration Committee, was well acquainted with the situation, *Ibid.,* § 1840.

was to be obtained only through a troublesome and often costly proceeding, involving unlimited red tape. This fact naturally operated with peculiar hardship upon the class of voters who were dependent upon weekly wages for their subsistence, although it was the enfranchisement of this class which had supposedly been effected by the act of 1867. For an artisan or labourer the trouble and loss of time consequent upon sustaining a claim or resisting an objection, was equivalent to a severe pecuniary fine. He might lose several days' wages or even permanent employment as the price of his attendance in the revising court. The courts were open in the daytime only, so that the workingman must choose between the franchise and the wages of at least a single day. If he attended during his luncheon hour the opposing attorney would consume the time with his speech, so that the hour would be up before the case was attacked. Under such circumstances it was hardly surprising that the working classes were often excluded as lodgers or, as in Sunderland, as occupiers. Nor could the labourers be blamed for complaining that parliament, having decided that a workingman was a fit and proper person to exercise the franchise, ought to allow him to come upon the register in the simplest and easiest way.[1]

But the red tape of the system itself, and the laxness of the overseers, aroused less complaint than the control of registration secured by the party associations. Their activity and power, which had resulted from too enthusiastic compliance with the early exhortations of Peel, had grown year by year, so that in many constituencies the voter was helpless without the assistance of the registra-

[1] 3 Hansard, ccvi, 580; *Parliamentary Papers*, 1868-1869, no. 294, "Minutes of Evidence," §§ 1648-1649, 1747. Of the 500 workingmen who were qualified in Sunderland, only 20 were registered voters.

tion attorney. Especially numerous were the complaints
directed against that power of registration agents which
rested upon the system of organized objections. The
statements made by agents before investigating committees, as well as in the House of Commons, show clearly
that the opportunities for disfranchisement through the
bringing in of wholesale objections, were so alluring that
the registration associations could not resist the temptation.[1]

According to an election manager, who was discussing
the registration system in 1869, a great political advantage could be gained at a very small expense by serving
objections wholesale; the sending out of thousands of
objections to the claims of political opponents was considered, in fact, the most advantageous method of spending electoral funds.[2] In all the constituencies where political power was at all evenly balanced it was apparently
considered a flagrant disregard of electoral tactics not to
scatter objections broadcast. Even if many of them
should fail in their purpose, a certain proportion of the
protested electors would be unable or unwilling to appear
in court and sustain their vote. The secretary of the
Liberal Association of Liverpool in 1865 himself made
out about three thousand objections of the nine thousand
issued in that constituency. Of these nearly a third were
said to be absolutely frivolous, sent out in the hope of
destroying good votes.[3] At Oxford, where there was an
electorate of five thousand, there were more than six hundred objections. In this instance most of those objected
to failed to appear; some attended the revising court to

[1] 3 Hansard, cxciv, 5; ccvi, 579.
[2] *Parliamentary Papers*, 1868-1869, no. 294, "Minutes of Evidence,"
§§ 142-143.
[3] 3 Hansard, ccvi, 579; *Parliamentary Papers*, 1868-1869, no. 294,
"Minutes of Evidence," §§ 90, 164.

sustain their qualification, but the attorneys talked at such length that the claimants preferred to surrender their vote; they left the court and their names were expunged.[1]

The post service of objection also played into the hands of those party agents who were intent upon the destruction of hostile votes. It will be remembered that the posting of the notice of objection to the address of the voter as it appeared in the overseer's list, was held to be effective service. The chance that this notice would not reach the voter at all, was a strong inducement to the sending out of such objections. In the case of workingmen, who changed their residence frequently, circumstances of peculiar hardship were apt to arise. If the postman, finding the house vacant, sent the notice to the dead-letter office, the disfranchisement of the voter was certain. The agent appearing in court need only say, "I have proved my notice of objection," throwing in the duplicate notice signed by the postmaster as evidence, and the name would be struck off. The same mischance might occur if, as often happened, the overseer inserted a wrong address in his list. Political agents would often make inquiries to ascertain if persons had left their houses, knowing that in such cases a notice sent out would be fatal.[2]

Personal attendance at the revision courts was not in theory necessary to rebut objections; a friend or an agent might, if furnished with sufficient authority, prove the claimant's qualification. But in practice, unless an attorney was appointed, attendance was essential. At least ninety per cent of those who succeeded in proving their qualification against objections had attended the court. In Chelsea the barrister refused to accept any evidence

---

[1] *Parliamentary Papers,* 1868-1869, no. 294, "Minutes of Evidence," § 98, and cf. 3 Hansard, ccxiv, 1937.

[2] *Parliamentary Papers,* 1868-1869, no. 294, "Minutes of Evidence," § 704.

except that of the man or his wife. It was soon observed that women did not like to go into the courts ·and in most cases could not be persuaded to; the workingman thus could not hope to depend upon his wife.[1] The practical necessity of attendance in the court was an important factor in the power of the registration association. Without the aid of the association's attorney, who took upon himself the burden of defence, the individual voter would often be unable to maintain his electoral rights. As the agents on both sides regularly objected to working class voters in the hope that they could not attend the court, labourers soon began to entrust the protection of their franchise to the party attorney.[2] And even those labourers who were not prevented by their work from attending, very generally refused to incur the trouble and expense involved, and promised their suffrages to the party which undertook the cost and bother of sustaining their claim and qualification. In the City of London the only lodger voters registered in 1868 were brought upon the list through the agency of a single man, and naturally voted as he directed.[3]

The sole protection against the abuse of the system of objections was the barrister's power of granting costs to the claimant if the objection was shown to be purely frivolous or vexatious. In counties, as a result of the act of 1865, the notice of objection to an occupation fran-

[1] *Parliamentary Papers,* 1868-1869, no. 294, "Minutes of Evidence," §§ 366, 417-421, 450-453, 2190.

[2] 3 Hansard, ccxiv, 1953; *Parliamentary Papers,* 1868-1869, no. 294, "Minutes of Evidence," §§ 232-235. The Radicals complained that "the franchise of the people was emptied into an attorney's brief bag, and without the aid of quibbling solicitors and the tricks of party associations, the workingman was unable to bear the burden of maintaining his own rights."

[3] *Parliamentary Papers,* 1868-1869, no. 294, "Minutes of Evidence," § 1309.

chise must state specifically the ground of objection; the objector might be fined for each separate ground of objection shown to be unjustifiable, and this though the name of the claimant might be expunged upon some other ground. It had also been enacted that costs might be awarded up to the amount of five pounds instead of twenty shillings as before.[1] In the case of the ownership franchise, however, the objector was not forced to specify more than the column in which the deficiency was supposed to occur.[2] In boroughs the objector need not state specifically his ground of objection, and costs could be granted only once for the objection as a whole, if it appeared frivolous.[3]

Practically speaking, the discretionary power of awarding costs was exercised so rarely and so inadequately by the barristers that the effects were nugatory. In Liverpool, during the revision of 1868, only four half-crowns were levied in costs; in Oxford, an agent of the Liberal Registration Association, after many applications for costs where his client's qualification had been sustained against objections, finally received a shilling.[4] The barristers generally made the rule that if they put pen to paper for the slightest correction in the qualification, no costs would be granted. Accordingly, a voter whose name, or the number of whose house, was inaccurately listed, received no costs for his attendance to correct an error of no importance and one which occurred through no fault of his. Costs were refused at Oxford because the

[1] 28 & 29 Vict., c. 36.

[2] "Sidney v. Dixon," 1871, *Law Reports, 7 Common Pleas*, 190; 1 Hopwood and Coltman, *Registration Cases*, 620.

[3] 3 Hansard, ccxiv, 1948.

[4] *Parliamentary Papers*, 1868-1869, no. 294, "Minutes of Evidence," §§ 106, 541, 544.

door of the person objected to had been recently painted over and the number obliterated.[1]

The organization of the system of objections and the practical control exercised through it by the party association was generally acknowledged. A party official known as "professional objector" had resulted; and notwithstanding the desire to limit the scope of the system expressed by representative men from both parties, the temptation proved too great for the electoral managers. Statistics proved that the more objections sent out, whether or not founded upon fair grounds, the better the party stood upon the register.[2] The power of the associations thus acquired did not escape severe criticism by many unprejudiced persons, and drew upon them the dislike of many reformers, who realized that the practical disfranchisement of a part of the labouring classes was due to registration tricks.[3]

The action of the associations was thus felt to be necessarily prejudicial to the independence of a constituency. It not merely supplied the means but it afforded a grave temptation to the exercise of illegitimate practices and corrupt inducements. It was proverbially and invariably difficult, if not impossible, to discriminate between money that was legitimately expended in registration, and money which under the guise of registration was practically employed for the corruption of a constituency. On the other hand, the associations could reply that their existence was justified and their operations excused by the inefficiency of the responsible registration authorities and

[1] *Parliamentary Papers*, 1868-1869, no. 294, "Report of the Select Committee on Registration of Voters," vi; "Minutes of Evidence," § 107.

[2] *Parliamentary Papers*, 1868-1869, no. 294, "Minutes of Evidence," §§ 91-98, 119.

[3] 3 Hansard, cxi, 1251.

by the state's abdication of functions which it alone should naturally control.[1]

There were obviously two possible paths, either of which might lead to a solution of the difficulty. The action of the party associations might be frankly recognized, and to the counterbalancing efforts of the rival parties might be entrusted the purity and accuracy of the electoral lists. This would involve a surrender of the old principle upon which legislation law had been hitherto established, namely that "registration is a business of the state and ought to be placed as far as possible beyond the influence alike of the apathy of the citizens, and the interested action of the political agents." There would also be necessary a better devised system of checks and balances, so that while the party associations might have full liberty of claiming for the real qualifications of their friends, and objecting to the fraudulent claims of their opponents, they should not also obtain the power of abusing that right. The other solution of the problem involved the elimination of the party associations, or a lessening of their influence, accompanied by such a reform of the system as would permit the action of the state to be really efficient. The system of objections and claims which gave such power to the party agents might then be disposed of. If the preliminary lists could be made accurate and complete once for all, the other difficulties would vanish.

The committee appointed to investigate registration conditions in 1868 reported in favour of the latter plan. Recognizing the inefficiency of the overseers and the careless fashion in which the lists were made up, they recommended that a single competent authority in each borough should be appointed to take charge of registration

[1] *Parliamentary Papers*, 1868-1869, no. 294, "Report of the Registration Committee," v.

and ensure the compilation of satisfactory preliminary lists. Holding the title of "Registrar of Voters," he should receive adequate remuneration for his work, and be assisted by a staff of competent and, if possible, expert assistants.[1] This scheme, warranted to a large extent by the successful example of the Scotch system and plausibly constructed in its details, was presented to the House of Commons in 1871.

Notwithstanding very continuous discussion, in which appeared little defence of existing conditions, the bill framed upon the committee's report in that year made very short progress, although it won the approval of Bruce, who spoke for the government.[2] In the following year a similar measure was introduced by Vernon Harcourt; the opposition was, however, too strong and the Liberal government was for the most part indifferent.[3] Both of these bills proposed to replace the incompetent overseers by trustworthy officials, and were designed to prevent the control of registration from falling into the hands of the political associations. The system of objections was to be rendered superfluous by throwing greater responsibility on the registration officers and by providing an official correction of lists prior to revision. Lodger voters were to remain on the lists from year to year, and the registrar of voters, assisted by the postman, was to make out complete lists of lodgers. The date of making claim was set on May 31 instead of July 20, thus giving the registrar seven weeks for the preparation of his lists and shortening the period of occupation to ten months. The evil of duplicate votes was met by a provision that the elector must select one single qualification; in case of

1 *Parliamentary Papers*, 1868-1869, no. 294, "Report of the Registration Committee," vii, viii.
2 3 Hansard, ccvi, 591.
3 3 Hansard, ccix, 374.

his failing to do so the revising barrister was empowered to expunge all the entries but one. The registrar was also to be given the power of objecting to double entries.[1]

Discussion of these registration bills did not follow party lines and in general the leaders of the government and of the opposition allowed their followers to vote as they pleased. The chief oppositions to the suggestions advanced, lay in the distrust of the proposed registrar of voters and in the belief that he would tend to become more and more a party man. Certainly the increased powers which the bills conferred upon the new officials, powers practically of secret revision, would have enabled them to exercise wide influence upon elections should they contract party affiliations. The office of registrar would become so desirable that elections for it must rapidly develop into keen political contests, and party strife would be extended into the smallest divisions of local government. Both Gathorne Hardy and Henley, whose opinion on electoral matters was deferred to upon both sides of the House, preferred the inefficiency of the overseers to the chance of political bias on the part of the proposed registrars.[2]

Following the failure of the bills of 1871 and 1872, the government introduced one of its own in 1873. The suggested measure was far less radical than the preceding proposals, in that it retained the overseers and provided no special registration officers. Its chief object, besides simplifying the process of revision, was the construction of one register for parliamentary and municipal voters. It left county registration untouched, except that the action of claims and objections was made the same as in boroughs, but proposed to strike at the control of party associations by increasing the difficulty of making objec-

[1] 3 Hansard, ccvi, 581-582.
[2] 3 Hansard, ccvi, 587, 592; ccxi, 1242.

tions. Every notice of objection must state specifically the grounds of objection; each ground was to be treated as a separate objection and costs were to be granted for each one that failed from any cause. The enfranchisement of lodgers was to be facilitated by allowing them to stay on the register from year to year without claim. Night courts of revision for each borough of more than ten thousand inhabitants were also provided in the hope of facilitating the claims of the working classes. As in 1872, the revising barrister was given the power of erasing all but one of each elector's qualifications, thus making double entries impossible.[1]

The bill of 1873 successfully passed the Commons but was checked in the Lords. Cairns insisted on the value of objections and felt that by curtailing their scope and effect, too broad an opportunity was presented for the manufacture of frivolous claims. The new liberty suggested for the lodgers, he opposed bitterly as being a Liberal party manœuvre, designed for the purpose of gaining adherents from the lower classes, especially in Liverpool. After brief discussion the measure was summarily thrown out by the upper House.[2] The provision in behalf of the working classes, that night courts of revision should be held in the larger boroughs, was, however, incorporated in a separate bill and became law.[3]

The failure of the bills of 1871 and 1872 in the Commons, and the general indifference displayed in 1873 when the Lords threw out the bill of that year, practically decided that the registration system should remain unaltered in its main lines. The public as a whole failed to understand the question, and accepted as a matter of course the control of the party registration associations.

---

[1] 3 Hansard, ccxiv, 1947-1952; ccxv, 715, 961; ccxvi, 1398-1399.
[2] 3 Hansard, ccxvi, 1399-1407.
[3] 36 & 37 Vict., c 70.

Indeed, the moment was at hand when organized party influence was to extend itself from the period of registration on to the election itself, by means of the caucus and similar organizations. For the most part the members themselves were disinclined to interfere with the party machinery, which was built up to a large extent on existing registration conditions. Under such circumstances all parties tacitly recognized that the activity of the party registration associations was essential to the securing of a pure and complete register, and that the original principle that registration was entirely a state business and ought to be placed beyond the influence of political agents, was an impractical theory. Mechanism provided by the state had proved insufficient and had been supplanted by party action. It was felt that the recognition of party endeavour, accompanied by an elaboration of the checks placed upon it, was not merely preferable to the construction of a new system but, under the circumstances, absolutely inevitable.

The legislation which thus openly recognized the function of party associations, at the same time that it imposed checks upon their activities, was embodied chiefly in two acts. By that of 1878, which was closely modelled on the bill thrown out by the Lords five years before, the machinery of registration was altered only so far as to render the preliminary lists more exhaustive, and prevent the action of party organizations from becoming vexatious instead of merely prophylactic. The associations were, however, allowed full scope, through the reformed system of claims and objections, for the completion and the purification of the register. Party spirit was not intruded into the act in any sense, the measure being constructed by a select committee and passed without opposition or comment. The act of 1878 was concerned entirely with boroughs and carried out the proposal made in 1873 for the establishment of a common register for parliamentary and municipal electors. That of 1885, which followed upon the extension of household suffrage to counties, assimilated the process of registration in counties to that of boroughs, and inaugurated a uniform system.

The prime object of these registration acts was to remove the occasion for vexatious objections and the opportunity for wholesale disfranchisement, by remedying the imperfection and impurity of the preliminary lists. Elaborate provisions were made for furnishing the overseers all the necessary information at first hand. Every registrar of births and deaths was to transmit to the overseers a true return of the names, ages, and residences of all persons dying within the parish, as well as the names and residences of those from whom the information was obtained. Such returns were to be made four times a year. The returning official of the poor of each parish was likewise to furnish the names of all those disqualified by parochial relief.[1] According to the information thus acquired, the overseers were to expunge names from the list and provide against insufficient or fraudulent claims. It was noted above that the list of persons entitled to vote upon the 31st of July was published by the overseers on the following day. This had proved in practice impossible. Accordingly, in future the list published on the 1st of August was to include persons qualified to vote upon the 15th of July. Further provision against deficiency in the register was made by repeating the enactment of 1869 with regard to the names of occupiers: compound occupiers were to be considered duly rated, their names entered in the rate-book, and thence transferred to the electoral register.[2]

---

[1] 41 & 42 Vict., c. 26, sec. 11-12.
[2] Ibid., sec. 7, 14.

A provision was also inserted to provide for the grievances of the lodgers, who had experienced almost insuperable difficulty in placing their names upon the list. In future the declaration annexed to the lodger's notice of claim was, for the purpose of revision, to be considered prima facie evidence of his qualification. These changes, which were introduced in boroughs by the act of 1878, were in 1885 extended to the counties.[1]

The system of objections, which had from the first formed an essential part of registration and which had aroused manifold complaints, was adhered to. Changes, however, were made in the hope of preventing objections from becoming a source of annoyance although leaving them efficacious in the elimination of fraud. Insignificant errors in the description of any qualification, as we have seen, had permitted vexatious objections to be made without danger of being held for costs. In future any person whose qualifying property was not clearly stated in the list, whether he had received notice of objection or not, was allowed to make a declaration correcting the misdescription.

The acts of 1878 and 1885, however, contained no provisions relative to the exact specification of grounds of objection, further than provided for in the previous acts. Until 1895 it was only by decisions of the courts that exact specification was shown to be necessary for the success of an objection. The Order in Council of 1895 especially provides for all objections in the case of occupiers, and makes plain that it is necessary to specify exactly the grounds of objection. In order to lessen the number of purely frivolous objections, the act of 1878 also altered the law which provided against the withdrawal of objections. Before 1878, objections entered upon slight grounds would probably have been often withdrawn when

[1] 41 & 42 Vict., c. 26, sec. 23; 48 & 49 Vict., c. 15, sec. 1.

the insufficiency of evidence was perceived; but objectors were not permitted to withdraw, once they had filed their objection, and many of the most frivolous character had accordingly been tried. Under the act of 1878 an objection may be withdrawn, but notice in writing to that effect must be signed by the objector and given to the person objected to, not less than seven days before the holding of the first revision court.[1]

Arrangements were also made with the purpose of redressing the grievance that the names of many persons of good qualification had been expunged at the revision courts because of non-appearance. After 1878 in boroughs, and 1885 in counties, if the person objected to failed to appear his name was not summarily expunged. The objector must offer a prima facie proof of his grounds, as if the person objected to were present; "it must be shown to the satisfaction of the revising barrister that there is reasonable ground for believing that the objection is well founded, and that, by reason of the person objected to not being present, the objector is prevented from discovering the truth respecting the entry objected to."[2]

Changes were also made in the law of costs, which had hitherto proved inadequate in the prevention of frivolous objections. The provision of the act of 1865 respecting costs for frivolous objections to names on the county lists was extended to the borough system. This compelled the barristers to grant costs ranging from half a crown to five pounds for every ground of objection frivolously or

[1] "Quinlan v. M'Carthy," 1890, 28 *Law Reports, Ireland*, 246; Registration Order, 1895, Schedules 2, 3, Form I; 41 & 42 Vict., c. 26, sec. 27.

[2] There is no appeal from the decision of the revising barrister as to whether or not prima facie proof has been given, "Douglas v. Smith," *Law Reports*, 1 *King's Bench*, 126; Mackenzie and Lushington, *Registration Manual*, 382-388.

vexatiously stated in a notice; and this, though the name of the person was expunged upon some other ground stated in the same notice of objection. Moreover, it was provided that whenever the name of a person objected to was not expunged, costs of forty shillings were to be paid by the objector to the person who had made good his claim.[1]

The evils attendant upon the existence of duplicate voters, which had been to a large degree accountable for the impurity of the register, were also remedied. Under the new registration acts, where the name of a person was entered more than once on a list of voters, the revising barrister was to receive proof that such entries related to the same person; he was then to retain one entry and mark the others as invalid for voting purposes. Any person might select the entry to be retained, except that a freeman's qualification must necessarily be first choice. If the voter himself made no selection, an order of choice was determined which the revising barrister should follow in his selection of entries.[2]

It can hardly be said that by these changes, none of them basic in character, the deficiencies of the registration system were satisfactorily remedied. But without question the system has operated more smoothly since 1885. The provision for the more complete information of the overseers helped to insure the perfection and the accuracy of the lists; unqualified persons found it more difficult, and compound occupiers found it easier, to acquire the suffrage. The strict control of duplicate entries removed a source of vexation and complication. The retention of partisan objections also proved a steady factor making for the purity of the lists; but at the same time, the improvement in the law of costs and the close supervision

[1] 41 & 42 Vict., c. 26, sec. 26-27.
[2] 41 & 42 Vict., c. 26, sec. 28.

of all objections, tended to prevent them from being used merely as a means of spitefully harassing opponents. In this respect the effect of the act of 1878 was in certain boroughs very striking and resulted in a greater extension of voting rights than had followed the act of 1867 itself.[1]

But the more satisfactory operation of the registration system was not entirely a result of the rather slight amendments introduced in 1878 and 1885. In all probability time rather than statutory change has been the great settling factor. It must be remembered that registration was new to England in 1832 and it would have been surprising had the process proved acceptable before the rough edges had been worn by years of practice. Slowness is a characteristic of the English and the half-century does not seem too long a period in which to accustom the newly enfranchised people to the mechanism of registration. Their adaptability is, however, equally marked and it is not astonishing that after testing the necessity of the system, they should accept it with that political phlegm that has permitted many an institution, impossible in theory, to work them in principle the utmost benefit.

Another reason for the improved working of the registration system was the organization of parties. It was not until the highly developed associations took over the work of registration from the scattered agents or unconnected societies that it was performed thoroughly and systematically. In the old days certain constituencies were marked by extreme activity on the part of registration agents, but such zeal was often confined to a single locality or to one party. But after 1885 those responsible for the success of their party in each constituency were closely supervised by the central organization, and

[1] See Dod, *Parliamentary Companion*, 1866, 1868, 1878, 1880, *passim*.

care was taken that their registration methods should be complete. And with the failure of the bribery system the importance of registration became greater and more clearly recognized.

In various respects, it is true, the system has continued to evoke complaints. No self-working system was introduced for the county voters qualified by the ownership franchise, and the freeholders were forced to make special claim. The same is true of the lodgers, who are placed in a worse position than the owners, since their names do not stand over from year to year. "Old lodgers" to be registered must send in their claims every year.[1] It results that the conditions existent before 1878 have not been greatly modified in this respect, and because of the conflictions, penalties, and fraud, frequently involved, the proportion of lodger voters is always small. It is true now, as it was in 1884, that because of registration conditions the lodger franchise is almost entirely an election agent's franchise, since it is hardly possible to bring one's name on the list without the aid of an agent.

Because of this difficulty and also because of the period of residence required prior to registration, the Radicals have long complained that the franchise is often a myth, and that thousands of the best citizens are effectually deprived of their rights, while the stationary classes of the slums are favoured. Broadhurst pointed out that because of the difficulties of registration he became a member of parliament before he acquired the right to vote for a candidate; and Lowell cites an instance of a university graduate who, because of migrations due to his schoolmaster's profession, was never able to qualify. Another cause of dissatisfaction, which, however, seems inevitable, is the discrepancy between the decisions of different revising barristers; such discrepancy naturally results in a liberal

[1] "Husant v. Halse," 1886, *Law Reports*, 18 *Queen's Bench*, 412.

enfranchisement in one constituency, while that of its neighbour is restricted.

Notwithstanding the existence of such irregularities and restrictions the registration system cannot be said to fail in its most important objects. In marked contrast to its early operation, it permits most of the persons qualified to place their names upon the register, and the opportunities that it affords for the creation of votes and for fraud are not numerous. The development of the system has tended in general to assist the democratization of the electoral system. In the first decades that followed the inauguration of electoral registration in England, the practical deficiencies of the process affected the suffrage to a very marked degree. The wide disfranchisement resulting from objections, from rate-paying requirements, and from the numerous complexities involved, did not fail to bar many from the franchise to which they believed themselves entitled. And many of those who succeeded in winning the vote did so only through the assistance of electoral agents. Inasmuch as the latter represented upper class interests, the practical influence of the aristocracy remained strong even though working through a middle class suffrage.

The acts of 1867 and 1869, however, simplified rate-paying requirements and removed one of the most important restrictions upon the operation of the franchise. There still remained the activity of registration associations and lawyers who were able by their system of objections to control the suffrage of a large part of the working class electors. The acts of 1878 and 1885 in reality authorized such control, although subjecting it to a closer supervision. The function of the party in the electoral system was thus recognized and its power over the individual voter consecrated. But the registration agents of the later régime represented not the aristocratic interests of the early period, but the new popular associations which rested, at least in name, upon the support of the masses. Thus in so far as the associations are democratic institutions, the later development, which places the control of registration in their hands, may be considered an important step in the direction of democracy.

CHAPTER XIII

ELECTORAL MORALITY AFTER 1854

The attack upon electoral corruption assisted the democratic
advance—Effect of the act of 1854—Lessened direct bribery in
general—Had no effect on certain boroughs—Bribery in Beverly,
Lancaster, Reigate, and elsewhere—Character of corrupt organizations—Sums paid for votes—Indirect corruption—Committee
work—Travelling expenses—Question of conveyance in the House
of Commons—Treating—Undue influence and intimidation—
Report of 1870—Expense of elections—Obstacles to reform—
Public opinion indifferent—Failure of election auditors—Their
abolition—The law of agency—Complicated by act of 1854—
Inefficiency of election committees—Character of desirable reform.

EVEN the limited transfer of electoral power from the
aristocracy of agricultural and commercial wealth
to the masses which was effected by the act of 1867 and
later complemented by the legislation of 1878, 1884, and
1885, would have been far less complete without the
accompanying reforms in electoral methods. The final
settlement of the registration system, as we have seen,
assisted the process. The compilation of the lists was left,
it is true, in the hands of the party registration associations; but these latter rested after 1885 upon a democratic basis, and instead of representing the interests of
the local squire or the aristocratic big-wigs of the party,
acted for the popularly constituted caucus organization.

But still more important as an auxiliary factor making
for a truly democratic franchise, was the gradual elimination of the more flagrant corrupt practices, accompanied
as it was by a reduction in the expense of elections. So

long as it was possible for the wealthy and influential classes to control a large number of constituencies through bribery and intimidation, the power of Whig and Tory aristocrats was strongly entrenched against Radical attack. It is with the almost complete disappearance of such practices that the democratic associations were able to organize the electorate enfranchised by the new qualifications, and successfully combat the class which had, till then, retained an almost exclusive monopoly of electoral power.

The Corrupt Practices Act of 1854 was a step of real importance towards the elimination of corruption. Like the Reform Act of 1832, it may claim the significance that attaches to the first in a series; without this rather halting attempt to meet the difficulties at hand, the more successful legislation of later years would have been impossible. With all its weak points it indicated a possible solution of the problem and one which, when completed, was destined to prove satisfactory; namely, the publication and examination of electoral expenses. The Corrupt Practices Act of 1883 was, it is true, so much stricter in degree as to almost differ in kind from that of 1854; but it rested, after all, upon the principles introduced by the earlier law.

But it cannot be denied that the act of 1854 was in some respects pitifully ineffective. It has been said that with all its minute provisions and penalties it made no change in political manners;[1] and this statement might hold true absolutely of some constituencies, while it is guilty of only mild exaggeration of the conditions existent in many others. So far as intimidation was concerned, the failure of the act was generally acknowledged. The secretary of the Liberal Association in Bristol called the

---

[1] Ostrogorski, *Democracy and Organization of Political Parties,* i, 469.

intimidation clause of the act waste paper; another reformer, after canvassing the opinions of a large number of electoral agents, asserted that in no constituency did the tenants, workmen, and debtors cast their votes with greater freedom than before.[1] And such opinions were invariably borne out by subsequent investigating committees, who witnessed the truth of Macaulay's prophecy that undue influence could never be checked by penal legislation.[2]

As to the other forms of corruption, the judgment of contemporaries differed widely. There was, as always, the pessimistic section who asserted that the effect of the act was incalculably slight. Berkeley, the advocate of the ballot, agreed with the *Times*, which denounced the legislation of 1854 as a "pompous profession" intended to be, and actually, inoperative.[3] A parliamentary whip told a committee of the Lords frankly that he always considered the act a dead letter, and that he believed its provisions were uniformly disregarded. Mellor, whose eyes were doubtless opened by contact with the notorious constituency of Great Yarmouth, called the act a mockery and a delusion.[4] Others, after talking with electoral agents, felt that although the minor expenses of contests were diminished by the act, the most objectionable features of electioneering still persisted.[5]

Such pessimistic conclusions were, however, rather the exception, and even those who attacked the act as inefficacious were generally willing to admit that the forms of corruption which continued, were not so much those of direct bribery, as of colourable payments and intimida-

---

[1] 3 Hansard, cli, 2116-2117; *Parliamentary Papers,* 1870, no. 115.
[2] 3 Hansard, cxliii, 982.
[3] 3 Hansard, cxliii, 979.
[4] 3 Hansard, clvi, 379.
[5] 3 Hansard, cli, 2119.

tion.[1] The mass of opinion seemed to coincide with the judgment of Grey and Palmerston, who, although they admitted the imperfection of the legislation, refused to consider it an absolute failure.[2] Such conclusions were borne out to a large extent by the record of elections voided because of corrupt practices, an index not altogether trustworthy, because of the conditions affecting the presentation and judgment of petitions, but capable of offering confirmatory evidence. From 1837 to 1852 the number of petitions and the number of voided elections increased steadily until, in the latter year, twenty-three seats were declared vacant because of corruption.[3] In the first election after the act of 1854 nine seats only were lost on that account, and in 1859 but one. The aggregate number of petitions presented and elections voided in the four general elections which followed the passing of the act, was less than that of the single election of 1852.[4] Moreover the number of cases in which corruption was so flagrant as to demand the appointment of a commission, was diminishing. During the fourteen years which followed the bribery act, there were seven commissions appointed; while six were necessary as a result of the single election of 1852.[5]

On the other hand the existence and practice of the less obvious methods of corruption in a large number of constituencies was generally admitted. And if bribery in its direct form was less prevalent after 1854, in a certain number of boroughs it continued unchecked either by punitive legislation or by the increase in the number of voters. At Beverly, where direct bribery had been the

[1] 3 Hansard, cxliii, 979; *Parliamentary Papers*, 1860, no. 329, "Minutes of Evidence," §§ 290, 332, 1070.

[2] 3 Hansard, cxlii, 986-990.

[3] *Parliamentary Papers*, 1866, nos. 77, 114.

[4] *Parliamentary Papers*, 1868-1869, no. 107; *Ibid.*, 1866, no. 77.

[5] *Parliamentary Papers*, 1868-1869, no. 281.

accepted custom, the election of 1854 was pure, but the evidence brought out later showed that such an improvement was due to adventitious circumstances and not to any change of sentiment on the part of the constituency, and the elections which followed were notably corrupt.[1] Of this borough the royal commissioners reported that but for the one exception of 1854, bribery and other corrupt practices had prevailed in every election; sometimes openly, extensively, and systematically, sometimes in various disguises and under different pretexts; but at every election a considerable proportion of the constituency expected and received a money consideration for their vote. Of the eleven hundred electors, about eight hundred were open to bribery. More than one-third of these were without political principles, locally known as "rolling stock"; two hundred and fifty others on either side expected to be paid, and otherwise would not vote, although they did not cast their ballots against their own party. In the four elections that followed 1850, the commissioners believed that not less than two-thirds of those who voted had either received or had been promised money.[2] A local magnate reported that "the system of corruption and bribery has been going on time out of mind in Beverly, and to that extent that it is impossible to arrest or counteract it."[3]

Beverly was by no means the only constituency of this type, although we may believe that such practices were confined to a moderately small proportion of the boroughs.

[1] *Parliamentary Papers,* 1870, no. c15, "Report of the Beverly Bribery Commission," vii.

[2] *Parliamentary Papers,* 1870, no. c15, "Report of the Beverly Bribery Commission," vii.

[3] *Parliamentary Papers,* 1870, no. c15, "Report of the Beverly Bribery Commission," vii. There were twenty-three persons in Beverly who received bribes at every election between 1867 and 1868, *Ibid.,* xxiii-xxxi.

The commissioners reported that at Bridgwater no election had taken place within the century, except under the influence of criminally corrupt practices. Neither the provisions of 1854 nor the increase in the number of electors in 1867 affected matters. The state of morality never varied whether the electorate were large or small. At least three-fourths of the voters were frankly corrupt.[1] At Totnes half of the electorate was regularly in receipt of bribes, the remainder being generally under the firm control of the landlord.[2] Here, as at Bridgwater, the purchase of votes arose largely from the efforts made by the weaker party to combat the influence of the local magnate, so that the elections were battles between intimidation and bribery.[3]

At Lancaster nearly all the freemen, who formed the mass of the electorate, received money bribes. In 1865 fourteen thousand pounds was spent by the two parties, of which the greater part went in this manner.[4] At Reigate, exactly half of the seven hundred voters were directly bribed, most of them workingmen, although more than a hundred tradesmen also sold their votes. In the latter town one elector consented to vote without being paid, but only on condition that his action should be kept secret; he stated that he should be forever ashamed of himself if the fact became public.[5] At Wakefield, of the eight thousand pounds expended by the two candidates,

[1] *Parliamentary Papers,* 1870, no. c11, "Report of the Bridgwater Bribery Commission," vi-vii.

[2] *Parliamentary Papers,* 1867, no. 3773, "Report of the Totnes Bribery Commission," ix.

[3] *Parliamentary Papers,* 1867, no. 3773, "Report of the Totnes Bribery Commission," xi.

[4] *Parliamentary Papers,* 1867, no. 3777, "Report of the Lancaster Bribery Commission," vii.

[5] *Parliamentary Papers,* 1867, no. 3774, "Report of the Reigate Bribery Commission," ix; *Ibid.,* "Minutes of Evidence," § 38033.

seven thousand was used in methods of corruption, and one-half of this was laid out in direct bribery.[1] In spite of the disfranchisement of the freemen at Yarmouth, similar conditions continued to prevail in that borough.[2]

The corruption which existed after 1854 in some of these boroughs is well illustrated by the manner in which candidates were selected, showing that the choice of a person to represent the constituency was almost entirely determined by his willingness and ability to spend money. Amongst the papers of one electoral agent was found a list of available candidates with their qualifications, from which it appears that although family connections and intellectual ability were of value, and political ideas so in a lesser degree, the real essential was wealth. There were instances where a chance acquaintanceship in a railway carriage between an agent and a wealthy manufacturer, led to the candidacy of the latter. The chief whips òf the party kept lists of openings, it is true, and recommendations from the *Carlton* or *Reform* carried great weight; but readiness to bribe was in the last instance the determining factor in the choice of a candidate. In at least one election, where a candidate had been already accepted, when it was learned that he planned to conduct a pure campaign, his committee waited upon him and requested him to withdraw.[3]

The candidate's success in the corrupt boroughs depended upon the approval of the established election agent, and in the attempts which sometimes took place to carry on a campaign unassisted, the futility of standing without the support of the recognized manipulator of the bribing

---

1 3 Hansard, clvii, 1632-1633.

2 *Parliamentary Papers*, 1867, no. 3775, "Report of the Yarmouth Bribery Commission," *passim*.

3 *Parliamentary Papers*, 1870, no. c10, "Report of the Bridgwater Bribery Commission," 6.

system was invariably demonstrated. The latter, colloquially known as "bribe agent," and ordinarily a tradesman or small solicitor, was backed by strong influence; he disposed frequently of large sums between elections which were often supplied by the magnate of the neighbourhood, who desired to keep ultimate control of local elections in his hands. The great asset, however, of the local bribe agent, and that which made him indispensable, was his intimate knowledge of the character and circumstances of each of the voters.[1]

The completeness of the corrupt organization varied greatly. In some boroughs, the methods of corruption were carefully planned out, and corrupt electioneering carried on constantly between elections; in others the bribery was haphazard and to a large degree unpremeditated. In Norwich, for instance, it was not until noon of the election day that the Conservatives, running behind, hastily procured money from the bank and scattered it about during the last hours of polling, in the hope of stemming the tide.[2] On the other hand in Beverly, the local bribe agent, a draper, gave up most of his time between elections to forming a system of corruption. All the institutions of the borough were brought under his control, and everyone owed his position to it; the town councillors themselves were elected by the money he found, and exercised their patronage as he directed; when it came to the time of parliamentary election he was complete master of the situation.[3] At Totnes, thousands of pounds were expended to hold the organization together between elections. Sometimes the party friendly society, as at

[1] *Parliamentary Papers*, 1870, no. c11, "Report of the Bridgwater Bribery Commission," xxi.

[2] *Parliamentary Papers*, 1870, no. c13, "Report of the Norwich Bribery Commission," *passim*.

[3] *Parliamentary Papers*, 1870, no. c15, "Report of the Beverly Bribery Commission," vii-ix.

Gloucester, served as an electoral organization of corrupt methods.[1]

In such instances, as well as in many of the boroughs where the system of bribery between elections was allowed to lapse, the method of procedure at election time was carefully organized. The local bribe agent was commander-in-chief, or if there were no regular permanent official of such a type, the party registration agent of the constituency might offer his valuable knowledge of the morals and solvency of the electors. The preliminary canvass was the initial operation, and upon it often depended the result of the election, although the voters could not be always depended upon, and where there was no permanent organization, would almost certainly turn to the other side if better terms were offered. Retaining fees of two guineas or more were sometimes paid as a preliminary earnest of the candidate's good will. "I asked for their votes," said one canvasser, "but you might as well ask for their lives, unless you had money to give them."[2] And elsewhere the candidate, when he attempted an honest canvass, was met with the invariable answer that the votes would be cast for "Mr. Most."[3]

In general, each party had a cashier who might be, and generally was, the local bribe agent, and to whom were entrusted the whole of the funds employed. Such funds were provided by the candidate himself and his wealthy backers, assisted by the magnate of the district; no money was collected from the constituency for illegal campaign expenses; the borough was there to receive, not to give.[4]

---

[1] 3 Hansard, clvi, 384.

[2] *Parliamentary Papers*, 1867, no. 3775, "Minutes of Evidence." § 24935.

[3] *Parliamentary Papers*, 1870, no. c11, "Report of the Bridgwater Bribery Commission," xxiii.

[4] At Norwich, in 1868, the working class candidate collected money from the poorer electors for his campaign; but the agents of

The borough and the country within seven miles was divided into districts, over each of which was set a captain, who dealt directly with the cashier and drew from him the money required within the district allotted to his charge. Under the captains were the sub-captains, who took charge of the separate streets, or particular families, or knots of voters working under the same employer. To the latter were joined a staff of assistants, whose duty it was to treat and drink with the voters, and collect them at the critical times of payment and voting. These men were naturally of the worst possible character and a large part of the money entrusted to them never found its way to the electors.[1]

The disbursement of bribes was often perfectly open, the bargaining and purchasing of votes being carried on in the streets. At Beverly a sub-agent describes going out into the market place, where the electors were waiting for the highest bidder, and openly asking how much they wanted for their votes; the cash was put down before the eyes of the whole town. At Bridgwater, concealment was not deemed necessary, for each side reckoned that the other would not dare "go on" with a petition, even if they presented one. Encounters and fisticuffs between the bribery agents of one party and the other, in their open competition for the purchase of votes, were by no means rare.[2] And a witness draws a pathetic picture of the frank disappointment expressed at Totnes when one candidate

the wealthy candidates never attempted to raise money for bribery by means of small subscriptions.

[1] Cf. the evidence submitted to the Commissions sitting at Beverly, Bridgwater, and Norwich in 1870, and those of Lancaster, Totnes, Reigate, and Yarmouth in 1867, *Parliamentary Papers*, 1870, nos. c15, c10, c13, and *Ibid.*, 1867, nos. 3777, 3776, 3774, 3775.

[2] *Parliamentary Papers*, 1870, no. c15, "Report of the Beverly Bribery Commission," x; *Ibid.*, no. c11, "Report of the Bridgwater Bribery Commission," xx.

withdrew, the wives of the electors coming down to the
Conservative hotel with baskets to carry away the sovereigns that were to be distributed, and loudly lamenting
their misfortune when it was announced that no contest
would be held.[1]

But in general some attempt at superficial concealment
was made. Often a stranger would be imported from
another constituency to distribute the money bribes and,
in parlance of the day, play the part of "the man in the
moon"; sometimes his incognito was so skilfully preserved that committees of investigation would have the
greatest difficulty in proving his connection with either
party. The voters might receive their money in a dark-
ened room; sometimes an aperture was made in a door
through which the money was pushed when the number
of the elector was called out. Ticket systems were also in
use, and on one occasion the electors were invited to
breakfast on the morning of polling day and each of them
discovered thirty shillings under his coffee cup.[2]

The sums paid for votes varied widely according to the
number of electors, their experience of corrupt elections,
as well as the personal circumstances of the voter bribed.
In Norwich, with a large constituency and a comparatively pure election, three half-crowns or a half-sovereign
was quite sufficient to win a vote. In fact one man obtained the suffrages of thirty electors by the expenditure
of thirty shillings in treating.[3] At Beverly the old system
of two sovereigns for a plumper and one sovereign for a
split vote was generally adhered to, although circum-

[1] *Parliamentary Papers*, 1867, no. 3773, "Report of the Totnes
Bribery Commission," ix.

[2] *Parliamentary Papers*, 1870, nos. c15, c11, c13, "Reports of
Beverly, Bridgwater, and Norwich Bribery Commissions," *passim*.

[3] *Parliamentary Papers*, 1870, no. c13, "Report of the Norwich
Bribery Commission," xiii-xiv.

stances sometimes ran the price up. A vote at Bridgwater had been known to bring ten pounds, and the tenants of the Duke of Somerset at Totnes received anywhere from sixty to one hundred and fifty pounds apiece for casting their ballots against his interest.[1] They naturally had to brave the penalty of certain eviction, which the landlord was not slow to inflict.

Such corruption as has been described was certainly not typical of all the boroughs in England, and we naturally ask in how many constituencies a pure election was an exception or an impossibility. The circumstances which led to exposure in each case were so exceptional, the difficulties which surrounded the presentation and successful prosecution of a petition so great, that we might infer that similar practices were existent in many other boroughs which were never brought to light. Such an inference is supported by the opinions of many persons, both in and out of parliament, well acquainted with electoral conditions. On the other hand, as we saw, the majority of elections voided after 1854 did not result from direct bribery, but from the less flagrant methods of corrupt electioneering. And the investigating committees after a thorough study of conditions believed that the direct purchase of votes was becoming more and more restricted to a small number of boroughs; in counties, they said, direct bribery was practically unknown. In all probability, bribery of the type described at Totnes and the other boroughs which were disfranchised in 1868 and 1870, did not affect a very wide circle of constituencies. In those boroughs, it is true, the system of corruption was ingrained so deeply that absolute disfranchisement was the sole remedy. But in a large number of other boroughs, of which Norwich and Gloucester furnish

[1] *Parliamentary Papers*, 1867, no. 3776, "Report of the Totnes Bribery Commission," x.

examples, direct bribery was doubtless exercised infrequently, in haphazard fashion, and affected but a small part of the electorate.

The circle of boroughs in which corruption assumed a less direct form was, however, far wider and, according to most of the witnesses examined, it was in this respect that the act of 1854 proved completely ineffective. Instead of the direct purchase of votes, prospective bribery was largely practised. The difficulty of detecting payments made long after the election, was great; and in the majority of cases, even if evidence leaked out a year or so later, nothing would or could be done.[1] Other methods of disguising bribery were general. Labourers who earned three to six shillings a day claimed and were paid a sovereign daily for loss of time in attending the nomination and the polls. Charitable subscriptions offered a veil of saintly white to throw over the corrupt traffic in the suffrages of the poor. The purchase of useless commodities at exorbitant rates was also used as a cloak to direct bribery.[2]

Still more general was the custom of appointing voters to perform nominal or fictitious services, for which such large sums were paid as to constitute actual bribery. It was an ordinary practice to engage a large number of paid canvassers who did no work and received a liberal salary.[3] At Gloucester, where, according to the commissioners, thirty canvassers would have been ample, two hundred and sixty were thus employed; at Hull in 1859,

[1] *Parliamentary Papers,* 1860, no. 329, "Minutes of Evidence," §§ 673, 917-919, 2875.

[2] *Parliamentary Papers,* 1860, no. 329, "Minutes of Evidence," §§ 152-158, 3310-3314; *Ibid.,* 1867, no. 3774, "Report of the Reigate Bribery Commission," x.

[3] *Parliamentary Papers,* 1860, no. 329, "Minutes of Evidence," § 415; *Ibid.,* 1867, no. 3774, "Report of the Reigate Bribery Commission," xii.

three hundred voters served in this respect, receiving
anything from half a crown to three pounds, and avoiding
all actual labour.[1] The custom of placing voters on the
campaign committees was also widespread. At Reigate,
a large proportion of mechanics and labourers were thus
employed and paid for their "services," which, as the commissioner reported, formed merely a plausible excuse for
the purchase of votes. At Lancaster, practically all the
freemen were placed upon the committees; this was the
invariable custom, and it was asserted that if it were not
done they would have deserted to the other side; many
served on the election committees of both parties. Com-
mitteemen were generally paid each week, at the rate of
five shillings for each day. They held committee meetings,
it is true, but all the evidence points to the fact that drink-
ing was the only business accomplished.[2]

A still more common method of covering up money payments for votes, was the entering of such sums under the
item of the electors' travelling expenses. This form of
disguised bribery was frequent in both counties and
boroughs; it was the more difficult to prevent, inasmuch as
the absolute prohibition of assistance to the outvoter would
have resulted in the practical disfranchisement of many of
the poorer voters, especially in the larger constituencies.
From early times it had been the custom to pay the expenses of all outvoters, and generally so to over-pay them
as to make the journey a profitable business excursion.

The legality of such payments was a matter of doubt,
and the conflicting opinions of legislators and jurists
prevented election committees from stopping the practice
of corrupt conveyance. On the one hand, Lord Mansfield

---

[1] 3 Hansard, clvi, 383.
[2] *Parliamentary Papers*, 1867, no. 3774, "Report of the Reigate
Bribery Commission," x; *Ibid.*, no. 3777, "Report of the Lancaster
Bribery Commission," xii.

had ruled that the payment of conveyance should be regarded as bribery; on the other, Russell considered it legal and permissible. In 1854 the latter attempted, without success, to sanction it directly by law.[1] In 1856 a candidate sent a circular to the electors, urging them to vote for him, and promising payment of all travelling expenses. A petition was brought against him, which on appeal was decided by the Exchequer Court to the effect that if corrupt intent were not proved, such payments were legal; the Lords, however, revised the decision, and once more the legality of the practice was in doubt.[2]

To settle the matter a bill was brought in by Walpole, in 1858, which legalized the payment of travelling expenses if made without corrupt intent. With a majority of the House of Commons, he believed it practically impossible to enforce any prohibition of such payments, and he asserted that prohibition would result in the wholesale abstention of electors from voting.[3] The measure was met by bitter opposition, led by the Radicals. They asserted that voting was a privilege and should not be remunerated, as for a favour received. Moreover, the custom of paying expenses swelled the candidate's account to such an extent as to make it impossible for any but the very rich to stand. The abolition of the member's property qualification, they maintained, must be without meaning if the ordinary electoral outlay were so high as to prevent the candidacy of poorer men. Moreover, whatever might or might not be proved as to corrupt intent, the fact remained that the payment of travelling expenses was a ready and common means for covering up bribery.[4]

Others, while admitting the force of these objections,

---

1 3 Hansard, cli, 2123-2124.
2 3 Hansard, cxliii, 980, 986; *Ibid.*, cl. 217.
3 3 Hansard, cli, 1491.
4 3 Hansard, cli, 1493, 2002.

believed it impossible not to provide some conveyance for
the voters, and proposed a compromise which was ultimately adopted. According to this compromise, the payment of money, or any valuable consideration, was forbidden; but it was to be legal to provide any sort of conveyance for the voters, either by the furnishing of vehicles
or railway tickets, or by reimbursing them for sums expended in actual travelling.[1] Notwithstanding annual
attempts to repeal this measure, both on the ground that
it covered up bribery and that it increased the cost of
elections, the conveyance of voters continued legal until
strictly modified in 1883.[2]

As a result, it was still possible practically to purchase
votes by an over-liberal payment of expenses; and enormous bills of conveyance were rendered by the electors, and
cheerfully settled by the candidates.[3] In Lancaster, in
1865, nearly nine hundred pounds was expended supposedly upon carriages and conveyances, although the
whole number of voters residing outside the town but
within the seven mile borough radius did not exceed three
hundred and thirty. In the opinion of the commissioners
such expenses should not have exceeded fifty pounds for
each side.[4] In Northamptonshire three thousand pounds
was spent in conveyance, and the returns from all the constituencies show that such expenditure was invariably one
of the major items.[5] The very indefiniteness of its char-

[1] 3 Hansard, cli, 1489, 1590, 1599.

[2] A provision was included in the Reform Act of 1867 which
limited conveyance to the counties and larger boroughs, 3 Hansard,
clvii, 1898.

[3] *Parliamentary Papers,* 1860, no. 329, "Minutes of Evidence,"
§§ 3106-3107, 3032-3033, 687-690, 1779-1781.

[4] *Parliamentary Papers,* 1867, no. 3777, "Report of the Lancaster
Bribery Commission," vii.

[5] *Parliamentary Papers,* 1857, no. 332, "Returns from Election
Auditors."

acter by no means detracted from its usefulness as a cloak
to more dishonest expenditure.

So far as treating was concerned, the investigation committee of 1860 decided that some slight improvement was
to be noted, although the penalties prescribed by the act
of 1854 had been of the most moderate character.[1] Such
optimism, however, resulted rather from the disgraceful
habits of the previous period, than from any clearly
marked virtue on the part of agents or voters after 1854.
The local committees still held their headquarters at the
public houses, and anyone claiming to offer assistance
might enter at any time and enjoy food and drink to a
practically unlimited extent.[2]

From the moment the canvass began, in many of the
boroughs, the poor spent most of their time in wandering
from one public house to another in search of refreshment.
One witness described his electoral function as that of
"fuddler" who kept by him a supply of shillings and small
change for the voters who came to him from time to time,
when they were dry of a morning. The Liberals had more
than forty public and beer houses in Lancaster in 1865,
and over a thousand pounds was spent on treating before
the election began. The commissioners reported that
"nothing could be more degrading than the effect of this
sort of canvass on voters; they struck work, they spent
the nights in public houses and the days in wandering
about, begging from the assistants on either side for a
few shillings to enable them to continue their debauch."
After the election in this instance, another thousand
pounds was spent in discharging outstanding public house

[1] *Parliamentary Papers,* 1860, no. 329, "Report of the Select
Committee," iv.

[2] *Parliamentary Papers,* 1860, no. 329, "Minutes of Evidence,"
§§ 237-239, 793-794, 835, 943-944.

accounts.[1] At one small borough five hundred pounds was
expended on each side at the public houses, and the commissioners did not trouble to make out a list of persons
treated there, since it would have contained the names of
practically all the voters in the constituency.[2] The act
of 1854 thus cannot be said to have exercised very strong
effect upon the practice of treating.

So far as the exercise of undue influence and intimidation was concerned, the results of that act were still less
beneficial. In all the really corrupt boroughs, such
methods continued to be practised as auxiliary to the
more direct method of bribery. In the constituencies
where most elections were comparatively pure, the investigating committees found as great difficulty as do historians in determining the exact truth of each specific alle-
gation of intimidation of workmen by masters, of tenants
by landlords, of tradesmen by customers, and of workingmen by each other.[3] Numerous instances occur in
some of the smaller boroughs, showing the part played in
elections by the magnates and great interests. In Totnes
farmers were admitted to holdings in the pasture lands
within the borough, only on the understanding that they
would vote for the Liberal candidate. Evictions from
holdings for "ratting" were not uncommon.[4]

[1] *Parliamentary Papers*, 1867, no. 3777, "Report of the Lancaster
Bribery Commission," xii.

[2] *Parliamentary Papers*, 1870, no. cll, "Report of the Bridgwater
Bribery Commission," xix, xxxv.

[3] Many witnesses were examined who alleged the existence of
intimidation in all the ways referred to. As soon as their evidence
became known in the locality, applications were received that witnesses on the other side should be examined, who denied the charges
brought against themselves, but usually attributed similar practices
to their opponents, *Parliamentary Papers*, 1870, no. 115, "Report of
the Select Committee on modes of conducting parliamentary elections,"
iv.

[4] *Parliamentary Papers*, 1867, no. 3776, "Report of the Totnes
Bribery Commission," v.

Sometimes, with the pecuniary assistance of the candidate, the old plan of buying up all the municipal offices was adopted; the party in power thus controlled the distribution of charities, which were used frankly for party purposes. "Freedom-brokers" were financed by the electoral agents, who thus created a powerful influence for their party amongst the freemen who had been assisted in taking up their freedom by the broker.[1] The influence of the great manufacturers in their locality was supreme, especially in the case of brewers; in one borough thirty-nine beer houses were owned by a single brewer, most of the publicans being voters and naturally active canvassers in the brewer's interest.[2] The influence of the Church in elections also continued to be great, and in the nonconformist denominations voting for a Conservative candidate was sometimes considered heresy, and was visited with expulsion from the congregation.[3]

That intimidation of such a kind was not extensively practised in a manner capable of legal proof, was evident from the rarity of returns voided on this ground. But this fact resulted rather from the defects of the law than from a paucity of provocation. It was, at least, certain that whether or not intimidation were widely practised, the fear of it prevailed extensively amongst that class of voters who were liable to its influence. Especially was this true during the canvass which preceded the election. It was then that undue influence in a modified form was

[1] *Parliamentary Papers,* 1870, no. c15, "Report of the Beverly Bribery Commission," xi-xiii.

[2] The sale of grains at reduced rates by the brewers to the cowkeepers who held the franchise was a valuable consideration and fortified the power of the brewers in the country towns, *Parliamentary Papers,* 1867, no. 3775, "Report of the Great Yarmouth Bribery Commission," x.

[3] *Parliamentary Papers,* 1870, no. c11, "Report of the Bridgwater Bribery Commission," xxv.

constantly at play, working upon the voters through private considerations, whether of interest, hope, or fear, and for political purposes.[1]

It was more difficult to obtain exact information of intimidation in the counties than in the boroughs. But the committee of 1870 were of the opinion that an influence exceeding, in greater or less degree, the legitimate influence which a popular and respected landlord must always exercise in his neighbourhood, was often brought to bear upon the tenant farmers and other voters in the agricultural districts. There were frequent instances when the tenants who had all signed the requisition to a candidate, voted against him and with their landlord; and it was rare to find a tenant who dared promise a vote until he had received an assurance from his landlord that he might vote as he pleased. The inducement to vote with the landlord might proceed frequently from the hope of future advantages to be gained rather than from the fear of injury to be inflicted. But the influence so employed, and utilizing whatever inducement, was incompatible with the exercise of a free suffrage.[2]

Thus whatever might be the improvement effected by the act of 1854, the electors did not yet really control the franchise that they were supposed to exercise. In some boroughs through direct bribery, in others and in the counties, through the more indirect forms of corruption and undue influence, ultimate power rested to a large extent with the upper and the upper middle classes. Nor did the increase of the electorate in 1867 alter matters very materially. In the larger constituencies, the dis-

[1] *Parliamentary Papers,* 1870, no. 115, "Report from the Select Committee on modes of conducting parliamentary elections." For instances of physical coercion, see the *Spectator,* April 7, 1866.

[2] *Parliamentary Papers,* 1870, no. 115, "Report from the Select Committee on modes of conducting parliamentary elections."

guised forms of bribery still continued and, in some of them, the proportion of voters open to corruption was definitely increased, although the price of votes fell.[1] In the traditionally corrupt boroughs, the new electors apparently regarded the suffrage as a financial melon, from the enjoyment of which they had been so long excluded that they intended to make up for lost opportunities. The general tenor of the commissioners' reports shows that the extension of the franchise had improved conditions no whit in such constituencies.[2]

Reformers pointed out also, and with some justice, that in another respect the franchise was not free. Because of the large sums demanded of a candidate it was not open to the electors to choose the sort of man they really wanted, and often they had merely a choice between evils. Since the contests called for a great financial outlay, the field was limited to an independent man of wealth, or to one wholly dependent upon aristocratic support, and subject to that influence.[3] In this respect the act of 1854, it is true, had effected a slight reform; but the length of the election accounts continued to provoke frequent complaints in the country, and numerous stillborn bills in parliament. Certainly there was nothing comparable to the amounts expended in pre-reform days, when Lambton spent thirty thousand pounds in a contest in Durham city, when fifty thousand was spent in Liverpool, and when the preparations for an uncontested election cost John Marshall seventeen thousand; while the Yorkshire contest of 1807, the "Austerlitz of electioneering," cost the three

[1] *Parliamentary Papers*, 1870, no. c13, "Report of the Norwich Bribery Commission," vi.

[2] *Parliamentary Papers*, 1870, no. c11, "Report of the Bridgwater Bribery Commission," xxxi; and cf. Ostrogorski, *Democracy and Parties*, i, 469.

[3] *Westminster Review*, lxxviii, 67; *Saturday Review*, February 22, 1868.

candidates anywhere from three hundred thousand to half
a million pounds.[1] Since then, and largely as a result of
the act of 1832, the sum total of a contestant's election
bill had decreased enormously; five thousand pounds spent
at a metropolitan election in 1852 was probably above the
average.[2]

For the decrease which continued after 1854, the act
of that year may be held in some degree responsible.
Such at least was the opinion of the day. In the corrupt
boroughs and in the places where there was tendency to
encourage corrupt practices, the effect of the legislation
was slight;[3] but in the counties and the large boroughs
there was a continual diminution in the expense of contested elections, and the accounts of all scrupulous candidates were certainly reduced.[4] It is difficult to state with
any degree of exactitude the sums expended, because of the
nature of the accounts furnished to the auditors, which
were frequently illusory; in some cases the published
accounts represented only half of the actual outlay. But
according to the election abstracts, the average cost of a
borough election in 1857 ran from two hundred to four
hundred pounds. In the metropolitan boroughs it was
high; at Finsbury and Tower Hamlets expenses ranged
from thirty-three hundred to forty-two hundred pounds,
and in Lambeth fifty-three hundred pounds was spent.
But in some boroughs, if the accounts do not lie, elections
were far cheaper: less than two hundred pounds at Bodmin

[1] Reid, *Durham,* i, 136; 3 Hansard, x, 243; xciv, 171; Roebuck,
Whig Ministry, i, 350; *Chambers Journal,* lviii, 513.

[2] *Parliamentary Papers,* 1854-1855, no. 227.

[3] *Parliamentary Papers,* 1860, no. 329, "Minutes of Evidence,"
§§ 452-454, 914-916, 922, 2971, 2978, 3064-3069.

[4] *Parliamentary Papers,* 1860, no. 329, "Minutes of Evidence,"
§§ 912-916, 919, 1742-1759, 1851-1853, 3064-3069, 1044, 1140. The
diminution in the cost of elections, however, proved later to be only
temporary.

and Bury St. Edmunds, and only eighty-nine pounds at Evesham. County elections were always more expensive, and in 1857 there was only one in which the credited expenditure was below a thousand pounds. In North Devon a candidate spent fifty-five hundred pounds, and in one division of Northamptonshire more than eight thousand pounds.[1]

In the election of 1868, because of the increase of the electorate and corrupt electioneering, and possibly also because of more accurate returns, the reported expenses were much higher. The average in boroughs ranged from four hundred to nine hundred pounds; two thousand was by no means an exceptional figure. In Bradford the loser expended seven thousand pounds for his chance of a seat, and in Westminster a successful candidate paid nearly nine thousand. In counties, the average ran from two thousand to four thousand pounds, and the least expended was thirteen hundred. In Middlesex the expenses of one member were nine thousand pounds, and in Durham, fifteen thousand.[2] Altogether the Radical complaint that the abolition of the former property qualification had not greatly widened the choice of candidates open to the electors, seemed to be not entirely without justification.

The obstacles which stood in the way of the elimination of corruption and the reduction of election expenses, were of various kinds, and generally similar to those existent before 1854. Of vital importance was the attitude of both people and legislature upon the question of bribery, direct and disguised. There is a wealth of testimony to

[1] *Parliamentary Papers*, 1854-1855, no. 171; *Ibid.*, 1855, no. 159; *Ibid.*, 1857, no. 332, "Returns from Election Auditors."

[2] *Parliamentary Papers*, 1868-1869, no. 424, "Abstract of Candidates' Expenses."

the fact that electoral corruption was not generally looked upon as an immoral act, and that all through the country there was an utter lack of moral sense connected with its practice.[1] On the one hand, the feeling prevailed amongst the people that the House of Commons was not serious in its attempts to eliminate corruption, and that this attitude extended throughout the wealthier classes: "Where the House is culpably lax is not in its legislative capacity, but as a body or club of individual members. It is a painful truth that a wealthy man known to have bribed, nay actually convicted of bribery, is not a whit the less respected by the majority of the members of the House. . . . No one admits that he thinks it morally right; a very few act as if they thought it morally wrong; but to the great body of society the offence operates practically as a recommendation rather than as an exclusion."[2]

Nor was this opinion unsupported by appearances and facts, and there was no lack of instances where members convicted of bribery came into the House on a later occasion without a social stain.[3] And the speeches of the eminent statesmen of the day did not always ring true in their denunciations of corrupt practices. Earl Grey, in his work on parliamentary government, did not hesitate to insist that bribery was not nearly so immoral or so dangerous as the current truckling to mob desire.[4] The son of the great reformer did not actually argue for bribery, but the effect produced upon the reader is that of

[1] *Parliamentary Papers,* 1860, no. 329, "Minutes of Evidence," §§ 290, 332, 371, 1068, 1070.

[2] *Westminster Review,* lxxvii, 65; 3 Hansard, clvi, 378.

[3] 3 Hansard, clxxxvi, 126-128.

[4] "To give money bribes to electors is not worse or rather not nearly so bad as to court their favour by flattering their passions and prejudices," Grey, *Parliamentary Government,* 120 (cited in *North British Review,* xxviii, 452).

philosophic tolerance and rather easy-going acceptance of the evil.

The actions of the candidates certainly seemed to display their willingness to fall in with the customs of the constituency. One candidate, of honourable name and station, admitted frankly that when asked, he supplied money to the election agent, "knowing perfectly well that it must go in bribery, but believing that bribery had become part of the constitutional system."[1] And it was no uncommon thing for an electoral committee, when the tide was going against the candidate, to hold a consultation as to whether corrupt methods should be adopted, or whether the election should be conducted honestly and the seat prayed for on petition. Policy or prudence might determine the character of the campaign, but rarely moral sense.[2]

On the other hand, since corruption was regarded in such a light by the upper classes, the poorer electors were not apt to oppose the system which benefited them richly. And everywhere one met with the complaint that until there was better state of public opinion among the voters, it was almost useless to pass stringent measures against bribery.[3] The belief was common that the experiments tried by parliament had been feeble and inadequate, chiefly because there had been "no adequate amount of indignation in the country against the crime."[4] Too often the attitude of the electors justified this complaint. Even when some sense of shame existed, the electors were accustomed to claim the usual payment for their votes as a right from the candidate of their own colour; and only

[1] *Parliamentary Papers,* 1867, no. 3773, "Report of the Totnes Bribery Commission," ix.

[2] *Parliamentary Papers,* 1867, no. 3777, "Report of the Lancaster Bribery Commission," x; *Ibid.,* "Minutes of Evidence," § 1583.

[3] 3 Hansard, clvi, 1075.

[4] *MacMillan's Magazine,* x, 192.

looked upon it as a bribe when they accepted it from the
candidate of the opposing party.[1]

Thus the advocates of political purity had to contend
against powerful opposition from two opposite quarters.
There was the natural appetite of the voters, which
demanded satisfaction, and which was especially rampant
in the smaller boroughs, where suffrages were extremely
valuable. On the other hand, there was the rich crowd of
suitors, whose sole hope of entering parliament lay in the
system of purchase. In the presence of candidates eager
to buy, and voters longing to be bought, the efforts of
those seeking to alter public opinion, in and out of the
House, were too often nullified.

Even the most sincere attempts to punish corrupt practices were thus prevented by the action of public opinion,
which combined with the loopholes left by the law to
further the escape of the guilty candidates. Russell had
believed that by the system of election auditors it would
be possible to check election expenses and prevent corrupt
outlay. But the auditors proved a bitter disappointment,
except in the boroughs where the method of electioneering
was impeccable, and where their services were not required.
It soon became evident that they were willing to pass any
account sent in and since they were fluctuating officers
they cared little for the exact performance of their duties.
Moreover they had no power of setting a maximum of
expenditure, so that in many cases election accounts rose
far above the sum that might have been expected from a
legitimate outlay.[2]

It is a matter of common knowledge that in many
boroughs complete accounts were never furnished to the

[1] *Parliamentary Papers,* 1870, no. c15, "Report of the Beverly
Bribery Commission," vii.

[2] *Parliamentary Papers,* 1860, no. 329, "Minutes of Evidence,"
§§ 2483-2498, 2510, 2734, 3121, 3154, 3183.

auditors.[1] The commissioners reported that at Gloucester the accounts were a farce, and the auditors only existed to deceive and delude the legislature and the public.[2] At Lancaster the accounts were prepared without any relation whatever to the real truth of the case; everyone connected with the conduct of the election admitted that "the duty devolving upon an election agent was to hand in a reasonably plausible account of what might have been expected to be the amount spent, if no recourse had been had on either side to any illegal practices or payments."[3] At Beverly the plan adopted on both sides, was to open two channels of expenditure: one open and pure, through which the regular and legal items were to pass; the other secret and impure.[4] Even when the expenses were duly entered, the election agents succeeded in concealing illegitimate expenses under the legal items, so that the accounts utterly failed to serve their purpose.[5]

Such a storm of protest was raised against the inefficiency of the auditors, even the government admitting that the system was futile, or worse, that in 1863 their office was abolished and their functions taken over by the returning officers.[6] The latter were to publish accounts of all payments within two months of the election, and such accounts could be entered only by the authorized agents of the candidate. Bills must be sent in within a month of the election or the right to recover was barred.[7]

[1] *Parliamentary Papers,* 1860, no. 329, "Report of the Select Committee," iv.

[2] 3 Hansard, clvi, 773.

[3] *Parliamentary Papers,* 1867, no. 3777, "Report of the Lancaster Bribery Commission," vii.

[4] *Parliamentary Papers,* 1870, no. c15, "Report of the Beverly Bribery Commission," xvi.

[5] *Parliamentary Papers,* 1860, no. 329, "Minutes of Evidence," §§ 2408-2410, 2461-2465.

[6] 3 Hansard, clvi, 1085.

[7] 26 & 27 Vict., c. 29.

The change, however, appeared to work no improvement, and the law was frankly declared a farce. It is certain that accounts continued to be "cooked," and that there soon grew up a system of evasion by which bills were not settled until all danger was past. In at least one case where fourteen thousand pounds was really spent, only twenty-five hundred was accounted for.[1]

The task of bringing home corrupt practices was thus not greatly facilitated by the system of published accounts. It was materially hindered by the complicated state of the law of agency. The parliamentary practice from early times had been that a return must be voided, not merely for the corrupt acts of the candidate himself but also those committed by his agent. The jurists considered that if the agents should play foul and the candidate enjoy the benefit of their actions, great mischief must arise. Hence it was assumed that the candidate must be responsible for the acts of his agent, nor could he exculpate himself by swearing that he never intended that anything illegal should be done at the election.[2] And it was certainly true that the greater part of corrupt acts were committed by persons who carefully abstained from allowing the member to know what they were going to do.

But the difficulty arose when it came to be asked who was the agent of the candidate at a parliamentary election. By the ordinary law of agency a person was not responsible for the acts of those whom he had not authorized, or even for acts committed beyond the scope of an agent's authority. Was the candidate to be held for the acts of a person who canvassed for him and made speeches

[1] *Saturday Review,* February 22, 1868; *Parliamentary Papers,* 1867, no. 3777, "Report of the Lancaster Bribery Commission," vii-xi.

[2] Per Blackburn, J., in Stalybridge, 1869, 1 O'Malley and Hardcastle, 67, 68; per Willes, J., in Tamworth, 1869, *Ibid.,* 81, 82.

in his favour, when he had not been specially requested by the candidate to assist him? Was a man who was authorized to get votes, without being distinctly employed, to be considered a responsible agent? Were members of a political club or association, working for a candidate, to be judged agents of that candidate? When did agency begin and when end? The law on all these points was doubtful to such an extent that it was extremely difficult to bring certain legal proof of agency and unseat the member, even when acts of bribery or corruption were freely admitted.[1]

The act of 1854 had rather complicated than explained matters. By requiring each candidate to name an authorized agent, it seemed to imply that all others working for the candidate were unauthorized, and that he would not be held responsible for their acts. It was a matter of frequent complaint after 1854 that an army of unauthorized agents were set loose; anyone from the *Carlton* or *Reform*, any "man from the moon" might carry on the most extensive corruption in behalf of the candidate, who remained absolutely safe. The act thus opened up a wider door to the practices which it aimed at excluding.[2] And in all the boroughs where there was a tendency towards corruption, the unauthorized, illegal or "bribe" agent existed: sometimes the party registration agent, sometimes a local tradesman, financed by the professional agents of London or by local magnates, and in rare cases by the party funds. The bribe agents held no intercourse with the candidate or the legal agent, who studiously avoided all knowledge of what was going on.[3]

[1] *Parliamentary Papers,* 1860, no. 329, "Minutes of Evidence," §§ 856-865.

[2] 3 Hansard, cxliii, 981.

[3] On one occasion when the candidate's agent was examined by a committee, he replied, "I really know nothing about the matter, I am only the legal agent," *Parliamentary Papers,* 1867, no. 3775,

As a result it was often impossible to connect the corruption either with the candidate or with his authorized agent, and unless evidence of wholesale corruption was forthcoming, the acts of the unauthorized agent would go unpunished, even if discovered.

It resulted that secret agency was becoming almost a regular profession, and the difficulty of meeting bribery in the daylight, and crushing it, increased enormously. A journalistic campaign was carried on by the *Saturday Review* in 1868 against this aspect of electioneering, which was regarded as the most difficult of all to cope with: "There is a hierarchy which administers the system of corruption, as complete and powerful as if it were the hierarchy of a national church. Its centre is in the London political clubs with their hangers-on, their *âmes damnées*, and their numerous and hungry tools, who live by serving a party. Its leading officers are wealthy, clever, influential lawyers, who pull the strings of provincial elections, select candidates, and introduce them to the right people; its executive is spread over all England, down to the smallest country town."[1] And later in the same year the journal returned to the attack, which, indeed, had not been entirely dropped: "Bribery in England is not merely a science or an art, it is a profession and a trade—a lucrative profession for the higher members of the hierarchy of corruption, a thriving and profitable trade for their instruments and tools."[2] Assuming journalistic exaggeration, it may nevertheless be admitted that the evils of unauthorized agency were such as to demand definite restriction, if corruption was to be eliminated from the boroughs.

"Minutes of Evidence," § 810. And cf. *Ibid.*, 1870, no. c11, "Report of Bridgwater Bribery Commission," xxxi.

[1] *Saturday Review*, February 22, 1868.
[2] *Saturday Review*, June 20, 1868.

But even admitting the insufficiency of the law, it would doubtless have been possible to track out the main lines of corruption had it not been for the inefficiency of the tribunal which tried all election petitions. For many years the system of testing the validity of elections had been the subject of complaint, and by 1867 was generally acknowledged to be ineffective in the disclosure of the real extent or character of corrupt practices. Jurisdiction over controverted elections had belonged to the House of Commons from the seventeenth century; the House was accustomed to name a committee to examine the complaint and report upon the validity of the election. In early days the bias of these committees was notorious, and their decisions were given invariably in accordance with the political sentiment entertained by the majority of the Commons.[1] The Grenville Act of 1774 embodied an attempt to end such abuses, by transferring the determination of petitions to a committee of the House, which was not elected but chosen by lot, and from the decisions of which it was hoped that party spirit would be excluded.

This system, although it persisted for nearly a century, never proved entirely satisfactory, and to the character of the committees was ascribed much of the difficulty experienced in running bribery to earth.[2] Their partiality was not entirely above suspicion, and their decisions

[1] Burnet, *History of England,* ii, 410; Hallam, *Constitutional History of England,* ii, 37; 3 Hansard, ii, 119.

[2] For examples of the weakness of the committee system, see *Parliamentary Papers,* 1836, no. 496; 1837-1838, no. 441, "Reports from the Select Committees appointed on the laws relating to the trial of controverted elections." The system was slightly reformed in 1839 (2 & 3 Vict., c. 38), and further in 1842 (5 & 6 Vict., c. 102), in the hope of obtaining an impartial tribunal and preventing corrupt compromises. But investigations held in 1852 and 1860 disclosed the failure of the petition system to function consistently, effectively, and with justice, *Parliamentary Papers,* 1852-1853, no. 775, "Report of the Select Committee," iii-iv; "Minutes of Evidence," §§ 23-25,

were often marked by a desire to save political friends.[1]
Even when they declared an election void, they were slow
to brand one of their colleagues as corrupt; frequently
when they had proved the bribery of an agent, they
stopped short, without examining the candidate himself.
Their legal knowledge was also inadequate and their
powers of cross-examination feeble.[2] This characteristic
was displayed in their utter inability to cope with sham
petitions, which were based upon purely frivolous grounds,
and presented merely in the hope that the respondent
would buy the petition off. In 1859 there were numerous
cases of such political blackmail; out of forty-four petitions, nineteen were withdrawn under the most suspicious
circumstances.[3] And of the serious petitions, many were
compromised in the hope of covering up the corruption
and blocking serious investigation. The failure of the
committees to cope with such electoral dodges was, in the
opinion of Disraeli, the chief weakness of the whole
electoral system.[4]

In general, the faults of the system for trying petitions
were such that even when the ground for a petition was

35-37, 68, 152, 169-172; *Ibid.*, 1860, no. 329, "Minutes of Evidence,"
passim.

[1] *Parliamentary Papers*, 1860, no. 329, "Minutes of Evidence,"
§§ 844, 2154-2156, 2549-2551, 3358. At Coventry in 1868 the member
himself was not called into the witness-box, nor did he dare enter
it to testify for himself. In this case the committee whitewashed
and exculpated a man they had not examined and of whose affairs
they knew nothing; and although they declared the election void,
they did not report extensive corruption, thus saving the borough
from further investigation, *Saturday Review,* April 4, 1868.

[2] 3 Hansard, xxvii, 975; *Parliamentary Papers*, 1860, no. 329,
"Minutes of Evidence," §§ 513-514, 866-882, 2245-2246.

[3] On the last day for presenting petitions, a large number were
invariably brought in intended only to be a weapon of "electoral
jobbing," 3 Hansard, clvi, 390; *Parliamentary Papers*, 1860, no. 329,
"Minutes of Evidence," § 3455.

[4] *Annual Register*, 1868, 38; 3 Hansard, cxc, 694-695.

most solid, the candidate defeated by corrupt methods hardly dared bring a petition. The expense of bringing witnesses to testify in London was great; many of them slipped away and the case was hushed up from lack of evidence. And even when the witnesses were secured, the inexperienced committees could not make them speak. The fear that disfranchisement of their constituency would follow their disclosures, generally sealed their lips, and the untrained members were helpless before a task which puzzled even the more expert commissioners.[1] The decisions of the committees were frequently conflicting, so that the petitioner could never be sure of the result, no matter how sure he was of his evidence.[2]

As illustrating the failure of the petition system to bring forth the extent of corruption, the electoral history of Bridgwater is illuminating. The commissioners reported that from 1832 to 1868 thirteen elections took place, every one of which was characterized by flagrant bribery. And yet only four petitions were presented, and only two of these brought to trial.[3] Clearly, if corrupt conditions were to be exposed and punished, an inquisitory tribunal of greater capacity or greater authority must be provided.[4]

It was inevitable that during the wave of electoral reform which came over the country in 1867 and 1868, something should be attempted for the reform of electioneering methods. The act of 1854, from which so much

[1] *Parliamentary Papers*, 1870, no. c13, "Report of the Norwich Bribery Commission," vi; *Ibid.*, "Minutes of Evidence," §§ 10344, 10392.

[2] *Parliamentary Papers*, 1860, no. 329, "Minutes of Evidence," §§ 508-510, 516-517, 844-850, 3335.

[3] *Parliamentary Papers*, 1870, no. c11, "Report of the Bridgwater Bribery Commission," ix.

[4] 3 Hansard, clvi, 380; *Saturday Review*, February 22, 1868; *Annual Register*, 1868, 38-39.

had been hoped, had altered the character of corruption to some extent, although the central pivot of its operation had failed because of the incapacity of the election auditors. But the forms of disguised bribery and intimidation which still persisted demanded attention, if the franchise of the people was to be something more than theoretical. This was realized clearly after 1867, when with an enormous increase in the electorate, the actual control of votes belonged, in many cases, not to the electors, but to the influences higher up.

The path of reform was indicated logically by all who understood conditions. The admitted failure of the House of Commons' committees meant the creation of a more capable tribunal, fitted for the impartial decision of cases, and for a searching examination into the customs of the constituency. And the sole hope of coping with the influence of intimidation in elections seemed to rest in a substitution of secret for open voting. With the acts of 1868 and 1872, which carried these ideas into effect, began a new era in the elimination of corrupt practices; and the act of 1883, which perfected the rather ineffective endeavour of 1854, realized in large measure the hope of excluding all the more direct and palpable methods of illegal influence from elections.

CHAPTER XIV

THE FINAL ATTACK UPON CORRUPTION AND EXCESSIVE ELECTION EXPENDITURE

Methods of attacking corruption—Improved tribunal for trial of election petitions—Secret voting—Effective publication and control of election expenses—Disfranchisement of incurable boroughs—Transference of jurisdiction over election petitions to courts—The act of 1868—Amended in 1879—General effect—Movement for introduction of the ballot—Report of 1870—Opposition and indifference in the Commons—Ballot Act carried in 1872—Effects—Partly nullified by the canvass—In certain boroughs merely lowered price of votes—Bribery in 1880—Indirect bribery and treating—Collective corruption—Rôle of the party associations—Expense of elections—The act of 1883—Maximum expenditure—Restraint of expenditure—Return of expenses—Definition of four kinds of corrupt practices—Illegal practices—Opposition to the act—Effects of the act—Expenditure lessened—Purity of elections furthered—Character of corruption that persisted—Democracy aided by the elimination of corruption.

THE elements of corruption which had survived the earlier attempts at purification were not to be dislodged by a single line of attack. In certain boroughs, as we saw, there remained strongly entrenched the traditions of the days when the sole issue of an election was the amount of money spent by the rival parties; here palliative remedies could not be utilized; the sole means of preventing bribery lay in the disfranchisement of the borough, a remedy which would throw the electors into the mass of county voters. Certain of the more obviously corrupt boroughs were thus treated in 1867; but the extent of disfranchisement was so limited that there remained many other incurables, which for the health of the whole must inevitably suffer ultimate excision.

In these boroughs, most of them small but some of good size, the increase of the electorate did not, we observed, raise the tone of electoral morality. The new voters, mostly of the poorer classes, displayed enthusiastic alacrity in adapting themselves to the customs of their predecessors. But in the larger boroughs and in those where bribery had never proved so profitable, the increase of the electorate doubtless assisted the efforts of those who sought to break up methods of direct corruption. But indirect and disguised methods, which were better suited to the control of an extended electorate, continued unabated, and with the passing of direct bribery, actually appeared to be increasing.

It was recognized that to cope with these types of disguised corruption there was necessary a tribunal capable of discovering and fearless in punishing the forms of illegal influence which had defied the rather lukewarm efforts of the House of Commons' committees. But the sentiment against the surrender of the House's final jurisdiction had always been too strong to permit the creation of an efficient instrument. In 1868, however, under the influence of the pervading reform spirit, Disraeli succeeded in transferring the decision of election petitions from the Commons to the courts. With all its imperfections, the new tribunal proved itself worthy of the unpleasant responsibility thrust upon it; and from the uncompromising efforts of the new election judges there resulted a notable improvement in the boroughs which were not incurable, although harbouring elements of political corruption.

But in the counties the great difficulty was not bribery or general treating so much as intimidation. The number of electors, the great area of the constituencies, and the difficulty of organizing the mechanism of corruption did not permit the system of electioneering established in the boroughs; but the fear of eviction, or the hope of favours, always determined the votes of the electors to a greater or less extent; and the £12 voters of 1867 proved as amenable to influence of such a sort as the £50 renters of 1832. To meet this influence the ancient manner of taking the poll was abolished and the hustings disappeared. Henceforth, in the hope of freeing the tenants from the illegitimate influence of their landlords, and of rendering the profits of bribery uncertain, votes were to be taken in secret.

But the safeguards by which the convictions of the voter were hedged remained yet incomplete. The court which tried petitions was by no means infallible, and it could not act unless a petition were first presented; and the motives which deterred the unsuccessful candidate from the presentation of a petition were strong. Nor did secret voting succeed in protecting the voter absolutely from undue influence, or from the temptations proffered him. The development of the system of canvassing soon nullified, to a large extent, the cover of secrecy afforded by the ballot. Bribery thus remained profitable, and although the position of the tenant who disagreed with his landlord was perhaps less unpleasant than before, the influence of the latter remained very great.

That influence it was, perhaps, impossible to eliminate; but the direct and indirect bribery which persisted could be attacked in another direction. So long as there were candidates who desired to buy seats, and who were willing to spend large sums for the satisfaction of their ambition, it was inevitable that there should be electors willing to sell their votes. It was too much to expect that the labourer would refuse a drink, a job for which he was vastly overpaid, or the price of his railway ticket trebled or quadrupled, when the offer was placed before him. The crux of the situation lay with the wealthy candidate who opened up the irresistible temptation. And the remedy lay obviously in a limitation of the amount which might be spent by the candidate, and the assurance that the accounts turned in by the candidate were accurate. In such a way public opinion, which could not be persuaded, might be forced to respect the provisions of the bribery laws.

The act of 1854 had, it is true, provided for the publication of all electoral expenses; but through its faulty mechanism the accounts were often illusory and the stipulations of the act proved ineffective. The act of 1883 not only saw to it that expenses were no longer covered up, but also set a limit within which the candidate must confine his outlay; notwithstanding inevitable evasions it made the expenditure of money for the corruption of a constituency extremely difficult.

Such, in its main lines, was the process by which the electoral customs of the early reformed period were transformed. The corruption formerly prevalent was confined to a few of the older boroughs, and even there it assumed generally a less direct form, and one less demoralizing in its effect upon the political morality of the community. In the country as a whole, although certain methods of influencing votes through the power of wealth persisted, as they must in any electoral system, the influence exerted was of a type which fifty years before would hardly have been considered corrupt.

The process of excising the incurable boroughs was carried through chiefly in the redistribution of 1885. It will not be forgotten that in 1867 four of the worst boroughs, Totnes, Reigate, Lancaster, and Yarmouth, lost their privilege of representation.[1] Three years later the

[1] *Parliamentary Papers*, 1867, nos. 3774, 3775, 3776, 3777, "Reports of Commissioners appointed to inquire into the existence of corrupt practices at Reigate, Yarmouth, Totnes, and Lancaster."

investigations of commissioners revealed the existence of conditions in Beverly and Bridgwater which would admit of no remedy; those two boroughs also suffered the same punishment.[1] The redistribution of 1885 was, however, the great factor in striking at that corruption which sprang from the extreme value of a vote in small boroughs, where each suffrage might be worth ten of those cast in a large town or county. By throwing into the counties the electors who had grown up on the traditions of the old régime, the act of 1885 helped materially to force on a new method of electioneering.

The first step in coping with corruption in boroughs whose habits were not considered incurable, was taken in 1868, by the transference of jurisdiction over controverted elections from the House of Commons to the courts. As we saw, the old tribunal had not proved effective, and by 1868 it was the general opinion in the country that committees of the House must inevitably err upon the side of leniency, even if they possessed the requisite legal ability. They would never be willing to put a stigma upon a gentleman, or convict and sentence him, after he had "parted freely from his money." And within parliament, the belief had gained ground that the competence and impartiality of the tribunal was of higher importance than the conservation of a constitutional principle. With reluctance, but with confidence, the leaders of both parties acknowledged that the time had come to surrender that final control over elections that had belonged to the Commons since the days of the Stuarts.

But although the House was generally agreed that the determination of petitions must be vested in a different tribunal, there was great variety of opinion as to the sort of body to which such weighty responsibility was to be entrusted. And it was only after long debate, succeeding

[1] *Parliamentary Papers*, 1870, nos. c10, c15.

the report of a select committee, that it was decided to
grant the jurisdiction over petitions to the Queen's
Bench division of the high court of justice.[1] The judges,
it is true, were by no means anxious to undertake the
onerous task, and accepted it only after various provisions were made ensuring the dignity of the election court,
and obviating any chance of derogating from the prestige
of the superior courts by the infusion of party strife.[2]
Many die-hard opponents of the new system fought to the
last moment against the proposed jurisdiction of the
judges, but in vain. The principle of the measure was,
however, carried by a majority of only twenty.[3]

The provisions of the act of 1868 were directed
especially against the withdrawal of petitions, corrupt
compromises, and the stoppage of investigations. No
petition might be withdrawn without leave of the court,
and such leave must be obtained through special application, and was only possible after lengthy and complex
procedure. If there was any suspicion of a compromise,
the judge was empowered to order the petitioner's security
to remain as surety for any costs that might be incurred
by another petitioner. And if the suspicion that the withdrawal resulted from a corrupt bargain was verified, the
judge was to see that the investigation was not stopped
by the withdrawal. Even the death of the respondent
was not to abate a petition. The act recognized clearly
the distinction between an ordinary suit and a petition
against an undue return, which was not considered to be
of a personal nature.

The tribunal before which the petitions were to be tried
was a single judge of the superior courts at Westminster.

[1] *Annual Register,* 1868, 37-40.
[2] *Parliamentary Papers,* 1875, no. 225, "Minutes of Evidence,"
§ 1733.
[3] *Annual Register,* 1868, 40-44.

The trial was no longer to be held in London, but in the county or borough from which the petition emanated, unless by special order of the judge. The demand for such local investigation had been voiced by many persons of experience in election matters, and was at the time conceded to be a great step in facilitating the disclosure of corruption. The judges were given the same power as the parliamentary committees in examination, and might force a witness to answer questions, even though he should incriminate himself personally, and they could call for any papers necessary for the establishment of evidence. They could, however, issue certificates of indemnity. It was the duty of the judge, after deciding the petition, to report to the House whether corrupt practices had been shown to exist, and whether they had been committed with the knowledge and consent of the candidate. If corruption was extensive, the judge was to draw up a special report, and the House upon receiving it was to order an inquiry, or take any other steps which the situation might seem to demand.[1]

The new tribunal proved to be not without its imperfections, but the transference of jurisdiction from the House of Commons was generally admitted to be a step in the direction of efficiency and justice. Almost without exception the witnesses examined in 1875 as to the working of the new system, believed that many of the faults of the

[1] The process of withdrawing a petition was purposely made complex in order to prevent corrupt compromises; if the judge suspected that the withdrawal was the result of a corrupt bargain, he was to insist on its being proceeded with; he might even order that the security furnished by the first petitioner should remain as security for any costs that might be incurred by succeeding petitioners, 3 O'Malley and Hardcastle, 2. For discussions on the bill, see 3 Hansard, cxc, 1141; cxci, 321; cxcii, 657, 2172; cxciii, 722, 1101, 1166, 1369, 1439, 1615, 1675, 1793, 1889. For opinion of the press, see Saturday Review, February 15, April 4, 1868.

earlier tribunal had been obviated.[1] The chief complaint aroused by the new system lay in the fact that the character, career, and reputation of a candidate lay at the mercy of a single judge from whom there was no appeal. The duty of deciding both the law and the facts seemed to many persons over-grave for a single legal officer. No suggestion was made by expert electioneers that the judges' decisions were actuated by personal or political bias; but the public were apt to impute political motives, as they had to the decisions of the committees, and the prestige of the new tribunal ran the risk of diminution.[2] The concurrence of opinion adverse to trial by a single judge led the investigating committee to recommend that in future the tribunal should consist of two judges, and that no member should be unseated, nor any person declared guilty of a corrupt act, unless both judges were agreed. Various suggestions to the effect that assessors should be appointed to decide upon questions of fact, were not approved; nor was the idea of appointing barristers or commissioners to the tribunal seriously considered.[3]

The recommendation of the committee was carried into effect by the act of 1879, which provided for two judges, and declared that if they differed as to whether the member was duly returned, they should certify that difference and the member should be deemed elected. If the judges determined that a member was not duly elected but differed as to the rest of the determination, they were to certify that

---

[1] *Parliamentary Papers,* 1875, no. 225, "Minutes of Evidence," *passim.*

[2] *Parliamentary Papers,* 1875, no. 225, "Minutes of Evidence," §§ 548-553, 641, 744, 1538-1543, 2400-2409, 2413-2421, 2681.

[3] *Parliamentary Papers,* 1875, no. 225, "Minutes of Evidence," §§ 240, 281, 779, 1192, 1348, 1371, 1770, 1806, 1971, 1987; "Report of the Select Committee appointed to inquire into the operation of the Corrupt Practices Act," iii.

difference, and the election was to be deemed void, but the petitioner was not to be seated.[1]

The act of 1879 made no change in the place of inquiry. To the surprise of many, the local investigations had not proved so far superior to the metropolitan investigations as election experts had promised. Agents alleged that it was more difficult to obtain the truth from the multitude of witnesses that now thronged the judge's court, than it had been from the few that could be brought to Westminster. And many testified that the local passions and prejudice of inquiry on the spot, interfered materially with the prosecution of justice.[2] Both the committee of investigation and the House of Commons were nevertheless decided in their approval of local inquiry, and the trials continued to be held in the county or borough which formed the site of the controverted election.

The results of the change in the petition system can hardly be separated from the effects of the other electoral reforms which were so nearly contemporaneous. That the act was successful to a very large degree, if not to the extent hoped for, may be accepted. The judges' decisions were by no means invariably in accord, and offenders sometimes escaped where a conviction might fairly have been expected.[3] But in general the excessive leniency of the committees was replaced by what seemed at the time rigorous severity, and which tended much toward the prevention of corrupt practices. Corrupt compromises were not entirely eliminated,[4] but they became far less frequent,

[1] 42 & 43 Vict., c. 58.

[2] *Parliamentary Papers*, 1875, no. 225, "Minutes of Evidence," §§ 189-204, 215-228, 230, 235-239, 259-268, 636-638, 859-866, 898-900, 923, 935, 1419, 1423, 2443.

[3] 3 Hansard, cclxxix, 1689.

[4] 3 Hansard, cclxxxv, 1347-1350; *Parliamentary Papers*, 1881, no. c2775, "Minutes of Evidence," §§ 3913, 3917, 5586, 5657, 21347, 21350; 3 Hansard, cclxxxvii, 1195.

RIVAL ROGUES

Commissioner Punch. "Gentlemen, your candour is charming. Not a pin to choose between you, you both deserve—penal servitude. *(Aside.)* And I hope—some day—you'll get it!!"

and after 1885 were doubtless as rare as they had been common a generation previous. One fact which testifies to the efficiency of the new tribunal, was the decreasing proportion of petitions which failed in their purpose. Of the sixty-one which were presented from 1868 to 1874, less than a third succeeded. But from 1874 to 1883 out of fifty-eight presented, all but twenty were successful. It would thus appear that petitions based upon slight grounds were less numerous, and that the new tribunal exercised greater severity and demanded closer adherence to the law than had been the custom in times past.[1]

The improvement in the system of petition trials, however, could have had but slight effect upon electoral morality, if it had not been followed by other reforms in which the problem was attacked from different angles. Numerous circumstances must always combine to deter an unsuccessful candidate from presenting a petition, even if his defeat had been secured by methods patently corrupt: the protraction of the trial, the expense of the action, the temptation of a compromise, the difficulty of securing reliable witnesses, all such circumstances tended to prevent the defeated candidate from petitioning against the return. And without a petition no investigation could take place. The rather haphazard inquisitorial method which rested upon the chance of a petition must be supplemented by measures of prevention. Of the attempts to prevent corrupt influence in the first place, the most notable in the period under discussion was the substitution of secret for open voting in 1872.

The movement for the ballot had, for nearly a generation, lost much of the practical force that had been imparted by the vigorous and skilful leadership of Grote. It is true that the Chartists, to whom the ballot was

---

[1] *Parliamentary Papers,* 1874, no. 219; 1880, no. 69; 1883, no. 325, "Returns of Election Petitions."

perhaps the dearest of all their points, had kept the matter of secret voting before the country; and the Radicals had never ceased to demand that it be discussed by the Commons.[1] But before 1862 the motion for leave to introduce a bill was invariably refused by varying majorities, and generally in a thin House. In that year Berkeley finally succeeded in gaining permission to bring in a bill, although his majority was won on a snap division; upon the second reading the measure was disposed of summarily.[2]

Notwithstanding the exertions of the *Ballot Society* and the spasmodic agitation incited by the Radicals, the years which preceded the second Reform Act witnessed no general demand for a change in the method of taking the poll.[3] Most of the Liberal leaders appeared to be as much opposed to secret voting as they had been a generation before. Argyll, writing to Gladstone, said: "It seems to me that it might succeed in counteracting some of the most legitimate influence exercised by one class over another, but that it will leave the poorer classes open to all the influences of corruption by which they can be moved." And again: "The motives under which men act in secret are as a general rule inferior to those under which they act in public."[4] Gladstone also declared in 1866 that his government would not view the ballot with favour either then or in the future.[5] And Grote himself, after the introduction of household suffrage, believed that the advantages of the ballot would be lost with the enormous exten-

[1] 3 Hansard, cxxxviii, 921; cxlii, 430; clvi, 771; clix, 4; clxii, 986; *Eclectic Review,* cix, 72; Molesworth, *History of England,* iii, 132.

[2] Berkeley's motion for leave to introduce was carried 83-50; the second reading was lost, 126-211, 3 Hansard, clxvii, 60, 1297.

[3] Berkeley's annual motion was lost by majorities ranging from 40 to 90, 3 Hansard, clxxi, 984; clxxvi, 36; clxxx, 416; clxxxiv, 971.

[4] Argyll, *Memoirs,* ii, 133.

[5] 3 Hansard, clxxxii, 24.

sion of the franchise, and admitted that the choice between one man and another signified far less than he used formerly to think it did.[1]

But in 1870 the question of the ballot became one of the first importance, and after being snubbed and summarily rejected for years by Liberal ministers, was brought forward in a government bill. The *volte face* was due in large measure to the demands of the advanced section of the Liberal party, and also to the influence of Bright in the cabinet, which more than counterbalanced the disgust with which Lowe regarded secret voting.[2] And there can be no doubt that many Liberals were sincerely converted as a result of the evils prevalent in the election of 1868, and the disclosures made the next year by the committee of investigation. Bruce, the Home Secretary, was one of the converts and Forster another. The latter still felt it better that an Englishman should record his vote in the light of day, but he was driven to the conclusion that for the prevention of intimidation, and for the avoidance of disorder, the ballot had become necessary. Gladstone also adopted the same point of view at the same time.[3]

The report of the investigating committee of 1870, of which Hartington was chairman, admitted the prevalence of corrupt practices and considered all possible remedies. The force of many of the objections to secret voting was not denied. But after studying conditions at home, and the operation of the ballot abroad, the committee was of the opinion that secret voting would not only promote the tranquillity of elections, but would also protect voters

---

[1] *Life of Grote*, 312-313.

[2] *Annual Register*, 1872, 65. *Punch* published a cartoon on March 27, 1869, showing Lowe looking with repulsion at "Little Boy Ballot," and saying, "His person's ugly, but he grows tremendously"; Bright is in the background with an expression of pride and patronage. See also 3 Hansard, cxciv, 1470.

[3] *Annual Register*, 1869, 16; Reid, *Life of Forster*, i, 530.

from intimidation and introduce a greater degree of freedom and purity than existed under the old system.[1] The tenor of the report, which was the first official recommendation of secret voting, determined the government in their belief that a change in the system of polling was necessary. In 1871 they introduced a bill.[2]

The details of the measure which provided for the mechanism of vote by ballot require no description, since readers of today are well acquainted with the system. It is curious to perceive that at the moment grave doubts were expressed as to the ability of the poorer classes to cast their votes correctly, and even Forster and Hartington went, with some nervousness, to watch a school-board election, to determine whether the difficulties of secret voting were insurmountable. It was said that on this occasion a distinguished member of the cabinet was unable to fill his voting paper unassisted.[3]

During the sessions of 1871 and 1872 long discussion took place in parliament upon the details of the measure, interspersed with speeches of virulent opposition, which almost without exception repeated the oft-spun arguments of past years. Shaftesbury believed the introduction of the ballot a direct dishonour inflicted by the country upon itself; it was, he said, an open avowal of cowardice and corruption, and he was prepared to witness the dissolution of the established church, a vital attack upon the Lords, and even trembled for the monarchy.[4] Russell, with many years of reforming experience behind him, believed that the ballot would increase personation,

---

[1] *Parliamentary Papers,* 1870, no. 115, "Report of Select Committee appointed to inquire into the present modes of conducting elections," 4–5.

[2] The government introduced a bill in the preceding year, but soon dropped it, 3 Hansard, cxcix, 268.

[3] Reid, *Life of Forster,* ii, 3.

[4] *Annual Register,* 1872, 66.

bribery, and fraud. All modern parliamentary history was, he said, a continuous and successful struggle for publicity; elections alone were to be secret and private.[1] Perhaps the most effective argument introduced in opposition was one first utilized by the *Fortnightly Review*, which attacked secret voting because it would lead to the absolute supremacy of the political associations; under the former system, the fluctuations of the poll could be followed and the electors could make up their minds how to vote; but in future, the success of the party candidate would depend entirely upon the previous arrangements of those in charge of the party organization.[2]

The measure introduced in 1871 was, after passing the Commons in haste, thrown out by the Lords on the plea that it was too late in the session to consider it thoroughly.[3] Reintroduced in the following year, the second reading was carried in a thin and inattentive House of Commons, and in the absence of the leaders of the opposition; at one time only two members were present.[4] Many of the Liberals appeared more anxious to neutralize the the effects of the bill than to secure its adoption, and Forster, who had it in charge, feared more than once that it would be lost because of the perfunctory manner in which some of the ministers who had no real love for it discharged their duty.[5] The final stages were passed without enthusiasm, and the great institutional change

[1] *Annual Register*, 1872, 71.

[2] Ostrogorski, *Democracy and Parties*, i, 159. It is interesting to note that the discussions on the ballot brought out the idea of the "mandate of the people": Salisbury pointed out that the question of secret voting had never been presented to the people, the government having gone to the polls as non-ballot politicians, *Annual Register*, 1872, 67.

[3] *Annual Register*, 1871, 36.

[4] *Annual Register*, 1872, 62-64.

[5] Reid, *Life of Forster*, ii, 5.

was completed, according to a contemporary account, "in spite of the all but unanimous hostility of the House of Lords, the secret disapproval of the House of Commons, and the indifference of the general community."[1]

Notwithstanding the uncertainty and dislike with which the ballot was regarded, its effects in certain directions were undoubtedly marked and salutary. The excitement and riots which had characterized the open nomination and polling were largely eliminated, and the factor of violence disappeared almost entirely from electoral contests.[2] The first election held under the new act took place at Pontefract and was watched with great interest. The Mayor in a letter to the *Times* reported that the familiar scenes of the old days were totally absent; the public houses were quiet, there was no drunkenness, no crowd around the polling places, and no difficulty in getting to the poll. At Preston the streets were nearly as quiet as on an ordinary day.[3] In the large industrial towns it was reported that the ballot worked admirably in lessening excitement and making for order. At Leeds, Liverpool, and Manchester, general satisfaction was expressed at the quietness of the proceedings.[4]

The fear that the system would tend to disfranchise the uneducated voters proved illusory. A small proportion of illiterates found difficulty in marking their ballots and

[1] *Annual Register*, 1872, 72. For debates on the ballot, see 3 Hansard, ccv, 1050; ccvii, 401, 560, 746, 1097, 1225, 1290, 1351, 1417, 1646, 1744, 1903, 1936, 1951; ccviii, 57, 89, 169, 218, 314, 320, 396, 590, 657, 791, 850, 1007, 1085, 1096, 1256; ccix, 172, 470, 1162, 1955; ccx, 677, 896, 1069, 1214, 1269, 1481, 1633, 1858, 1936; ccxi, 107, 510, 665, 843, 1421, 1800; ccxii, 15, 157.

[2] *Parliamentary Papers*, 1876, no. 162, "Minutes of Evidence," §§ 931-934, 1002-1003.

[3] *Annual Register*, 1872, 74.

[4] *Parliamentary Papers*, 1875, no. 225, "Minutes of Evidence," §§ 769-772, 1066; *Ibid.*, 1876, no. 162, "Minutes of Evidence," §§ 49, 56, 229, 321, 344, 369, 505, 600.

some votes were cast out because of irregularities; but the number was trifling.[1] Nor was the belief that personation would be facilitated under the new system justified by the results.[2] But the prophecy that the power of the associations would be increased proved more accurate; henceforth it became difficult to manage elections in which the great mass of voters were left to their own inspiration on the day of the poll, unless preliminary arrangements were made, and a closely knit organization provided.[3]

The main purpose of the ballot was, however, not completely realized, and corrupt influence was by no means banished from elections. It is probable that secret voting tended to mitigate the force of undue influence, and it is certainly true that no petitions alleging intimidation were upheld after 1872.[4] But the borough electors were not liberated from the pressure exercised by employers and fellow workmen; and the county voters followed the orders of the landed aristocracy in 1874 and in 1880 as implicitly as they did in 1868. The protection offered the political conscience of the voter soon proved slight; by demanding pledges, the agent was often able to exert as strong influence as in the days of open voting.[5] And by organizing the canvass to a degree hitherto unknown, the party associations soon began to acquire an ascendancy over the elector as great as, or greater than, that formerly possessed by the aristocracy.[6] In times past the landlord told

---

[1] *Parliamentary Papers,* 1876, no. 162, "Minutes of Evidence," §§ 199, 270-279.

[2] *Parliamentary Papers,* 1876, no. 162, "Minutes of Evidence," §§ 162, 197, 341.

[3] Ostrogorski, *Democracy and Parties,* i, 172.

[4] *Parliamentary Papers,* 1876, no. 162, "Minutes of Evidence," §§ 1092, 1111, 1129-1135.

[5] Cf. 3 Hansard, cclxxvi, 1733.

[6] Ostrogorski, *Democracy and Parties,* i, 458, 463. Notes in a canvasser's book illustrate the methods employed: "Paralysed, wants help to get change of air or rides out"; "very favourable and poor";

his tenants to vote for a given candidate and they had no alternative but to obey. Tradesmen were ordered by their customers, and workmen by their employers to vote in a specified direction and they did so. Such customs were, to a certain extent, destroyed by the ballot. But the new power of intimidation, exercised by the agents of the caucus organization was soon to play a rôle of authority, quite as despotic and no less effective than that of the landed and business aristocracy.

The effect of the ballot upon the forms of corruption other than intimidation doubtless varied in different constituencies. In the boroughs where the traditions of the old-time corruption were not strong, and where electioneering methods were generally honest, the ballot was said to have discouraged the introduction or the spread of bribery. Many witnesses agreed that secret voting was effective in this respect; and a few declared that bribery was driven entirely from their constituencies.[1]

But in the traditionally corrupt boroughs, the chief effect of the ballot was merely to decrease the price of votes, which in some places fell from five pounds to five shillings.[2] In constituencies of this type, possibly a score in number, every election was conducted upon corrupt methods, and the evil rather increased after 1872. The Macclesfield commission reported in 1881 that while it seemed doubtful whether any election in the borough had been fought on really pure principles, "the corruption of

"promised, wants a little drop"; "wants a better pension, was a warden at the jail"; "wants to be seen, cash"; "wife wants liquoring up," *Parliamentary Papers,* 1881, no. c2796, "Report of the Sandwich Bribery Commission," xii.

[1] *Parliamentary Papers,* 1875, no. 225, "Minutes of Evidence," §§ 769-772, 1066; *Ibid.,* 1876, no. 162, "Minutes of Evidence," §§ 58-59, 176-177.

[2] *Parliamentary Papers,* 1881, no. c2853, "Report of the Macclesfield Bribery Commission," 1-3.

the last election was far more widespread and far more open than had been the case at any previous parliamentary election, at all events of recent years, though the bribes were in most cases trifling in amount."[1] The Sandwich report showed that bribery was not merely unchecked by the ballot, but that many voters were enabled to take bribes from both sides. Apparently neither party was slow to bribe from fear of bribing in vain. At Boston the agents felt it necessary to make more corrupt bargains than had previously been the case, when the exact number that could be counted upon was known.[2]

In these boroughs and elsewhere, direct bribery was still the custom, and affected a large part of the constituency. The man in the moon persisted, and the ancient practices of chaining doors and passing money out through the cracks or through broken panes of windows were by no means extinct.[3] In one town, since the Conservatives were not able to rent an empty house for the purpose desired, they erected a tent close by the polling booth, within which sat a respected justice of the peace, who made the bargains and passed out the money.[4] At Sandwich, where the seductions of drink proved insufficient, forty-five hundred pounds was expended in direct purchase of votes,

[1] *Parliamentary Papers*, 1881, no. c2853, "Report of the Macclesfield Bribery Commission," 14.

[2] *Parliamentary Papers*, 1881, no. c3796, "Report of the Sandwich Bribery Commission," xv; no. c2784, "Report of the Boston Bribery Commission," viii.

[3] *Parliamentary Papers*, 1881, no. c2824, "Report of the Chester Bribery Commission," xiv; no. c2841, "Report of the Gloucester Bribery Commission," 12-13. In Macclesfield the bribery was "open, fearless and confiding"; no disguise was attempted and no anxiety felt by the corrupt agents. Many were bribed twice on the same side, and more than 200 were bribed on both sides, *Ibid.*, no. c2853, "Report of the Macclesfield Bribery Commission," 12-13.

[4] *Parliamentary Papers*, 1881, no. c2853, "Report of the Macclesfield Bribery Commission," 9.

and of the thousand electors corrupted, nearly all received money bribes. At Gloucester, although the amount spent was less striking, more than half of the electors were bribed directly, and the same was true of Macclesfield.[1]

But though in some constituencies corruption remained as direct and all-pervading as it had been before the introduction of the ballot and the reform of the petition system, in the majority of boroughs the proportion of voters corrupted was far smaller and the bribery of a more indirect character. The commissioners of 1881 reported the belief that towns like Oxford, Canterbury, and Knaresborough were not corrupt as a whole, and that there was very little direct buying and selling of votes. It also appeared that much, if not most, of the bribery was committed by irresponsible persons, and without the sanction of the candidate, his agent, or even of the party organization. The methods of corruption in general use were becoming more indirect; possibly no less pernicious, but certainly different from those of the old days.[2]

The means by which votes were corruptly obtained when direct bribery was not utilized were various. Corrupt employment of voters was not unusual, and had the same practical effect as direct purchase. A host of canvassers, bookmen, messengers, and watchers, were hired by each party, far in excess of the number actually required and receiving munificent wages for little or no work. At Chester, where eighty-eight clerks were admitted to be all that the situation demanded, four hundred

---

[1] *Parliamentary Papers*, 1881, no. c2796, "Report of the Sandwich Bribery Commission," viii-x; no. c2841, "Report of the Gloucester Bribery Commission," 12-13; no. c2853, "Report of the Macclesfield Bribery Commission," 12-14.

[2] *Parliamentary Papers*, 1881, no. c2856, "Report of the Oxford Bribery Commission," 10; no. c2775, "Report of the Canterbury Bribery Commission," x; no. c2777, "Report of the Knaresborough Bribery Commission," 7.

and eighty were hired and paid. At Boston twelve hundred were employed. And in many other constituencies the amount spent upon this "colourable employment" was vast. The tradesmen and labourers also found rich profits in making flag-poles, flags, and rosettes, for which the contending parties cheerfully paid exorbitant prices if the vendor were an elector. At Sandwich the Conservatives spent eight hundred pounds in such fashion in 1880, and their opponents more than six hundred pounds.[1]

Treating and gifts also played their part in the electioneering, and although the gross customs of the earlier days had been softened, public houses were generally thrown open at election time, and breakfasts and luncheons for the voters were served in lavish profusion. In some boroughs the party which could secure the bulk of the public houses was considered certain to secure the majority of the electors. At times a hundred voters might be seen in the bar pledging their fidelity to the political publican who furnished the liquor without stint.[2] Gifts of coal, or groceries, or even money were not generally considered bribes by the recipients; at Macclesfield it was said that many voters who would not desert their side for a bribe of any amount did not feel it dishonourable to accept a few shillings after polling, "if money was going."

[1] *Parliamentary Papers*, 1881, no. c2824, "Report of the Chester Bribery Commission," vii, xv; no. c2784, "Report of the Boston Bribery Commission," vii, viii; no. c2796, "Report of the Sandwich Bribery Commission," viii, xiii, xvi; no. c2853, "Report of the Macclesfield Bribery Commission," 7. Watchers at the polls frequently used their position as an excuse for taking bribes.

[2] "The great weapon of parliamentary warfare at Chester is beer," *Parliamentary Papers*, 1881, no. c2824, "Report of the Chester Bribery Commission," xiv-xv; cf. also no. c2775, "Report of the Canterbury Bribery Commission," viii; *Ibid.*, "Minutes of Evidence," §§ 9159, 12353. For other illustrations, see *Parliamentary Papers*, 1875, no. 225, "Minutes of Evidence," §§ 169, 174, 181, 896-897, 2279-2281; 3 Hansard, ccli, 778; ccliii, 436.

This they took as a sort of compliment and without any feeling of degradation.[1] The payment of travelling expenses also persisted as a source of corruption; it is true that the act of 1867 had declared such payment illegal in all but the widely extended boroughs and the counties; but there was constant evasion of the law, and even when applied the penalty for its infringement was absurdly small.[2]

With the growth of the electorate, collective corruption became the economical method of influencing votes, and under the ballot proved as productive of results as individual bribery. General treats, picnics, and entertainments, became the custom. The Conservative excursions at Chester were famous for giving the maximum amount of refreshments at a notoriously insufficient price. In 1879 it was said that twenty-two hundred and eighty-one persons took the trip arranged, and returned from the shore, firm and enthusiastic supporters of Disraeli's policy.[3] Gradually the habit of holding such entertainments during the period between elections became the practice; and the importance of the continual "nursing" or "salting" the constituency by the candidate or member increased as direct bribery began to disappear. It is not

[1] Parliamentary Papers, 1881, no. c2853, "Report of the Macclesfield Bribery Commission," 15.

[2] At the election of 1880 more than £750,000 was expended upon the conveyance of voters; even in the small borough of Boston £542 was spent. The resulting increase in the cost of elections was a matter of bitter complaint on the part of the Radicals, who declared that while the property qualification for voters had been lowered, that for members was in reality raised, so that only rich men could sit in the House, 3 Hansard, ccli, 866; cclxxxiii, 698; Parliamentary Papers, 1881, no. c2784, "Report of the Boston Bribery Commission," viii.

[3] Parliamentary Papers, 1881, no. c2824, "Report of the Chester Bribery Commission," xi.

without interest to note the swelling expenditure of the member as the year of the general election approached.[1]

Upon such indirect forms of corruption the ballot had little or no effect, and even when the illegal influence was generally recognized, it was difficult to unseat the member. Part of the difficulty was caused by the unsettled state of the law of agency, which, as before, did not define exactly who constituted an electoral agent. It resulted that the offence was rarely brought home to the sitting member. The newly organized political associations made the most of this opportunity and worked zealously and without scruple for the candidate of their party, and generally without endangering his seat. By disclaiming agency they could practise all sorts of indirect corruption in comparative safety.[2]

The associations took an active part in the election of 1880, and were probably accountable for much of the corruption then carried on. Of the money used for corrupt purposes at the Oxford bye-election of that year, at least three thousand pounds came from the Conservative Association.[3] At Gloucester the Liberal registration association was utilized for the corrupt disposal of party funds.[4] The Conservatives complained loudly that a circular of the Liberal Central Office suggested how the law might be violated with impunity and yet a safe majority

[1] As at Sandwich, where in 1877 Brassey subscribed £489; in 1878, £551; and in 1879, £573, *Parliamentary Papers*, 1881, no. c2796, "Report of the Sandwich Bribery Commission," xv. Cf. also *Ibid.*, no. c2784, "Report of the Boston Bribery Commission," viii; no. c2775, "Report of the Canterbury Bribery Commission," ix; *Ibid.*, "Minutes of Evidence," §§ 7553, 9818, 9821, 10409, 10429, 10490.

[2] *Parliamentary Papers*, 1875, no. 225, "Minutes of Evidence," §§ 153-168, 581-583, 1130-1134, 1678, 2765, 2931.

[3] *Parliamentary Papers*, 1881, no. c2856, "Report of the Oxford Bribery Commission," 9.

[4] *Parliamentary Papers*, 1881, no. c2841, "Report of the Gloucester Bribery Commission," 3, 6.

be secured. The candidate, his agent, and committees were all to resign from the association, which could henceforth claim that all connection with the candidate had been severed, and the acts of the organization could not be construed as those of an agent.[1] This plan was carried into effect at various places, notably at Chester; here the commissioners reported that "a general notion appears to have been abroad in the city that the Liberal Association might bribe and treat freely, without endangering the seats of the candidates."[2]

The reform in the tribunal of petitions and the introduction of the ballot obviously did not succeed in securing that complete purity of election which was sought. Their effects were salutary, and cannot be minimized; but the reports of the commissioners of 1881, who proceeded to a thorough evisceration of electioneering habits, showed that further legislation was necessary, if the methods of indirect bribery were not to prove as pernicious as had the old-fashioned bribery. And gradually the impression gained strength that the real fault lay not so much with the electors corrupted, as with the agents and candidates, who by their lavish expenditure exposed the poorer classes to seductions against which their principles of honesty were not proof. This belief was expressed by the Chester commission: "There are probably electors upon every register whose scruples are not strong enough to resist the proffered temptations of bribes and treats. So long therefore as the practice of subscribing to the funds of elections is continued uncontrolled, purity of elections is hopeless."[3]

---

[1] 3 Hansard, ccliii, 71.

[2] *Parliamentary Papers*, 1881, no. c2824, "Report of the Chester Bribery Commission," vi. Cf. also 3 Hansard, cclii, 1615; Ostrogorski, *Democracy and Parties*, i, 470–471.

[3] *Parliamentary Papers*, 1881, no. c2824, "Report of the Chester Bribery Commission," xvi.

The sums subscribed and expended were not merely large, but were for the most part increasing. In certain of the larger boroughs it was becoming customary to lay out three or four thousand pounds and the average for the boroughs was between five hundred and a thousand pounds. In the smaller boroughs, where the legitimate cost of a seat should not have been large, the amount expended proved generally a true norm and test of the amount of corruption. The county seats were coming to cost generally as much as five thousand pounds and in a comparatively small constituency, such as Montgomery, twelve thousand was spent.[1] The gradual but distinct increase in the cost of elections was illustrated with clarity by the case of Oxford.[2]

As we observed, the provisions of the law of expenses were futile because of the failure, in the first place of the auditors and then of the returning officers, to enforce true accounts. At times the officials entrusted with the duty of examining election returns were unable to bring forth any return whatever.[3] Illegal expenses were constantly concealed under various harmless items, and completely fictitious accounts were often handed in. A vast deal of corruption was habitually covered up by the sums entered under the head of conveyance, committee rooms, or posting expenses. Frequently the sums expended for illegal or corrupt purposes were not entered at all.[4] One agent

[1] *Parliamentary Papers,* 1874, no. 358, "Return of charges made to candidates by the returning officers."

[2] In 1868 the two Liberal candidates spent £2,310; in 1874 they spent £2,632; in 1880 they spent £3,275, *Parliamentary Papers,* 1881, no. c2856, "Report of the Oxford Bribery Commission," 6, 12-13.

[3] 3 Hansard, cclviii, 1247.

[4] *Parliamentary Papers,* 1875, no. 225, "Minutes of Evidence," §§ 432, 1211-1217, 1221-1223, 1475, 1480, 1553; *Ibid.,* 1881, no. c2853 "Report of the Macclesfield Bribery Commission," 16; no. c2856, "Report of the Oxford Bribery Commission," 16; no. c2784, "Report of the Boston Bribery Commission," vi-vii; 3 Hansard, ccli, 779.

reported that he considered that "the election expenses are the legal and proper election expenses, and that any illegal and improper payment is not an election expense which ought to be returned to the returning officer."[1] At Gloucester the published accounts of the candidates in 1880 included only a quarter of the whole sum expended.[2]

It was the general impression that if the law could be enforced, corrupt practices might be largely curtailed. The Sandwich commission reported that "if the law compelled a strict audit and provided that candidates declare their real expense, bribery as at Sandwich would not have been possible."[3] It was also felt that the number of agents and employees, in fact all the expense of the electoral contest, should be strictly limited in proportion to the number of electors; this would make the covering up of expenses more difficult and would tend to remove the temptations proffered to the voters.[4]

In the hope of striking a decisive blow at corrupt electioneering, these suggestions were considered by Gladstone's administration, and were incorporated into a bill, which was presented in 1882. In the following year a similar measure passed the legislature, and determined the chief characteristics of electioneering in the United Kingdom.

The principle of the new act was practically an increase in the severity of penalties, and the enactment of a sumptuary law regarding election expenses.[5] The act might be

1 *Parliamentary Papers,* 1881, no. c2777, "Report of the Knaresborough Bribery Commission," 11.

2 *Parliamentary Papers,* 1881, no. c2841, "Report of the Gloucester Bribery Commission," 3-4.

3 *Parliamentary Papers,* 1881, no. c2796, "Report of the Sandwich Bribery Commission," xv.

4 *Parliamentary Papers,* 1876, no. 162, "Minutes of Evidence," §§ 502-503, 546-547.

5 One of the best short descriptions of the act of 1883 is to be found in 3 Hansard, cclxxxiii, 697.

divided into three parts. One included the punishments
which were to be inflicted; another created and defined new
illegal practices; and the third consisted of schedules
delimiting the amount that might be spent in the various
constituencies. The latter was in reality the vital portion.
As Raikes said, the real importance of the act was contained in the postscript, like a lady's letter. The main
hope for the efficiency of the measure lay not so much in
the punitive provisions, which had been tried in less rigorous form before, but in the supervision of expenditure.

The amount of money that might be spent was determined, as had been suggested in 1875, by the number of
electors in the constituency. If the number of electors in
a borough did not exceed two thousand, the maximum
expenditure was limited to three hundred and fifty pounds.
In boroughs with an electorate of more than two thousand,
there was allowed three hundred and eighty pounds, and
an additional thirty pounds for every additional thousand electors. In the counties six hundred and fifty
pounds was the maximum conceded for an electorate of
less than two thousand; sixty pounds more was allowed if
the number of electors passed the two thousand line; and
sixty pounds extra for every additional thousand electors.

The kind of expense that the candidates might incur
was defined as closely as the amount; and all sums paid out
must be included in one of the five categories drawn up
by the act. The number of employees was strictly limited.
One election agent, a polling agent to keep watch at each
polling booth, and messengers and clerks in proportion to
the number of electors were provided for. But none of
these employees, who were paid, might vote. Paid canvassing, which had offered a ready cover to indirect
bribery, was thus eliminated. One committee room was
permitted for every five hundred electors, and the expense
of public meetings, postage, advertising, and similar items

was also included. For matters of a miscellaneous sort, not strictly forbidden, two hundred pounds was conceded. Each candidate might also incur personal expenses to the amount of one hundred pounds, which was outside of the general sum allowed. The charges of the returning officer were not included in the stipulated sum of expenses.

The stringency of the rules which provided for the regular and accurate return of expenses was also increased. The candidate must name a single agent, who alone had the right to settle expenses incurred in any manner whatsoever. The agent must give notice through the papers that nothing might be ordered or paid for save by himself. All bills should be sent to the agent within a fortnight after the election, and must be paid within the month; the settlement of any account after this time was made an illegal practice. Before the lapse of thirty-five days the agent was to send to the returning officer a certified statement of all sums expended, together with the receipts, which must be attached to every item exceeding two pounds. The member might not take his seat until he had made a declaration, certifying to the truth of the accounts.

In other respects the provisions of the act did little more than amend those established by previous legislation, but it clarified much that was doubtful, and increased the penalties inflicted upon candidates or electors who were convicted of corruption. Treating was defined as before, but was now included in the category of corrupt practices, and involved a penalty equal to that of bribery. The definition of undue influence caused some discussion; it was finally held to result from threats of spiritual as well as temporal injury, and provision was thus made against priestly intimidation.[1]

The four kinds of corrupt practices, namely, bribery,

[1] *Annual Register,* 1883, 116.

treating, undue influence, and personation, were all liable to the same punishment. The candidate, if personally guilty, could not ever be returned to the House of Commons by the constituency in question. If guilty by his agents, he could not be returned by that constituency for a period of seven years. Apart from the validity of the election, a conviction for corrupt practices might be followed by a year of imprisonment, with or without hard labour, and a fine of not more than one hundred pounds. Any elector convicted of corrupt practices could not be registered during the ensuing seven years, nor could he hold any public or judicial office during that period.

The act of 1883 also enumerated a series of illegal practices. These included the payment of travelling expenses, or the hiring of conveyances, banners, ribbons, bands, or any marks of distinction. The surpassing of the sum of expenses allowed by the law, or the payment of any sum not directly authorized, was also included in the category of illegal practices. The candidate proven personally guilty of illegal practices, might not represent the constituency involved for seven years; if guilty by his agent, he was disqualified during the existing Parliament. An elector guilty of illegal practices lost his political rights for five years. The commission of an illegal practice might also be punished as a misdemeanour by a fine of one hundred pounds.

The complaint that corruption, even when its existence was notorious, escaped unpunished, was met by the appointment of a special official. He was known as the Director of Public Prosecutions, and was to attend the trial of petitions and obey any directions given him by the court for the examination of witnesses or the prosecution of offenders. If, in his opinion, proceedings ought to be instituted, he was to prosecute upon his own responsibility. Such an official had been provided for in

1879; but owing to the doubt which surrounded the scope of his functions the position had been of no importance in the punishment of corruption.[1]

The limitation of election expenses, the minute definitions of corrupt and illegal practices, and the severity of the penalties imposed by the act of 1883 were not accepted without protest. Members complained that the new law was too rigid and full of pitfalls for the honest man; it was based, they said, upon principles of heroic virtue to which the constituencies had not yet attained; it was impossible to make people moral beyond the tone of feeling which prevailed in their own particular district.[2] Others, like Cross, who approved of the principles of the act, felt that the details were too severe, and believed that the very severity of the penalties would result in their remaining a dead letter.[3] The provisions which forbade the payment for, or the hiring of, conveyances were, curiously enough, opposed by the Conservatives as being favourable to the Liberals; they believed that the result would be the disfranchisement of county electors, who were regarded as the mainstay of Conservative strength. The Radicals naturally complained that an unfair distinction was made between the rich who could furnish their own carriages, and the poor who could not.[4]

The limitation of expenditure met with opposition on

[1] *Parliamentary Papers*, 1875, no. 225, "Minutes of Evidence," §§ 845-856, 872-875, 2242-2250; 3 Hansard, ccliii, 1638; cclxxxvi, 745.

[2] 3 Hansard, cclxxix, 1652.

[3] *Annual Register*, 1883, 114.

[4] 3 Hansard, cclxxix, 1654-1655; cclxxxiii, 702. The Radicals also objected to the refusal of the government to provide that the expenses of the returning officers should be paid by the constituency as a whole. They asserted that the payment of official expenses by the candidates was not merely a barrier to democracy, but that it also offered an opportunity for bribery, *Annual Register*, 1883, 115. In 1868 they had made a similar attempt to throw official election expenses upon the constituency, *Ibid.*, 1868, 41.

the ground that it was too strict. It was pointed out that in Oxford only five hundred pounds was to be allowed, although in 1880 the Home Secretary and his colleague had spent three thousand pounds. Others were of the opinion that the scale was unfair; that it was liberal for large or small boroughs, but scanty for those of a moderate size. Moreover, the candidate for a small constituency with two seats was at an advantage with the candidate for a constituency of the same size which had but one.[1] The feeling, indeed, was widespread that the chances of the practical success of the act were not rosy.[2] But to every assertion that the law would not work, Henry James replied that the old system of electioneering certainly would not work under the act; but the object of the legislation was to alter the system.[3]

That answer foreshadowed with some accuracy the actual effects of the act of 1883. Not merely did its provisions prove practical, but because of them electioneering conditions were radically transformed. It is, of course, a certainty that the extension of the suffrage and the redistribution of 1885 were important factors in that transformation. A different attitude on the part of the agents must have resulted from an increased electorate and the comparative equality in the value of votes; direct bribery of individual electors would have proved too expensive, if it could have been made possible, to provide for it on a large and organized scale. But the change in the methods

[1] 3 Hansard, cclxxix, 1656-1658.

[2] It was asserted that the persons successful at the following election would all be second candidates, since the first candidates would be disqualified because of corrupt practices, 3 Hansard, cclxxxiii, 701.

[3] 3 Hansard, cclxxix, 1698-1700. James showed that it was possible to poll 19,000 votes for £914, since this had been accomplished in Hackney, while in Southwark under the old system of indirect purchase it cost £8000 to poll 9000 votes.

of influence, which was perhaps inevitable, was rendered sharper and more far-reaching by the legislation of 1883. Almost immediately corrupt practices, where they did not disappear, assumed a totally different character from that which marked the tactics of electioneering in the previous period.

In its chief purpose, the limitation of the expenses of an election, the success of the act was unquestionable. Although the cost of a seat in the Commons is still so high as to narrow the range of candidates and operates as a serious barrier to democracy, the sums expended after 1883 were small in comparison to those of the earlier period. In the election of 1886 the ordinary amount spent in a borough contest was about three hundred and eighty pounds; in counties it was rather less than six hundred pounds. The average cost per vote in the former was not far from five shillings, while in the latter it was about three shillings.[1] In the elections of the following years the expense of elections changed very slightly. The total expenditure for all elections actually decreased, partly because of many uncontested seats. But even when hotter contests took place the sums expended did not approach those laid out before 1883.[2] In the election of 1906 five hundred pounds was by no means a low figure for a contested borough election; but in 1880 it had been only in an uncontested election that so little was required; in towns like Greenwich, Halifax, Southwark, and York anywhere from three thousand to five thousand pounds had been spent. And in 1880 there was no contested election in counties which did not require at least a thousand pounds; five thousand was an ordinary sum; and seats for

---

[1] *Parliamentary Papers,* 1886, no. 45, "Return of charges made to candidates by the returning officers."

[2] *Parliamentary Papers,* 1893, no. 423; 1896, no. 145, "Returns of charges made to candidates."

Durham and Montgomery cost more than twelve thousand. But in 1906 a thousand pounds was a high figure for a contested county election.[1]

The effect of the act of 1883 upon the purity of elections cannot be so clearly traced. It is difficult to estimate the extent of corruption which still persisted, and equally difficult to determine how far the provisions of the act were responsible for the undoubted improvement in electoral conditions. It is, however, certain that both the number of petitions and the number of elections voided on account of bribery diminished after the enactment of the new law. Thus in 1880 thirty-three petitions were presented, of which twelve were sustained and the members unseated.[2] But in the election of 1885 there were petitions against only seven members on the ground of corrupt practices, and only one of the petitions was sustained. In the election of the following year three petitions were presented, leading to the unseating of a single member only; in 1892 we find that two members were unseated for corrupt practices and in 1895 but one again.[3] It is true that in the election of 1906 a petition was presented which resulted in the appointment of a royal commission, showing that cases of gross bribery were by no means eliminated.[4] But the mere fact that the appointment of a single commission caused great discussion as to the effect-

[1] *Parliamentary Papers,* 1880, no. 382; 1906, no. 302, "Returns of charges made to candidates."

[2] *Parliamentary Papers,* 1883, no. 325, "Return of election petitions."

[3] *Parliamentary Papers,* 1886 (Sess. 1), no. 177, "Shorthand writers' notes of the . . . judgments delivered at the trial of election petitions"; *Ibid.,* 1887, no. 90, "Shorthand writers' notes of . . . judgments"; *Ibid.,* 1893-1894, no. 25, "Shorthand writers' notes of . . . judgments"; *Ibid.,* 1897, no. 347, "Report from the Select Committee on Election Petitions."

[4] *Parliamentary Papers,* 1906, no. cd3268, "Report of the Royal Commission."

iveness of the system of 1883 indicates that electoral morality is of a markedly different character from that of a generation previous.

The enormous advance made in the direction of the purity of elections is also indicated by the nature of the charges incorporated in the election petitions that have been sustained by the judges. Bribery in its direct form has doubtless not entirely disappeared from electioneering. But it has become so infrequent that we do not find it advanced in any successful petitions since 1883. Wherein bribery has formed ground for the voidance of an election it appeared in its more insidious but less blatant method of allowing unreasonable time off to vote, in paying railway fares to voters, or in philanthropic gifts. Thus when an agent wrote to a freeman, who said that the expense of a trip prevented his coming to vote, that the affair could be arranged, the two successful candidates were unseated.[1] The gift of tickets entitling the bearer to food, coal, or groceries has formed the grounds of a successful petition for bribery, even when the distribution of the tickets was overseen by a philanthropic society. Such methods of corruption are doubtless as mischievous in their effects on the voter as the purchase of a vote with money, but they argue a great change in electoral customs and standards from those of earlier times.

Still greater stringency has been exercised by the courts in dealing with treating. This is not unnatural, since treating has become that particular form of corruption which can be practised to advantage; for the enlargement of the constituencies as well as the penalties of 1883 have made it difficult to carry on the old-fashioned form of bribery with success. Hence elections have been voided for causes which before 1883 would probably have been

[1] *Parliamentary Papers*, 1887, no. 90, "Shorthand writers' notes of . . . judgments."

regarded as negligible. Deficits in entertainments given by political associations cannot be covered by the agents of candidates; and where refreshments are offered they must be paid for according to their real value; nor may refreshments be given to workmen on election day.[1]

The practical success of the act of 1883 cannot be said to be vitiated by the constant evasions of many of the minor provisions, and the disguised forms in which corrupt influence still continued to be exercised. It was inevitable that some loopholes should have been left, for which the foresight of the legislators could not provide. The difficulties which persisted were many of them the same as those prevalent before 1883. The law of agency has remained undetermined, so that it has been possible for the caucus association to exercise influence in a more than doubtful fashion by severing all apparent connection with the candidate. Especially has this been true of the period between elections, when both the party association and the candidate spend large sums in nursing the constituency. Because of the indulgence of the judges, who have not considered that the electoral period began before a dissolution, vast influence, of a type which during the election

---

[1] *Parliamentary Papers,* 1887, no. 90; 1893-1894, no. 25; 1896, no. 63; 1906, no. 198, "Shorthand writers' notes of . . . judgments." In one instance some sports were held under the auspices of the Conservative Association, which were announced by large bills in Conservative colours, and at which the Conservative candidate presided; political addresses were delivered; there was a deficit when it came to paying the expenses of these sports, which was covered by the agent of the successful candidate. This was held to be collective bribery by treating. In Hexham, in 1892, a deficiency of £35 incurred in giving a series of dances and entertainments, and which was made up by the Conservative Association, led to the unseating of the successful candidate. When at Rochester conversazioni were arranged by a committee of the political association and threepence only charged for the refreshments furnished, it was held that corrupt treating was taking place.

would certainly be considered corrupt, can be exercised without danger.

For the same reason the amount of money expended upon a seat is very frequently not represented by the candidate's account. The association, which is not supposed to be acting as agent, may hire large numbers of workers, spend large sums under cover of the legitimate registration charges, and not endanger the seat. Frequently the information gathered by the association at great expense, and invaluable for the campaign, is sold for a nominal sum to the candidate or his agent.

In general the associations have set their face against bribery and have made for purity of elections. But whenever they choose to exercise influence in a manner which approaches the corrupt, it is almost impossible to bring their derelictions from the legal path home to the candidate. The greatest of election authorities has said that "an election inquiry has been more frequently baffled from a failure in the proof of agency than from all other causes put together."[1]

Again the trial of petitions has not been entirely satisfactory, notwithstanding the improvements made in 1868. The cost of the trial is invariably so great as to discourage many defeated candidates who believe themselves unfairly beaten. The protraction of the trials was one of the great complaints of the system in 1898, and doubtless often tended to prevent the bringing forward of a petition. And notwithstanding the comparative severity of the judges,

[1] Rogers, *Elections,* ii, 360. For a brief discussion of the methods of evading the act of 1883, see Lowell, *Government of England,* i, 232-238; Ostrogorski, *op. cit.,* i, 438-439, 472-480. For the unsettled question of agency, see *Parliamentary Papers,* 1887, no. 90; 1893-1894, no. 25; 1896, no. 63; 1906, no. 198, "Shorthand writers' notes of . . . judgments"; especially see the cases of Norwich (1887), Rochester, Hexham, Montgomery, and Stepney (1893), Lancaster, Lichfield, and Shoreditch (1896), Great Yarmouth (1906).

the tendency to require a proof of corrupt intent allows candidates to escape conviction when their guilt appears reasonably clear to the lay mind. Thus because of the cost and the protraction of the trial and the uncertainty of the result, as well as the unpopularity which accrues to a petitioner, it is a fact that certain cases of corrupt elections are never brought before the notice of the public. And because of the difficulty of procuring evidence of a satisfactory sort, punishment is not applied, even when the facts are clear.[1]

But even recognizing the existence of bribery in a few of the older boroughs, and the existence of indirect corrupt influence in many of the larger constituencies, the advance made in the past half-century in purity of elections cannot be questioned. It is inevitable that the voters should be influenced in some manner or other. The flexibility of political influence is well known; at one time it is embodied in patent, flagrant, and unashamed corruption; under different conditions it becomes insidious and impalpable. In earlier days a constituency was purchased like a church living or an army commission. It was the property of the buyer, who did as he would with his own. Such customs fell into disuse with the passage of time, and individual voters were bought with money or presents. Then instead of purchasing individuals the candidate bought whole communities, by entertainments and picnics. The step between this stage and that in which classes and trades are won by promises of legislation is not very broad.

But the difference between the early methods by which electors were influenced and those now in vogue is so great that Ostrogorski seems equipped with over-blue spectacles,

---

[1] *Parliamentary Papers*, 1897, no. 347, "Minutes of Evidence," § 1005; appendix; *Ibid.*, 1898, no. 340, "Report of the Select Committee on Election Petitions," iv.

when he says that only the forms of corruption have changed. For the forms have changed so absolutely that the very nature of electioneering has been transformed. And the study of conditions before 1869 and even in 1880 induces a feeling of surprise that the change has been so great and the vestiges of the old system of corruption so slight.

The position of the reform of electioneering methods in the development of electoral democracy is certainly one of great importance. The corruption of a constituency was, after the destruction of nomination, one of the most vital factors in the electoral power of the aristocracy and upper middle class. That power was shaken only slightly by the legislation of 1854, which, it is true, improved conditions in the larger constituencies and lessened the extent of direct bribery. But all the indirect forms of intimidation and corruption still persisted, and were bulwarks of the influence exercised by the wealthy and well-connected. The reform of the petition system in 1868 and the introduction of the ballot in 1872, were of assistance in breaking down that influence; for the inefficiency of the House of Commons' committees was substituted the stern severity of the judges; the ballot, while it may not have developed new sources of democratic strength, inevitably made for purity and freedom of election.

But more stringent provisions were necessary if the spread of indirect corruption was to be checked amongst the men who had been lately enfranchised and whose poverty rendered them an easy object of plutocratic control. For the moment enfranchisement ran the risk of total perversion. Nor could democracy proceed upon its path, if election expenses were to increase with the same rapidity as the increase in the number of voters.

Such provisions were furnished by the Corrupt Practices Act, which sought to curtail the irregular and illegitimate expenditure that had grown up in place of the old-fashioned bribery. And so plainly did the Radicals perceive that legislation of this type was necessary if the position of the Whigs and Tories was to be captured, that the caucuses furnished the most sincere coöperation in bringing the reform to a successful issue. The act of 1883 thus stands as a landmark in the development of democracy in England, and must be classed with the legislation of the two succeeding years, which extended the franchise and reformed the distribution of electoral power.

CHAPTER XV

DEMOCRATIC SUFFRAGE IN THE COUNTIES: THE FRANCHISE ACT OF 1884

Reform waves—The legislation of 1883, 1884, 1885—Franchise and redistribution—The movement for franchise reform—Demonstrations in 1883 and 1884—General consensus as to necessity of reform—Attitude of various elements—Gladstone's plan—Its simplicity and moderation—General acceptance of the principle of the bill—Demand for concurrent redistribution—Compromise arranged—Radical attack upon plural voting—Gladstone insists upon retention of freehold qualification and county voting rights of borough freeholder—Attack upon university representation—The franchise for women—General character of the act as passed—The ancient right voters—Importance of the freeholders in counties—Effect of ownership vote on party strength—The new county voters—Ratio of voters to population in counties and boroughs—Advantage of rural divisions disappeared—General regularity in relative size of electorate—Summary of franchise development from 1832 to 1884.

STUDENTS of constitutional development have not failed to observe that the legislatures of a democracy are subject to what may be termed periodic waves of reform, under the impulse of which the remodelling of the outworks and sometimes the basic structure of government proceeds apace. An impatience with mere tinkering, a desire for real "finality," characterizes the attitude of the legislators. A lassitude of the question so long discussed and a desperate acquiescence in the leap in the dark paralyzes their powers of resistance to the demand for reform. It was such a wave that caught the Tory government of Disraeli in 1867 and 1868, inducing the enactment of household suffrage in boroughs, as well as the change in the petition system; its force sufficed to introduce the ballot in 1872, despite the indifference of Liberals and the hostility of Conservatives. It was a similar wave, during the second Gladstone administration, that led to the culminating events in the period of electoral development which we are surveying.

Of certain aspects, characteristic of the electoral changes which together go to make up what is called the third reform, something has been said. The Registration Act of 1885 completed the development of the process which was designed to transform the elector from a potential to an active factor, in the system of elections. As a result of this and the analogous act of 1878 the party associations were left with full scope for their activities, although restrained in large measure from the vexatious and illegitimate practices which had denatured the intended operation of the franchise. The influence of the new associations in registration now became more complete even than that of the earlier registration associations, and was tacitly admitted as part of the system. But that influence tended in the direction of democracy, for the new party federations were, at least ostensibly, organized upon a popular basis; whereas the efforts of the older registration associations had been exerted, with but few exceptions, in the interest of the aristocracy and the upper middle classes.

The Corrupt Practices Act of 1883 was an aspect of the same wave of electoral reform, and was almost identical in its tendency. It was supported by the democratic associations and it brought into existence new conditions of electioneering largely to their advantage. Wealthy candidates from the upper middle class could no longer hope for success unless supported by the association, deprived as they were of the opportunity of purchasing the seat directly. The influence of both the landed and the capitalistic aristocracy was limited by the rigorous definition of corrupt practices. The curtailment of election expenses was also to the advantage of the associations, since it enlarged enormously the circle of possibilities from which a candidate might be adopted. For the tyranny of the aristocracy was substituted that of the caucus; but the latter at all events sprang from the masses themselves and rested upon popular support.

The reforms in registration and in the conduct of elections, important as they were, can nevertheless be considered only subsidiary to the more essential question of the franchise and the redistribution of seats. It was the settlement of these latter problems that made the reform wave of 1884 and 1885 one of such vital importance in electoral history. Upon that settlement is based to a large extent the democratic character of the British government. The act of 1867, as we saw, could hardly be regarded as a final solution. The democratic franchise then introduced was confined to the borough constituencies, which in population and wealth were inferior to the counties, which were excluded from the new voting rights. It was inevitable that the latter should demand the logical extension of the household franchise on sentimental as well as on practical grounds. Anomalies comparable to those of the pre-reform period had arisen as a result of the favour shown to boroughs, and the age was no longer one which tolerated anomalies. The question of redistribution also demanded attention. The redistribution of 1867 had been slight to a degree, and even at the time it was recognized that the settlement then effected could be only temporary. Franchise and redistribution as practical questions are closely correlated, and, as the Conservatives pointed out in 1884, cannot be taken up separately. From motives of convenience, however, we may follow the example set by Gladstone and proceed to consider each in order.

The question of extending household suffrage to the counties was brought to a position of the first importance in 1877, when Hartington, at that time leader of the Liberal opposition, signified his approval of Trevelyan's motion. Three years later the Liberal success at the polls rendered it practically certain that a government measure would be introduced, and the leaders of the party considered that definite pledges had been given to such effect. Little impatience, however, was evinced either in the country or in the Commons, and the subject of reform, when discussed, turned rather in the direction of the expected redistribution and the vexatious problem of proportional representation. In the new Gladstone Parliament matters of foreign policy, the unseemly struggle over the position of Bradlaugh, and the acute crisis resulting from Irish policy and Irish disturbance, occupied both ministry and opposition. Electoral reform, in so far as it was taken up in government bills, was confined to the elimination of corruption and the limitation of election expenses.

Such radical reform as would have resulted from the assimilation of county and borough suffrage must, in any event, have been a subject for an old and not a young Parliament. The acknowledgment that the representative system was imperfect ought to be speedily followed by a dissolution; and in spite of the confidence with which Liberals looked to the urban industrial districts, and even to the agricultural labourers, a dissolution was not desired by the mass of the party. There was the possibility, not remote, that the already embarrassing influence of the Radicals would be increased by an appeal to the country; in any case a general election was not desirable at the existing juncture of Irish affairs. The Conservatives,

sure of the counties under the franchise in force, held to
the policy of "quieta non movere," at least so far as the
suffrage was concerned.

But in the fourth year of Gladstone's Parliament the
spirit of reform gathered momentum. The Corrupt Practices Act had centred attention upon the electoral system, and recalled to the public the franchise pledges of the
administration. Reformers began to emphasize the
advisability of redeeming those pledges before the Parliament became moribund. The agitation was led by the
Radicals, who, under Chamberlain's guidance, utilized the
caucus organization for the purpose of airing the question. During the autumn of 1883 meetings were constantly organized to rouse enthusiasm for the extension
of the franchise. Chamberlain himself sounded the rally-
call in a letter to the Battersea Radical Association, and
shortly afterwards a suffrage meeting of fifty thousand
persons was held at Newcastle-upon-Tyne. On the 17th
of October a monster conference was convened at Leeds,
where there assembled delegates from five hundred Liberal
associations, all of which were unanimous in their support of household suffrage for the counties.[1] In January
of 1884 a deputation, representing two hundred and forty
thousand delegates from all the trades unions in the
United Kingdom, waited upon Gladstone and urged him
to act.[2] By the following March four hundred and fourteen different meetings had been held, in all of which the
principle of enfranchisement was insisted upon as one of
burning importance.[3]

With such pressure from outside, and with such re-

---

[1] *Annual Register,* 1883, 165, 175-176.

[2] 3 Hansard, cclxxxvi, 1552.

[3] In one week of April fifty meetings were held in Northumberland, according to Burt, and numerous associations were formed in
order to promote enfranchisement, 3 Hansard, cclxxxvi, 1862.

formers as Chamberlain, Dilke, and Trevelyan in the cabinet, the government could hardly have refused to take the question up, even had the opposition to reform amongst the old Liberals been general. It is true that in certain quarters enthusiasm for the measure was by no means keen. Gladstone himself, although he recognized the necessity and desirability of extending the franchise, feared, and would have been glad to escape from the burden of carrying through the details of a complex reform bill.[1] Hartington had not succeeded in conquering his doubts of the electoral capacity of the agricultural labourers; he believed that were it not for the pledges given, the necessity for change was not pressing.[2] Courtney, while he favoured the principle of extension, would have been glad to see the measure postponed until a definite settlement, including woman's suffrage and proportional representation could be obtained. But Radical pressure in and upon the cabinet was strong enough to insure the introduction of a government bill. Goschen admitted in a speech at Ripon that, while he could not approve of reform, it was hopeless to attempt to stem the rising tide.[3] And even Salisbury and Northcote, who complained that the moment was inopportune and demanded that no step be taken without adequate redistribution, dared oppose no direct protest to the principle of extension.[4]

The character of the reform thus demanded by Radicals, accepted by Liberals, and unopposed by Conserva-

[1] He realized the necessity of following up franchise reform with a redistribution, and protested that the heavy burden ought to fall on younger shoulders.

[2] Hartington said: "The equalization of the franchise presses, I think, mainly on account of the pledges which we have given; not much for any other reason," *Life of the Duke of Devonshire*, i, 395.

[3] *Annual Register*, 1884, 10.

[4] *Annual Register*, 1884, 7.

tives, differed widely. As to the extension of household franchise into the counties, there was practically no dispute. Thus would be eliminated the most striking anomalies which allowed the franchise to part of the urban working class and excluded another quota of the same class, merely because they lived outside of the borough boundary.[1] Change of work, causing the labourer to change his residence, would no longer deprive him of his vote. The half million miners of whom, according to Burt, few possessed the franchise, would thus be placed on a par with those who happened to reside within the boundaries of such towns as Morpeth and Merthyr Tydvil.[2] The four hundred thousand tradesmen and artisans of the urban districts would have the same rights as their fellows in the represented towns; and the vote which had been given in 1867 to the seventy-five thousand agricultural labourers of the large rural boroughs would now be extended to a million of the same class in the counties.

There were certain persons in 1884 who opposed such extension. Randolph Churchill demanded that the sincere desire of the agricultural labourers for the franchise should first be expressed more distinctly;[3] and some of the older Tories opposed, with the arguments of 1831, any extension whatever of the electorate, and any increase in

1 As in Walker-on-Tyne, which with a population of 21,500 had neither municipal nor parliamentary representation, although it was but a quarter of a mile from the Newcastle boundary, 3 Hansard, cclxxxvi, 1554.

2 3 Hansard, cclxxxvi, 1861.

3 He said at Edinburgh in December, 1883, that if he saw the agricultural labourers in a great state of excitement, holding meetings, tearing down railings,—then he would admit that they wanted the vote, had made up their minds to have it, and were therefore fit for it. Chamberlain complained that such an attitude was a direct incitement to violence and outrage, 3 Hansard, cclxxxvi, 951.

the power of numbers. But such direct opponents were few. On the other hand, those who agreed on the principle of extension were divided into two main camps: some desired to mitigate the democratic effects of the extension; others considered that extension by itself would be entirely inadequate.

The Conservatives were determined that redistribution should accompany the introduction of the household franchise in the counties, in order that the new country urban electors might be prevented from swamping the agricultural element. It was all very well, they argued, to give the vote to those who deserved it, but care must be taken to preserve the rights of existing voters which were in danger of practical extinction. Others advocated the preservation of existing rights by means of some system of minority representation. Of these, Goschen was the most outspoken in doubting the capacity of the agricultural labourers and in his desire to blunt the electoral weapon about to be presented to them.[1] Sir John Lubbock and Courtney also advocated some scheme of proportional representation, although they based their plea on different grounds. Less timorous than Goschen, they sought an escape from the element of blind chance which had vitally affected the elections of 1874 and 1880.

On the other hand many considered that no finality was to be found in the household franchise and demanded the introduction of manhood suffrage. Chamberlain himself regarded household suffrage in counties as merely a step, and advocated the simpler and more democratic qualification, although he admitted that the time was not yet pro-

---

[1] 3 Hansard, cclxxxvi, 1343. Goschen pointed out that in 30 out of 95 county divisions the urban and industrial would entirely outvote the agricultural. Since it was the urban, the gregarious classes which were chiefly being enfranchised, there would be an entire transfer of political power from the agricultural to the urban, *Ibid.*, 1878.

pitious.[1] But those for whom Broadhurst acted as spokesman, destined not long after to be the organizers of the Labour party, declared that nothing but manhood suffrage would satisfy them.

A more numerous element confined their democratic enthusiasm to an attack upon the older franchises by which the upper classes were benefited. Of these the most important was the 40s. ownership franchise in counties, which had so long served as the basis for manufactured votes. These faggot votes, at one time the mainstay of the middle class Radical attack upon the corn laws, were now supposed to favour unduly the Whig and Conservative elements. At all events, the ownership vote was becoming more and more an outvote, and in many constituencies was exercised by those who had votes elsewhere in such a way as to distort the true sentiment of the community. With this attack upon the ownership franchise was included a protest against the other forms of plural voter, such as the town freeholder voting in counties and the university elector. According to Hartington, the sentiment against the property franchise and the plural voting resulting from it, was so strong that if it had not been for Gladstone's desire to retain it, the freehold suffrage would have been extinguished.[2]

Gladstone's guidance of the reform question ensured indeed a policy of moderation.[3] Like his bill of 1866, that of 1884 pursued a middle course between the demands of the Conservatives for immediate guarantees which would prevent the annihilation of existing votes, and the claims of the extreme Radicals for more complete democracy. Redistribution and the question of minority representation were left for future consideration. Manhood suffrage

---

[1] *Annual Register,* 1883, 183.

[2] *Life of Duke of Devonshire,* i, 404.

[3] For an epitome of press opinion, see *Annual Register,* 1884, 98.

and the destruction of certain forms of electoral privilege, on the other hand, were not included in his plan.

That plan was as simple as is possible in the case of a Reform Bill. In the counties, the old ownership franchises, which gave the vote to freeholders, copy- and lease-holders, were retained. In addition to these was introduced the threefold form of borough qualification: the £10 occupation, the household, and lodger franchises. The county suffrage was thus given the same breadth as that of the boroughs. The £50 rental qualification was abolished, saving existing rights; but the £12 occupation franchise of 1867 was retained, although the practical result of the new qualifications in counties would be to render it largely a dead letter. In boroughs the ancient right franchises of the old pre-reformed régime were specially preserved, as were the qualifications of 1867.[1]

The main effect of the bill was thus simply to extend the borough franchise to counties. Existing qualifications were not abrogated nor were any new franchises created. An apparent exception was to be found in what Gladstone termed the service franchise; this constituted as occupiers persons who inhabited a dwelling house by virtue of any office, service, or employment, provided that the master or employer was not resident. This clause did not in reality create a new kind of franchise. It was merely intended to alter the inference of law that a servant or employee who occupied his master's tenement for the better perform-ance of his duties, was not to be regarded as a tenant. By the correction of this legal inference, stewards and agents could now be registered under the household occu-pation franchise in boroughs and counties.[2]

[1] 3 Hansard, cclxxxv, 106-183.
[2] This inference had been established by several cases, notably "Clark v. Overseers of Bury St. Edmunds," 1 *Common Bench Reports, New Series, 23*; 3 Hansard, cclxxxviii, 1383-1392.

In describing his measure, Gladstone made no attempt
to introduce arguments for the extension of the franchise.
The prime minister tacitly laid upon his opponents the
burden of proof, and invited them to show reason why the
change should not be made; the principle of such extension had already, in his opinion, been approved by fifteen
years' experience. "I take my stand," said he, "upon the
broad principle that the enfranchisement of capable citizens, be they few or be they many—and if they be many
so much the better—is an addition to the strength of the
State."[1]   More pains were taken, indeed, to justify the
retention of the ancient, and especially the property,
franchises than to demonstrate the necessity of household
suffrage in counties.

The country and the Commons accepted Gladstone's
bill either as beneficial or as inevitable. The press agreed,
almost without a dissenting voice, that his proposals were
the acme of moderation, and the objections brought out
by the debate on the second reading were not numerous.
Some Conservatives, like Raikes, disapproved of the
identity of the franchise in counties and in boroughs,
quoting Russell as their authority; to these Bright
answered by referring to Disraeli, and his bill of 1859
which proposed such identity.[2]   Others believed that the
agricultural interest in parliament would be annihilated;
that the farmers, whether tenants or freeholders, would be
practically disfranchised.[3]   Hartington admitted that the
supremacy of the tenant farmers would be terminated, but
denied that agricultural interests would suffer thereby.[4]   A
few Conservatives did not fear to express their frank dis-

[1] 3 Hansard, cclxxxv, 107.
[2] *Annual Register*, 1884, 104; Murdoch, *History of Constitutional
Reform*, 297.
[3] 3 Hansard, cclxxxvi, 691.
[4] Murdoch, *Constitutional Reform*, 297, 302.

trust of the agricultural labourers, considering them grossly ignorant and careless of politics. Others objected that numbers were to be enfranchised at the expense of intelligence and property, and complained that the ratio of responsible to irresponsible electors, always low, was about to be lessened.[1]

Opposition on such scores was, however, scattered, and had it not been for the quarrel over redistribution, the bill might have passed without difficulty. The sentiment of the front opposition bench was expressed by Cross, who admitted that he had never opposed the principle of extension; in his opinion it was illogical to maintain an electoral distinction between the suburbs of great towns and the towns themselves, when in the habits and pursuits of the people no such distinction existed.[2] Ritchie, speaking for the younger Conservatives, insisted that they had always believed it impossible to preserve an artificial barrier between voters of the same class, and that it had always been merely a question of time before the barrier was broken down.[3]

On the other side of the House the arguments of the Liberals and Radicals were briefly expressed. Chamberlain complained that as a result of the restricted franchise the endowments of the country poor were misappropriated and the country labourers were robbed of their land. Shaw Lefevre demanded the franchise as the first of a series of remedies for rural debilitation, which followed upon the immigration of the best men from villages to towns.[4] Forster answered the old Tory objection by asserting that the doctrine of numbers already pervaded the

[1] 3 Hansard, cclxxxvii, 805.
[2] 3 Hansard, cclxxxvi, 1230.
[3] 3 Hansard, cclxxxvi, 935.
[4] 3 Hansard, cclxxxvi, 956, 1245; Murdoch, *Constitutional Reform*, 320.

representative system and must pervade it. The act of
1867 had made this clear, and the measure under consideration would merely complete the process; the basis of
popular power was to be determined not by property or
interest, but by numbers—human beings.[1] Forster's
speech seemed to give point to the fear already expressed,
that household suffrage in counties was but an installment
and that the end was not yet.[2]

But though Liberal arguments were left practically
unanswered, and approximate concord upon the cardinal
principle of the bill was secured, the Conservatives did
not conceal their repugnance to the bill itself. The entire
party protested against the extension of household suffrage to Ireland, not without the sympathy of many of
the Liberals, especially Hartington, who had some difficulty in concealing his sentiments.[3] In fact some of the
staunchest supporters of the government could hardly
restrain the fears evoked by the prospect of Parnell's
absolute dominion over the sister isle. Others objected
that, because of foreign and colonial affairs, the moment
was inopportune for basic reform; they pointed out that
the main principle of the bill, so far as it affected the
miners and the urban districts, might easily be attained
by a rearrangement of boundaries. But the great objection to this measure was that it included no provision for
the protection of the old voters who were now likely to be
snowed under by the force of numbers. "You are bound,"
said Sir Michael Hicks-Beach, "to take some measure to
secure that the classes who are the best educated, the most

---

[1] 3 Hansard, cclxxxvi, 1196.

[2] 3 Hansard, cclxxxv, 458.

[3] 3 Hansard, cclxxxvii, 1119; *Life of the Duke of Devonshire,*
i, 395. Hartington, like the Conservatives, did not wish franchise
without redistribution. For a comparison of his views with those
of Chamberlain, see *Ibid.,* 396-397.

cultivated, who pay the whole of the direct taxation, shall have some means of being heard in parliament."[1]

Various schemes were suggested in the hope of neutralizing the political power which was now about to be offered to the masses. One member advocated the German electoral system of plural voting, which gave two or more votes according to the amount of taxes paid.[2] Others were in favour of allowing persons rated above a certain amount to vote for one member, and those rated at less than the fixed sum to vote for the second member.[3] The sentiment for a system of minority or proportional representation was also strong, and was voiced by influential members. But the demand of the Conservatives for a redistribution of electoral power, which should accompany the franchise reform, was the crux of the situation. They feared lest in the event of a dissolution, the old constituencies, swamped by the new voters, should return a Parliament hopelessly radical; such a Parliament, handling redistribution according to their own lights, might indefinitely postpone the return of the Conservatives to power, or of the landed interest to that influence which was claimed for it.[4] Gladstone's refusal to accede to the demand for immediate redistribution determined Tory opposition to his measure.

The question of reform in 1884 was thus fought out, not on principles, but upon the method of procedure. The

[1] 3 Hansard, cclxxxvi, 1307.

[2] 3 Hansard, cclxxxvii, 1540.

[3] 3 Hansard, cclxxxvi, 1560.

[4] *Annual Register*, 1884, 2, 87. "The Tory leaders believed that unless the allotment of seats went with the addition of a couple of million new voters, the prospect would be ruinously impossible to their party, and they offered determined resistance to a jockeying operation of this kind. At least one very eminent man among them had privately made up his mind that the proceeding supposed to be designed by their opponents . . . would efface the Tory party for thirty years to come," Morley, *Gladstone*, iii, 126.

parliamentary tactics of the struggle do not, perhaps, require detailed description. The motions, direct and indirect, brought forward by the Conservatives in the hope of forcing the prime minister to annex or at least to outline a plan of redistribution, were all opposed by Gladstone and negatived by his obedient majority. He refused to load his bill with more than it would carry, and commanded his forces to keep the decks light, lest the measure founder. Of argument there was little; he bade his party waste no time in debating amendments, and when, after speaking for five minutes on a capital point, he was taxed with curtness, he replied, "Our object in this bill is, as far as we can, to make curt speeches."[1]

Failing in the Commons, the Conservatives trusted to the Lords, who justified such confidence by refusing to pass the measure without sufficient guarantee of an immediate Redistribution Bill. The Conservative leaders, Salisbury and Cairns, did not, indeed, raise the question of franchise at all, and the discussion was centred almost entirely upon the tactics of the government.[2] It was not until the autumn of 1884, when the aroused temper of the masses and the inflexibility of the upper House threatened a crisis, that a compromise was arranged, and the constitutional revolution which took place twenty-seven years later, was avoided. The Conservatives agreed that the bill when reintroduced, should be allowed to pass, but only upon the understanding that a scheme of redistribution should be meanwhile presented. The bases of that scheme were to be arranged by the opposing leaders.[3]

The Franchise Act, which was accordingly passed in the

[1] 3 Hansard, cclxxxviii, 557.

[2] *Annual Register,* 1884, 139-152; Murdoch, *Constitutional Reform,* 367.

[3] For the details of the compromise and the manner in which it was carried through, see Morley, *Gladstone,* iii, 126-139.

autumn session of 1884, differed only slightly from the bill
originally presented by Gladstone. From the Radicals
there emanated constant complaints that the reform was
entirely inadequate, and they offered not a few amendments, in the hope of imparting a more democratic character to the measure, and of removing some of the electoral
opportunities which still remained open to the wealthy
classes. Radical complaints had no effect in altering the
lines of the act, but the voting strength aroused by certain
amendments showed that the strongholds of the aristocracy were destined to ultimate extinction. Of these
amendments the most significant were those presented in
the hope of destroying the system of plural voting.

As plural voting rested chiefly upon the property qualification in counties, it was against this 40s. franchise, and
the faggot votes manufactured from it, that the most
strenuous efforts were made.[1] In the years which immediately preceded the introduction of Gladstone's measure
faggot voting had been the object of much adverse criticism, and the Liberals never wearied of recounting the
elections which had been affected, if not decided, by votes
manufactured under the property franchise.[2] In Scotland, and especially in Midlothian, the abuse was rampant;
and in many of the English counties utter strangers to the
constituency frequently held the balance of electoral
power by means of created votes. In West Somerset a
single tithe rent charge was divided amongst thirty-three
merchants of Bristol; the latter had no real interest in the
county and never came there except to vote.[3] The abolition of such opportunities for the creation of votes was in
1883 loudly demanded by the Liberal press.[4] In the Com-

---

[1] *Annual Register,* 1884, 5.
[2] 3 Hansard, ccli, 861; *Annual Register,* 1879, 37.
[3] 3 Hansard, cclxxxvi, 932.
[4] *Spectator,* November 10, 1883.

mons, Fawcett and Jesse Collings insisted, with others, that the 40s. franchise should not be suffered to continue; that in any case residence should be annexed as a necessary condition, and plural voting as well as created qualifications be destroyed at a single blow.[1]

The Conservatives, in answer, referred to the Liberals themselves, and to Bright especially, as the fathers of the system of manufacturing votes.[2] It was the Liberal party which in the registration movement of the Anti-Corn Law League had first demonstrated the possibilities of the 40s. franchise. With acrimonious pleasure they quoted Cobden's famous saying that nothing better could be done for a boy of twenty-one than buy him a freehold qualification. The prime minister, however, removed the burden of defence from Conservative shoulders, by refusing to insert residence as a necessary condition of the property qualification. Without sympathizing with plural voting, Gladstone was unwilling to legislate against established rights. One change, however, he admitted, by restricting property qualifications which depended upon rent charges in such a way as to render difficult the creation of faggot votes. The opportunities of the plural outvoter were thus narrowed to a certain extent.[3]

But in a different direction another and a more determined attack was made upon plural voting. This took the form of a demand that borough freeholders be deprived of their right to vote in counties, and that university representation be abolished. It will be remembered that the borough freeholder had been the object of warm dispute in 1831 and in 1859. In the debates over the first Reform

1 3 Hansard, cclxxxvi, 685.
2 3 Hansard, cclxxxvi, 688.
3 3 Hansard, cclxxxv, 119; cclxxxviii, 1792-1824. Gladstone made use of his retention of the property franchise to prove that the bill was not constructed upon party lines, 3 Hansard, cclxxxvi, 1841.

Bill the Liberals had advocated the right of the urban
freeholder to vote in the county, notwithstanding the protests of Peel and Praed. This right was attacked by
Disraeli in 1859, who provided in his unsuccessful Reform
Bill of that year that the freeholder should vote in the
place where his property lay. Again in 1867 the Tories
would not have been displeased if a similar provision could
have been inserted in the second Reform Act. But the
Liberals were able to prevent any change. By 1884 it was
reckoned that more than one hundred and twenty thousand
town freeholders were voting in the counties; many of them
had numerous votes in other constituencies, and as early
as 1867 there is an instance of a man with eighteen votes.[1]

Against this bulwark of plutocratic strength, which was
generally reckoned to the advantage of the Whigs, the
Radicals joined with Tories. Both strove with emulous
violence to place the franchise, in this respect, on a "one
man, one vote" basis. The Radicals hated plural voting
in any form. The Conservatives, while they were willing
to accept such advantages as plural voting in general
offered, considered the right of the freeholder in boroughs
unfair to the freeholder in counties. On the one hand, the
county vote of the town freeholder was attacked by Broadhurst, as a concession to ancient and aristocratic
monopoly; on the other it was assailed by Gorst, as the
anomalous bulwark of urban privilege.[2]

Various amendments were proposed which, if they had
been carried, would have prevented long years of Liberal
complaint. The suggestion that any elector, in borough
or county, might vote once as owner and once as occupier
received scant respect; such a provision would have re-

[1] Porritt, "Barriers against Democracy in the British Electoral
System," in *Political Science Quarterly*, xxvi, no. 1.
[2] 3 Hansard, cclxxxvi, 1552, 1559, 1825; cclxxxviii, 547-555.

moved the anomaly, but would have resulted in the complete establishment of plural voting.[1] On the other hand, the amendments of Leighton and M'Laren were approved by individuals from all parties. The latter proposed that a claimant with qualifications in different constituencies must elect one and vote in that alone. Had this suggestion been accepted plural voting would have ceased in England in 1884.[2]

The Liberal government, however, opposed the amendment. True to his Whig principles, Hartington objected now, as always, to the disfranchisement of the borough freeholder; Gladstone, while he cautiously refused to disclose his true opinion upon plural voting, was unwilling to see the disfranchisement of so many votes as were involved. And Sir Henry James, who in 1882 had bitterly attacked the plural voting freeholder, and still admitted his dislike of the system, must, as member of the government, perforce defend its policy.[3] From the front opposition bench Cross admitted the anomaly of the county vote of the borough freeholder, although he opposed any change upon the same ground as that advanced by Gladstone.[4] Many of the Liberals doubtless agreed with Morley, who while defending the principle of "one man, one vote," was unwilling to trouble the government and believed that the question could wait.[5] M'Laren's amend-

[1] 3 Hansard, cclxxxviii, 564, 1906, 1932.

[2] 3 Hansard, cclxxxvii, 1543-1546; cclxxxviii, 1395; Murdoch, *Constitutional Reform*, 352.

[3] 3 Hansard, cclxxxviii, 557, 1402, 1546.

[4] 3 Hansard, cclxxxviii, 566.

[5] 3 Hansard, cclxxxviii, 1399. Men like Forster and Walter, who approved of the bill in general, regretted bitterly the retention of the opportunities for plural voting. The Radical Labouchere, who must have secretly approved the Conservative attack on the plural-voting freeholder in boroughs, refused to vote for a Conservative amendment, *Ibid.*, cclxxxv, 408; cclxxxvi, 1195; cclxxxviii, 561.

ment was accordingly disposed òf by an overwhelming majority.[1]

Another attack upon plural voting centred about the representation of universities, and the non-resident university voter. This university franchise was bitterly assailed by Broadhurst in the early stages of the bill, and also received a severely unfavourable analysis at the hands of Morley.[2] So strong was the feeling that it is possible that if the government had possessed a free hand, this stronghold of country clergymen subject to Tory direction would have disappeared. But the question was necessarily relegated for discussion to the debates upon redistribution, and the ministers then found their hands tied by the pledges given to the leaders of the opposition.

There was also presented an amendment along a different line, the adoption of which would have saved Liberals of the following generation much worry. Ever since 1832 there had been spasmodic demands for the extension of the franchise to women, although at no time did the question come within the range of practical politics. In 1832 Hunt presented a petition from a lady in Yorkshire, who claimed that as she paid taxes she ought to vote.[3] In the following year Disraeli discovered a fashionable suffragist in the person of Bulwer's mother-in-law.[4] A clause advocating the voting rights of women was included in the first draft of the People's Charter in 1837, and ten years later Holyoake began a feminist agitation which was, however, chiefly confined to a demand for the extension of the civil rights of women.[5]

[1] 43-235, 3 Hansard, cclxxxviii, 1407.
[2] 3 Hansard, cclxxxvi, 925, 1557, 1565.
[3] 3 Hansard, xiv, 1086.
[4] Monypenny, *Disraeli*, i, 233.
[5] Kent, *The English Radicals*, 360; Holyoake, *Sixty Years of an Agitator's Life*, i, 222.

The question was first seriously laid before parliament
in 1867, when Mill, after moving for a return of the
number of women excluded from the franchise on account
of sex, proposed an amendment for the removal of the
existing disabilities. Though he denied that the claim was
based on abstract right, he insisted that it was a question
of practical justice; since taxation and representation
went hand in hand, women taxpayers should be admitted
to equal privileges with men.[1]

After 1870 the question was annually brought before
the Commons by Jacob Bright, although it received scant
attention.[2] Of the more prominent Liberals, Courtney
was heartily in favour of extending the vote to women,
and in 1879 himself brought in a motion to that effect.
His argument rested entirely upon utilitarian grounds,
of which the most important were the necessity of removing the grievances of the women, and the improved
quality of candidates which would result.[3] John Bright,
on the other hand, displayed slight sympathy, frankly
admitted his fear of the influence which priest and parson
would have upon female voters, and declared himself convinced that the alleged grievances of women were either
imaginary or exaggerated.[4] In 1883 the motion was again
brought forward and lost; but the majority was by no
means overwhelming, and amongst the minority were
counted such influential figures as Fawcett and Dilke.[5]

Hence when the amendment in favour of female suffrage

---

[1] 3 Hansard, cclxxxiv, 996; Murdoch, *Constitutional Reform,* 250.

[2] 3 Hansard, ccvi, 68; ccxi, 1; ccxv, 1194; ccxxviii, 1658; ccxxxiv,
1362; ccxl, 1800.

[3] *Annual Register,* 1879, 39.

[4] *Annual Register,* 1876, 53.

[5] The motion was lost, 114-130; Gladstone, Bright, Bryce and
Hartington voted against it, 3 Hansard, cclxxxi, 664-722; *Annual
Register,* 1883, 136.

was proposed to the bill of 1884, it was not considered a forlorn hope, nor could the question longer come within the definition of a "parliamentary crochet." The debate was long and non-partisan; for the most part the arguments were practical, although some speakers found difficulty in evading the temptations to deliver abstract disquisitions upon feminine nature. Perhaps the strongest argument in favour of the amendment was the position of the thirty thousand women tenants, who themselves farmed their land; the labourers whom they hired would, under the new act, all become voters although they themselves were excluded.[1] But this, and the other well-worn arguments, made no impression upon Gladstone; without revealing his own opinion upon the innate merits of the amendment, he refused once again to overload his bill with matter that might be decided at another time. He drew with him a smaller proportion of the party than usual, but sufficient to negative the amendment by a two to one majority. Many of the leading figures, both Conservative and Liberal, went into the lobby with the tellers of the minority.[2]

The failure of all attempts to extend the scope of the bill of 1884 left it imbued with the character that Gladstone had sought; it was as moderate as was consistent with the elimination of the chief anomalies that had characterized the suffrage since 1867. The demands of the Conservatives for safeguards against the overwhelming force of numbers were indeed refused, or, at least, put off

---

[1] 3 Hansard, cclxxxvi, 928; *Annual Register,* 1884, 132-135. For an exposition of the position of the question in 1878 and 1884, see the *Saturday Review,* xlv, 775, and *National Review,* v, 60.

[2] The motion was lost, 135-271. Lord Randolph Churchill and Lord John Manners both agreed in favour of woman suffrage, Murdoch, *Constitutional Reform,* 283; 3 Hansard, cclxxxvi, 625; cclxxxviii, 1942-1964; cclxxxix, 92-204.

for later discussion. But the Radical attacks upon the existing barriers to democracy, upon the ancient property franchise, the town freeholder, the university elector, and the plural voter in all his forms—all such attacks failed absolutely. The basis of the suffrage since 1884 has thus failed to approach complete democracy. Old privileges and anomalies still remained, counteracting to some extent the newly won power of the masses in the counties.

The vestiges of the ancient electoral system, it is true, lost most of their influence in elections, and except in the counties have drawn forth but few complaints from the advocates of pure democracy. In the boroughs, after 1885, the ancient right voters numbered thirty-five thousand only, and were to be found in only fifty-six constituencies. In most of these boroughs the influence of the relics of the old system was negligible. At Taunton there were but four potwallers as reminder of the most picturesque of ancient franchises; in Westminster, the freemen who had once furnished inspiration to the genius of Hogarth, were represented by a single voter. And the loosely interpreted inhabitant franchise of Preston, which in the eighteenth century would have allowed a regiment quartered there overnight, to vote on the morrow, was accountable for only twenty-two electors.[1]

In ten boroughs, however, the ancient right voters formed more than ten per cent of the electorate, and in fifteen others they were at least an appreciable element. In the city of London, the liverymen, comprising a quarter and more of the voters, exercised a very real influence upon elections; almost all of them were plural voters with suffrages in other constituencies. The freemen of Stafford also were more than a fourth of the electorate,

---

[1] *Parliamentary Papers,* 1886, no. 44.

and those of Coventry could almost hold their own against all other types of voter combined.[1]

But with these exceptions the ancient franchises in boroughs have been of small practical importance since 1884; in the counties, on the other hand, the old property qualification was responsible for a fifth of the registered electorate. It is true that the absolute supremacy of the freeholder was departed, but he could influence where he once controlled.[2] After the reform the ownership electors formed thirty per cent or more of the voters in twenty-five divisions. These were, for the most part, the more thinly populated districts of the non-industrial counties, such as Appleby in Westmoreland, Wells in Somerset, Eskdale in Cumberland, and Tewkesbury in Gloucester. In a few of the busiest divisions of Yorkshire and Lancashire, it is true, the proportion of freeholders was high. At Pudsey, in the West Riding, for instance, nearly half of the voters held ownership qualification, most of them being out-voters of the type repugnant to Radicals.[3] But in general the registers of the manufacturing divisions showed only a small proportion of freeholders. In such typical indus-

		Ancient Right Voters	Total Electorate
[1]	London . . .	7,552	29,152
	Stafford . . .	820	3,264
	Coventry . . .	4,772	9,736

Parliamentary Papers, 1886, no. 44.

[2] The county electorate in 1886 was composed thus:

Ownership voters	508,554
Occupation voters	2,020,650
Lodger voters	8,937
Total county electorate . . .	2,538,141

Ibid.

[3] In Shipley, Yorkshire West Riding, the proportion of ownership voters was nearly as high, and in Stretford and Bootle, Lancashire, the ownership voters formed more than a third of the electorate, *Ibid.*

trial divisions of Lancashire as Gorton and Radcliffe, only four per cent of the voters were owners.

The fifteen years which followed the act of 1884 saw a slight decrease in the number of property owning electors, and by the end of the century their position in the electorate was becoming less and less important. In 1886 they formed twenty per cent of the county vote, in 1902 only sixteen per cent. And there were but twenty divisions where a quarter or more of the electors voted upon the ownership qualification.[1] Such a development was not unnatural, since the occupiers increased with the population, whereas the number of freeholders depended upon property and had approached its limit even in 1886.

No statistics are in existence showing without question what proportion of ownership electors possessed votes in more than one constituency. The number of plural voters has been estimated at close to half a million, which would mean that five-sixths of the owners were plural voters. That a very large part of the ownership vote is an out-vote will probably not be questioned. It has also been asserted that eighty per cent of the plural voters are affiliated with the Conservatives.[2] The accession of the Liberal Unionists, who had always controlled a large proportion of the town freeholder vote, doubtless transformed what had formerly been a factor of Conservative weakness into one of strength.

But in reality the ownership vote has probably affected Conservative strength in elections rather less than is

[1] From 1886 to 1902 the ownership electors decreased from 508,000 to 493,000 in England and Wales. The occupation voters on the other hand increased from two millions to two millions and a half. In Stretford and in Wimbledon, Surrey, the ownership voters still formed, however, more than a third of the electorate, *Parliamentary Papers*, 1886, no. 44; 1902, no. 70.

[2] Porritt, "Barriers against Democracy," in *Political Science Quarterly*, xxvi, no. 1, p. 8.

popularly supposed. Liberal leaders have implied, if not asserted, that seventy seats in England and Wales have been regularly carried for Conservatives by freehold voters.[1] But in the constituencies where the property electors are most numerous the Conservative advantage in elections has been far less marked than might have been expected. Of the elections held in constituencies where the property vote exceeded forty per cent, only slightly more than a half were carried by the Conservatives between the years 1886 and 1910. Some of the seats won by them were invariably safe, but no more so than neighbouring seats where there was no property vote at all. This has been true of constituencies like Fareham in Hampshire or Bootle in Lancashire, in which the property vote has been large, and of Basingstoke or Widnes in which the ownership vote has been almost entirely lacking.

It is also true that in several of the divisions in which the freehold vote has been strikingly great, such as Shipley, Forest of Dean, or Tavistock, Liberal or Labour success has been almost invariable. A high proportion of owners thus does not by any means insure Conservative success. That the ownership vote has tended generally in favour of the Conservatives, probably will not be denied. But whether its abolition, or the restriction upon its exercise will affect the balance of parties as much as has been expected, may be doubted.[2]

The great numerical increase consequent upon the Reform Act of 1884 is naturally to be found in the county occupation voters. The borough electorate was indeed

[1] Asquith, Speech at Oxford, March 18, 1910. And Unionists have admitted that the majority of the Unionists in plural voters is 400,000 to 100,000, Finlay, Speech of April 27, 1914, *Liberal Magazine*, May, 1914. Cf. also 4 Hansard, lii, 1237; *Annual Register*, 1912, 144, 161-165; Lowell, *Government of England*, i, 214.

[2] *Parliamentary Papers*, 1886, no. 44; 1902, no. 70; McCalmont, *Parliamentary Poll Book*.

reinforced by nearly two hundred thousand electors, but this gain of about eleven per cent resulted almost entirely from the enlargement of borough boundaries. In the counties the number of electors was nearly tripled, increasing from nine hundred thousand to two and a half millions. Proportionately the total increase of the electorate in 1884 was not so large as in 1867; but absolutely the number of new electors was nearly twice as great as at the time of the preceding reform.[1]

The lodger franchise in counties, as in boroughs, was responsible for comparatively few new voters. There were only twelve divisions where they numbered as many as a hundred, and in all England and Wales only nine thousand county lodgers were registered. The next fifteen years saw the lodger vote tripled in counties, but at the end of the century in both counties and boroughs there were not more than one hundred and thirty thousand lodger voters on the electoral lists. In the metropolitan constituencies alone, were they of any electoral importance; in nine of these constituencies they formed a tenth and in three a seventh or more of the electors.

The householder occupation franchise thus has qualified the bulk of the registered voters since 1884. The ancient rights and the lodger qualification have been of

[1] The per cent of increase in 1832 was 49; in 1867, 88; in 1884, 67. The per cent of increase in borough voters in 1867 was 134; of county voters in 1884, 162. Absolutely the reform of 1832 added 217,000 voters; that of 1867, 938,000; that of 1884, 1,762,000. After the reform of 1884 the electorate was made up as follows:

Occupation voters in boroughs . .	1,749,441
Occupation voters in counties . .	2,020,650
Ancient right voters in boroughs . .	35,066
Ownership voters in counties . . .	508,554
Lodgers in boroughs	57,684
Lodgers in counties	8,937

Parliamentary Papers, 1886, no. 44.

small practical importance except in a few constituencies. The property franchises, although assailed bitterly because of their anti-democratic tendencies, have represented less than a fifth of the county voters, and even where they have been strongest have not always turned the tide in a Conservative direction. Of the four million electors registered in 1886 all but about a half million were those qualified by the democratic occupier franchise; and in 1902 they formed eighty-eight per cent of all the voters in England and Wales.[1]

The extent to which the franchise has been rendered democratic is realized more clearly by considering the proportion of voters to population. The special privilege of the boroughs, which previous to 1884 was characteristic of the system, has been removed. In 1883 one man in every seven inhabitants possessed the vote in boroughs; in counties, only one man in fourteen was enfranchised. After the Reform Act of the next year, conditions were so far equalized that in counties the ratio of electors to population was rather more than one in six, and in boroughs, rather less than one in six. Naturally the proportion of electors varied in different parts of the country, and still more in individual constituencies. Such variations were inevitable, depending as they must upon the intensity of political feeling in the particular section, as well as upon the by no means uniform decisions of the revising barristers. But conditions of the law of franchise itself no

---

[1] In 1902 the electorate of England and Wales was composed as follows:

Occupation voters in boroughs . .	2,229,381
Occupation voters in counties . .	2,570,928
Ancient right voters in boroughs . .	26,038
Ownership voters in counties . .	493,694
Lodgers in boroughs	93,421
Lodgers in counties	32,894

Parliamentary Papers, 1902, no. 70.

longer affected particular classes or sections with such irregularity as before 1884.

Until the enactment of the third Reform Act it was in the industrial divisions of the counties that the suffrage was least extended; after the act, the urban county divisions, like Wimbledon and Pudsey, could show a ratio of more than one in four, thus approximating manhood suffrage. And it was in the rural divisions of Basingstoke or Carmarthen, that the low proportion of one elector to eight inhabitants was to be found. In general, however, the extent of the suffrage was almost exactly the same in agricultural and in industrial divisions.[1] In North Durham and in Herefordshire, the ratio of electors to population was identical; and the average ratio of ten typically urban divisions differed only by a fraction from that of ten rural divisions.[2] The majority of the boroughs showed a proportion of electors to population which approximated closely to that of the counties. It is notable, however, that while the county divisions in the vicinity of the metropolis could boast of a widely extended suffrage, in the metropolitan boroughs the ratio of voters was low, in some as low as one in ten. In Liverpool and Manchester, also, the proportion of registered electors was below the average.[3]

Slight variations in the extent of the suffrage still existed, it is true, even after the franchise of 1885 had been

[1] Thus in the Northwestern county divisions the ratio of electors to population was one in 5.7; in the Eastern counties it was one in 4.5.

[2] In the rural divisions the ratio was one in 5.3, in the industrial divisions it was one in 5.2. In a pronounced urban division like North Durham the ratio was one in 5.1, exactly the same as obtained in agricultural Herefordshire. The lowest ratio in these typical divisions was to be found in the rural West Sussex and the Isle of Wight: one in 6.

[3] In Liverpool it was one in 8.7; in Manchester, one in 7.4; in Bristol, one in 7.7; in Wolverhampton, one in 6.9. But the very fact

put into operation for fifteen years. From group to group such variations were hardly noticeable; in general the county suffrage was very slightly more extensive than that of the boroughs. Thus in the Midland counties one man in five inhabitants was registered, and in the boroughs one man in six only; and the disparity between the eastern counties and boroughs was equally noticeable. The lowest proportion of electors was still in the metropolitan boroughs, where the ratio fell below one in seven; in Tower Hamlets only ten per cent of the inhabitants were registered. In Pudsey, in the West Riding, on the other hand, the proportion of electors rose to nearly a third of the population.[1]

But in general the exceptions which deviated from the average ratio were few, and ordinarily the deviations were slight. So far as any guiding principle can be discovered, the higher ratio was maintained in the agricultural divisions, where it was rarely less than one in five; in the industrial constituencies the average was slightly less. The property franchise in the counties naturally increased the ratio there, and accounted to some extent for the high proportion of registered electors in certain sections. The rural population was also less subject to migratory habits than the urban, and less affected by the residential requirements. The generally regular operation of the franchise at the beginning of the century was, perhaps, considering the anomalies existent before 1884, the striking characteristic of the suffrage.

The act of 1884 was the culmination of the process begun in 1832. The legislation of the latter year introduced the occupation franchise in both counties and

that the ratio of electors must be differentiated by decimal points indicates the enormous advance made in the regularity of the operation of the franchise.

[1] *Parliamentary Papers,* 1902, no. 70.

boroughs, setting an arbitrary standard of value, and preserving the difference between the two kinds of constituencies by demanding a higher value in the counties. In 1867 the standard of value was not required in boroughs and that of the counties was lowered. In 1884 the process was logically completed by accepting as qualification in counties as in boroughs simply the occupation of a house. The next step, that which would involve absolute manhood suffrage, naturally belongs to a different epoch, and to a generation still more completely separated from the older electoral traditions.

The process which transformed the £10 and the £50 occupation franchises of 1832 into the household suffrage of the present day led, as we have seen, both to a change in the composition and to an increase in the size of the electorate. The act of 1832 was in its first effects by no means a democratic measure. A large proportion of the few labourers who had previously possessed the right of vote were disfranchised; the new electors in boroughs, wherever they could vote independently, voted with narrow middle-class interests in view. And the new county electors were the tools of the landed aristocracy. Moreover the increase in the number of voters was small, partly because the franchises were themselves narrow, partly because of the restrictions of the registration system.

But the importance of the act of 1832, so far as it was concerned with voting rights, cannot be minimized. Besides opening up the close boroughs, a process which affected the balance of parties rather than of classes, it provided for an automatically increasing electorate, and in so doing sounded the knell of aristocracy. Before the Reform Act, the county electorate could not increase in proportion to the population, except by the creation of faggot votes; and the increase of the number of borough voters, under the ancient right franchises, was bound to

be spasmodic and slow. But the introduction of the £10
occupation franchise and the £50 tenancy qualification not
merely enfranchised certain persons and their descendants;
it rendered possible the growth of the electorate as wealth
increased and as numbers multiplied. The reform itself
introduced only some two hundred thousand voters; but
in the succeeding generation the electorate was increased
by more than six hundred thousand.

That increase would not have made England democratic,
even had the manifold electoral conditions which preserved
the power of the landed aristocracy and upper middle
class not been in existence. It could, however, exert
enough force, supported by the opinion of the unenfranchised, to liberalize the legislature to some extent, and
finally force on the logical step: the removal of the standard of value attached to the qualification in 1832. The
introduction of household suffrage in 1867 was by no
means a democratic revolution, inasmuch as more than
half of the population were not affected by it, and the £12
franchise in counties was a poor substitute for the household franchise. In the latter constituencies the landed
aristocrat was actually more supreme than ever.

But the act of 1867 was a far greater step in advance
than had been either desired or intended by one or other
of the chief .parties. In its immediate effects upon the
electorate it was the most striking of all three; the increase
in the number of electors far transcended that of 1832 and
was proportionately greater than that of 1884; henceforth
the majority of voters in the boroughs were workingmen
and the democratic franchise was firmly established. Controlling power, it is true, was still left in the hands of the
upper and upper middle classes, but the forward step was
unquestionable. And the extension of the democratic
franchise to the counties was merely a matter of time; for
otherwise a vast anomaly would have been perpetuated, in

a day when electoral anomalies were no longer defended on
the ground of either prescriptive right or practical value.
Theoretically the act of 1884 was merely the complement
of that of 1867, although the importance of the results
then achieved demands a far more dignified description.

It is at the same time an interesting and significant
fact that the ancient right voter in boroughs, and the freeholder in counties still persisted after 1884. The anomaly
of privilege, vested in the London liveryman, the freeman
of Coventry, the plural-voting freeholder, or university
voter, was not destroyed. A uniform doctrinaire principle of suffrage was not advanced in any of the three acts,
nor was the franchise based in any respect upon the doctrine of the innate voting rights of man.

Actually, however, the approach to manhood suffrage
was so close, that the most progressive could afford to
wait until the twentieth century before putting the franchise on a purely democratic basis. The reform in electioneering methods and the settlement of registration
conditions accomplished in 1883 and 1885, went far, in
combination with the new suffrage, towards completing
the transfer of predominant political power from the aristocracy and middle classes to the nation as a whole. So
far as the electoral aspect of the question was concerned,
the process only demanded for its completion along broad
lines, a thorough redistribution of seats. This was accomplished in 1885.

CHAPTER XVI

THE DETERMINATION OF ELECTORAL POWER: THE REDISTRIBUTION ACT OF 1885

Importance of the question of redistribution—Anomalies of the distribution of seats—No proportional relation between votes cast and members elected—Movement for redistribution in the Commons—Opposition of Disraeli—Attitude of parties after 1880—No general demand for equal electoral districts or periodic redistribution—Question of proportional representation—The preferential vote—The second ballot—Single-member districts—Opposition—Radical attitude of Conservative leaders—Gladstone's theory of centrifugal representation—The Redistribution Bill—Influence of Conservative ideas—Disfranchisement—New seats—Division of the counties—Opinion on the measure—Attack on university representation—Effects of Redistribution Act—Equality of voting values in county divisions—Anomalies that still persisted—Significance of the redistribution of 1885.

THE determination of the suffrage in 1884 was by no means an easy task, nor, as we have seen, was it one upon which complete unanimity of opinion was possible. It was, however, of a less complex character and productive of far less discordance than the redistribution of electoral power. The extension of the franchise, vital as it was in the minds of the legislators, had about it a comparatively abstract character which was totally lacking in the question of distribution, where party and personal interests were affected in a fashion by no means indirect.[1]

[1] "From a tactical point of view the extension of the franchise is a comparatively simple operation; redistribution is one of extreme difficulty, magnitude, and danger," Holland, *Life of the Duke of Devonshire,* i, 394.

The practical importance of this question in determining the character of government, was indeed hardly less than the primary question of the suffrage; as Bright had shown years before, no matter how extended the franchise, the power of the masses could be easily reduced to nil by the manipulation of redistribution. And in 1884, when the future of the suffrage was practically settled, not a few could be found to agree with Dilke that the redistribution of electoral power as greatly transcended the mere extension of the franchise in importance, as it did in difficulty of treatment.[1] That the question of redistribution demanded attention was insisted upon by all Radicals and admitted by most Liberals after 1872. Many persons really pressed the extension of the franchise less for its own sake than to force a redistribution, which was in their eyes the main issue of the moment.[2]

The numerical anomalies against which they protested in the name of democracy, and also because they desired a final settlement, were by no means slight. The counties, with a population greater by over a million than that of the boroughs, returned one hundred and ten less members.[3] And the difference between the representation of individual

[1] 3 Hansard, ccxxxv, 505-506.

[2] These feelings were voiced by Dilke, who at Glasgow in 1883 said that identity of franchise was chiefly valuable as being the first step in redistribution, which was to be the keynote of politics, and "the means of putting an end to the tyranny of the few over the many," *Annual Register*, 1883, 178.

		Population	Members
[3]	Counties . . .	13,688,902	187
	Boroughs . . .	12,285,537	297

Parliamentary Papers, 1886, no. 47. Only three million of the six million householders were voters, and of these three million, a third returned two-thirds of the House of Commons, 3 Hansard, cclxxxv, 167.

constituencies was still more anomalous; the ratio of seats
to population in Liverpool was one to one hundred and
eighty-five thousand, in Calne one to five thousand. Nor
was the anomaly less striking in that the electoral advantage, in an age of industry and democracy, was altogether
with the agricultural constituencies and those dominated
by a landed aristocracy. In the industrial county divisions of the Northwest, there was but one member to
every one hundred and fifty thousand inhabitants; in the
rural boroughs of the Southwest the proportion was one
to twelve thousand. The slight redress offered to the
industrial and commercial centers in 1867, was soon obliterated by the growth and shifting of wealth and population. Each year new material was furnished for Radical
speeches, in which was emphasized the doctrine that size
and representation must go hand in hand.[1]

Certain effects of these anomalies were made patent in
the elections of 1874 and 1880. In a representative system where two-thirds of the members were returned by
one-fourth of the electorate, and where the minority in
one large borough would furnish a majority in five or six
small boroughs, the relative strength of parties in the
House might easily not be in proportion to their strength
in the country.[2] The element of blind chance necessarily
played a major part. In 1874 the Conservatives, who
polled barely thirty thousand more votes than the Liberals,
had a majority of eighty-two members over their opponents; they thus won seventy-two seats more than they
were entitled to on a strictly proportional basis. In 1880,
on the other hand, the Liberals carried eighty-nine seats

[1] *Supra,* Chap. XI.
[2] 3 Hansard, ccxxv, 1533-1554; Murdoch, *History of Constitutional Reform,* 266.

too many, in proportion to the total poll.[1]   Salisbury
stated that notwithstanding the Liberal majority of two
hundred thousand, if only two thousand electors had voted
differently, the Conservatives would have had a majority
in the House of Commons.[2]   In various counties the distribution of seats produced surprising results.   Lancashire
with only two thousand more Conservatives than Liberals
in a total electorate of two hundred thousand, returned
twenty-two of the former and only eleven of the latter.[3]
To equalize the value of a vote and to establish a proportional relation between the votes cast and the members
elected, was, in the minds of many a more pressing necessity than the extension of the franchise.

When, owing chiefly to the efforts of Dilke, the subject
of redistribution was brought up in the Disraeli administration, the Conservatives refused to admit the advisability of any change.   One of the chief objections advanced to the extension of the franchise by Disraeli was
that it would involve a large measure of redistribution.
Freely confessing the existence of the anomalies against
which Dilke inveighed, he did not scorn to resuscitate his
arguments of twenty years previous, and again declared
his belief in the benefits resulting from electoral anomalies;
it was through their agency, he asserted, that the parliamentary system had worked as well as it had.   From the
practical point of view Disraeli's further argument was

[1] 3 Hansard, ccxciv, 738.   The following table illustrates the
anomaly:

Liberal votes, 1874,	934,000	Liberal seats, 1874,	230
Conservative votes, 1874,	978,000	Conservative seats, 1874,	312
Liberal votes, 1880,	1,199,000	Liberal seats, 1880,	335
Conservative votes, 1880,	1,022,000	Conservative seats, 1880,	208

On a strictly proportional basis the Conservatives had 72 seats too
many in 1874, and in 1880 the Liberals had 89 too many.

[2] 3 Hansard, cclxxxv, 168.

[3] McCalmont, *Parliamentary Poll Book*.

possibly stronger. It was impossible, he contended, to
obviate anomalies in distribution without inaugurating a
commission of parliamentary revision and a periodical
redistribution; this he objected to on various grounds,
but chiefly because it would afford frequent opportunities
for gerrymandering. The distribution of political power
after all, said he, was not a matter of abstract right, but
of expediency. That twenty thousand votes were necessary in one constituency for the election of a member,
while three hundred and fifty were sufficient in another,
was perhaps an offence to the principles of symmetry;
but it was preferable to a system of equal electoral districts which would involve continual organic change. The
problem of proportional representation was avoided altogether by Disraeli.[1]

The prime minister's supporters for the most part
echoed his sentiments heartily, and there was no lack of
hostility expressed towards any measure which, by altering
the character of the electoral system, would crush out its
life and variety. The Conservatives favoured by chance
in the election of 1874, and still looking for support to
the small rural boroughs, had not yet begun to feel the
necessity for change, and argued that time should be taken
to try out the existing law.[2]

The Radicals, although they had small hope of success
in the near future, aired the question continually, both in
and out of parliament. That opinion was not yet far
advanced may be inferred from the fact that the advocates
of change considered it necessary to disprove elaborately
the arguments brought forward in favour of the small
boroughs, which but a few years later were tacitly and
almost unanimously condemned.[3]   The reformers were

[1] *Annual Register*, 1874, 61; 3 Hansard, ccxxv, 1546.
[2] *Annual Register*, 1877, 64.
[3] 3 Hansard, ccxxv, 1537.

often vague and by no means agreed as to the character of the proposed redistribution. Edmond Fitzmaurice declared himself prepared for a disfranchisement of one hundred and fifty seats; Dilke, on the other hand, hoped to avoid disfranchisement altogether by means of grouping the smaller boroughs.[1] On the question of proportional representation there was a wide variety of opinion. Some reformers advocated the cumulative vote, and others the alternative vote; while yet others desired to chop up the constituencies into single-member districts. All the Radicals, however, were agreed that the existing system could not remain unreformed, and lost no opportunity of expatiating upon the increase in electoral anomalies which resulted from the growth of the industrial and the decadence of the rural constituencies.

With the accession of the Liberals to power in 1880, the question assumed a different aspect. The Whigs had shown themselves ready to accept the principle of redistribution when they voted for Trevelyan's resolution in 1877; they therefore considered themselves pledged to carry through some changes, now that they could be incorporated in a government measure. But their opinion as to the extent of redistribution necessary, was by no means bold. The Conservatives, on the other hand, became the party of progress and casting aside for the most part the traditions which had so long determined their electoral policy, found themselves not widely separated from the extreme Radicals. Their fear was no longer that the basis of the representative system would be destroyed by the extinction of small constituencies, but rather that the extension of the franchise would be enacted without a sufficiently large measure of redistribution. From their point of view it was essential that the rural vote of the counties should not be swamped by the urban electors who were

[1] *Annual Register*, 1877, 62, 64.

about to be enfranchised.[1] Redistribution accompanied
by a rectification of boundaries would offer protection, and
they feared postponement to a later Parliament when conditions might be more unfavourable. Moreover, the election of 1880 had proved the existence of the Tory workingman, and the electoral progress of the Conservatives in
the metropolis and certain industrial centres rendered them
more gracious towards the doctrine that representation
should depend upon population. The over-representation
of the smaller boroughs they also felt to be less desirable,
now that those constituencies were no longer bulwarks of
Tory strength.

Thus, as it became obvious that the franchise was soon
to be extended, all parties looked upon a measure of redistribution as inevitable, and the discussion centred not so
much upon its advisability as upon its extent.[2] For the
most part opinion was not divided upon party lines. A
few of the Radicals, supported by a still smaller section
of the Liberals, did not fear to propose that the system of
equal electoral districts be adopted, and the principle of
absolutely uniform representation approved. From the
strictly logical point of view, if identity of suffrage were
established in counties and boroughs, there was much to
be said for this contention. Even Disraeli admitting in

[1] Morley, *Life of Gladstone,* iii, 126. Hartington himself took the
same point of view, and nearly resigned in 1883 because Gladstone
did not plan to bring in redistribution with the franchise bill, Holland,
Life of the Duke of Devonshire, i, 401-402. Cross showed that in
Northeast Lancashire there would result 147,000 urban voters from
the new franchise and only 70,000 rural voters; the latter would
therefore be totally swamped, 3 Hansard, cclxxxvi, 1231. Salisbury
also insisted at Reading that redistribution must accompany the new
franchise, *Annual Register,* 1883, 179. See also 3 Hansard, cclxxxvi,
620; cclxxxvii, 760.

[2] *Annual Register,* 1883, 179. Parties differed also as to whether
redistribution should accompany franchise reform or be deferred
to a later session.

1874, that the trend of forty years of reform had been in the direction of equal electoral districts, considered them logically necessary, if household suffrage were extended to the counties.[1] The principle of uniform representation was supported warmly by the *Spectator*, which advocated a distribution of seats in exact proportion to population; it also demanded, for the avoidance of constant tinkering, an automatic periodical redistribution.[2]

But slight favour was accorded to such advanced opinion even by the more progressive spirits. Chamberlain himself denied his allegiance to the principle of mathematically equal districts, provided that the value of a vote in different constituencies were equalized.[3] Leatham protested against periodical redistribution, as an unfortunate device of American democracy which would absolutely destroy the individuality of the constituency.[4] Salisbury agreed with him, and a writer in the new *National Review* prophesied the absolute ascendancy of the caucus and the tyranny of the party wire-puller as a result of equal electoral districts.[5]

But although such a democratic reorganization as was implied by the introduction of equal electoral districts and periodical redistribution, was advocated by only a few, various shades of opinion combined to urge that population be taken as a basis for the distribution of seats. Many of those who inclined to this view were members of the Conservative party. Salisbury, while he protested against equal districts and their attendant evils, warmly sup-

[1] *National Review,* ii, 635.

[2] *Spectator,* January 26, 1884. Sir Henry Tyler attempted to introduce the principle of exact proportion to population in place of arbitrary figures, since the latter would have only temporary effect, 3 Hansard, ccxciv, 688.

[3] 3 Hansard, cclxxxvi, 962.

[4] 3 Hansard, cclxxxvi, 674.

[5] *Annual Register,* 1884, 214; *National Review,* ii, 816.

ported the criterion of population and urged the electors
not to rest until the representation of Manchester was
doubled and that of the metropolis tripled.[1] And although
Cross dissented from the principle of an exactly proportionate distribution, the Tory benches as a whole cheered
enthusiastically when its adoption was suggested by
Chamberlain. The effects of the principle would hardly be
to the advantage of the Conservative party in Birmingham, but they were in consonance, theoretically and practically, with the growth of Tory democracy, and would
serve at all events to weaken the Irish contingent.[2] In
general, the moderate opinion of both Conservatives and
Liberals agreed on preserving the individuality of the
old constituencies. As to the extent of redistribution, the
Conservatives showed themselves rather more prepared
for a large measure than their opponents. Raikes advocated a disfranchisement which would render available one
hundred seats, and evidently feared that the government
would err on the side of timidity.[3] Shaw Lefevre, on the
other hand, inclined to a transfer of only fifty or sixty,
most of which should go to the metropolis and the Northwest.[4]

Few, whether Whigs or Tories, cared to take up the
defence of the smallest boroughs. Here and there in a
debate, notwithstanding the years that had passed and
the numerous theories which had gone over the falls, a
phrase or a sentence echoed the words of Croker and
Wetherell. The value of the strong men returned by the

[1] In his speech at Manchester, August 9, 1884, *Annual Register*,
1884, 157.

[2] 3 Hansard, cclxxxvi, 961.

[3] 3 Hansard, cclxxxvii, 763.

[4] *Annual Register*, 1884, 8; *Spectator*, January 26, 1884. But
Bright proposed to disfranchise all boroughs with a population of
less than 30,000, according to which plan England and Wales would
have lost 108 boroughs and 140 seats, *National Review*, ii, 34.

small boroughs, the representation of interests as opposed
to the blind dominion of numbers, still received their meed
of praise, but rather in the tone of a eulogy of the depart-
ing, than of an optimistic defence.[1] And when a writer
dared to question the future, and doubt the practical
superiority of the coming constituency, he was forced to
admit at the same time that the collection of "micro-
cosmical hamlets" which constituted a typical borough,
was a ludicrous anachronism, and that the day had passed
when the electors in such a place could claim peculiar
privileges on the ground of inherent right. In the minds
of most the small boroughs were condemned, not only as
illogical absurdities, but as practical failures.[2]

Opinion was also agreed, for the most part, that the
smaller boroughs escaping disfranchisement might be
grouped, so as to raise the population of each to twenty
thousand. This plan was warmly advocated by Fawcett,
who saw in it a means of escape from equal electoral districts, while at the same time the necessary seats could
be found for the industrial sections. A similar suggestion
was that the boundaries of the smaller boroughs should
be enlarged, so as practically to transform them into
county divisions. The surrender of one member by the
moderate-sized towns was also looked upon with very
general favour.[3]

There was thus no very decided division of opinion either
as to the fact or as to the main characteristics of the
redistribution. All accepted it as inevitable, and few
advocated a very conservative or a thoroughly democratic
measure; the preservation of the smallest boroughs on the

[1] 3 Hansard, cclxxxvii, 801; Murdoch, *History of Constitutional
Reform*, 378.

[2] *National Review*, i, 246; 3 Hansard, cclxxxv, 409.

[3] *Annual Register*, 1884, 10; 3 Hansard, ccxxv, 1543; ccxciv, 727-
728; *MacMillan's Magazine*, l, 249; *Spectator*, November 10, 1883.

one hand, and the adoption of equal electoral districts on the other, were alike condemned. Opinion, indeed, was by no means unanimous as to whether an exact proportion to population should be followed in the distribution of seats. But if a regular and even ratio was impractical, without conditions worse than the existence of electoral anomalies, nearly all desired so much exactness as should make it certain that the will of the country was being expressed, and that something like order and principle was replacing chaos and privilege.[1]

Something more than a redistribution, however, was necessary if the element of chance was to be eliminated, and if the varying opinion of the country was to be fairly represented in the House of Commons. No matter how carefully the seats were distributed, the minority of the voters might return a majority of the members, or conversely the opinions of a large minority might go entirely unrepresented. In order that the ideas of the voters might be represented in proportion to their number, special precautions must be devised; and it was on this question of proportionate representation that opinion was most sharply divided. Impelled by different motives both Conservatives and Liberals were sincerely desirous of finding some device which would render the character of the legislature more representative. The Conservatives, notwithstanding their professions, sought protection from the new democracy; the philosophical Liberals were driven by their enthusiasm for justice in the abstract.

The fear of both Tories and Whigs that a wide enfranchisement of one class without precautions would destroy the representation of the other classes, was demonstrated plainly in the discussion of proportional representation. "When political power was vested in the aristocracy," said

1 *MacMillan's Magazine*, l, 241.

Sir Michael Hicks-Beach, "its abuse was restrained by the fact that the ultimate political power rested with the people. But when political power is given to those with whom physical power rests, you have the absolute certainty that the minority will be placed in a position in which they can have no possible appeal against the decision of the majority."[1] Goschen, in arguing the same point, pointed out that the anomalies which were on the brink of destruction were, in fact, the varieties which often protected minorities. In proportion as the system based upon population did away with anomalies, and placed electoral power in the hands of large aggregates of population, in that proportion it would be necessary to search out securities for the minority.[2]

For some of the Liberals, of whom Courtney and Lubbock were the most eminent, fear of democracy was not so much the keynote as their love of justice and their desire that the strength of the party in the House should represent its voting strength in the country. They had no difficulty in showing that a small majority in one constituency might counterbalance a large majority of the opposing party in another. Two small majorities might outvote a single overwhelming majority; thus the representatives of the minority might outnumber those of a majority as easily under a system of uniform representation, as they could in the days of the small boroughs. As Lubbock pointed out the majority of a majority may be and often is a minority; the majority on a division in parliament is

---

[1] 3 Hansard, cclxxxvi, 1308.

[2] 3 Hansard, cclxxxvi, 1875; *Annual Register,* 1884, 112. "The system," he said at another time, "must be a truly representative system. It must represent all classes, and there may be fear that a liberal enfranchisement of one class without any precautions will mean the taking away of representation from other classes," 3 Hansard, cclxxxv, 423. Blennerhasset also showed the importance of the question, *Ibid.,* 397.

arrived at by eliminating two minorities, which taken together might largely outnumber the so-called majority. Chance, he asserted, was too often the determining factor, and chance must be eliminated as far as possible.[1]

Another contingency and one that affected the Radicals especially, was the division of votes which resulted when two candidates of the same party, or of allied parties, presented themselves. Such a division frequently threw the election into the hands of their common opponent. Numerous instances had occurred when a Conservative, standing alone against a Radical and a Liberal, had been returned, although the majority of votes cast was by no means in his favour.[2]

The devices suggested for the obviation of such infringements of pure democracy were numerous, and warm discussion in the press and parliament ensued, which were based partially upon theoretical abstractions and partially upon observation of the systems prevailing in other countries. On the platform the question of proportional representation was not so widely aired, and the country at large, puzzled by the difficulty of the subject, remained cold to the arguments and counter-arguments. But to not a few it appeared that upon a proper solution of this problem depended the value of a man's vote, and the whole result of the redistribution of political power.

The system of minority representation which had been introduced into the three-member constituencies in 1867, found few supporters. It had given rise to the caucus, and its extension would mean the practical despotism of the new political associations, which were disliked and feared by many members of the House. It was useless in bye-elections, and the minority members felt themselves in an uncomfortable position; if they wished, or were

[1] 3 Hansard, cclxxxv, 450; ccxciv, 739.
[2] McCalmont, *Parliamentary Poll Book, passim.*

forced to retire, a seat was immediately resigned to the other side. So unpopular was this minority provision that more than one motion for its abrogation had been made.[1] Another plan was suggested which was strongly advocated by Courtney and Lubbock and which enjoyed the patronage of the *Proportional Representation Society*. This plan was based upon the principle of the scheme first outlined by Hare. The great local communities were to be left undivided, and represented by the number of members that their population warranted. Each elector was to have but one vote; if the candidate for whom he voted received enough ballots for election without his vote, it might be transferred to a second candidate who was to be indicated by the voter upon his ballot. Thus no votes would be wasted, and the element of chance would be excluded so far as was humanly possible.[2]

This preferential, or transferable, vote awoke the warmest enthusiasm amongst those who understood the system, or who believed that the voters could understand it.[3] The balance of press opinion was, however, hostile, the editor of the *Spectator* declaring himself incapable of understanding this, or any other, plan of proportional representation that had been suggested.[4] In the House of Commons there were few inclined to vote for the adoption of the transferable ballot. Morley attacked it warmly as a hollow disguise for the old Tory distrust of the people.[5] Even those who approved of its principle felt that it would be impossible to induce the people to accept

1 3 Hansard, cclxxxv, 410.

2 *Annual Register,* 1879, 38; 3 Hansard, ccxciv, 740, 1806.

3 A writer in the *Daily News* (March 3, 1883), claimed that many of the stereotyped objections to the single alternative vote resolved themselves on examination into little more than thinly veiled accusations of ignorance and stupidity against the nation.

4 *Spectator,* December 1, 1883.

5 3 Hansard, cclxxxvi, 1566.

a system for the discussion of which real mathematical knowledge was necessary; and even a philosopher like Arthur Balfour believed that the crusade for this type of proportional representation was hopeless.[1]

The more popular scheme in the country, not for the protection of the minority, but rather to prevent the success of a minority candidate in a three-cornered contest, was the second ballot. This had been much pressed by Radical orators and had actually been incorporated in bills during the sessions of 1872 and 1882. It was again suggested in the House of Commons in 1885 and approved by such ministers as Chamberlain and Dilke. But the Conservatives were naturally opposed to the second ballot, and many of the Liberals objected to it on the ground of the delay, anxiety, and expense which would result from its adoption.[2]

The plan generally advocated by the Conservatives was the division of the constituencies into single-member districts. It was hoped that a fairly proportional representation would result from this arrangement, since a minority in one constituency would probably be represented by a majority of the party in another. Sections which had formerly been swamped by hostile contiguous districts would be granted independent representation under the single-member system. The Liberal press, with some exceptions, favoured this plan, adducing the opinion of Cobden, who shortly before his death had advocated single-member districts in preference to Mill's scheme of minority representation.[3] Single-member districts were

[1] 3 Hansard, ccxciv, 1839. Bryce favoured elections by different systems in different boroughs, but on the whole believed that the example of the United States proved the value of single-member districts, 3 Hansard, ccxciv, 744.

[2] 3 Hansard, ccxciv, 1808, 1922.

[3] Cobden's letter appeared in the *Times,* June 2, 1868. The *Spectator* believed in the single-member district, insisting that it

also approved by the government, although without enthusiasm. Gladstone admitted that it was a choice of evils, but disliking the preferential vote, he confessed his conversion to the single-member constituency, which had been justified by experience all over the world. Dilke believed that the disappearance of the small borough and the introduction of one-seat districts would practically destroy the element of luck in elections.[1]

The single-member constituency was bitterly opposed by a small section of the Liberals, both because they distrusted its effects upon the character of the constituency, and also believed that the system would prove a poor substitute for the preferential ballot. Both Lubbock and Courtney feared that the division of the larger constituencies into units would destroy the individuality of the borough. "There is all the difference in the world," said the former, "between the constituency which is whole in itself, and another which is a mere fragment of a larger body."[2] Courtney opposed it on the ground that the members for the new type of constituency would completely lose their representative character, and would become nothing but delegates of ward interests. He also pointed to the failure of the single-member district abroad as a means for securing a proportional representation. Various cases in the United States were cited, notably at New Haven and Boston, where minorities had defeated majorities under this system. So strongly did Courtney feel that he resigned his position in the government rather than accept this type of constituency.[3]

Goschen also was disturbed by the prospect of single-

---

was stupid first to ascertain the majority of a constituency and then multiply its significance by two (November 22, 1884).

[1] 3 Hansard, ccxciv, 686, 1816.
[2] 3 Hansard, ccxciv, 732.
[3] *Spectator*, December 6, 1884; 3 Hansard, ccxciv, 660-680.

member constituencies, largely from the fear that members would reflect too closely the opinions of their district, and that class divisions would develop in the House. The strength and glory of British politics, he asserted, had been that the master and servant, the manufacturer, foremen, and factory hands, had all canvassed and voted for the same man, and that the member represented not a class but a party. There was danger lest the new districts might force a member to represent the class interest prevailing in his constituency, and lest there should be representatives of the proletariat in the east end of London and those of the plutocracy and aristocracy in the rich districts of the west end: "Let us beware that the single-member constituencies do not develop into one class constituencies, whose members will come here feeling themselves responsible, not to the whole people of the country, but to the particular class living in the district by which they are returned."[1]

The opposition to the single-member districts had no effect, however, upon the policy of the government. The hands of the ministers, indeed, were by no means free, since the plan of redistribution as presented to the House of Commons was agreed upon by the chiefs of each party; and it could not be seriously altered without upsetting the compromise, according to the terms of which the Conservative peers agreed to pass the Franchise Bill. Important amendments in the bill were thus impossible, and the measure in large part represented Conservative ideas; more especially was this apparent in the adoption of single-member districts and in the wide extent of disfranchisement.

The Conservative leaders showed themselves in general distinctly more radical than their opponents. Sir Michael

[1] 3 Hansard, ccxciv, 719.

Hicks-Beach confessed to Hartington that he might have preferred no change at all, if there had been no extension of the franchise; but under the circumstances he did not shrink from a large disturbance of existing areas. His suggestions went far beyond anything advocated by Hartington; in his opinion no borough with a population of less than twenty-five thousand should be represented at all and no borough under eighty thousand should have two members. He believed in single-member districts and insisted that the distinction between town and country should be preserved. He also favoured the granting of representation as nearly as possible in proportion to population. Salisbury also astonished Gladstone by his radical attitude, and Randolph Churchill was outdistanced by none but Chamberlain.[1]

Gladstone, on the other hand, although progressive in his ideas upon the franchise, was a conservative as to redistribution. As early as 1872 he had foreseen the necessity of some redistribution; and he now admitted that the measure must be a large one, and nearer to that of 1831 than to that of 1867. But he did not desire one larger than was absolutely necessary nor one which would destroy the ancient electoral traditions of the country. He warmly opposed anything like equal electoral districts, and his desire to respect the individuality of the constituency rendered him reticent in praise of the single-member constituency. Nor was he in favour of a sweeping disfranchisement of the small boroughs with their great historical associations. On the question of preserving the distinction between town and country, Gladstone was at one with the Conservatives.[2] He differed with them, how-

1 Holland, *Life of the Duke of Devonshire*, ii, 56-58; Morley, *Life of Gladstone*, iii, 138.

2 *Annual Register*, 1872, 65; 1884, 91; Murdoch, *History of Constitutional Reform*, 274-275; *Spectator*, March 1, 1884; Holland, *Life*

ever, in declaring that seats need not be alloted in proportion to population; the large and thickly populated districts, especially in the metropolis, did not, in his opinion, require so high a proportional share of representation as the distant and scattered populations.[1]

This theory of centrifugal representation, as it came to be called, was attacked both by Conservatives and Radicals. Salisbury and Lord George Hamilton pointed out that the sections for which it would be of advantage, namely, Cornwall, Wales, and Scotland, were Liberal strongholds; whereas the metropolis and thickly populated centres were becoming more and more Conservative.[2] Forster, disregarding the effect upon party, declared that while Gladstone's theory might have been true in the day of the stage coach, it was absurd under the conditions of modern transportation, mail, and telegraph service. He believed that London from its very concentration had less power of expressing public opinion than the outlying districts; and he maintained that the amount of taxes paid by metropolitan citizens justified them in their demand for a full ratio of representation.[3]

The influence of the radical tendencies of the Conservatives, and the sacrifice of many Liberal ideas, was made apparent when the Redistribution Bill was presented to the House on December 1, 1885. Gladstone's hope of preventing a sweeping disfranchisement was not realized, for the measure provided that all boroughs with populations under fifteen thousand should pass into the counties, and that boroughs with less than fifty thousand inhabi-

---

of the Duke of Devonshire, i, 403; ii, 51. Hartington agreed with Gladstone on all essential points, Ibid., 50.

[1] 3 Hansard, cclxxxv, 129.
[2] Annual Register, 1884, 156; 3 Hansard, cclxxxvi, 969.
[3] 3 Hansard, cclxxxv, 463; cclxxxvi, 1194.

tants were not to return more than one member. Although
the Conservative standard of twenty-five thousand and
eighty thousand for absolute and partial disfranchisement respectively, was thus not embodied in the bill, the
transfer of seats was larger than would have resulted
from the Liberal line, which they hoped to draw at ten
thousand and forty thousand.[1]

It would, perhaps, be unfair to assert without qualification that the attitude of each of the parties was determined by party interest. But it should not be forgotten
that the towns of between ten and fifteen thousand inhabitants had shown very marked Liberal tendencies. On the
other hand, the new Tory democracy had begun to show
its effects chiefly in the large industrial centres, and the
Conservatives would naturally not have been sorry to
see the standard of population raised for two-member
constituencies. The provisions of the bill, which disposed
of boroughs upon which the Liberals were inclined to look
with favour while they left two seats to towns not included in the Conservative plan, thus very obviously
represented a compromise.[2]

The result of the disfranchisement was to liberate one
hundred and thirty-six seats in England and in Wales.
Seventy-two boroughs returning seventy-nine members
were thrown into the counties, and thirty-six boroughs
lost one member. There were also thrown into the counties
six large boroughs of the type of East Retford and Shore-

---

[1] 3 Hansard, ccxciv, 715.

[2] The Liberals lost most by the disfranchisement, 58 Liberal seats
being extinguished and only 37 Conservative. On the other hand,
the towns which retained specially privileged representation (those
of from 15,000 to 50,000 inhabitants with one member, and those of
above 50,000 and less than 100,000 with two members), returned three
times as many Liberals as Conservatives, McCalmont, *Parliamentary
Poll Book*. See also *Quarterly Review*, clix, 240.

ham; these were all large rural constituencies which, as a result of the assimilation of the franchise, would in any case have been county divisions in all but name. London city lost two seats, Pembroke and Haverfordwest were combined, a seat was taken from Rutland and Hereford counties, and Macclesfield and Sandwich were disfranchised for corrupt practices.[1]

With the seats which had been taken from Beverly and Bridgwater in 1870, and the increase in number of the members of the House, one hundred and forty-two seats were made available for distribution. Of these, sixty-four were assigned to the English and four to the Welsh counties; the remaining seventy-four went to the boroughs. In general the policy of granting full representation to the thickly populated industrial centers was followed. The metropolitan boroughs received thirty-nine new members, and the manufacturing towns of the Northwest eighteen. The large towns, such as Manchester, Sheffield, Birmingham, and Liverpool, were given from three to six new seats apiece. The industrial county divisions were likewise favoured; Lancashire received fifteen new members and the West Riding thirteen. In the arrangement of the new constituencies the Conservative principle of single-member districts was followed. All of the counties were cut up into one-seat constituencies, and the same system was also applied to the new boroughs, as well as to the large towns. Liverpool was thus divided into nine separate districts, and Tower Hamlets into seven. The districts were only approximately equal in popula-

[1] The largest towns were well treated. Birmingham with 450,000 inhabitants had 7 seats, whereas Oldham, Newcastle, and Stoke, which together had 450,000, had only 6 seats together. Sheffield with 250,000 had 5 seats, while Oldham and Newcastle, with an aggregate population of 300,000, had only 4 together. Seven towns, including the metropolis, had 100 seats.

tion and electors, some in the same borough being twice as large as others.[1]

The redistribution as outlined in the bill, was received, if not with enthusiasm, at least in the spirit of resignation generally evoked by compromises. The advocates of proportional representation objected warmly to the single-member districts, and the dissection of the boroughs was by no means popular. Amending motions on these points were, however, lost by large majorities. Goschen regretted that Gladstone had been so far influenced by the Conservatives as to treat the large towns so liberally, and the *Quarterly Review* complained that the House could in future hope for no higher a character than that of the American House of Representatives.[2] The *Spectator*, on the other hand, would have liked a wider scheme and one more mathematically exact in the proportions of distribution; but it admitted that if the old lines of representation were to be adhered to, the measure had touched the limits of progressive possibility. Notwithstanding some complaint that the urban element would swamp the rural in the county divisions, it was generally conceded that the boundary commissioners had done their best to carry out the Conservative demand that town and country be strictly delimited.[3]

All attempts to seriously alter the measure in committee failed. The most striking in the democratic sense was Bryce's attack on the representation of the universities, which had already been foreshadowed during the franchise debates. Much of the hostility expressed towards university representation resulted from the fact that it was an anomalous privilege, and afforded an opportunity for the plural voter. Bryce, however, did not rest his case on

[1] See Appendix, No. 8.
[2] *Quarterly Review*, clix, 242.
[3] *Spectator*, October 11, 1884; *Saturday Review*, lix, 535.

the anomalous character of university representation,
for he saw no harm in anomalies, if they were useful and
practical. But be believed that the representation of the
universities was bad for them, because it intruded political
consideration into educational questions. In some cases,
he asserted, the evil was carried so far as to run candidates
for academical appointments on purely political grounds;
frequently the scholarly merits of the candidates had less
to do with a university appointment than political services
rendered or expected.[1]

Bryce also objected that there were no constituencies
less independent than the universities, and none more at
the mercy of agents and political wire-pullers. The electors had often no real connection or interest with the university, and the members were "not really members for
the university at all. They knew nothing about the university. They were the members for a large number of
persons scattered over the country, and not for true universities as teaching bodies." Trinity, Dublin, was assailed as a constituency which served to provide ex officio
seats for law officers of the crown under Conservative
governments; and as for the Scotch universities, "the time
has now arrived," said Bryce, "when it becomes desirable
to dismiss this device of the Stuart kings to the limbo to
which so many other of their devices have been relegated."[2]

The universities were defended by their members, and
with some ability. "In a Parliament of six hundred and
seventy members," said Gibson, "surely it is not too much
to ask that its dead level of representation be broken by
the interposition of university members, men whose business it is—in addition to representing what they conceive

[1] Porritt, "Barriers against British Democracy," 24, in *Political
Science Quarterly*, xxvi, no. 1.
[2] Porritt, "Barriers against British Democracy," 25-26, *Ibid*.

to be the wants of the whole country—to exercise the special function of considering the claims of education, and the requirements of the law, the church, and medicine." Northcote also argued, as a good Conservative, the importance of preserving some counterbalance, however slight, against the power of mere numbers. No defence of university representation was put forward by the government, and Dilke admitted the force of Bryce's arguments, and emphasized them by a reference to his own dislike of the plural voter. But he also announced the inability of the government to accept an amendment which was not included in the compromise made with the Conservatives, and Bryce's motion was rejected by a large majority.[1]

The failure to remove the anomaly of university representation, like the defeat of proportional representation, did not seriously affect the apathetic content with which the act, as passed, was received. The Radicals rejoiced in the disappearance of the small boroughs, and the Liberals congratulated themselves upon the favour shown the towns of moderate size; each party was naturally disappointed, however, that their special demands had not been more completely satisfied. The Conservatives regretted, on traditional grounds, the almost total disappearance of the numerous small constituencies in which property influence was strong, but they approved of the single-member districts and the concentration of power in the metropolis. At the same time the hard-shell Tories were by no means displeased at the partial survival of many numerical anomalies.[2]

---

[1] Porritt, "Barriers against British Democracy," 27-28, *op. cit.*

[2] On certain points not mentioned above, keen dissatisfaction reigned in certain quarters; both Bryce and Goschen disapproved of the increase in the number of seats, a provision which the government carried 137-25, 3 Hansard, ccxciv, 715, 741, 2002. And Arnold complained bitterly of the retention of the 16 boroughs of less than

These anomalies became in a way more striking than before, since they were now the exception, whereas previously they had been the rule. Generally speaking the electoral advantages possessed by the southern and the agricultural constituencies disappeared in 1885. The industrial Northwest gained forty-eight seats and lost only eight, and the enormous accession of strength to the metropolis, forty-two members in all, has been noted. In the Southwest, on the other hand, thirty-three borough seats were disfranchised, so that even with the seven new county members there was a net loss of twenty-six seats. The southeastern group lost fourteen members, the south-midland lost eleven, and the west-midland ten.[1] The counties of the southern seaboard, instead of returning half of the House of Commons as in unreformed days, were represented after 1885 by little more than a sixth.

The redistribution satisfied in broad lines, and for the moment, the Conservative contention that seats should be assigned according to population. This was especially true of the county divisions, where the ancient traditions were more generally disregarded and where a closer approximation to mathematical exactness was possible than in the boroughs. Not merely was the former electoral disadvantage of the counties removed, so that a county and a borough member represented on the general average the same number of inhabitants, but the ratio of seats to population was made regular throughout the county divisions. The average ratio for all England and Wales was one member to about every fifty-two thousand inhabitants. In the Northwest and the Southeast the ratio was slightly below the average, and in the East and Wales rather above

20,000 inhabitants, when the whole active municipal life of the country was sacrificed to obtain what was called a redistribution according to population, 3 Hansard, ccxciv, 702.

[1] See Appendix No. 5.

it.[1] But the proportional disadvantage of the concentrated centres of population and of industry as opposed to agriculture disappeared. In Middlesex, the south-midland, south-western, midland, and northern groups, whether of an urban or a rural character, the proportion of county members to population was practically the same.

This regularity was even to be found between separate constituencies, although it was not so perfect as to suggest a real approximation to the principle of equal electoral districts. In the Isle of Wight, it is true, a member represented seventy-three thousand persons, whereas in Rutland or Radnor he represented only twenty thousand. But such discrepancies, which were determined by geographical causes or the unwillingness to deprive a county of separate representation, were rare. The disparity which had existed between the electoral strength of the industrial and the agricultural parts of Warwick, for instance, disappeared entirely. The proportion of seats in the urban divisions of the West Riding of Yorkshire was the same as in the rural constituencies of Buckingham. And South Lancashire, which before the redistribution had only a third the proportional strength of Cheshire, was given practically her full quota of seats.[2]

[1]

			Ratio of seats
Northwestern counties	.	.	one to 57,000
Southwestern counties	.	.	one to 57,000
Eastern counties	.	.	one to 44,000
South Welsh	.	.	one to 47,000
North Welsh	.	.	one to 48,000

Parliamentary Papers, 1886, no. 44.

[2]

			Ratio of seats
Yorkshire West Riding	.	.	one to 57,733
Buckingham	.	.	one to 57,619
South Lancashire	.	.	one to 57,713
Cheshire	.	.	one to 54,383

In the boroughs, however, while some of the industrial centres were given enough seats to raise their electoral power to a point not far from the average, the retention of the smaller boroughs of between fifteen and thirty thousand inhabitants, gave undue proportional weight to the districts in which they were situated. The proportion of borough members in the Southwest was twice that of the Midlands, and the towns of the southwestern group had also double the electoral strength of those in the Northwest in proportion to their population.[1] But the anomalies which had worked to the disadvantage of the large commercial and manufacturing towns were at least diminished. The metropolitan group of boroughs, which had always been under-represented, returned a member to every sixty-five thousand inhabitants; and the disadvantage of the industrial Northwest and Midlands was due not so much to their low ratio as to the high proportion in the southern boroughs.

By comparing individual constituencies it can be seen at a glance that the principle of exact proportion to population was by no means followed out to its completion. The representatives of one hundred and forty thousand persons could offset in a division those of nearly half a million. York, with a smaller population than Middlesborough, had two members to the latter's one. Durham had representation proportionately four times that of Gateshead.[2]

[1]

		Ratio of seats
Southwestern boroughs	. .	one to 28,000
Northwestern boroughs	. .	one to 58,000
Midland boroughs .	. .	one to 56,000
Metropolitan boroughs	. .	one to 65,000

[2]

		Ratio of seats
York . .	. . .	one to 30,000
Middlesborough	. .	one to 72,000
Durham	. . .	one to 15,000
Gateshead	. . .	one to 65,000

Windsor with a population of fifteen thousand had equal
strength with Croydon, which had seventy-eight thousand
inhabitants. And the advocate of the past glories of the
electoral system must have been comforted to note that in
ten constituencies the number of electors per member was
less than twenty-seven hundred, while in nine others there
were more than fourteen thousand electors per member.[1]

Thus in spite of the fact that the redistribution was
based upon population and the representation granted to
the industrial centres far exceeded the desires of the Liberals, and actually equalled the expectations of Radicals and
Conservatives, the survivals of the old system protected
many numerical anomalies. The redress of industry's
disadvantage was not niggardly, the very small boroughs
were eliminated, and something like a regular proportion
of representation was established, especially in the county
divisions; but a completely democratic system was not
introduced. And the advance toward uniformity of representation made in 1885 could not continue, nor indeed be
maintained, without provisions for a periodical redistribution. Inevitably the anomalies then preserved must become
greater, and new ones spring up, with the growth of popu-

See also:

Rochester	.	.	.	.	one to 21,000
Portsmouth	.	.	.	.	one to 64,000
Winchester	.	.	.	.	one to 17,000
Dudley	.	.	.	.	one to 87,000

[1] The ten boroughs where the number of electors per member was
smallest were: Durham, Bury St. Edmunds, Winchester, Salisbury,
Pontefract, Taunton, Penryn and Falmouth, London University,
Windsor, Whitehaven. In Durham there were only 2,000 electors.
The nine constituencies where there were at least 14,000 electors
were: Newcastle-upon-Tyne, Huddersfield, Handsworth (Staffordshire), Nottingham, Dudley, Bootle (Lancashire), London City,
Wimbledon (Surrey), Shipley (Yorkshire), *Parliamentary Papers*,
1902, no. 205.

lation in certain districts and the rise of new industries and interests.[1]

[1] The anomalies of the distribution of seats in recent years have received wide publicity and scarcely need description. A few instances will suffice to show the representative disadvantage of industrial constituencies in 1902:

	Ratio of seats
Metropolitan county divisions .	one to 102,000
Northwestern county divisions .	one to 77,000
Southwestern county divisions .	one to 52,000
North Welsh county divisions .	one to 49,000

Comparing individual constituencies in the same part of the country the advantage of the rural is obvious:

	Ratio of seats
Dartford (Kent) . . .	one to 109,000
Ashford (Kent) . . .	one to 67,000
Walthamstow (Essex) . .	one to 185,000
Saffron Walden (Essex) . .	one to 43,000
Romford (Essex) . . .	one to 217,000
Banbury (Oxford) .	one to 40,000
Tyneside (Northumberland) .	one to 100,000
Kendal (Westmoreland) .	one to 32,000
East Glamorgan . . .	one to 105,000
Leominster (Hereford) .	one to 44,000

A similar comparison of boroughs throws the same light upon the state of distribution:

	Ratio of seats
Croydon	one to 133,895
Winchester	one to 19,000
Hanley	one to 100,000
Stafford	one to 20,000
Birkenhead	one to 111,000
Whitehaven	one to 19,000
Middlesborough . . .	one to 116,000
York	one to 37,000
Cardiff district . . .	one to 167,000
Montgomery district . .	one to 17,000

Parliamentary Papers, 1902, no. 70. And see, especially, *Ibid.,* 1910, no. cd5163.

We may not, however, yield to the temptation of laying undue stress upon electoral anomalies after 1885, nor should we underrate the importance of the redistribution of that year. It is no exaggeration to say that with its destruction of the small boroughs, its introduction of the single-member district, and its recognition of populous and industrial centres, and following upon the electoral reforms of the two preceding years, it opened a new political epoch. This must have been true, even apart from the accident of the Home Rule dispute, which disorganized one of the chief parties. Already, under the old electoral system, the political atmosphere was being transformed and the tone of politics changing. But the democratization of the representative system which culminated in 1885 facilitated the change, perhaps, as much as any other one factor.

CHAPTER XVII

Conclusion

THE growth of democracy in elections had been slow and it is to be traced out in various directions. The Reform Act of 1832 found the electoral system completely under the control of the peerage and the landed or mercantile aristocracy. Through the close boroughs the House of Commons was dominated by the upper classes, and the open boroughs were, for the most part, at the disposal of the party which furnished the most funds. The lower House, supposedly representative of the common people, was thus the nominee of a restricted and privileged order.

The act of 1832 struck fiercely at this power of the aristocracy. Many of the close boroughs were opened by the introduction of the £10 franchise, and none were so easily controlled by the patron as in pre-reform days. A large number of the family and saleable boroughs disappeared entirely and their place was taken by the new industrial towns, in which there were no pre-reform traditions to break down and which represented an entirely new factor in the electoral system. The introduction of the new borough franchise, moreover, furnished an opportunity to a large class of the community for expressing its opinions at the polls.

But the absolute sway that had been wielded by the landed and commercial aristocracy was by no means destroyed by the act of 1832, nor was full power of representation granted to the middle class, which was supposedly made the controlling force. Entirely apart from the influence vested in the great landlords by centuries of tradition, nomination to the House of Commons by borough patrons still persisted. The small boroughs, generally representative of aristocratic interests, held the balance of power in the Commons. Without exception the rural and agricultural constituencies were in possession of far greater electoral power than the industrial districts which were the centres of middle class strength. And through the Chandos clause, which was granted to the aristocracy as compensation for the destruction of nomination boroughs, the nobles and squires secured a dominating position in the counties.

Aristocratic control was also fortified by the manipulation of the registration system and the exercise of corrupt influence. The process of registration was so complicated that a large number of qualified persons did not trouble to become registered electors. The party agents did not fail to seize their opportunity. On the one hand they agreed to obtain the vote for persons too lazy, too busy, or too poor to secure it themselves, stipulating that their protegés should vote according to instructions; on the other hand they utilized the red tape of the system to disfranchise their opponents. Partisan interests thus secured very wide influence over the composition of the electoral lists, and in general exercised that influence in behalf of the aristocracy. That the power of the upper classes in elections was also maintained by means of corruption and intimidation is well attested. Only too often the votes of the electors represented not the opinions of their own class so much as the orders of the bribe agents and the stewards, acting for the class higher up. For all of these reasons the domination of the landed and commercial classes in elections outlived the attack made upon nomination in 1832 and continued to characterize the representative system. It was weakened but by no means crushed.

But the first Reform Act was but the beginning of the transformation, and merely pointed the way to further developments. Herein lay its great importance. Once the electoral traditions of centuries were broken down, it proved not too difficult to continue and expand the process of democratization. That process was developed by a large number of reforms. The act of 1867, by establishing a truly democratic franchise in boroughs and adding a vast number of new electors, broke down aristocratic control in many constituencies. The conservative tendencies of the two chief parties were at once affected by this new factor of democratic strength; inevitably they began to succumb to the pressure brought to bear by those politicians for whom success at the polls was the matter of prime importance. Moreover, the control of the upper classes that had been exercised through corruption weakened under the altered conditions of electioneering. The reform in the petition system effected in 1868, as well as the Corrupt Practices and Ballot Acts of 1854 and 1872, tended to render elections a more actual norm and test of the real opinions of the voters. At the same time the increase in the size of the constituency rendered direct bribery more difficult. The influence which the upper classes had exercised through registration agents was also weakened, after 1867, inasmuch as the new popular associations began to assume almost exclusive control over the composition of the electoral lists.

It is essential to remind ourselves, however, that the power of the aristocracy in elections was still great even after 1867. The elective franchise was democratic only for the inhabitants of represented boroughs. The qualified electors in counties formed a small proportion only of the total county population; they were for the most part under the control of the landlords and, almost without exception, voiced the interests of the landed aristocracy when they came to the polls. The franchise was thus one of privilege in that it excluded the masses dwelling outside of the represented towns; and it was the more undemocratic in that it depended upon the hap of residence.

The electoral system was also undemocratic because of the distribution of electoral power. The redistribution of 1867 was limited and failed to grant to the large industrial centres the representation which they claimed was due their wealth and importance. In every instance the electoral power of rural and agricultural constituencies far exceeded that of the manufacturing sections in proportion to their population. And the representatives of the small rural boroughs could still outvote the members for the great textile, mining, and shipping districts of the Midlands, Northwest, and North.

More than one official investigation showed, moreover, that if electoral corruption had been diminished, it was still the moving force in many of the smaller boroughs. In these constituencies the enfranchisement of 1867 was running the risk of total perversion, for the masses there were almost as completely under the sway of the upper classes as in the old days of nomination. The form of electoral institutions may have been democratic in these boroughs; their essence was aristocratic. Nor could the process of democratization be developed, so long as the cost of contesting a seat remained so high as to restrict the circle of candidates to a knot of wealthy plutocrats or men who were backed by plutocratic interests.

Thus, notwithstanding the vast increase in the borough electorate and in spite of the efforts made to insure freedom of elections, the system remained essentially undemocratic in many respects. The exclusion from the franchise of the county population, both rural and urban, the uneven distribution of seats, the influence of the upper classes maintained by corruption, the exaggerated expense of contesting a seat,—all these circumstances tended to oppose barriers to the development of a real electoral democracy.

Most of these bulwarks of aristocratic power were levelled by the electoral reforms that took place from 1883 to 1885. It is not quite exact to say that the legislation of these years made the system democratic, for much of the process of democratization was intangible, going on gradually and imperceptibly between 1867 and 1884. It is true, however, that the electoral system was a democracy in its main lines soon after 1885, just as shortly before that year the electoral power of the aristocracy was very great. The granting of household suffrage to the counties removed the most striking anomalies of the franchise, and redressed the grievances that weighed upon the miners and artisans in unrepresented towns and the agricultural labourers in country districts. By the redistribution of seats the metropolis and the industrial centres received representation in rough proportion to their wealth and population; if the maxim "one vote, one value" was not perfectly realized, at least the equality of voting values was far more closely approximated than ever before. The Corrupt Practices Act of 1883 was also of advantage to the cause of democracy in elections since it transformed methods of electioneering. It reduced the expense of contesting a seat and extended the circle of possible candidates. If corrupt purchase of votes, whether individually or wholesale, was not entirely eliminated, it was to be found in a smaller number of boroughs and assumed a far less blatant form than previously. Where in earlier days the electors informed the canvassers that their votes would be cast for "Mr. Most," they began to respond to less sordid arguments. Political education began to replace political purchase.

It is true that the democratic principle in elections was not carried into full effect. The complexities of the franchise and the registration system, since 1885, have been such that many persons have been excluded from the right to vote whose qualifications, in all essential characteristics, seemed equal or superior to those of actually constituted electors. The persistence of the ownership and university franchises, which permit a man to become a plural voter, is directly opposed to the democratic ideal that is expressed by the slogan "one man, one vote," and which refuses to accept the argument that those who possess a special stake in the country should be allowed to exercise a greater voting power than those who possess a smaller stake. In the third place the distribution of seats effected in 1885 made no provision for a periodic redistribution. With the passing of each year, the shifting of industry and population has given rise to electoral anomalies that are at total variance with truly democratic principles. Other barriers to perfect democracy have also persisted. The parliamentary franchise has been refused to women, the system of voting for candidates representing single-member districts has failed to secure a really proportional representation, and the official expenses of elections continue to be thrown upon candidates.

Despite such undemocratic survivals, however, the epoch of reorganization which made of England an electoral democracy may fairly be said to have been completed by the reforms of 1883, 1884, and 1885. The introduction of a democratic franchise, the redistribution of seats, the breaking down of aristocratic control in the process of electioneering, and the establishment of an impartial tribunal for the decision of election petitions, have transferred ultimate power in elections from the privileged few to the mass of the people. To the regular development of England as a political and social democracy the growth of this democratic electoral system has, without question, borne a close relation. The acquiescence of the upper classes in the reforms which robbed them of electoral power, and their trust in the political capacity of their fellow countrymen, have been of the utmost importance; for they enabled England to undergo gradually an inevitable political and social transformation which otherwise could not have been secured without the shock of revolution. That which was effected in France by the convulsions of 1848 and 1870, and may conceivably result in Germany as an aftermath of war, was peacefully obtained in England because the parliamentary machine was continually kept in touch with the pulse of public opinion.

BIBLIOGRAPHICAL NOTE

THE materials upon which the foregoing study is based
and to which reference is made in the footnotes, are
well known to nineteenth century historians; because of
this fact no formal bibliography has been appended. The
legislative enactments referred to are to be found in the
published series of *Public General Statutes*, appearing
annually since 1830, and published since 1888 under the
title of *Public General Acts*. The *Chronological Table
and Index of the Statutes* (1335-1895) will be found convenient for hasty reference.

Of vital importance for the historian who studies the
conditions preceding and resulting from the legislative
reforms, is the series of *Parliamentary Papers*, commonly
known as Blue Books. Before the nineteenth century
reports of committees were generally printed in the
Journals. In 1773 a selection of the more valuable papers
not printed in the Journals was made and published. In
1811 further volumes of reports, eleven in number, were
published, to which Hansard appended an index and a list
of the reports printed in the Journals with their subject
matter. In 1825 the series was enlarged upon the recommendation of a committee which advocated the publication
of Commissioners' Reports and other papers of interest
and importance, as well as reports of committees. Finally
in 1837 the public circulation of *Parliamentary Papers*
was fully established.

From 1830 to 1835 the *Papers* were classified under
four headings: Finance Accounts, Estimates and Account-
ings, State Papers, and Slave Papers. From 1835 to

1850 the headings varied. Since 1851 the classifications have been Bills Public, Reports from Committees, Reports from Commissioners, Accounts and Papers, the two latter categories including the larger part of the material published. In 1820 there were but twelve folio volumes of *Parliamentary Papers*. By 1850 they had increased to fifty-seven volumes, and in 1900 there were one hundred and eleven volumes with invaluable information upon every branch of national activity.

There is a general index of the material published in these *Papers* from 1801 to 1852; since then indices have appeared every decade. A general catalogue of *Parliamentary Papers*, covering the period 1801-1900, has also been published by P. S. King, which lists and briefly criticises the most important returns.

The quality of the *Parliamentary Papers* relating to the electoral system, especially since the middle of the century, is excellent and they constitute an official source of the first importance. The returns of electoral statistics that appeared soon after 1832 are not always to be relied* upon implicitly, but their value is only slightly vitiated by occasional misprints and mathematical errors which can be easily corrected. Unfortunately the few available statistics that deal with electoral conditions immediately before the first Reform Act are woefully marred, either by careless compilation or wilful misrepresentation.

For the study of electoral corruption and the registration system the reports of the investigating committees furnish valuable résumés of electoral conditions, the points which required remedy, and the kinds of remedy suggested. The evidence given before these committees also enables us to gain an insight into methods of corruption as well as the large number of petty difficulties which offered serious obstructions to the successful operation of the registration system. In general the statements of the witnesses are not coloured by party or class bias, but the tendency of the witness is often to overstate his point and his evidence cannot always be accepted at its face value. The cumulative result of the evidence, however, points in one direction, namely that the influence of the aristocracy in elections continued to be preponderant until after the beginning of the third quarter of the century.

Supplementing the *Parliamentary Papers* on the subject of electoral corruption are the series of published reports of cases tried before the Election Committees, Election Judges, and Revising Barristers.

Hansard's *Parliamentary Debates* have been constantly utilized, not merely for studying the opinions of noted individuals and rival parties, but chiefly because of the mine of invaluable information there contained. Facts of the greatest significance, well-nigh drowned in the rhetoric of debate, are to be retrieved from Hansard; frequently these facts are to be found in the less important debates and are apt to be furnished by persons of lesser note. The series is too well known to require description.

In the category of semi-official authorities mention should be made of McCalmont's *Parliamentary Poll Book*, which is essential for information on the results of elections in separate constituencies from 1832 to 1906. It includes alphabetical lists of candidates as well as members, thus supplementing the *Parliamentary Paper* of 1874 which contains a list of members. Miscellaneous material, often valuable, is also to be found in Dod's *Parliamentary Companion*, published annually since 1833. As a brief résumé of the more important events and speeches connected with parliamentary reform, the *Annual Register* may also be consulted.

Of secondary literature dealing with the electoral system and its reform in the nineteenth century there is great dearth. The system before 1832 has been exhaustively treated by Mr. and Mrs. Porritt in their admirable *Unreformed House of Commons*, a thorough acquaintance with which is essential to an understanding of the earlier period of reform. Veitch, in his *Genesis of Parliamentary Reform*, studies the movement which culminated in the first Reform Act, and Butler's *The Passing of the Great Reform Bill* provides us with an excellent description of the crisis of 1831-1832.

On the effects of the first Reform Act and the operation of the electoral franchise after 1832, however, there are few details published. Books dealing with the modern electoral system and its reform fall generally into one of three categories: the parliamentary histories of the Reform Bills, the legal abstracts of the legislation enacted, and the general works upon the modern English constitution. Of the first, nearly all are concerned with the manner of passing rather than the matter of reform. Apart from the above-mentioned work of Mr. Butler, Roebuck's *History of the Whig Ministry* is valuable as a presentation of the Radical point of view, and Molesworth's *History of the Reform Bill of 1832* still remains a useful, brief description of parliamentary manœuvres during the critical period, although its value has been largely diminished by the appearance of Butler's recent study which covers the same ground. The *History of the Reform Bills of 1866 and 1867* by Homersham Cox, although tinged with a very strong Liberal bias, is for that reason a valuable expression of the Gladstonian point of view, and also contains excellent material culled from official documents. There are also two books each of which attempt a survey of reform legislation: Heaton's *The Three Reforms of Parliament* and Murdoch's *History of Constitutional Reform*. The former is lucid but slight, and the latter is dry in the extreme, merely presenting a badly proportioned epitome of the debates in parliament, with no consideration beyond the superficial parliamentary detail of the moment.

The scope of each of the above-mentioned works is confined entirely to franchise reform and redistribution; no attention whatever is given to the development of the registration system and the efforts made to check electoral corruption in its various forms. Obviously the relation between these latter aspects of electoral reform and franchise reform is vital, and without the changes in registration and the prevention of corrupt practices the legislation of 1832, 1867-1868, 1884-1885, would have been of far less effect. For this reason Dickinson's brief *Development of Parliament* is of the utmost value and will be found invariably suggestive to the highest degree.

The legal works upon parliamentary reform contain abstracts of the acts themselves and constitute useful epitomes of the legislation. Most valuable are *Rogers on Elections* (*ed.* Powell, 1897 ; *ed.* Williams, 1906), Fraser's *The Law of Parliamentary Elections and Election Petitions*, and Mackenzie and Lushington's *Registration Manual*. They contain a wealth of cases illustrative of the operation of the electoral system, although they are in no sense histories. Halsbury's collection of *The Laws of England* is also invaluable for purposes of reference.

The general works dealing with the modern English political system are naturally of great value, especially for the more recent period. Ostrogorski's *Democracy and Parties* contains much that is useful for the study of electoral corruption and the operation of the registration system, and Lowell's *Government of England* covers the existing electoral system and devotes some space to parliamentary representation. Franqueville's *Le Gouvernement et le Parlement Britannique* contains perhaps the best published description of the development of the franchise and the electoral system since 1832, although it is of necessity extremely brief. May's *Constitutional History of England* includes an excellent account of parliamentary reform and the causes leading to it, and Gneist in his *Das heutige englische Verfassungs- und Verwaltungsrecht* devotes some pages to the subject. But neither touch in detail upon the effect of the reforms upon the numbers of parliamentary voters and the distribution of electoral power.

There is little periodical literature of value dealing with the electoral franchise. The two most important articles are by Edward Porritt ("Barriers against Democracy in the British Electoral System" in the *Political Science Quarterly*, xxvi, no. 1) and by John Lambert "Parliamentary Franchises, Past and Present" in the *Nineteenth Century*, December, 1889). The latter from his long experience on the Poor-law Board was excellently qualified to write an authoritative work on the entire electoral system; but his article is too short to be of serious weight, and his figures are marred by inaccuracies and misprints. Party literature on reform is extensive; when not published in the periodicals, it is generally to be found in pamphlet form, and may be run down in Watt's *Bibliotheca Brittanica* under the word "Reform."

APPENDICES

APPENDIX NO. 1

THE ELECTORATE AND THE REFORMS IN ENGLAND AND WALES

	County Electorate	Borough Electorate	Total Electorate		Increase	% Increase
1831	247,000*	188,391*	435,391 ⎫		217,386	49
1833	370,379	282,398	652,777 ⎬			
1866	542,633	514,026	1,056,659 ⎫		938,427	88
1869	791,916	1,203,170	1,995,086 ⎬			
1883	966,721	1,651,732	2,618,453 ⎫		1,762,087	67
1886	2,538,349	1,842,191	4,380,540 ⎬			

* These figures obtained from an unpublished *Parliamentary Paper*, cited by John Lambert in "Parliamentary Franchises," *Nineteenth Century*, December, 1889. The county electorate is estimated. The form of the above table is the same as that published by Mr. Lambert, but his figures have been corrected from published *Parliamentary Papers*.

EFFECT OF REFORMS ON BOROUGH AND COUNTY ELECTORATES

			Increase	% Increase	Total Increase
1832	County	. .	123,379	49 ⎫	217,386
	Borough	. .	94,007	49 ⎬	
1867-1868	County	. .	249,283	45 ⎫	938,427
	Borough	. .	689,144	134 ⎬	
1884-1885	County	. .	1,571,628	162 ⎫	1,762,087
	Borough	. .	190,459	11 ⎬	

APPENDIX NO. 2

ARRANGEMENT OF COUNTY AND BOROUGH GROUPS

Metropolitan
Middlesex
Metropolitan Boroughs

Southeastern
Kent
Surrey
Sussex
Hampshire
Isle of Wight

South Midland
Berkshire
Bedfordshire
Hertfordshire
Buckinghamshire
Oxfordshire
Northamptonshire

Eastern
Huntingdonshire
Cambridgeshire
Rutlandshire
Lincolnshire
Yorkshire East Riding
Norfolk
Suffolk
Essex

Southwestern
Wiltshire
Dorsetshire
Devonshire
Cornwall
Somerset

West Midland
Gloucestershire
Herefordshire
Shropshire
Worcestershire
Monmouthshire

Midland
Staffordshire
Warwickshire
Leicestershire
Nottinghamshire
Derbyshire

Northwestern
Cheshire
Lancashire
Yorkshire West Riding

Northern
Durham
Northumberland
Cumberland
Westmoreland
Yorkshire West Riding

South Wales
Radnorshire
Pembrokeshire
Carmarthenshire
Glamorganshire
Cardiganshire
Brecknockshire

North Wales
Carnarvonshire
Denbighshire
Montgomeryshire
Anglesey
Flintshire
Merionethshire

APPENDIX NO. 3

REDISTRIBUTION OF 1832

Groups	Counties		Boroughs	
	With-drawals	Assign-ments	With-drawals	Assign-ments
Metropolitan . . .	—	—	—	10
Southeastern . . .	—	9	36	3
South Midland . .	—	6	9	—
Eastern	—	9	10	—
Southwestern . .	—	9	69	3
West Midland . .	—	7	5	5
Midland . . .	—	10	—	7
Northwestern . . .	—	6	3	17
Northern . . .	—	6	11	18
South Wales . . .	—	2	—	2
North Wales . . .	—	1	—	—
Total . . .	—	65	143	65

8 seats assigned to Scotland
5 seats assigned to Ireland

APPENDIX NO. 4

Redistribution of 1867-1868

Groups	Counties		Boroughs	
	With-drawals	Assign-ments	With-drawals	Assign-ments
Metropolitan . . .	—	—	—	4
Southeastern . . .	—	4	8	1
South Midland . .	—	—	5	—
Eastern	—	6	8	—
Southwestern . . .	—	4	17	—
West Midland . . .	—	—	6	—
Midland	—	4	1	2
Northwestern . . .	—	7	5	7
Northern . . .	—	—	2	4
South Wales . . .	—	—	—	1
North Wales . . .	—	—	—	—
Total . . .	—	25	52	19

1 seat assigned to London University
7 seats assigned to Scotland

APPENDIX NO. 5

REDISTRIBUTION OF 1885

Groups	Counties Withdrawals	Counties Assignments	Boroughs Withdrawals	Boroughs Assignments
Metropolitan . . .	—	5	2	39
Southeastern . . .	—	5	20	1
South Midland . .	—	1	12	—
Eastern	1	5	14	4
Southwestern . . .	—	7	33	—
West Midland . . .	1	4	16	2
Midland	—	1	12	9
Northwestern . .	—	30	8	18
Northern . . .	—	6	12	—
South Wales . . .	—	3	4	1
North Wales . . .	—	1	1	—
Total . . .	2	68	134	74

2 seats available by raising numbers of the House
4 seats withdrawn from Beverly and Bridgwater

APPENDIX NO. 6

ANALYSIS OF THE REDISTRIBUTION OF 1832

Disfranchisement　　　　　　　　　　　　　　　　　　　*Seats*

55 double-seated boroughs absolutely disfranchised　.　110
1 single-seated borough (Higham Ferrers) disfranchised　1
30 boroughs lose 1 seat apiece　.　.　.　.　.　30
Weymouth and Melcombe Regis lose 2 seats .　.　.　2

Total number of seats available　.　.　.　.　143

Enfranchisement

26 counties divided　.　.　.　.　.　.　.　52
10 counties receive 1 seat apiece　.　.　.　.　.　10
Yorkshire receives 2 seats　.　.　.　.　.　.　2
Isle of Wight separated from Hampshire　.　.　.　1
22 large towns receive 2 seats apiece　.　.　.　44
21 moderate-sized towns receive 1 seat apiece　.　.　21

Total number of seats assigned　.　.　.　.　130

4 seats given to Ireland
8 seats given to Scotland
1 seat given to Dublin University

APPENDIX NO. 7

Analysis of the Redistribution of 1867-1868

Disfranchisement   *Seats*

3 double-seated boroughs disfranchised for corrupt practices   6
1 single-seated borough disfranchised for corrupt practices   1
3 double-seated boroughs (of less than 5000 population)   6
4 single-seated boroughs (of less than 5000 population)   4
35 boroughs lose 1 seat apiece   35
                                                                             —
        Total number of seats available   52

Enfranchisement

10 counties redivided into 3 instead of 2 divisions . .   20
Lancashire receives 3 seats   3
Yorkshire West Riding receives 2 seats   2
Chelsea and Hackney receive 2 seats apiece . . .   4
Liverpool, Birmingham, Manchester, Leeds, Salford,
        Merthyr Tydvil receive 1 seat apiece . . .   6
9 moderate-sized towns receive 1 seat apiece . . .   9
London University receives 1 seat   1
                                                                             —
        Total number of seats assigned   45

        Scotland receives 7 seats

APPENDIX NO. 8

Analysis of the Redistribution of 1885

Disfranchisement   Seats

7 double-seated boroughs (of less than 15,000 population)   14
65 single-seated boroughs (of less than 15,000 population)   65
6 double-seated boroughs (large rural constituencies)   .   12
2 corrupt double-seated boroughs   4
36 double-seated boroughs lose 1 seat apiece   .   .   .   36
City of London loses 2 members   2
Haverfordwest combined with Pembroke   1
Rutland and Herefordshire lose 1 seat apiece .   .   .   2

                                                                  ———
Total number of seats available by disfranchisement   136
Seats available by raising numbers of House   .   .   .   2
Seats available by disfranchisement of Beverly and Bridg-
        water, 1870   4

                                                                  ———
Total number of seats available   142

Enfranchisement

39 seats given to metropolitan boroughs   39
25 seats given to existing English boroughs   .   .   .   25
9 new provincial boroughs created in England   .   .   9
1 seat given to Swansea   1
64 seats given to English counties   64
4 seats given to Welsh counties   4

                                                                  ———
Total number of seats assigned   142

APPENDIX NO. 9

Ratio of Electors to Population
BOROUGH GROUPS

		1866	*1869*	*1884*	*1886*
Metropolitan	.	one in 15.1	10	9.6	8
Southeastern	.	one in 14.3	7.9	7.9	7
South Midland	.	one in 13.6	6.3	6.8	6.2
Eastern	.	one in 14.5	5.9	6.1	6.5
Southwestern	.	one in 16.8	8.7	7.5	7.5
West Midland	.	one in 16	6.6	7	8.7
Midland	.	one in 17.5	6.1	6.3	5.9
Northwestern	.	one in 20.4	7	7.2	6.8
Northern	.	one in 16.6	6.3	6	5.5
South Wales	.	one in 25.1	6.6	7.2	6.2
North Wales	.	one in 9.7	6.6	6.6	6.5

COUNTY GROUPS

Metropolitan	.	one in 24.9	14.6	10.2	5.5
Southeastern	.	one in 23	13.7	13.1	5.6
South Midland	.	one in 22.5	16.6	16.6	5.5
Eastern	.	one in 20.9	15	15.1	4.6
Southwestern	.	one in 20.3	15.3	13.8	5.5
West Midland	.	one in 17.2	12.8	13.8	5.3
Midland	.	one in 19.8	13.9	13.5	5
Northwestern	.	one in 25.2	15.7	15.7	5.7
Northern	.	one in 16.5	13.5	13.5	5.4
South Wales .	.	one in 18.6	11.5	13.2	5.3
North Wales	.	one in 19.9	11.9	11.7	5.2

APPENDIX NO. 10

RATIO OF MEMBERS TO POPULATION

BOROUGH GROUPS

		1866	1869	1884	1886
Metropolitan	.	one in 137,000	124,000	157,000	65,000
Southeastern	.	one in 13,000	16,000	21,000	42,000
South Midland	.	one in 8,000	10,000	14,000	30,000
Eastern	.	one in 12,000	14,000	22,000	39,000
Southwestern	.	one in 8,000	11,000	12,000	28,000
West Midland	.	one in 19,000	18,000	25,000	49,000
Midland	.	one in 32,000	34,000	47,000	56,000
Northwestern	.	one in 49,000	48,000	67,000	58,000
Northern	.	one in 17,000	20,000	30,000	46,000
South Wales	.	one in 28,000	25,000	37,000	49,000
North Wales	.	one in 18,000	18,000	22,000	23,000

COUNTY GROUPS

		1866	1869	1884	1886
Metropolitan	.	one in 184,000	184,000	197,000	53,000
Southeastern	.	one in 72,000	59,000	84,000	57,000
South Midland	.	one in 47,000	47,000	50,000	52,000
Eastern	.	one in 66,000	53,000	60,000	44,000
Southwestern	.	one in 68,000	56,000	56,000	50,000
West Midland	.	one in 51,000	51,000	59,000	53,000
Midland	.	one in 63,000	52,000	59,000	52,000
Northwestern	.	one in 171,000	111,000	152,000	57,000
Northern	.	one in 57,000	57,000	70,000	54,000
South Wales	.	one in 53,000	54,000	63,000	47,000
North Wales	.	one in 48,000	48,000	53,000	48,000

INDEX

INDEX